ธป

โกร

THE SALE OF GOODS

To
Sir Rupert Cross
In admiration and friendship

THE
SALE OF GOODS

P. S. ATIYAH, M.A., B.C.L.
of the Inner Temple, Barrister-at-law
Professor of Law in the
University of Warwick

FIFTH EDITION

Pitman

PITMAN PUBLISHING LIMITED
39 Parker Street, London WC2B 5PB

Associated Companies
Copp Clark Ltd, Toronto · Fearon–Pitman
Publishers Inc, Belmont, California
Pitman Publishing New Zealand Ltd, Wellington
Pitman Publishing Pty Ltd, Melbourne

Fifth edition published in Great Britain 1975
Reprinted 1978

Printed in Great Britain by
The Camelot Press Ltd, Southampton

ISBN 0 273 00872 2

FOREWORD

TEACHERS of Commercial Law have long felt the need for an up-to-date narrative textbook of modest dimensions on the Law of Sale of Goods. Section-by-section commentaries on an Act may sometimes be convenient to practitioners but they are not ideal for teaching purposes, especially when the arrangement of the Act is not altogether satisfactory—and despite the praise justly lavished on Sir Mackenzie Chalmers's draftsmanship, the Sale of Goods Act was, perhaps, his least happy effort in this and other respects. Hence Mr. Atiyah's book fills a gap and, to my mind, fills it admirably.

Though this book is a short one in comparison with most modern textbooks, it is neither elementary nor superficial. Far from avoiding the difficult byways, Mr. Atiyah leads his readers down them with the zeal of the true explorer and sometimes arrives at unexpected conclusions. With some of these conclusions one may quarrel, but the book is none the worse for that. The essential feature of a student's textbook is that it should arouse the reader's interest and make him think and argue. And a desirable, if rare, feature of a practitioner's book is that it should suggest to him novel lines of argument. Mr. Atiyah's book possesses both of these features. His arguments are always clearly and attractively presented and supported by the results of serious and often original research.

It gives me real pleasure to commend this book as a valuable addition to the library of a commercial lawyer, whether he be a teacher, student or practitioner.

L. C. B. GOWER

FROM THE PREFACE TO THE FIRST EDITION

THE object of this book is to state within a moderate compass the modern English law of sale of goods. I think I may fairly use the word modern, for the treatment is based almost exclusively on the Sale of Goods Act, 1893, and on cases decided thereunder. It seemed to me, rightly or wrongly, that sixty years after the Sale of Goods Act was passed the time had come to discard most of the older cases and to rely on modern authorities only. In this respect I have tried hard to be loyal in the spirit as well as in the letter to the injunctions of Lord Herschell in *Bank of England* v. *Vagliano Bros.*,[1] and to confine the citation of cases decided before 1893 to those situations in which the interpretation of the Act is doubtful, or in which terms had acquired a technical meaning before that time.

PREFACE TO THE FIFTH EDITION

IT is, perhaps, a sign of the times that it is now statutory change which is the main impetus to a new edition of a work of this nature. This edition has been necessitated mainly by the radical alterations made to the law of sale by the Supply of Goods (Implied Terms) Act, 1973, and the Consumer Credit Act, 1974. These two Acts have required a great part of the book to be rewritten.

The process of revision and, I hope, improvement has continued. Academic and judicial development in the law of damages since the book was first published have been substantial, and this part of the book has been extensively re-written for the first time since 1957.

University of Warwick   P. S. A.

[1] [1891] A.C. 107. A passage from his speech is set out on p. 1.

CONTENTS

PART I
NATURE AND FORMATION OF THE CONTRACT OF SALE

CHAPTER 1
INTRODUCTORY

CHAPTER 2
DEFINITION AND NATURE OF THE CONTRACT OF SALE

CHAPTER 3
FORMATION OF THE CONTRACT

CHAPTER 4
FORMALITIES

CHAPTER 5
SUBJECT MATTER OF THE CONTRACT

CHAPTER 6
THE TYPES OF OBLIGATION CREATED

PART II
THE DUTIES OF THE SELLER

CHAPTER 7
THE EXISTENCE OF THE GOODS

CHAPTER 8
THE DUTY TO PASS A GOOD TITLE

CHAPTER 9
THE DUTY TO DELIVER THE GOODS

CHAPTER 10
THE DUTY TO SUPPLY THE GOODS AT THE RIGHT TIME

CHAPTER 11
THE DUTY TO SUPPLY GOODS IN THE RIGHT QUANTITY

CHAPTER 12
THE DUTY TO SUPPLY GOODS OF THE RIGHT QUALITY

CHAPTER 13
CONSUMER PROTECTION

CHAPTER 14
EXCLUSION OF SELLER'S LIABILITY

PART III
THE DUTIES OF THE BUYER

CHAPTER 15
THE DUTY TO PAY THE PRICE

CHAPTER 16
THE DUTY TO TAKE DELIVERY

PART IV

THE EFFECTS OF THE CONTRACT

CHAPTER 17
THE TRANSFER OF PROPERTY

CHAPTER 18
RISK AND FRUSTRATION

CHAPTER 19
TRANSFER OF TITLE BY A NON-OWNER

PART V

EXPORT SALES

CHAPTER 20
EXPORT SALES

CHAPTER 21
EXPORT AND IMPORT LICENCES

CHAPTER 22
BANKERS' COMMERCIAL CREDITS

CHAPTER 23
THE UNIFORM LAWS ON INTERNATIONAL SALES

PART VI
THE REMEDIES OF THE SELLER

CHAPTER 24
REAL REMEDIES

CHAPTER 25
PERSONAL REMEDIES

PART VII
THE REMEDIES OF THE BUYER

CHAPTER 26
REJECTION OF THE GOODS

CHAPTER 34
THE REMEDIES OF THE CREDITOR

CHAPTER 35
THE REMEDIES OF THE DEBTOR

TABLE OF STATUTES

(Page numbers in bold type indicate that the section referred to, or a part of it, is set out verbatim in the text)

TABLE OF CASES

PART I

NATURE AND FORMATION OF THE CONTRACT OF SALE

CHAPTER 1

INTRODUCTORY

THE SALE OF GOODS ACT, 1893

THE law of sale of goods is contained partly in the Factors Act, 1889, partly in the Sale of Goods Act, 1893, as amended by later Statutes, and partly in the rules of common law left untouched by the Act. The Sale of Goods Act is a codifying statute, and the proper method of interpreting such a statute was laid down by Lord Herschell in *Bank of England* v. *Vagliano Bros.*—[1]

> I think the proper course is in the first instance to examine the language of the statute and to ask what is its natural meaning, uninfluenced by any considerations derived from the previous state of the law, and not to start with inquiring how the law previously stood, and then, assuming that it was probably intended to leave it unaltered, to see if the words of the enactment will bear an interpretation in conformity with this view.
>
> If a statute, intended to embody in a code a particular branch of the law, is to be treated in this fashion, it appears to me that its utility will be almost entirely destroyed, and the very object with which it was enacted will be frustrated. The purpose of such a statute surely was that on any point specifically dealt with by it, the law should be ascertained by interpreting the language used instead of, as before, by roaming over a vast number of authorities in order to discover what the law was, extracting it by a minute critical examination of the prior decisions.

Lord Herschell then went on to observe that in exceptional cases reference to earlier decisions may still be permissible. Firstly, where the provisions of the Act are ambiguous, earlier cases may help to resolve the ambiguity; and secondly, where a term has acquired a technical meaning, previous cases may be cited to illustrate this technical meaning. It is scarcely necessary to add that where a point is not covered by the Act older decisions are still in force and must be followed.

Despite this warning and its subsequent repetition in later cases, it cannot be said that it has always been taken to heart by courts or

[1] [1891] A.C. 107, at pp. 144-5. These observations were made with reference to the Bills of Exchange Act, 1882, but they apply to all codifying statutes alike.

1

writers. Indeed, there are indications in the speeches in the House of Lords in *Ashington Piggeries, Ltd.* v. *Christopher Hill, Ltd.*[1] that Lord Herschell's remarks may now need qualification. In particular, in the interpretation of provisions of the Act relating to implied terms Lord Diplock said that the Act "ought not to be construed so narrowly as to force on parties to contracts for the sale of goods promises and consequences different from what they must reasonably have intended."[2]

The Sale of Goods Act makes no attempt to codify the general principles of contract law. Indeed it expressly leaves them untouched, for Sect. 61 (2) enacts that—

> The rules of the common law, including the law merchant, save in so far as they are inconsistent with the express provisions of this Act, and in particular the rules relating to the law of principal and agent and the effect of fraud, misrepresentation, duress or coercion, mistake, or other invalidating cause, shall continue to apply to contracts for the sale of goods.

Despite this section no exposition of this subject would be complete without some account of the general rules of the law of contract in so far as they have some special bearing on the law of sale of goods.

As will appear during the course of this book, the Sale of Goods Act has not proved one of the more successful pieces of codification undertaken by Parliament towards the end of the nineteenth century. The principal reason for this may well be that there has been a change in the type of sale of goods cases coming before the courts. The nineteenth century cases on which the Act was based were, in the main, sales between business men or organisations, i.e. sales by manufacturers and suppliers. Since the Act was passed, however, a large proportion of the cases coming before the courts appear to have been sales by retailers to the consuming public.[3] In view of the very different social and economic nature of these transactions, both of which are in law sales of goods, it is not surprising that an Act devised principally for the one has not always worked satisfactorily for the other. It is now noticeable that one of the principal trends of modern legislative change is to discriminate between consumer and non-consumer transactions.

[1] [1972] A.C. 441.   [2] At p. 501.
[3] Is this because business men nowadays tend to prefer arbitration to litigation in the courts?

CHAPTER 2

DEFINITION AND NATURE OF THE CONTRACT OF SALE

DEFINITION

SECT. 1 (1) of the Act defines a contract of sale of goods as—

> a contract whereby the seller transfers or agrees to transfer the property in goods to the buyer for a money consideration, called the price.

Subsect. (3) gives different names to the two transactions—

> Where under a contract of sale the property in the goods is transferred from the seller to the buyer the contract is called a sale; but where the transfer of the property in the goods is to take place at a future time or subject to some condition thereafter to be fulfilled the contract is called an agreement to sell.

SALE DISTINGUISHED FROM OTHER CONTRACTS

A contract of sale of goods must be distinguished from several other transactions which are normally quite different from a sale of goods, but which in particular circumstances may closely resemble such a contract, namely (1) a contract of exchange, (2) a contract of bailment, (3) a contract of hire-purchase, (4) a contract of loan on the security of goods, (5) a contract for skill and labour, (6) a contract for labour and materials, and (7) a contract of agency.[1] These distinctions were formerly of importance mainly in connection with Sect. 4 of the Act. This section, which was originally part of Sect. 17 of the Statute of Frauds, 1677, required contracts of sale of goods of the value of £10 and upwards to be evidenced in writing, whereas for the other types of contract listed above there was no such requirement. Since the repeal of Sect. 4 by the Law Reform (Enforcement of Contracts) Act, 1954, this particular point has ceased to be of importance, but it may still be necessary to decide whether a contract is a contract of sale of goods for, of course, the other provisions of the Sale of Goods Act also apply only to such contracts. It must be added, however, that as the Act is largely, though by no means entirely, declaratory, the law may well be the same

---

[1] In former editions a contract for the transfer of a possessory interest in a chattel was also distinguished from a sale of goods. As a result of the Supply of Goods (Implied Terms) Act, 1973, it is now clear that such a contract should be treated as a sale of goods, see further, *post*, p. 53.

whether or not the Act applies. Indeed, there has been a noticeable tendency for the courts to model the common law contracts on the Sale of Goods Act, and in particular to imply terms in these contracts very similar to those implied by the Act.[1] In *Young & Marten, Ltd.* v. *McManus Childs, Ltd.*[2] the House of Lords expressed strong views on the undesirability of drawing unnecessary distinctions between different classes of contract. Unfortunately it seems probable that one result of the Supply of Goods (Implied Terms) Act, 1973, may be to hinder this development in the future. Since the changes made by this Act are clearly not declaratory, it is difficult to see how the Courts could modify implied terms in other contracts to keep them in line with contracts of sale. Quite possibly, therefore, the distinction between a sale and the various other types of contract may assume greater importance again in the immediate future.

In cases under Sect. 4 it was necessary to draw a firm line between contracts of sale and other types of contract, but for other purposes there seems no reason why it should not sometimes be possible to hold that a contract is partly a contract of sale, and partly something else.[3] Thus a contract for the provision of a meal in a hotel is apparently a contract of sale,[4] and so is a contract for the construction of machinery.[5] Yet such contracts are also in a sense contracts for skill and labour, and there seems no reason why terms should not be implied with regard to the seller's skill and labour at common law which should avail the buyer even if the terms implied by the Sale of Goods Act are, for some reason, excluded. More to the point now will be the possibility of holding that a contract falls under the Supply of Goods Act of 1973 so as to restrict the exclusion of implied terms[6] even in cases where, taken as a whole, the contract is not a sale of goods. It remains to be seen whether this degree of ingenuity is within the capacity of the courts.

Before considering the distinction between contracts of sale and the other types of contract mentioned above, one preliminary point needs emphasis. A contract of sale is first and foremost a *contract*, i.e. a consensual transaction based on an agreement to buy and an agreement to sell. So where an out-patient at a hospital obtains drugs at the hospital dispensary, even on payment of a statutory prescription charge, this is not a contract of sale at all. The patient has a statutory right to receive the drug, and the hospital a statutory obligation to

[1] See e.g. *G. H. Myers & Co.* v. *Brent Cross Service Co.*, [1934] 1 K.B. 46; *Samuels* v. *Davis*, [1943] K.B. 526; *Stewart* v. *Reavell's Garage*, [1952] 2 Q.B. 545; *Ingham* v. *Emes*, [1955] 2 Q.B. 366.
[2] [1969] 1 A.C. 454.
[3] See, e.g. *Watson* v. *Buckley*, [1940] 1 All E.R. 174.
[4] *Lockett* v. *A. & M. Charles, Ltd.*, [1938] 4 All E.R. 170.
[5] *Cammell Laird & Co., Ltd.* v. *Manganese Bronze and Brass Co., Ltd.*, [1934] A.C. 402.
[6] *Post*, p. 132.

supply it.[1] It seems the position is the same with respect to drugs and other medical appliances supplied by a chemist under the National Health Service.[2] It would, however, be a mistake to conclude that the patient would necessarily be remediless in such circumstances if defective drugs were supplied, even in the absence of negligence. Although the transaction is not a sale, and the terms implied under the Sale of Goods Act probably do not apply, it is thought that it would still be open to the courts to impose obligations on the supplier analogous to those under the Act. As was said by Lord Upjohn in discussing an analogous question in *Young & Marten, Ltd.* v. *McManus Childs, Ltd.*, "It would be most unsatisfactory, illogical and indeed a severe blow to any idea of a coherent system of common law, if the existence of an implied obligation depended upon such a distinction."[3]

But, as already noted, the terms to be implied will probably be analogous to those in the original Sale of Goods Act and not those implied by the 1973 Act.

Sale and Exchange

The fact that the consideration must be in money, and that the term "goods" is defined by Sect. 62 so as to exclude money, serves to distinguish a sale from an exchange in the ordinary case. But a coin which is a curio piece may be "goods" even though it is legal tender, and there may be a sale of such a coin. In such an event the coin does not possess the usual negotiable qualities of money, and if the sale is by a thief he cannot pass a good title thereto.[4]

The position is less clear where goods on the one hand are exchanged for goods plus money on the other. Is this a contract of sale or of exchange? In *Aldridge* v. *Johnson*[5] a contract for the exchange of 52 bullocks with 100 quarters of barley, the difference in value to be made up in money, was treated without argument as a contract of sale, but the case was fought on an entirely different point. One view is that the answer depends upon whether the money or the goods are the substantial consideration. The decision in *Robinson* v. *Graves*[6] lays down an elastic test of this nature for distinguishing contracts of sale from contracts for skill and labour, and now that the repeal of Sect. 4 has removed a natural bias against contracts of sale, a similar approach may well be justified here.

However, it may well be that, if the parties envisage the transaction as a sale, and use terminology more appropriate to a sale, the contract would be held to be such even if the substantial consideration is supplied in goods rather than money. In the motor trade it is, of

---

[1] *Pfizer Corpn.* v. *Minister of Health*, [1965] A.C. 512.
[2] *Appleby* v. *Sleep*, [1968] 1 W.L.R. 948, 954.
[3] [1969] 1 A.C. 454, at p. 473.
[4] *Moss* v. *Hancock*, [1899] 2 Q.B. 111.
[5] (1857), 7 E. & B. 885.   [6] [1935] 1 K.B. 579.

course, a common occurrence for a person to "trade-in" an old car in part-exchange for a new one, and if the transaction relating to the new car is treated by the parties as a sale it is improbable that the courts would treat it as anything else, even if the dealer's "allowance" for the traded-in car does not fall far short of the price of the new one. It seems that the transaction relating to the old car would also amount to a sale, even though no money actually passes, if, as is usual, the parties fix a notional price which is set off against the price of the new car.

Sale and Bailment

A bailment is a transaction under which goods are delivered by one party (the bailor) to another (the bailee) on terms which normally require the bailee to hold the goods and ultimately to redeliver them to the bailor or in accordance with his directions. The property in the goods is not intended to and does not pass on delivery though it may sometimes be the intention of the parties that it should pass in due course, as in the case of the ordinary hire-purchase contract. But where goods are delivered to another on terms which indicate that the property is to pass at once the contract must be one of sale and not bailment. In *Chapman Bros.* v. *Verco Bros. & Co. Ltd.*[1] farmers delivered bags of wheat to a company carrying on business as millers and wheat merchants. The wheat was delivered in unidentified bags which were identical to those in which other farmers delivered wheat to the company. The terms of the transaction required the company to buy and pay for the wheat on request by the farmer, or failing such a request, on a specified date, or to return an equal quantity of wheat of the same type; but there was no obligation to return the identical bags. Although the contract referred to the company as "storers" it was held by the Australian High Court that this transaction was necessarily one of sale as the property passed to the company on delivery.

Sale and Hire-Purchase

Contracts of hire-purchase resemble contracts of sale very closely, and indeed in practically all cases of hire-purchase the ultimate sale of the goods is the real object of the transaction. Nonetheless, in a legal sense the distinction is clear and important, though its importance has been greatly diminished by the Consumer Credit Act, 1974. A sale is a contract whereby the seller "transfers or agrees to transfer the property in goods to the buyer," that is to say, as soon as the contract is made the ultimate destination of the goods is determined even though the property is not to pass for some considerable time, for example until all the instalments of the price have been paid. A con-

[1] (1933), 49 C.L.R. 306; see also *South Australian Insurance Co.* v. *Randall* (1869), L.R. 3 P.C. 101.

tract of hire-purchase, on the other hand, is a bailment of the goods coupled with an option to purchase them which may or may not be exercised. Not until the option is exercised will there be a contract of sale.

The similarity between the two transactions is accentuated by the artificial nature of most hire-purchase agreements. This is brought out by consideration of three points. Firstly, as already observed, the real object of a contract of hire-purchase is almost invariably the sale of the goods. Secondly, the amount which the hirer is bound to pay under the contract is usually far in excess of the amount which he would have had to pay if he were really hiring the goods. And thirdly, the legal purchase price for which the hirer has the option to buy the goods is frequently nominal only, and in fact is often not exacted in practice.

Under the provisions of the Consumer Credit Act, 1974 (first enacted by the Hire-Purchase Act, 1965), a conditional sale agreement in which the price is payable by instalments is, for most purposes, assimilated to a hire-purchase agreement, with the result that a "sale" of goods by instalments can now take only one of two forms.

1. The contract may be a genuine contract of sale in which the buyer is bound to buy, and to pay the whole price, and the seller is bound to sell. The property in the goods will pass at once with a purely personal obligation to pay the price in instalments. In this case there is an absolute contract of sale, and obviously the buyer can pass a good title to a third party; and, should he go bankrupt, the seller has no claim to the goods.

2. Alternatively, the passing of the property may be made conditional on the payment of the instalments (or a number of them). Under the Hire-Purchase Act, 1965, it made virtually no difference whether this transaction was drafted as a sale, or in the traditional form of a contract of hire, together with an option to purchase. Under the Supply of Goods Act, 1973, this is no longer wholly true. In that Act the sections dealing with sales, and not those dealing with hire-purchase, apply to conditional sales. But this is of little moment because the wording of the two sets of provisions in that Act is virtually identical. It therefore remains true to say that for most purposes there is no distinction between a conditional sale and a hire-purchase contract. In either event the agreement takes effect as a hire-purchase agreement, and in either event the "buyer" is unable to pass a good title to the goods should he purport to sell them before the property has vested in him. The exception for motor vehicles also applies in both cases.[1] Again, in either event, the property remains in the seller (in the one case, until the condition is satisfied, in the other, till the option is

exercised) and the seller would be able to claim the goods should the buyer become bankrupt before the property has vested in him.

Quite apart from any question of re-sale by the buyer, it is important to note that a transaction under which a person "buys" goods on hire-purchase is often, and in the motor trade, is usually, a complex transaction involving three and not two parties. In such a case the seller sells the goods to a finance company which lets them on hire-purchase terms to the "buyer". It follows that the "buyer" has no contractual relations with the seller, and although the latter may be liable in tort for negligence[1] he cannot be sued on the terms implied by the Sale of Goods Act, which create liability even in the absence of negligence.[2] But if the seller gives an express warranty to the "buyer" in consideration of which the latter enters into the contract of hire-purchase with the finance company to which the seller has sold the goods, then the seller can be held liable on this separate contract of guarantee.[3] The finance company may also be liable on the terms implied by the Supply of Goods (Implied Terms) Act, 1973. Under the Consumer Credit Act, 1974, it would be more correct to refer to the buyer as the debtor, and to the seller as the supplier, but the principles themselves are not changed.

Hire-purchase contracts were developed in England towards the end of the nineteenth century, and it is impossible to understand why they came into existence without an appreciation of the legal context which already existed. There was clearly a need for a form of contract of sale of goods on credit, under which the seller could reserve some security interest in the goods. Consumers wanted to buy on credit, and financiers who were willing to supply the credit wanted security. Two obstacles existed to achieving this desired end through the most obvious legal methods. On the one hand, the seller might simply sell and deliver the goods on credit while expressly stipulating that the property in the goods should remain his until the buyer had paid the price. This is a conditional sale, and it did give the seller *some* security: it protected him against the possibility of the buyer's insolvency. But it did not protect him against the possibility that the buyer might sell the goods to a third party before he had paid the whole price. Even though the seller had reserved the property in the goods, Sect. 25 (2) of the Sale of Goods Act[4] enabled a person who had "bought or agreed to buy goods" to pass a good title to a third party. In *Lee* v. *Butler*[5] the Court of Appeal held that this provision clearly applied where the buyer was in possession of the goods under an agreement to buy the goods and pay the price in instalments.

---

[1] *Herschtal* v. *Stewart & Ardern, Ltd.*, [1940] 1 K.B. 155.
[2] *Drury* v. *Victor Buckland, Ltd.*, [1941] 1 All E.R. 269.
[3] *Brown* v. *Sheen & Richmond Car Sales, Ltd.*, [1950] 1 All E.R. 1102.
[4] *Post*, p. 205.
[5] [1893] 2 Q.B. 318.

The alternative way of achieving the desired result was for the seller to sell and deliver the goods outright to the buyer but to require the buyer to grant him a mortgage, or charge, or a right to repossess the goods in the event of the buyer's failure to pay the instalments. At common law it was possible to create a charge of this nature on goods which would be binding even on third parties. Most probably, a legal arrangement of this nature would still have been caught by Sect. 25 (2) of the Sale of Goods Act, but there was a more fundamental objection to this device. The whole essence of this scheme is that one person, the buyer (A), should have the possession of goods and be entitled to the use of them as though he were the owner, while another person, the financier (B), should actually have a charge or mortgage on the goods. Now this kind of transaction is one which is frowned upon by the law because third parties may be induced to do business with, or give credit to, A in the belief that he is the unencumbered owner of the goods in question. And if A becomes insolvent they will then find that B has a prior claim to the goods. It is generally thought to be unfair that B should be able to do this unless he has in some way publicised his transaction with A. Accordingly the Bills of Sale Acts of 1878 and 1882 require a transaction of this kind to be made by a written instrument called a bill of sale which is required to be registered under the Acts.

The Bills of Sale Acts had two great disadvantages. First, they required some degree of publicity—that was their whole purpose, of course—and borrowers may have disliked this requirement. But secondly, they rapidly attracted a body of extremely technical case law, and it became easy to fall foul of the Acts by accident so that the security granted (and in some cases the right to interest also) might become void. The result was a search for a legal form of sale which enabled the seller to retain security in the goods without falling foul of the Bills of Sale Acts and which also gave protection against bona fide purchasers from the buyer. The contract of hire-purchase was the answer and its efficacy was upheld by the House of Lords in two cases in 1895. In *Helby* v. *Matthews*[1] it was held that a person in possession of goods under a hire-purchase agreement had not "bought or agreed to buy" them within the meaning of Sect. 25 (2) of the Sale of Goods Act. This meant that the buyer, or the "hirer" as it now became more correct to call him, could not dispose of the goods to a third party in contravention of the agreement, and the seller's (or "owner's") security was thus protected. And in *McEntire* v. *Crossley Bros.*[2] it was held that a hire-purchase contract did not fall within the Bills of Sale Acts; those Acts, it was held, only applied where an owner of goods granted a charge, or right to seize the goods to another party, while in the hire-

[1] [1895] A.C. 471.
[2] [1895] A.C. 457.

purchase contract the hirer was not owner at the time he granted the right to seize the goods.

With the blessing of the House of Lords to the legal arrangements, the way was paved for the great commercial expansion of the use of hire-purchase contracts. For the next forty years the use of the contract spread throughout the entire field of consumer purchasing of goods other than purely consumable or perishable goods; and it also began to be used in some commercial situations.

As time went on, it became increasingly obvious that the contract of hire-purchase was being used as a form (in effect) of secured sale. Instead of borrowing the money to buy the goods, and mortgaging the goods to the lender as a security, the consumer entered into a hire-purchase contract with the financier. While this achieved similar results from the financier's point of view, at least in the sense that it gave him the security he wanted, it created a good deal of difficulty because the legal form of the transaction did not reflect the fact that, as a mortgagor, the hirer had an "equity" in the goods. In the land law it has for centuries been recognised that a mortgage is a security device (no matter what its form) and that the mortgagor has an "equity" in the land mortgaged. This "equity" meant that for most purposes the mortgagor was treated as owner of the land and the mortgagee's interests were confined to using the land as a security for repayment of the loan. So long as the mortgagee obtained repayment, plus interest, the mortgagor was always entitled to the residuary "equity". These familiar principles of the land law were not recognised as applicable to hire-purchase contracts; and so long as total freedom of contract prevailed, much hardship to the consumer resulted. For example, if the hirer paid nine-tenths of the price and defaulted in payment of the final instalment the finance company might seize the goods and resell them, retaining the proceeds for itself. Abuses of this kind led to the gradual legislative recognition of the hirer's equity. These reforms began with the Hire-Purchase Act, 1938, and were greatly extended and strengthened in the Hire-Purchase Acts of 1964 and 1965. But these reforms did not touch the basic problem that the form of the hire-purchase contract was recognised as creating a sharp difference between a hire-purchase and a sale of goods. The law continued to distinguish sharply between the legal rights and duties of a consumer who borrowed money to buy goods, or bought them on credit, or acquired them under a hire-purchase contract.

A movement for reform began to attract support under which hire-purchase contracts, as a separate legal contract, would be abolished. If a person wanted to buy goods by instalments he would, in law, buy those goods under a contract of sale of goods; if he did not have the cash to pay the full price down, he could borrow the money from a third party (such as a finance company, or a bank), or alternatively he could buy on credit from the actual seller. If necessary, the law could then provide some simple process to enable the buyer to "mortgage" the goods to the lender by way of security. This movement for reform began to grow after the general adoption throughout the United States of the Uniform Commercial Code, Article IX of which proceeded along these lines. Then in 1971 the Crowther Committee on Consumer Credit examined this problem at length as part of a general enquiry into the whole field of consumer credit.[1] This Committee proposed the abolition of hire-purchase contracts and the enactment of legislation along lines similar to those of the American Uniform Commercial Code. This recommendation was not wholly accepted by the Government. Partly because there was some disagreement with the idea that a hire-purchase agreement was always based on a "fiction", and partly because the public and the trade were familiar with the concept, it was felt to be going too far to abolish the contract altogether. Consequently the Consumer Credit Act, 1974, retains the hire-purchase contract. It is, however, very important to appreciate that although the name and form of hire-purchase as a distinct contract have been retained, the substance of the matter is very different. The Hire-Purchase Acts have been almost entirely repealed by the Consumer Credit Act, and the rights and duties of the parties involved in a hire-purchase contract now differ hardly at all from those of parties to a sale of goods in which the consumer has obtained credit, whether from the seller or a third party. The principal remaining differences are all concerned with the problem of the seller's security right to the goods. The Crowther Committee's recommendations as to the law relating to the use of chattels as security remain to be implemented pending further examination by the Government. In the meantime, a contract of hire-purchase (or of conditional sale) remains the principal method by which a financier or seller can reserve a security interest in the goods sold; a sale on credit, without any reservation of property, means that the seller retains no security rights in the goods.[2]

Sale and Loan on Security

Parties sometimes enter into, or go through the motions of entering into, a contract to sell goods with the intention of using the goods as a security for a loan of money. If the owner of goods (A) wishes to borrow money on the security of the goods he may charge or mortgage them to B on the understanding that (1) A will retain possession of the goods, (2) A will repay B what he has borrowed together with interest, and (3) B will have a right to take the goods from A if and only if A fails to repay the loan or interest at the agreed time.

Partly in order to evade the Bills of Sale Acts but partly for other reasons, parties sometimes enter into this kind of transaction in the

[1] Cmnd. 4596.   [2] See further on hire-purchase contracts, *post*, p. 320.

form of a sale—thus A would "sell" his goods to B, though retaining possession of them and only giving B the right to seize them in certain events. In modern times this kind of transaction is almost invariably reinforced with a hire-purchase agreement. A "sells" the goods (usually a motor vehicle) to B for a cash price and then B lets the same vehicle to A under a hire-purchase contract. Under Sect. 61 (4) of the Sale of Goods Act—

> The provisions of this Act relative to contracts of sale do not apply to any transaction in the form of a contract of sale which is intended to operate by way of mortgage, pledge, charge or other security.

Moreover, in analysing a transaction of this nature the courts have always insisted that the substance of the transaction and not merely its form must be examined. If the transaction is "really" a loan on the security of the goods the Bills of Sale Acts will apply and if it is un-registered (as it nearly always is) the contract is void and the chargee will be unable to seize the goods, or even to recover the agreed interest though the actual loan itself will be recoverable as money had and received.[1] If on the other hand the parties "really" intend the transaction to be a genuine "sale" followed by a genuine "hire-purchase" contract the transaction will be valid and the two contracts will take effect according to their terms. For instance, in *Kingsley* v. *Sterling Industrial Securities, Ltd.*,[2] Winn, L.J., said—

> In my definite view the sole or entirely dominant question upon that part of the appeal to which I have so far adverted is whether in reality and upon a true analysis of the transactions and each of them, and having regard in particular to the intention of the parties, they constituted loans or sales. It is clear upon the authorities that if a transaction is in reality a loan of money intended to be secured by, for example, a sale and hiring agreement, the document or documents embodying the arrangement will be within the Bills of Sale Acts; it is equally clear that each case must be determined according to the proper inference to be drawn from the facts and whatever the form the transaction may take the court will decide according to its real substance.

It might have been thought that such an approach would usually lead to the transaction being struck down since in most such cases the parties do not "really" intend the goods to be "sold."[3] This is borne out by the fact that the sale price will rarely be fixed by the market price of the goods but will depend on the amount the seller wishes to raise, though doubtless the market price will normally represent at least the maximum which the buyer will pay or lend. Moreover, there is never any intention in such transactions for the possession of the goods to be given unless the seller defaults in payment of the hire-

---

[1] *North Central Wagon Finance Co., Ltd.* v. *Brailsford*, [1962] 1 W.L.R. 1288.
[2] [1967] 2 Q.B. 747, 780.
[3] See Fitzpatrick, [1969] *Journal of Business Law*, 211.

purchase rental; hence the implied conditions under the Supply of Goods Act would be absurdly inappropriate. Nevertheless the modern tendency has been to uphold the genuineness of these transactions though judicial disagreements are frequent.[1] The difficulty is to formulate any criterion by which the "real intention" of the parties may be judged. The most recent pronouncements on this issue tend to take at their face value the intention of the parties as expressed in the written documents which they have executed. The argument that these documents are "shams" because they do not express the "real intention" of the parties has been rejected unless it is shown that both parties do not intend the documents to operate according to their terms. Thus in *Snook* v. *London and West Riding Investments Ltd.* Diplock, L.J., said—

> As regards the contention of the plaintiff that the transactions between himself, Auto Finance and the defendants were a "sham," it is, I think, necessary to consider what, if any, legal concept is involved in the use of this popular and pejorative word. I apprehend that, if it has any meaning in law, it means acts done or documents executed by the parties to the "sham" which are intended by them to give to third parties or to the court the appearance of creating between the parties legal rights and obligations different from the actual legal rights and obligations (if any) which the parties intend to create. But one thing, I think, is clear in legal principle, morality and the authorities (see *Yorkshire Railway Wagon Co.* v. *Maclure*[2] and *Stoneleigh Finance Ltd.* v. *Phillips*),[3] that for acts or documents to be a "sham," with whatever legal consequences follow from this, all the parties thereto must have a common intention that the acts or documents are not to create the legal rights and obligations which they give the appearance of creating. No unexpressed intentions of a "shammer" affect the rights of a party whom he deceived. There is an express finding in this case that the defendants were not parties to the alleged "sham." So this contention fails.[4]

These refinancing transactions are not prohibited by the new legislation, although the Consumer Credit Act has the result of conferring upon the "seller" the protection of the general provisions relating to the provision of credit. It is, however, possible that the Supply of Goods Act of 1973 may indirectly affect the situation. Because of the restrictions on the right of the parties to contract out of that Act,[5] financiers may become more reluctant to enter into a transaction of this nature; what is more, because of the absurd consequences which

---

[1] See *Stoneleigh Finance, Ltd.* v. *Phillips*, [1965] 2 Q.B. 537; *Kingsley* v. *Sterling Industrial Securities, Ltd.* (*supra*); *Snook* v. *London and West Riding Investments, Ltd.*, [1967] 2 Q.B. 786.
[2] (1882), 21 Ch. D. 309, C.A.   [3] [1965] 2 Q.B. 537.   [4] [1967] 2 Q.B. 786, 802.
[5] There were, of course, similar restrictions in the previous Hire-Purchase Acts. But the new Act makes no specific provision, as the old one did, for second-hand goods. It is therefore more likely that a refinancing transaction could involve the owner in liability for the quality or fitness of the goods.

could follow, the courts may be more inclined to hold that such transactions are not genuine sales but fall within the Bills of Sale Acts.

Sale and Skill and Labour

The distinction between contracts of sale and contracts for skill and labour has agitated the courts for many years, and though its importance was greatly diminished by the repeal of Sect. 4 of the Act, it still cannot be ignored. Indeed, as previously noted, the distinction could well become more important again as a result of the Supply of Goods Act of 1973. It was thought for many years that *Lee* v. *Griffin*[1] laid down that, if a contract would result in the transfer of the property in goods from one party to another, then it must be a contract of sale. This view was exploded in *Robinson* v. *Graves*[2] where it was held that a contract to paint a portrait was a contract for skill and labour and not a contract for the sale of goods, despite the fact that it was the object of the contract to transfer the property in the completed portrait to the defendant. Greer, L.J., stated the law as follows—[3]

> If the substance of the contract . . . is that skill and labour have to be exercised for the production of the article and . . . it is only ancillary to that that there will pass from the artist to his client or customer some materials in addition to the skill involved in the production of the portrait, that does not make any difference to the result, because the substance of the contract is the skill and experience of the artist in producing the picture.

On the other hand in *Cammell Laird & Co., Ltd.* v. *Manganese Bronze & Brass Co., Ltd.*,[4] the House of Lords held that a contract for the construction of two ships' propellers was unquestionably a contract for the sale of goods.

In modern times another distinction between contracts of sale of goods and contracts for skill and labour has emerged which is sometimes of the greatest importance. In a contract of sale of goods the seller's obligations with regard to the goods sold are normally "strict" in the sense that they extend to latent defects and do not depend on proof of negligence.[5] But in a contract for skill and labour—or a contract for services as it would be more normally termed today—the party rendering the services is usually held to undertake only to exercise all due skill and care and is not liable in the absence of negligence. The distinction is well illustrated by the decision of the New York Court of Appeals in *Perlmutter* v. *Beth David Hospital*[6] in which the plaintiff was given a blood transfusion in the defendants' hospital. The blood was contaminated with jaundice viruses which, according to the expert

[1] (1861), 1 B. & S. 272.   [2] [1935] 1 K.B. 579.
[3] [1935] 1 K.B. at p. 587.   [4] [1934] A.C. 402.
[5] *Post*, p. 99.   [6] (1955), 123 N.E. 2d. 792.

evidence, were not detectable by any scientific tests, and the plaintiff suffered injury in consequence. The plaintiff was a paying patient at the hospital and in the account rendered to him he was charged a separate sum for the cost of the blood itself. The plaintiff claimed that the blood had been "sold" to him and that the defendants were therefore liable for "defects" in the blood on the basis of implied warranties.[1] But the majority of the Court held that the transaction was one of services only and that the supply of the blood was merely incidental to those services, and an English Court would almost certainly concur with this decision.

On the other hand, in *Dodd* v. *Wilson*,[2] the plaintiff contracted with a veterinary surgeon to inoculate his cattle with a serum, which the surgeon did, using vaccine which he had himself bought from suppliers of vaccine. It was held that this was not a contract of sale but that nevertheless the surgeon impliedly warranted the vaccine to be fit for the purpose for which it was supplied. Hence he was liable despite the fact that he was not himself guilty of negligence.

It is by no means easy to distinguish these cases. Perhaps what underlies the distinction is that human blood for transfusion is not ordinarily thought of as the subject of commerce which is bought and sold,[3] whereas cattle serum clearly is ordinarily the subject of contracts of sale. And although in *Dodd* v. *Wilson* the contract between the plaintiff and the surgeon was not one of sale, the learned judge evidently did not wish to deprive the plaintiff of the remedy which he would undoubtedly have had, if he had himself bought the serum and merely obtained the services of the defendant to inoculate his cattle with the serum. In fact the surgeon brought in his suppliers as third parties to the case and the suppliers brought in the manufacturers as fourth parties. Since the transactions between these parties, and between the surgeon and his suppliers, were clearly contracts of sale, the liability was in fact passed down the line to the manufacturers.

Sale and Labour and Materials

A contract for the supply of goods to be installed or fitted into a building or construction is normally regarded as a contract for labour and materials and not a contract for the sale of goods. Although such a contract may differ in some respects from a contract of sale—in particular with respect to the time when the property in the materials passes to the buyer or client[4]—the House of Lords has recently stressed the undesirability of drawing unnecessary distinctions between these types of contract with regard to the implied duties of the supplier.[5] It should make no difference to the duties of a supplier of household

[1] See *post*, p. 80 [2] [1946] 2 All E.R. 691.
[3] See Titmuss, *The Gift Relationship* (Harmondsworth, 1973).
[4] See *Pritchett & Gold & Electrical Power Storage Co.* v. *Currie*, [1916] 2 Ch. 515, *post*, p. 151.
[5] *Young & Marten, Ltd.* v. *McManus Childs, Ltd.*, [1969] 1 A.C. 454.

installations whether the supplier sells them as goods or agrees also to install them as fixtures.[1] But once again the Supply of Goods Act means that the terms to be implied in such contracts will probably differ in the future; and even more important, perhaps, is that exclusion clauses which would be void in a sale will be valid if the contract is for labour and materials.

Sale and Agency

It may, at first sight, seem a little odd that it is thought necessary to distinguish a contract of sale of goods from a contract of agency, but in a certain type of case the distinction may well be a fine one by no means easy to draw. Where, for example, A asks B, a commission agent, to obtain goods for him from a supplier or from any other source, and B complies by sending the goods to A, it may well be a fine point whether it is a contract under which B sells the goods to A, or is a contract under which B acts as A's agent to obtain the required goods from other sources.

It is important to distinguish between the two transactions for a number of reasons. For one thing, if the transaction is an agency there may be privity of contract between the buyer and the agent's supplier which will enable action to be brought between them [2] On the other hand, if it is a sale, there will be no privity between the buyer and the seller's own supplier. Other reasons for distinguishing the relationship of agent and seller may be that the duties of a commission agent are less stringent than those of a seller, and in the event of a breach of contract the measure of damages may be different. Thus if a seller delivers less than he is bound to deliver under the contract the buyer can reject the whole,[3] but if, despite his best endeavours, a commission agent delivers less than his principal has ordered he has committed no breach of contract and the principal is bound to accept whatever is delivered.[4] Again, should the commission agent deliver goods of the wrong quality he will only have to pay as damages the actual loss suffered by the buyer.[5] On the other hand should a seller be guilty of such a breach he may have to pay as damages the buyer's probable loss of profit. So also an agent who merely introduces a seller to a buyer is not necessarily warranting the seller's title to sell; whereas if he is himself buying and reselling, such a warranty is invariably implied.[6]

Where one person contracts to manufacture goods for another out

---

[1] Ibid.   [2] *Teheran–Europe Corpn.* v. *Belton, Ltd.,* [1968] 2 Q.B. 545.
[3] Sect. 30 (1), see p. 67, *post.*
[4] *Ireland* v. *Livingston* (1872), L.R. 5 H.L. 395. Similarly in the case of late shipment: *Anglo-African Shipping Co.* v. *J. Mortner, Ltd.,* [1962] 1 Lloyd's Rep. 610.
[5] *Cassaboglou* v. *Gibb* (1883), 11 Q.B.D. 797.
[6] See *Warmings Used Cars, Ltd.* v. *Tucker,* [1956] S.A.S.R. 249, where it was held that the defendant did not warrant title although the transaction was a sale; but it seems that the defendant might more properly have been treated as a mere agent.

of materials to be supplied by that other, it may again be doubtful whether the manufacturer is a seller or an agent.[1]

In the converse position, where a person contracts to dispose of the goods of another, it is again necessary to decide whether the relationship between the parties is that of buyer and seller or principal and agent. In the latter case the agent is not a buyer, and therefore cannot pass a good title to a third party without the principal's actual or apparent authority.[2] The relationship between the principal and the agent depends, of course, on the terms, express or implied, of the contract between them; but in many cases the agent will have the goods on "sale or return" or similar terms in which case, although the transaction is not strictly a sale, the Sale of Goods Act applies.[3]

NUMBER OF PARTIES

It has been decided that the requirement that the property be transferred from one party to another means that there must be two distinct parties to a contract of sale. In *Graff* v. *Evans*,[4] decided in 1882, eleven years before the Act was passed, it was held that the transfer of intoxicating liquor by the manager of an unincorporated club to a member for money was not a "sale" within the Licensing Act but merely a transfer of special property. The basis of the decision was that the member was himself a part owner of the liquor and that consequently the transaction was a release of the rights of the other members to the "purchaser". It might have been thought, therefore, that when Sect. 1 (1) of the Act specifically enacted that—

. . . There may be a contract of sale between one part owner and another

the basis of *Graff* v. *Evans* had been swept away. But in *Davies* v. *Burnett*[5] a Divisional Court followed the earlier case and the Sale of Goods Act was not even referred to. This view of the law has now been accepted for so long that it is unlikely to be upset by a higher court.[6]

It should be observed that, though the Act contemplates two distinct parties to the contract, viz. a buyer and a seller, it does not follow that the buyer cannot be the owner of the goods; for the seller may be a person having legal authority to sell them, for example a sheriff acting in execution of a writ of *fi. fa.* However, if a person contracts to buy his own goods from someone else, under the mistaken impression that the goods belong to the seller, it seems clear that he can

[1] Cf. *Dixon* v. *London Small Arms Co., Ltd.* (1876), 1 App. Cas. 633; *Hill & Sons* v. *Edwin Showell* (1918), 87 L.J.K.B. 1106.
[2] *Edwards* v. *Vaughan* (1910), 26 T.L.R. 545.
[3] Sect. 18, Rule 4.   [4] (1882), 8 Q.B.D. 373.   [5] [1902] 1 K.B. 666.
[6] In any event the particular difficulty in question has been met by legislation: see Part II of the Licensing Act, 1964, which regulates the "supply" of liquor in clubs. See also *Carlton Lodge Club* v. *Customs & Excise Commissioners*, [1974] 3 All E.R. 798.

recover any price paid on the ground of total failure of consideration. *A fortiori* if he has not yet paid the price the seller cannot sue him for it. This does not mean that such a contract is necessarily void.

THE PRICE

Sect. 8 of the Act is as follows—

(1) The price in a contract of sale may be fixed by the contract, or may be left to be fixed in manner thereby agreed, or may be determined by the course of dealing between the parties.

(2) Where the price is not determined in accordance with the foregoing provisions the buyer must pay a reasonable price. What is a reasonable price is a question of fact dependent on the circumstances of each particular case.

We have already seen that the price must be paid in money, and that strictly speaking the contract will not be a contract of sale of goods if the consideration is in some other form. There are, it is true, dicta in *Koppel* v. *Koppel*[1] indicating that a contract to transfer goods in return for services is a sale of goods but these seem to have been *per incuriam*.

Sect. 8 has given rise to more difficulty than might have been thought. The section assumes that a contract has been made by the parties and then proceeds to explain the methods by which the price can be ascertained. But the first point which must be considered in an action on the sale is whether a contract has in fact been finally agreed upon by the parties; and the absence of an agreement as to the price (or even as to the mode in which the price is to be paid[2]) may provide good evidence that the parties have not yet reached a concluded contract. The second problem concerns the question whether the parties can make a binding contract in which they agree to fix the price at some future date. When Sect. 8 says that the price can be "left to be fixed in manner thereby agreed" does this exclude the possibility that "the manner" may simply require the parties to agree on the price? There is undoubtedly some support for this view in the difficult case of *May & Butcher* v. *The King*.[3] The House of Lords here held that an agreement for the sale of goods at a price to be later fixed by the parties was not, in the circumstances of the case, a concluded contract; but the later case of *Hillas & Co., Ltd.* v. *Arcos, Ltd.*[4] shows that we cannot regard the earlier case as laying down any general rule and that that case is best regarded as one where the parties had not in the circumstances arrived at a concluded agreement. In *Foley* v. *Classique Coaches, Ltd.*,[5] the Court of Appeal held that an agreement to supply petrol "at a price to be agreed by the parties" was a binding contract as the parties had clearly evinced an intention to be bound. The price to be paid was a

---

[1] [1966] 1 W.L.R. 802, at p. 811.
[2] See *Ingram* v. *Little*, [1961] 1 Q.B. 31, *per* Sellers, L.J., at p. 49.
[3] [1934] 2 K.B. 17n.   [4] [1932] All E.R. Rep. 494.   [5] [1934] 2 K.B. 1.

reasonable one, presumably under Sect. 8 of the Act, though in fact no reference was made to it in the judgments.

In the Australian High Court suggestions have been made that Sect. 8 is "anomalous" and is not to be extended;[1] and it has also been suggested in the same case that the section only applies where the goods have been delivered and accepted, and that it has no application to a purely executory contract.[2] Despite the high authority of these dicta, they seem to have little to commend them, and they have not been followed even in Australia.[3]

Sect. 9 runs as follows—

(1) Where there is an agreement to sell goods on the terms that the price is to be fixed by the valuation of a third party, and such third party cannot or does not make such valuation, the agreement is avoided; provided that if the goods or any part thereof have been delivered to and appropriated by the buyer he must pay a reasonable price therefore.

(2) Where such third party is prevented from making the valuation by the fault of the seller or buyer, the party not in fault may maintain an action for damages against the party in fault.

An agreement for the sale of goods at a valuation to be made by a third party must be distinguished from an agreement for sale at a valuation without naming any third party who is to make the valuation. In the former event, Sect. 9 applies and if the third party does not make the valuation the contract is avoided, subject to the effect of Sect. 9 (2). But in the latter event (for example, a sale of stock "at valuation") the agreement is in effect an agreement for sale at a reasonable price and, if no valuer is agreed and the parties otherwise fail to come to some arrangement for valuation, the contract will stand as a contract for sale at a reasonable price under Sect. 8.[4]

The sort of situation which is probably envisaged by Sect. 9 (2) is, for example, a refusal by the seller to allow the valuer access to the goods, thereby preventing him obtaining the necessary material for making his valuation. It is a little difficult to imagine circumstances in which the buyer could prevent the valuer making his valuation but no doubt this was inserted *ex abundanti cautela* to meet all possible contingencies.

CONVEYANCING EFFECT OF THE CONTRACT

Some comment must be made here on the words "A contract of sale of goods is a contract whereby the seller *transfers . . . the property*

[1] *Hall* v. *Busst* (1960), 104 C.L.R. 206.

[2] Ibid., at p. 234. The basis for this view is the words in Sect. 8 (2) providing that "the buyer must pay a reasonable price". It is argued that, if the contract is executory, the seller's only remedy is for damages and not the price (see *post*, p. 271). But this seems to confuse the buyer's contractual obligations with the seller's remedies in the event of non-performance by the buyer.

[3] *Wenning* v. *Robinson* (1964), 64 S.R. (N.S.W.) 157.

[4] Ibid.

in goods" in Sect. 1 (1). As is clearly apparent from these words the actual contract may suffice to transfer the property in the goods, that is to say it operates both as a conveyance and a contract. Attention is frequently drawn to this as though it were a remarkable rule, and a contrast is often made with the corresponding provisions of Roman law in which a sharp line was drawn between the contract and the conveyance. There is some point in this contrast, but a note of caution should be sounded against pursuing it too far, for remarkably few results follow in English law from the transfer of property by the mere agreement which would not in any event follow from the transfer of property by delivery. This topic will be more fully examined later (pp. 141 *et seq.*).

It is possible that these words in Sect. 1 (1) may also have the effect of bringing a transaction within the scope of a contract of sale even though it would be difficult to say that the object of the transaction was the transfer of the property in any goods. For example, if a person organises a party for which he sells tickets entitling the purchaser of the ticket to help himself to drinks, it seems that a sale takes place when this happens, although it would be difficult to say that there was a contract of sale of goods arising from the mere sale of the ticket.[1] On the other hand the courts have shown little inclination to make use of this analysis in civil cases. Thus in the case of a contract for work and materials the courts have not said that there is a contract of sale within the Act when property in the materials eventually passes to the party ordering the work and materials.[2]

[1] See *Doak* v. *Bedford*, [1964] 2 Q.B. 587 *per* Paull, J., at p. 596, but cf. Lord Parker, C.J., at p. 594.
[2] See *Young & Marten, Ltd.* v. *McManus Childs, Ltd.* (*supra*).

CHAPTER 3

FORMATION OF THE CONTRACT

OFFER AND ACCEPTANCE

THOUGH Part I of the Act is entitled "Formation of the Contract" it is somewhat paradoxical that there is nothing in it which regulates the actual formation of the contract of sale of goods. The only section which deals with this subject is Sect. 58 in Part VI governing the sale of goods by auction.

We are left to infer from Sect. 61 (2) that a contract of sale of goods is formed according to the ordinary principles of the common law, that is to say by offer and acceptance. As there is nothing in these rules of special significance in the law of sale of goods this subject need not be enlarged upon here.

AUCTION SALES

The first two subsections of Sect. 58 are as follows—

(1) Where goods are put up for sale by auction in lots, each lot is prima facie deemed to be the subject of a separate contract of sale:

(2) A sale by auction is complete when the auctioneer announces its completion by the fall of the hammer, or in other customary manner. Until such announcement is made any bidder may retract his bid:

No difficulty arises here and no comment is thought necessary. The next two subsections however, give rise to more difficulty.

(3) Where a sale by auction is not notified to be subject to a right to bid on behalf of the seller, it shall not be lawful for the seller to bid himself or to employ any person to bid at such sale, or for the auctioneer knowingly to take any bid from the seller or any such person: Any sale contravening this rule may be treated as fraudulent by the buyer:

(4) A sale by auction may be notified to be subject to a reserve or upset price, and a right to bid may also be reserved expressly by or on behalf of the seller. Where a right to bid is expressly reserved, but not otherwise, the seller, or any one person on his behalf, may bid at the auction.

The effect of these subsections may be considered under three heads.

Auction Sale Expressly Subject to Reserve Price or Right to Bid

Firstly, where the auction is expressly advertised subject to a reserve price or to the right of the seller to bid, subsect. (4) preserves the seller's right not to sell below the reserve price, or to bid himself or to employ one (but no more than one) person to bid on his behalf, as the case may be. But as we have seen subsect. (2) preserves the common law rule that no contract of sale comes into existence until the seller accepts a bid. Subsect. (4) therefore has independent force only where the auctioneer knocks the goods down below the reserve price by mistake. The effect of such a mistake was discussed in *McManus* v. *Fortescue*.[1] In that case the printed catalogue at an auction sale stated that each lot was subject to a reserve price, but the auctioneer knocked the goods down to the plaintiff for less than the reserved price by mistake. Recollecting the reserve price the auctioneer then refused to sign a memorandum of sale.[2] It was held by the Court of Appeal that an action against the auctioneer must fail. Since the sale was expressly subject to a reserve price the auctioneer could not be made liable for breach of warranty of authority. An action against the owner would presumably also have failed as the auctioneer's authority was known to be limited and was in fact exceeded. It is a fair inference that had the sale not been notified to the public as being subject to a reserve price the seller would have been liable as the buyer would have been able to rely upon the auctioneer's apparent authority.

Auction Sale with No Express Statement as to Reserve Price or Right to Bid

Where nothing is said about any reserve price or right of the owner to bid, a distinction must be drawn between the two cases. In the former case the effect of Sect. 58 (2) is that the auctioneer is still entitled to decline to accept any bid. In the latter case however, subsect. (3) applies, and the buyer may set the contract aside, or presumably may sue for damages. Even where a reserve price is notified the owner is still not entitled to bid unless this right also is expressly reserved, and if he does so bid and the reserve price is reached the contract may be treated as fraudulent by the buyer. If the reserve price is not reached however, although the seller may have wrongly bid himself, no one will have suffered damage so as to entitle him to sue the seller.

Auction Sale Expressly Advertised Without Reserve

The effect of an express notification that the sale will be without reserve is left obscure by the Act. It is at any rate clear that Sect. 58 (2) prevents any contract of sale coming into existence if the auctioneer refuses to accept a bid. There remains the possibility that the auctioneer may be held liable on the basis that he has contracted to sell the goods to the highest bidder, a device sanctioned by the Court of Exchequer Chamber in *Warlow* v. *Harrison*.[3] The difficulties of this

---

[1] [1907] 2 K.B. 1.
[2] If he had signed, *semble*, he would have been liable: *Fay* v. *Miller*, [1941] 2 All E.R. 18.
[3] (1859), 1 E. & E. 309.

case have been explored by two learned writers in 68 *L.Q.R.* 238, ibid., 457, and 69 *L.Q.R.* 21. Put briefly these are (*a*) the fact that the highest bidder cannot be identified until the hammer has fallen and we are postulating a case where the auctioneer has not accepted any bid; and (*b*) the apparent lack of consideration for the auctioneer's promise. Neither of these seems to be a fatal objection, for the person who had made the highest bid when the goods were withdrawn should prima facie be able to claim that he was the highest bidder, and the lack of consideration in any strict sense is a feature common to most cases of breach of warranty of authority by an agent, as for example in *Collen* v. *Wright*.[1]

Bidding Agreements

Certain undesirable auction practices by buyers are dealt with by the Auctions (Bidding Agreements) Act, 1969. The purpose of this Act (and the earlier Act of 1927 of the same name) is to prevent dealers from agreeing to abstain from bidding at a sale so that goods may be purchased at less than their true value if no other party is interested in bidding. Sect. 3 of the new Act provides that where such an agreement is made the seller may avoid the contract and recover the goods, or, in default, any loss he has suffered (viz., the difference between the sale price and the true or fair price) from any party to the agreement. It is, however, difficult in practice to control these bidders' "rings" because of problems of proof. Moreover, the Act does not prohibit a genuine agreement to buy the goods on joint account, and in practice it may well be difficult to distinguish such an agreement from one whereby one dealer agrees not to bid for one item and another dealer agrees not to bid for another item.

MISTAKE IN THE OFFER OR ACCEPTANCE

Certain kinds of mistake, although traditionally treated as part of the generic subject "Mistake" (as they were in the first edition of this book), are really part of the law of offer and acceptance. These cases, usually referred to nowadays as cases of "mutual" and "unilateral" mistake, involve a denial by one of the parties that an agreement has ever been reached on the ground that the intention of the parties, judged objectively or subjectively as the case may be, never coincided. However, the expressions "mutual mistake" and "unilateral mistake" are somewhat misleading. The important question is not whether a mistake is one-sided or two-sided, but whether or not the mistake has prevented an agreement from coming into existence. In deciding whether the parties have in fact agreed, or must be taken in law to have agreed, the first thing to determine is whether it is a case where the parties' intentions are to be judged objectively or subjectively, for until

[1] (1857), 8 E. & B. 647.

this is done it is obviously impossible to say whether the intentions are the same; and hence, whether the parties have agreed.

Where neither party is aware of the other party's real intentions the law is clear that the offeree is entitled to judge the offerer's intentions objectively. If, so judged, the intentions coincide, then there is an agreement, and if the other requirements of the law are satisfied, a contract. For example, in *Tamplin* v. *James*,[1] the defendant agreed to buy a public house under a mistaken impression that a certain field was included in the sale. There was nothing in the sale which should have led the buyer to this mistake, and the seller was unaware of it. Applying the objective, reasonable man, test the Court of Appeal held that the buyer was liable on the contract for the sale of the public house without the field. The objective test in these cases means no more than that the parties are bound by what a reasonable man would have regarded as their intentions.

It may happen that even on the application of the objective test it is still not possible to spell out any definite contractual agreement between the parties and in such a case there is no contract. For example, in *Raffles* v. *Wichelhaus*,[2] the plaintiff agreed to sell and the defendant agreed to buy a consignment of cotton *ex Peerless* from Bombay. In fact there were two ships of that name, one leaving Bombay in October and the other in December. The seller was thinking of the later and the buyer of the earlier ship, that is to say they misunderstood each other's intentions. It was held that there was no contract and the buyer was not liable for refusing to accept the consignment arriving in the later ship.[3]

In such circumstances the main practical reason for holding that there is no contract is that the "agreement" is in fact no agreement, because its meaning is not sufficiently certain. The requirement of certainty, while it may for reasons of convenience be treated independently, is really no more than a requirement that an offer must be certain in order to be capable of being converted into a contract by acceptance.

It only remains to add that cases in which the contract will be held void on these grounds are necessarily rare for the application of the objective test will usually produce a definite result.

Where, on the other hand, one party is aware, or ought reasonably to be aware, that the other party's intentions are not the same as his own, the mistaken party's intentions cannot be judged objectively and the party who is not mistaken cannot hold the other to a contract on the terms intended by him. Thus in *Smith* v. *Hughes*,[4] the defendant

---

[1] (1880), 15 Ch. D. 215.   [2] (1864), 2 H. & C. 906.
[3] *Scriven* v. *Hindley*, [1913] 3 K.B. 564, another case of sale of goods, is open to the same explanation.
[4] (1871), L.R. 6 Q.B. 597.

bought some oats from the plaintiff but refused to take delivery on the grounds that the oats were not old, as he had thought, but new oats. In ordering a new trial on the ground of misdirection the Court drew a distinction between these two possibilities—

(a) If the defendant mistakenly thought that the goods were old, then, in the absence of warranty by the plaintiff, the defendant would be bound by the contract even though the plaintiff was aware of the mistake.

(b) On the other hand, if the defendant mistakenly thought that the plaintiff was offering to sell him the oats *as old oats*, and the plaintiff was aware of the mistake, then the defendant would not be liable for refusing to accept the oats, presumably because there would have been a binding contract to sell old oats, and the oats not being old, the defendant would have been entitled to reject them.

It is important to note that in neither case would the contract have been void.

The principle to be applied in cases of mistake as to the person is exactly the same although the application of this principle in this case may make the contract void. Firstly, a person cannot accept an offer which he knows is not intended for him, but for some third person.[1] And, secondly, a person cannot hold another to an acceptance when he knows that that other was intending to accept an offer not made by him, but by some third person.[2] It should be noted that knowledge of the mistake by the one party is essential if the contract is to be held void. It cannot be said that one party is simply unable to accept an offer not intended for him, for a person can accept an offer not intended for him if he reasonably thinks it was so intended.[3]

It is also essential that there should be some identifiable third person for whom the offer or acceptance was intended if the contract is to be held void.[4] For if there is no such third person the usual analysis is that the mistaken party does intend to contract with the other party although he is mistaken as to his attributes.[5]

These principles all go back to the late nineteenth century, if not earlier, and are well illustrated by two leading cases from that period which have caused trouble ever since. In *Cundy* v. *Lindsay*[6] a swindler named Blenkarn ordered some goods from the plaintiffs in a letter in which he signed his name so as to resemble that of Blenkiron & Co., a firm known to the plaintiffs. Although the address of Blenkarn was

---

[1] *Boulton* v. *Jones* (1857), 27 L.J. Ex. 117. It must be inferred that the plaintiff knew that the defendant intended to contract with Brocklehurst, and with him alone.

[2] *Cundy* v. *Lindsay* (1878), 3 App. Cas. 459.

[3] *Upton R.D.C.* v. *Powell*, [1942] 1 All E.R. 220; cf. Blackburn, J., in *Smith* v. *Hughes* (1871), L.R. 6 Q.B. 597, at 607.

[4] *King's Norton Metal Co., Ltd.* v. *Edridge* (1897), 14 T.L.R. 98. On this point see Glanville Williams in 23 *Can. Bar Rev.* 271.

[5] See J. Unger in 18 *M.L.R.* 259 replying to J. F. Wilson in 17 *M.L.R* 515.

[6] *Supra*, footnote 2.

not the same as that of Blenkiron & Co., they were both in the same street. The plaintiffs, without noticing the discrepancy in the street number, despatched the goods to Blenkarn who promptly disposed of them to the defendants, who bought in good faith and for value. It was held by the House of Lords that no contract existed between the plaintiffs and Blenkarn, and the case had to be decided as though Blenkarn had stolen the goods; at no stage had the plaintiffs voluntarily decided to entrust the possession of their goods to Blenkarn. On the other hand in *King's Norton Metal Co.* v. *Edridge*,[1] a swindler ordered goods under a false name, which was not that of any identified third party, and the plaintiffs despatched these goods on credit, on the strength of the order. Once again the swindler disposed of the goods to the defendants. The Court of Appeal rejected the plaintiff's claim on the ground that this was a simple case of a contract voidable for fraud, and not a contract wholly void. The distinction has long been thought to rest primarily in the presence in the earlier case of the identifiable third parties, Blenkiron & Co., with whom the plaintiffs thought they were dealing.

The application of these cases to situations where parties have dealt with each other face to face has proved particularly troublesome. In *Phillips* v. *Brooks*,[2] a swindler bought some jewellery in a shop by representing himself to be "Sir George Bullough" a real third person known by name, but not personally, to the jeweller. It was held that there was a voidable contract. On the other hand, in *Ingram* v. *Little*[3] a different result was arrived at. Here, a swindler (H) representing himself to be a certain P. G. M. H. of Caterham, a real person not known personally to the plaintiffs, bought a car from them. The Court of Appeal (Devlin, L.J., dissenting) held that there was no contract at all between the plaintiffs and H. Sellers, L.J., summarised the views of the learned judge below, with which he agreed, as follows—

> The judge, treating the plaintiffs as the offerors and the rogue H as the offeree, found that the plaintiffs, in making their offer to sell the car not for cash but for a cheque . . . were under the belief that they were dealing with, and therefore making their offer to, the honest Mr. P.G.M.H. of Caterham, who they had reason to believe was a man of substance and standing. H, the offeree, knew precisely what was in the minds of the two ladies [sc., the plaintiffs] for he had put it there, and he knew that their offer was intended for Mr. P.G.M.H. of Caterham, and that they were making no offer to, and had no intention to contract with him, as he was. There was no offer which he, H, could accept, and therefore there was no contract.[4]

However, in *Lewis* v. *Averay*,[5] yet another case of a similar nature in which a swindler bought a car in return for a cheque by representing

[1] (1897) 14 T.L.R. 98.   [2] [1919] 2 K.B. 243.   [3] [1961], 1 Q.B. 31.
[4] At p. 49.   [5] [1971] 2 All E.R. 507.

himself to be a well-known television star, the Court of Appeal threw doubt on *Ingram* v. *Little*. In this case the Court emphasised that where parties are dealing with each other face to face there is a strong presumption that there is a contract between them. But only Lord Denning, M.R., suggested that *Ingram* v. *Little* was wrongly decided. It was also said to be surprising if the result of such cases was to turn, as suggested by Sellers, L.J. in *Ingram* v. *Little* on the swindler's state of mind. However, this is largely inherent in the House of Lords' decision in *Cundy* v. *Lindsay*, although admittedly that decision did not concern agreements arrived at face to face.

The distinctions drawn in some of these cases are very fine ones; for instance *Ingram* v. *Little* is scarcely distinguishable from *Phillips* v. *Brooks* and *Lewis* v. *Averay*. So too, *Cundy* v. *Lindsay* is barely distinguishable from *King's Norton Metal Co.* v. *Edridge*. Of course fine distinctions do not necessarily mean that the distinctions are inherently unsound. It is the business of the law to draw distinctions and fine distinctions are often a necessary consequence. But these cases involve fine distinctions which are based on abstract concepts rather than on real social or commercial distinctions. It is, of course, clear that the only purpose of drawing these distinctions is to decide whether the contract is void or voidable and hence whether or not a bona fide purchaser should be protected. But whether or not the bona fide purchaser should be protected should depend on more substantial considerations than those which decide these cases. It is true that distinctions can be drawn between these cases which to some degree are more real than those which the courts drew. For instance, in *Phillips* v. *Brooks* the plaintiff was a shopkeeper who dealt in jewellery, whereas in *Ingram* v. *Little* the plaintiffs were two private sellers. Plainly a shopkeeper who sells goods on credit to someone not known to him by sight, and accepts a cheque in return, is, in many respects, in a very different situation from a private seller. On the other hand, the plaintiff in *Lewis* v. *Averay* was also a private seller and yet he was held not protected. Equally, in comparing *Cundy* v. *Lindsay* with the *King's Norton* case, it is clear that the sellers in the latter case consciously took a much greater commercial risk than the sellers in the former case. In the *King's Norton* case sellers fulfilled an order by delivering goods on credit to a company of whom they had never heard and without any attempt to secure payment in advance. In *Cundy* v. *Lindsay* the sellers did at least think they were dealing with buyers known to them by repute. These distinctions may well be valid, and they may even have influenced the actual decisions. But they are not the distinctions drawn by the courts, which appear elusive and theoretical. The courts themselves now seem unhappy with the law they have created but their response is usually to distinguish cases "on their facts" which may achieve justice but tends to create uncertainty.

The result is that proposals have been made to abolish the distinction between void and voidable contracts, and to protect the bona fide purchaser in both cases alike.[1]

[1] See the Twelfth Report of the Law Reform Committee discussed, *post*, p. 218.

CHAPTER 4

FORMALITIES

REPEAL OF SECT. 4

In 1954 the Law Reform (Enforcement of Contracts) Act repealed Sect. 4 of the Act which had for so long been a blot on our jurisprudence, with the result that nearly all contracts for the sale of goods can now be made by word of mouth, irrespective of the value of the goods sold.

Sect. 3 of the Sale of Goods Act enacts—

> Subject to the provisions of this Act and of any statute in that behalf, a contract of sale may be made in writing (either with or without seal), or by word of mouth, or partly in writing and partly by word of mouth, or may be implied from the conduct of the parties.
>
> Provided that nothing in this section shall affect the law relating to corporations.

Since the repeal of Sect. 4 the opening words of Sect. 3 have been deprived of their meaning since there are no other provisions in the Act relating to formalities. The only exceptions which need to be noted to the general effect of Sect. 3 are contracts of hire-purchase or credit-sale which come within the provisions of the Consumer Credit Act, 1974; and contracts for the purchase of a British ship or of a share therein which come within Sect. 24 of the Merchant Shipping Act, 1894. Detailed consideration is given to the Consumer Credit Act later.[1]

It is possible, also, that contracts for the sale of goods may sometimes also be contracts for the sale of an interest in land within the meaning of Sect. 40 of the Law of Property Act, 1925, and may therefore be unenforceable if there is no note or memorandum in writing of the contract. This possibility arises from the fact that the definition given to "goods" by Sect. 62 of the Sale of Goods Act includes "emblements, industrial growing crops, and things attached to or forming part of the land which are agreed to be severed before sale or under the contract of sale." There can be little doubt that this definition embraces certain goods, i.e. *fructus naturales*, at any rate in some cases, which at common law were regarded as being an interest in land. The fact that since 1893 these are "goods" within the meaning of the Sale of Goods Act does not rule out the possibility that they may at the same time be land within the meaning of the Law of Property Act.[2]

---

[1] See *post*, p. 334.
[2] See Hudson, "Goods or Land?" in (1958) 22 *Conveyancer*, 137. The title of this article is somewhat inapt, for the question is not "Goods or land?" but "Goods only or goods and land?".

BILLS OF SALE

A further word needs to be said on bills of sale within the Bills of Sale Acts to which reference has already been made in distinguishing contracts of sale from loans on the security of goods.[1] Strictly speaking these Acts do not require a contract of sale to be in writing or in any particular form. There is nothing to prevent a person buying goods under an oral contract, and allowing the seller of them to remain in possession of them, so far as the Bills of Sale Acts are concerned. But in practice a buyer who does not obtain possession of the goods would almost invariably wish to have some written evidence of the sale and if the sale is in writing, or is evidenced in writing (even by a mere receipt), the Acts will apply.

Under the Act of 1878 a sale of goods which is evidenced in writing, and under which the seller remains in possession is void against trustees in bankruptcy and persons seizing goods in judicial execution, unless the sale is made by a written instrument called a bill of sale and registered in accordance with the Act.[2] No particular form is required for a bill of sale under the Act of 1878.

The above provisions only apply if the first transaction is a genuine sale. If it only takes the form of a sale but is intended to operate as a security the Sale of Goods Act does not apply at all by reason of Sect. 61 (4). Such a transaction is covered by Sect. 8 of the Bills of Sale Act, 1882, which avoids the transaction *in toto*, that is, even as between the immediate parties, unless it is made by a registered bill of sale.[3] Moreover, a bill of sale by way of security must be made in the form prescribed in the Schedule to the Act of 1882 and failure to comply again renders the bill wholly void.

---

[1] *Supra*, p. 9.
[2] Bills of Sale Act, 1878, Sect. 8, which is still in force as regards sales despite its apparent repeal by Sect. 15 of the Act of 1882.
[3] Nevertheless, sums advanced on an unregistered bill of sale are apparently recoverable as money had and received: *North Central Wagon Finance Co., Ltd.* v. *Brailsford*, [1962] 1 W.L.R. 1288.

CHAPTER 5

SUBJECT MATTER OF THE CONTRACT

MEANING OF "GOODS"

THE term "goods" is defined by Sect. 62 as including "all chattels personal other than things in action[1] and money . . . The term includes emblements, industrial growing crops, and things attached to or forming part of the land which are agreed to be severed before sale or under the contract of sale."[2]

The only point which requires comment is the meaning of the latter part of this definition. Since the products of the soil must always be sold with a view to their ultimate severance "under the contract of sale" it appears that, whether or not they are also land within the meaning of Sect. 40 of the Law of Property Act, 1925, they are now always goods within the meaning of the Act. It is, however, still necessary to distinguish the products of the soil or "things attached to or forming part of the land" on the one hand, from the actual land itself, or interests therein, on the other. The sale of sand from a quarry for example, is not a sale of things attached to or forming part of the land, but a sale of an interest in the land itself. Thus in *Morgan* v. *Russell*[3] it was held that the sale of cinders and slag which were not definite or detached heaps resting on the ground, was not a sale of goods, but a sale of an interest in land, and therefore the Sale of Goods Act did not apply. Similarly, in *Mills* v. *Stokman*,[4] a quantity of slate which had been quarried and then left on some land as waste material for many years, was held to be part of the land, and not goods. The slate was "unwanted dross cast on one side with the intention that it should remain on the land indefinitely, and, by implication, that it should form part of the land."[5]

DIFFERENT TYPES OF GOODS

Sect. 5 of the Act is as follows—

(1) The goods which form the subject of a contract of sale may be either existing goods, owned or possessed by the seller, or goods to be manufactured or acquired by the seller after the making of the contract of sale, in this Act called "future goods."

---

[1] And therefore shares are not goods.
[2] The part omitted deals with Scots law. Scottish technical terms are omitted throughout.
[3] [1909] 1 K.B. 357.　　[4] (1966–67), 116 C.L.R. 61.　　[5] *Per* Barwick, C.J., at p. 71.

(2) There may be a contract for the sale of goods, the acquisition of which by the seller depends upon a contingency which may or may not happen.

(3) Where by a contract of sale the seller purports to effect a present sale of future goods, the contract operates as an agreement to sell the goods.

The subject matter of the contract of sale may be either existing goods owned or possessed by the seller; or future goods; or (a possibility not mentioned by the Act) a *spes*, or chance.

Existing Goods

Little need be said here except to point out that existing goods may be either specific or unascertained, and that important consequences follow from this distinction, e.g. in relation to the application of Sect. 6, and in connection with the passing of the property. These will be discussed later.[1]

Future Goods

Future goods include goods not yet in existence, and goods in existence but not yet acquired by the seller. It is probably safe to say that future goods can never be specific goods within the meaning of the Act.

This certainly seems to be true of those parts of the Act dealing with the passing of property. There remains some doubt about a number of other sections, such as Sects. 6 and 7, which apply to contracts for the sale of specific goods. In cases under Sect. 7 of the Act future goods, if sufficiently identified, may be specific goods in the limited sense that their destruction may frustrate the contract. In *Howell* v. *Coupland*[2] a sale of 200 tons of potatoes to be grown on a particular piece of land was held to be a sale of specific goods despite the fact that they were not existing goods for the purpose of the common law rules of frustration. Failure of the crop was thus held to avoid the contract. Since the Act was passed it is largely immaterial whether this result is arrived at by application of Sect. 7 or not, because the same result may be arrived at by holding the contract to be a sale within Sect. 5 (2) dependent upon a contingency.[3]

The most important question in connection with future goods, the passing of the property, will be dealt with later.[4]

---

[1] Pp. 44 and 147, *post*.

[2] (1876), 1 Q.B.D. 258. Similarly, in *Goldsborough Mort & Co., Ltd.* v. *Carter* (1914), 19 C.L.R. 429, the Australian High Court held (before the enactment of the Sale of Goods Act in New South Wales) that a sale of "about" 4,000 sheep pastured on certain lands was a sale of specific goods though the sheep were not then specifically identified.

[3] *Re Wait*, [1927] 1 Ch. 606, at p. 631, *per* Atkin, L.J.; *H. R. & S. Sainsbury* v *Street*, [1972] 1 W.L.R. 834.

[4] P. 155, *post*.

A Spes

The sale of a *spes*—a chance—must be distinguished from the contingent sale of future goods, though the distinction is not so much as to the subject matter of the contract but as to its construction. Thus it is possible for a person to agree to buy future goods from a particular source and to take the chance (or, in language appropriate to the sale of goods, the risk) of the goods never coming into existence. For example a person may agree to buy whatever crop is produced from a particular field at a fixed price. Such a transaction comes perilously close to a gamble, but as the seller stands to gain the same amount in any event it appears that the sale cannot be a wager within Sect. 18 of the Gaming Act, 1845.[1]

A transaction such as that in *Howell* v. *Coupland* is thus open to at least[2] three possible constructions—

1. It may be a contingent sale of goods within Sect. 5 (2), in which case if the crop does not come into existence the contract will not become operative at all and neither party is bound; or

2. It may be an unconditional sale, that is, the seller may warrant that there will be a crop in which case, if there is no crop, he will be liable for non-delivery; or

3. It may be a sale of a mere chance, that is the buyer may take the risk of the crop failing completely in which case the price is still payable.

Despite the fact that Sect. 5 which expressly deals with the subject matter of the contract, classifies the types of subject matter as either existing or future goods, there is in fact a much more important classification which cuts right across this one. This is the distinction between specific and unascertained goods, which is of the greatest importance in connection with the passing of the property and risk in the contract of sale. Specific goods are goods "identified and agreed upon at the time a contract of sale is made,"[3] for example this particular car, or this particular load of wheat. Unascertained goods are not defined by the Act, but they seem to fall into three main categories—

1. Goods to be manufactured or grown by the seller, which are necessarily future goods.

2. Purely generic goods, for example 100 tons of wheat, or the like, which must also be future goods, at least where the seller does not already own sufficient goods of the description in question to appropriate to the contract. Where the seller does own such a quantity of the

---

[1] See *Ellesmere* v. *Wallace*, [1929] 2 Ch. 1.
[2] At least three, because it is now clear that, where part only of the crop has perished, yet other possibilities are available, see *H. R. & S. Sainsbury* v. *Street*, [1972] 1 W.L.R. 834, discussed *post*, p. 45.
[3] So defined by Sect. 62.

goods it is not easy to apply the "future goods"/"existing goods" distinction. In one sense the goods appear to fall within the definition of "existing goods" in Sect. 5 (1), but on the other hand until the goods are appropriated to the contract the mere fact that the seller has sufficient goods for that purpose seems irrelevant. In either event it seems that nothing turns on the distinction.

3. An unidentified part of a specified whole, for example 100 tons out of a particular load of 200 tons of wheat; these may be either future or existing goods within the meaning of Sect. 5.

It will be seen that the distinction between the third type of unascertained goods and specific goods is only a matter of degree, and in a particular case it may be slight indeed. Thus if A agrees to sell to B 12 of the 13 bottles of port now in his cellar, this is a sale of unascertained goods because they are not identified, but it is obvious that such a transaction has more affinities with a sale of specific goods than with a sale of purely generic goods. It is also true, although less obviously, that the distinction between the second and third kinds of unascertained goods is only a matter of degree. The more detailed is the description of the *genus* the more it comes to resemble a sale from a specified bulk or stock. It will be seen later that the failure of the Act to draw these distinctions has led to unfortunate results. In particular the classification of the third of the above three types as unascertained has led to difficulties in connection with the passing of property and risk, and also in connection with the doctrine of frustration.

CHAPTER 6

THE TYPES OF OBLIGATION CREATED

THE CORE OF THE CONTRACT

THERE has been much discussion in recent years over the need to distinguish the fundamental obligation created by a contract from ancillary obligations, however important, and whether conditions or warranties.[1] The reason for drawing such a distinction arose mainly when the contract contained a clause exempting one of the parties from liability in the event of a breach of contract. Until recently such a clause could exempt a person from liability for a breach of warranty or condition, but there was a strong principle of construction under which an exemption clause, however sweeping, was prima facie not to be construed as protecting a party from the effect of a complete failure to perform the fundamental obligation imposed by the contract.[2] Moreover, it seemed that, if there was a breach of the fundamental obligation, or (which is not quite the same thing) a fundamental breach of the contract, the innocent party might be entitled to bring the contract to an end, or it might terminate automatically notwithstanding the provisions of an exemption clause. And in this event the exemption clause would not avail the guilty party.[3] It appears that, subject to one possible qualification mentioned below, it was only in relation to exemption clauses that these rules had any significance and their practical importance will now be greatly reduced by the Supply of Goods (Implied Terms) Act, 1973.[4]

In the second edition of this book it was suggested that there might be another reason why it could be important to distinguish between the core of the contract and conditions and warranties. It was there suggested that there could be no acceptance, and hence no loss of the right to reject goods where there was a complete non-performance of the contract. In the third edition, as a result of the decision in *Charterhouse Credit Co., Ltd.* v. *Tolly*,[5] this suggestion had to be modified, if not altogether rejected. In this case the Court of Appeal had no difficulty in holding that the hirer of a car under a hire-purchase agreement had affirmed the contract and accepted the goods despite a fundamental breach by the owner in supplying a car with a defective rear axle. And

[1] See Melville, 19 *M.L.R.* 26; Cheshire & Fifoot, *Law of Contract*, 8th ed., pp. 134–41, Guest, 77 *L.Q.R.* 98 and cf. Reynolds. 79 *L.Q.R.* 534.
[2] *Suisse Atlantique Société D'Armement Maritime S.A.* v. *N.V. Rotterdamsche Kolen Centrale*, [1967] 1 A.C. 361.
[3] *Harbutt's Plasticine* v. *Wayne Tank Co., Ltd.*, [1970] 1 Q.B. 447.
[4] *Post*, p. 131.   [5] [1963] 2 Q.B. 683.

it seems clear that the Court contemplated the possibility of a buyer "accepting" goods delivered by the seller even where there was a delivery of goods wholly different from those sold, e.g. a horse instead of a tractor.

But doubts have now been cast on the decision in *Charterhouse Credit* v. *Tolly*[1] and the suggestion previously made may now be put forward again. As will be seen later,[2] there are circumstances in which a buyer can be treated as having accepted goods even though he has no knowledge of defects in them, and it is arguable that there may be circumstances in which a buyer would be held not to have accepted the goods if there has been a breach of a fundamental term, although a breach of condition would not help him.[3] For example, suppose that A agrees to sell peas to B but sends him beans instead. If B, in ignorance of the substitution but having had an opportunity to examine the goods, resells and delivers the goods to C, it seems that B would not thereafter be precluded from rejecting the goods. In the *Suisse Atlantique* case Lord Reid suggested that such a delivery could not properly be treated as a delivery under the original contract at all, but only as an offer to enter into a new contract.[4] On the other hand if A had merely been guilty of a breach of condition, B would, in such circumstances, have lost his right of rejection.[5]

CONDITIONS

The term condition is not defined by the Act, but Sect. 11 (1) (*b*) states that—

> Whether a stipulation in a contract of sale is a condition, the breach of which may give rise to a right to treat the contract as repudiated, or a warranty, the breach of which may give rise to a claim for damages but not to a right to reject the goods and treat the contract as repudiated, depends in each case on the construction of the contract. A stipulation may be a condition, though called a warranty in the contract:

This paragraph therefore explains the term condition by reference to its legal effect, but it does not explain how a condition is to be distinguished from a warranty. It is enough here to say that in its usual meaning a condition is a term which, without being the fundamental obligation imposed by the contract, is still of such vital importance that it goes to the root of the transaction. The importance of a condition in contracts for the sale of goods is that its breach, if committed

---

[1] *Suisse Atlantique* case, *supra*.
[2] *Post*, p. 291.
[3] In Treitel, *Law of Contract*, 3rd ed., p. 711, this is suggested to be the reason why a breach of Sect. 12 (1) is not affected by Sect. 11 (1) (*c*), but cf. Reynolds, 79 *L.Q.R.* at 543 and 549.
[4] [1967] 1 A.C. at p. 404.
[5] See Sects. 34 and 35 of the Act as amended, *post*, pp. 288–9.

by the seller, may give the buyer the right to reject the goods completely and to decline to pay the price, or if he has already paid it,
to recover it.[1]

WARRANTIES

The term warranty is defined by Sect. 62 as "an agreement with
reference to goods which are the subject of a contract of sale, but collateral to the main purpose of such contract, the breach of which gives
rise to a claim for damages but not to a right to reject the goods and
treat the contract as repudiated." This definition thus explains both
the meaning and the legal effect of a warranty. The term "collateral",
though hallowed by usage, is not very happily chosen, for it may give
the impression that a warranty is a term which is somehow outside the
contract, whereas it is in fact a term of the contract.[2] In practice one
would not go far wrong if one were to say that, subject to a clear
contrary intention, a warranty is a minor term of the contract, while a
condition is a major term.

REPRESENTATIONS

From terms of the contract it is necessary to distinguish mere statements or representations, which are not part of the contract but may
have serious consequences nonetheless. On the details of this topic
reference must once again be made to the standard works on Contract.[3]
It is, however, necessary to say a few words on the distinction between
a warranty and an innocent misrepresentation.

Whether a statement is or is not a part of the contract is said to
depend upon the intention of the parties, but this most elusive criterion
is almost useless in this connection.[4] This has become especially so
since the courts have been prepared to hold that an oral statement
may override the written terms of a contract. It is probably true to
say that the courts are now much readier to interpret a statement as
a term of the contract than they were a hundred years ago. This tendency may be illustrated by contrasting the two cases of *Hopkins* v.
Tanqueray[5] and *Couchman* v. *Hill*.[6] In the former case the defendant,
who was offering his horse for sale by auction, gave an assurance to
the plaintiff on the day before the sale that the horse was perfectly
sound. It was held that this statement was a mere representation and

---

[1] The term condition has a large number of other meanings. See Stoljar, 69
L.Q.R. 485: "The Contractual Concept of Condition." See also Montrose (1960),
C.L.J., p. 72.

[2] See Stoljar, 15 *M.L.R.* 425, at 430-32.

[3] See Cheshire & Fifoot, *Law of Contract*, 8th ed., pp. 109-15; Treitel, *Law of
Contract*, 3rd ed., Chapter 9.

[4] Except, of course, where the contract in terms states that the truth of a statement
is warranted by the party making it, as, e.g. in *Liverpool & County Discount Co.,
Ltd.* v. *A.B. Motor Co.* (*Kilburn*), *Ltd.*, [1963] 1 W.L.R. 611.

[5] (1854), 15 C.B. 130.   [6] [1947] K.B. 554.

not a term of the contract. In the second case the defendant was offering his heifer for sale by auction. In reliance on an assurance given by the defendant and also by the auctioneer that the heifer was unserved, the plaintiff bid for and bought the animal. This statement was held to be a term of the contract. In a strictly technical sense there is no conflict between these cases because questions of intention must depend upon all the circumstances of the case, and superficial similarities may hide underlying differences.[1] It would be more realistic, however, to admit this general change of attitude on the part of the courts. It is in fact uncommon, and becoming increasingly so, for a court to hold that a material statement made by one of the parties to a contract is only a misrepresentation. This is particularly true of statements made by a seller in a contract for the sale of goods.

The tendency these days frequently appears to be for the courts to hold a statement to be a term of the contract when they think it reasonable to impose liability in damages on the person making the statement, and vice versa. Thus to attempt to decide whether a statement is a term of the contract or a mere representation without reference to the result is, in many cases, to put the cart before the horse. On the one hand a statement as to the quality or state of the goods by a seller will almost invariably be held to be a term of the contract if the seller is a dealer in the goods. So in *Dick Bentley (Productions), Ltd.* v. *Harold Smith (Motors), Ltd.*,[2] where a dealer, in selling a car told the buyer that it had done only 20,000 miles, this was held by the Court of Appeal to be a warranty and not a mere representation. On the other hand, in *Oscar Chess, Ltd.* v. *Williams*,[3] where a person selling a second-hand car in part exchange for another innocently misrepresented the age of the car (relying on the log book, which was in fact forged), the Court of Appeal held the statement to be a mere representation. These cases provide some evidence that the courts are approaching the not irrational principle that, in the absence of a clear intention one way or the other, a statement is a term of the contract where the person making it had, or could reasonably have obtained, the information necessary to show whether the statement was true. But it will be necessary to consider later whether the use now being made by the courts of Sect. 13 of the Act does in truth leave intact the age-old distinction between a contract term and a representation.[4]

---

[1] The earlier case was not cited in *Couchman* v. *Hill* and in an editorial note in [1947] 1 All E.R. 103 it was suggested that the decision in the later case might otherwise have been different. But in *Harling* v. *Eddy*, [1951] 2 K.B. 739, the Court of Appeal held the two cases to be distinguishable. The correct explanation of *Hopkins* v. *Tanqueray* may well be that the auction was held at Tattersalls where, by custom, sales were without warranty. See also *Schawel* v. *Reade*, [1913] 2 Ir. R. 81.
[2] [1965] 2 All E.R. 65.
[3] [1957] 1 W.L.R. 370; see also *Routledge* v. *McKay*, [1954] 1 W.L.R. 615.
[4] See *Beale* v. *Taylor*, [1967] 1 W.L.R. 1193, discussed *post*, p. 72.

It is unnecessary in a work of this nature to make more than a cursory reference to the possibility of an action for negligent misrepresentation at the suit of a buyer, whether or not he is able to establish that the representation amounts to a term of the contract. Although it is now clear that an action for negligent misrepresentation will lie in some circumstances even at common law,[1] it will not often be possible for a buyer to pray in aid this cause of action in a case where the representation is not a term of the contract.[2] But this is now of little importance for, under Sect. 2 (1) of the Misrepresentation Act, 1967, a contracting party is given a statutory cause of action for negligent misrepresentation against the other contracting party. Since the onus of disproving negligence is placed on the representor it seems probable that claims based on negligent misrepresentation will in future frequently be joined with claims for damages for breach of condition or warranty. It has, moreover, recently been held that damages for loss of bargain, i.e. damages according to *contractual* principles, can be awarded under the Act.[3]

[1] *Hedley Byrne & Co., Ltd.* v. *Heller & Partners, Ltd.*, [1964] A.C. 465.
[2] But this did happen in *Esso Petroleum, Ltd.* v. *Mardon* [1975] 1 All E.R. 203.
[3] *Watts* v. *Spence, The Times*, 12 February, 1975.

PART II

THE DUTIES OF THE SELLER

CHAPTER 7

THE EXISTENCE OF THE GOODS

NO IMPLIED CONDITION THAT THE GOODS EXIST

IT might have been thought that in a sale of specific goods there would be an implied condition on the part of the seller that the goods were in existence at the time when the contract was made. Since the seller warrants, as we shall see shortly, that he has a right to sell the goods, and since he is in many cases responsible for defects in the quality of the goods, it seems that *a fortiori* he should be liable if he has sold non-existent goods. Nevertheless, this is not generally so, for Sect. 6 enacts that—

> Where there is a contract for the sale of specific goods, and the goods without the knowledge of the seller have perished at the time when the contract is made, the contract is void.

This section has been commonly understood to confirm the decision of the House of Lords in *Couturier* v. *Hastie*.[1] The defendant in that case was a *del credere* agent who sold, on behalf of the plaintiffs, a cargo of corn shipped from Salonika. Before the date of the sale the cargo had been lawfully sold by the master of the ship. The purchaser repudiated the contract and the plaintiffs sued the agent whose liability depended on whether the purchaser would have been liable. It was held that the defendant was not liable and it has for many years been thought that the case was decided in this way on the ground that the contract was void for mistake. It has, however, been convincingly demonstrated by a learned writer[2] that the decision does no more than illustrate the well-known principle that if the seller cannot deliver the goods the buyer is not bound to pay the price, a rule affirmed by Sect. 28 of the Act. If the buyer had brought an action for non-delivery then the Court would have had to decide a very different question. This might have been whether the contract was void for mistake, but a better approach would have been to regard it as a question of construction. In other words, did the defendant contract that the goods existed, or

---

[1] (1856), 5 H.L.C. 673.   [2] C. J. Slade in 70 *L.Q.R.* at 396-7.

was there an implied condition that if there were no goods there would be no contract? This apparently was the view of Lord Atkin in *Bell* v. *Lever Bros., Ltd.*,[1] for in the course of his judgment he said—

> This brings the discussion to the alternative mode of expressing the result of a mutual mistake . . . The proposition does not amount to more than this that, if the contract expressly or impliedly contains a term that a particular assumption is a condition[2] of the contract, the contract is avoided if the assumption is not true.

Looking at the problem as one of interpretation the facts of *Couturier* v. *Hastie*[3] were open to at least three possible constructions—

(1) There might have been an implied condition precedent that the goods were in existence, in which case if they were not neither party would be bound; or,

(2) The seller might have contracted, or warranted, that the goods were in existence, in which case he would be liable for non-delivery, and the buyer would not be liable for non-acceptance; or,

(3) The buyer might have taken the risk of the goods having perished, in which case he would be liable for the price even in the absence of delivery, and the seller would not, of course, be liable for non-delivery.

In *Couturier* v. *Hastie*[3] the House of Lords merely decided that the contract could not be construed in the third of the above three ways, but the House did not decide, as it was not called upon to decide, whether the proper interpretation was of the first or second types above.[4] A decision between these two possibilities would only have been necessary if the buyer had sued for non-delivery. Such a decision was necessary in *McRae* v. *Commonwealth Disposals Commission*[5] where the defendants contracted to sell to the plaintiffs a shipwrecked tanker on a certain reef. After the plaintiffs had incurred considerable expenditure in preparing a salvage expedition it was discovered that not only was there not, and had never been any tanker, but also that the reef was non-existent. The High Court of Australia approached the case on the basis that the defendants were liable for breach of contract unless they could establish that there was an implied condition precedent that the ship was in existence. Manifestly, on the facts of the

---

[1] [1932] A.C. 161, at 224, 225.
[2] I.e. a condition precedent.
[3] (1856), 5 H.L.C. 673.
[4] It is for this reason that the interpretation of *Couturier* v. *Hastie* given in *Cheshire & Fifoot*, at p. 207 still appears to me, with great respect, to be wrong. The learned authors appear to assume that the H.L. actually held the contract void, but this they did not, and could not do, as the question was not in issue. It was not even argued that the contract was void, but only that the buyer had not bought a "chance." Nor does the word "void" appear in the judgments either in the Exchequer Chamber at 9 Ex. 102 or in the H.L. For a full discussion of this case see the present writer's article in 73 *L.Q.R.* 340.
[5] (1951), 84 C.L.R. 377.

case, no such condition could be implied. On the contrary the Court concluded that—

> The only proper construction of the contract is that it included a promise by the Commission that there was a tanker in the position specified. The Commission contracted that there was a tanker there.[1]

In this connection, the earlier decision of the same Court in *Goldsborough, Mort & Co., Ltd.* v. *Carter*,[2] is also of great interest, although this case (like *Couturier* v. *Hastie*) was decided at common law. In this case the defendant agreed to sell "about" 4,000 sheep pastured on certain lands at a price per head. It was agreed to muster and count the sheep on a certain date and the contract also stated that if it should be found that there were less than 4,000 sheep the buyer would take and pay for the actual number delivered. In fact there had been conditions of severe drought in the area and these were followed by cold winter rains, with the result that, on muster, only 890 acceptable sheep were found. The buyer claimed damages for the short delivery, but his claim was rejected. Griffith, C.J., treated the contract as one for the sale of specific goods and said—

> It is an implied condition of such a contract that at the time of making the contract or before the time of performance the chattels are or will be in existence (*Couturier* v. *Hastie*), and, further, that they shall still be existing when the time comes for performance (*Howell* v. *Coupland*).

But the majority of the Court held that this principle was displaced in the particular circumstances of the case on the true construction of the contract. Since the seller did not know how many sheep there were and since the buyer was aware of the possibility of shortage and had agreed to take what number were delivered, it was held that the contract was only for the sale of such sheep as existed and could be delivered on muster.

If this is the correct approach, and it is submitted that it is, the impact of Sect. 6 of the Act on the problem must next be considered. In terms the section clearly contemplates a case where the goods have existed at one time, but have perished before the contract was made, so that a case such as *McRae* v. *Commonwealth Disposals Commission*[3] would not come within it at all. Consequently the common law position remains and the result should be that arrived at by the High Court of Australia. But this does not answer the question where the goods have in fact existed but have perished before the contract was made. If a seller in effect contracts that the goods are in existence is he entitled to avoid all liability on the ground that Sect. 6 applies and the contract is void? Such a result would be most extraordinary and it is submitted that it could be avoided by giving a liberal interpretation to Sect. 55 (1) of the Act (as amended) which runs—

[1] At p. 380.   [2] (1914), 19 C.L.R. 429.   [3] (1951), 84 C.L.R. 377.

Where any right, duty, or liability would arise under a contract of sale of goods by implication of law, it may be negatived or varied by express agreement or by the course of dealing between the parties, or by usage, if the usage be such as to bind both parties to the contract. . . .

At first sight it might appear that this section would not prevent the operation of Sect. 6 in a case such as that being considered for the whole effect of the section is to prevent any right duty or liability arising; but in preventing the principal obligations from arising Sect. 6 may give rise to other rights and duties, e.g. as to the return of the price.[1] In any case the clear object of the section is to enable the parties to vary, by agreement, all those provisions of the Act which do not affect third parties. Moreover, anomalous results would follow if Sect. 6 were held to be a rule of law to be applied irrespective of the intention of the parties. Since the section is limited in various ways (e.g., in that it only applies to a sale of specific goods, and only applies also where the goods perish) closely parallel cases may fall just within or just outside the section. Those outside will be settled according to the true construction of the contract. It would be unfortunate if those just on the other side of the line had to be determined by a rigid application of Sect. 6. It is submitted, therefore, that if, on the true construction of the contract, it appears that the seller is contracting that the goods do exist, Sect. 6 will not apply and the seller will be liable for non-delivery.[2] Moreover, if the seller has been negligent in not discovering that the goods have perished, the courts will probably be more ready to construe the contract in this way.

The only effect of Sect. 6 is thus to give rise to a presumption, in the cases to which it applies, that the seller is not contracting that the goods exist. Where, on the other hand, as in *McRae* v. *Commonwealth Disposals Commission*, the goods have never existed at all, Sect. 6 cannot apply, and the presumption would appear to be that the seller is contracting that the goods exist.

Although this problem may appear to be of greater academic than practical importance, it is perhaps unfortunate that Sect. 6 was written into the Act at all in its present form. It should, of course, be remembered that *Couturier* v. *Hastie* was decided before the invention of modern methods of communication and on the facts of that case, in the year 1856, it might well have been reasonable to hold that the seller was not contracting that the goods were in existence. If the identical facts were to recur today, however, it is in the highest degree improbable that the seller would not be aware of the sale of the cargo even before it occurred, and if he were not it would most probably be due to his own negligence.

---

[1] I am grateful to a learned reviewer for drawing my attention to this point: see 75 *L.Q.R.* 417; cf. Treitel, *Law of Contract*, 3rd ed., pp. 222–3.

[2] In *Joseph Constantine S.S., Ltd.* v. *Imperial Smelting Corpn.*, [1942] A.C. 154, at pp. 184–5, Lord Wright clearly intimates his opinion that Sects. 6 and 7 of the Act merely embody common law rules of construction.

The sort of facts to which Sect. 6 may be applied today may well differ considerably from the *Couturier* v. *Hastie* situation. For example, in *Barrow, Lane & Ballard, Ltd.* v. *Phillip Phillips & Co., Ltd.*,[1] the plaintiffs contracted to sell to the defendants 700 bags of nuts which were believed to be lying in certain warehouses. In fact 109 of the bags had disappeared, presumably by theft, at the time when the contract was made, and a further 450 disappeared before the buyers attempted to obtain delivery two months later. On the face of it, one would have thought this was a plain case. The sellers had sold a specific parcel of 700 bags of nuts when in fact there were only 591 to deliver. This would seem, therefore, to have been a simple case of breach of contract by the sellers. In fact, however, owing to the operation of Sect. 6 the contract was held void, and the sellers would probably not have been held liable in damages to the buyers.

Sect. 6 gives rise to three other difficulties which will be considered in the next three sections.

Meaning of "Specific Goods"

"Specific goods" are defined by Sect. 62 as "goods identified and agreed upon at the time a contract of sale is made." In most cases this is clear enough, and serves to distinguish such cases from contracts of sale of future or generic goods. Thus, if A contracts to deliver 1,000 tons of wheat to B this is not a sale of specific goods and A's obligations are unaffected by the fact that he had a particular 1,000 tons in mind which have, unknown to him, perished before the date of the contract. Some cases, however, are not so clear. What of a contract to sell 200 tons of potatoes to be grown on a particular piece of land? In *Howell* v. *Coupland*[2] (a case dealing with subsequent destruction, now covered by Sect. 7 of the Act, see *post*, p. 170) it was held that this was a sale of specific goods for the purposes of the common law rules of frustration. However, the modern tendency appears to be to confine the meaning of "specific goods" under the Act to cases of existing goods which have actually been identified or agreed upon. Thus in *Re Wait*,[3] a case to be considered at length later, it was held that a sale of 500 tons out of a cargo of 1,000 tons of wheat on a particular ship was not a sale of specific or ascertained goods within the meaning of Sect. 52 of which specific performance could be ordered. Similarly in *H. R. & S. Sainsbury* v. *Street*[4] it was held that a sale of 275 tons of barley to be grown on a particular farm was not a sale of specific goods. The effect of the perishing of the goods in such circumstances must, therefore, be a matter for the common law, rather than Sect. 6 of the Act.

---

[1] [1929] 1 K.B. 574.   [2] (1876), 1 Q.B.D. 258.
[3] [1927] 1 Ch. 606.   [4] [1972] 1 W.L.R. 834.

Effect of Part of Goods Perishing

Where there is a sale of specific goods, part of which have perished before the date of the sale, the effect of Sect 6 is now somewhat obscure. In *Barrow, Lane & Ballard, Ltd.* v. *Phillip Phillips & Co., Ltd.*, the facts of which have been given above, Wright J. (as he then was), emphasising that he regarded the 700 bags of nuts as an indivisible parcel of goods, held that the contract was avoided by Sect. 6. However, it must be stressed that the actual claim in that case was for the price of the missing 109 bags. In fact the sellers delivered the bags which were available when delivery was required, and the buyers paid the price without question. The buyers, however, refused to pay for the missing 109 bags which is hardly surprising, since their loss would probably not have been covered by their insurance, while it probably was covered by the sellers' insurance. It seems strange to say that the whole contract here was void when the sellers in fact delivered and the buyers paid for a substantial part of the goods. This would imply that the terms governing the sale of these other bags were not the terms agreed upon by the parties, but terms "implied by law". It would also mean that if the sellers had refused to deliver the remaining bags they would not have been liable to the buyers. That conclusion would seem particularly suspect in the light of *H. R. & S. Sainsbury* v. *Street*.[1] In this case the defendant agreed to sell a crop of about 275 tons of barley to be grown by him on his farm. In fact, owing to general crop failure, only some 140 tons were produced which the defendant sold and delivered to a third party at a substantially higher price. McKenna J. held that, although the contract was frustrated as to that part of the crop which failed, this did not exonerate the defendant from offering the crop actually produced to the plaintiffs. Somewhat puzzlingly, he did not seem to regard the plaintiffs as being obliged to take the 140 tons,[2] which suggests that the seller but not the buyer was bound by the contract in the events which actually occurred. What is at any rate clear is that, treating the problem purely as a common law question of construction, there are three additional possible constructions of the contract to be added to those dealing with total perishing of the goods.[3] These are that if part of the goods perish—

(4) The seller may be obliged to deliver the balance and the buyer may be bound to take it; or

(5) The seller may be obliged to tender delivery of the balance to the buyer who is not bound to take it; or

(6) The seller is not bound to tender delivery to the buyer, but if he does so, the buyer is bound to take it.

Although *H. R. & S. Sainsbury* v. *Street* was decided at common law,

[1] [1972] 1 W.L.R. 834.
[2] Perhaps because of Sect. 30 (1), see *post*, p. 67.
[3] *Supra*, p. 41.

it would seem very odd if, on parallel facts falling within Sect. 6, a different result had to be arrived at. It would seem, therefore, that the buyers in the *Barrow Lane & Ballard* case may have been entitled to insist on delivery of the bags of nuts remaining notwithstanding Sect. 6.

Meaning of "Perish"

Barrow, Lane & Ballard, Ltd. v. *Phillip, Phillips & Co., Ltd.*[1] is also material on the next point, viz the meaning of the word "perished". Read literally this might be thought to cover only physical destruction, but in fact it is submitted that it should be construed to cover also perishing in a commercial sense. Although this point was not argued in this case the decision supports this contention. There are no other English cases precisely in point under Sect. 6, but several cases on freight and insurance law deal with a very similar question, that is whether there has been a total loss of goods. On this topic one cannot do better than quote the pungent observations of Esher, M.R., in *Asfar & Co., Ltd.* v. *Blundell*—[2]

> The first point taken on behalf of the defendants, the under-writers, is that there has been no total loss of the dates . . . The ingenuity of the argument might commend itself to a body of chemists, but not to business men. We are dealing with dates as a subject matter of commerce; and it is contended that, although these dates were under water for two days, and when brought up were simply a mass of pulpy matter impregnated with sewage and in a state of fermentation, there had been no change in their nature, and they still were dates. There is a perfectly well known test which has for many years been applied to such cases as the present— that test is whether, as a matter of business, the nature of the thing has been altered.

Mutatis mutandis these remarks could apply equally to the meaning of the word "perish" in Sect. 6. The only case which is inconsistent with this view is *Horn* v. *Minister of Food*[3] which was a case under Sect. 7 of the Act. Morris, J., here held that potatoes which had so rotted as to be worthless had not perished within the meaning of Sect. 7 because they were still potatoes, but in any event he held that the section did not apply because the risk in the goods had already passed to the buyer, and the section is excluded in such a case. His remarks on this point are therefore *obiter* and it is submitted with the greatest respect that they cannot be supported.

It should, however, be noted that if a wide meaning is given to the word "perish" it becomes all the more important that Sect. 6 of the Act be treated only as a rule of construction. For (as will be seen later) a seller is usually under stringent obligations as to the quality and fitness of the goods to be supplied under the contract. So, for example,

---

[1] [1929] 1 K.B. 574.   [1896] 1 Q.B. 123, 127.   [3] [1948] 2 All E.R. 1036.

a seller who contracts to sell a specific load of potatoes will be liable for breach of his implied obligations if he delivers unmerchantable potatoes, and it will be immaterial whether they were unmerchantable before the contract was made. It would therefore be strange if the seller's position were improved where the potatoes were so rotten as to be no longer describable as "potatoes" so that he could rely on Sect. 6 of the Act. Yet such a result was arrived at in the New Zealand case of *Turnbull* v. *Rendell*[1] where the seller agreed to sell 75 tons of "table potatoes" from a specific crop, some of which were still undug. At the time of the contract the potatoes were so badly affected with secondary growth that they no longer answered the description "table potatoes." Prima facie one would have thought, therefore, that there was a breach of Sect. 13 of the Act (that the goods must answer their description)[2] but in fact the buyer's claim for damages was rejected. The Court held that the potatoes had "perished" within the meaning of Sect. 6 of the Act and the contract was therefore void. At all events there seems no inclination to extend the meaning of "perish" by analogy to cases where the seller is responsible for the unavailability of the goods. Thus it has been held no defence for a seller who is sued for non-delivery to prove that, after agreeing to sell the goods to the plaintiff, he sold and delivered the goods to another buyer.[3]

Even granting that Sect. 6 covers perishing in a commercial sense a difficulty still exists in the case of goods lost by theft. Suppose, for example, that A sells his car to B, which unknown to them both, has just been stolen. It may be a long time before the police give up all hope of tracing the car, and until this happens the vehicle can hardly be said to have perished even in a commercial sense, but what is to happen in the meantime? The validity of the contract can hardly depend upon the activities of the police. The insurance cases are not of much assistance here because a theft can clearly be a commercial loss, and of course this is often the whole object of the insurance, while it is not so clear that a stolen car can be said to have perished even commercially. *Barrow, Lane & Ballard, Ltd.* v. *Phillip Phillips & Co., Ltd.,*[4] is distinguishable from such a case because there the nuts had in all probability been dispersed by sale after the theft, and indeed some or all of them might well have been consumed by the ultimate purchasers. Whether a stolen article can be said to have perished, therefore, is a question which is still open and awaits solution by the courts.

[1] (1908), 27 N.Z.L.R. 1067.   [2] *Post*, p. 71.
[3] *Goodey* v. *Garriock*, [1972] 2 Lloyd's Rep. 369 at p. 372.
[4] [1929] 1 K.B. 574.

CHAPTER 8

THE DUTY TO PASS A GOOD TITLE

THE SELLER'S RIGHT TO SELL THE GOODS

AMONG the most important terms implied by the Act in a contract of sale of goods are those relating to the seller's duty to pass a good title to the goods. Sect. 12 (1) (*a*), as amended by the Supply of Goods (Implied Terms) Act, 1973, is as follows—

> In every contract of sale, other than one to which subsection (2) of this section applies, there is—
>
> (*a*) an implied condition on the part of the seller that in the case of a sale, he has a right to sell the goods, and in the case of an agreement to sell, he will have a right to sell the goods at the time when the property is to pass;

The first difficulty in interpreting this section arises from the ambiguity of the word "right". The question whether the seller has a right to sell the goods cannot be answered until it is known precisely what it is which the seller must transfer to the buyer. The Act itself does not provide a very clear answer to this problem. All we have is the statement in Sect. 1 (1) that "a contract for the sale of goods is a contract whereby the seller transfers or agrees to transfer the property in goods to the buyer," and the definition of the term "property" in Sect. 62 as "the general property in goods and not merely a special property." In other words unless the seller has a right to pass the general property to the buyer he will be in breach of Sect. 12 (1) (*a*). But what is meant by a "right" to sell the goods? The natural and primary meaning of the word "right" in Sect. 12 (1) is in fact "power"; in other words the seller must have the power to pass the general property in goods to the buyer. It appears, however, from the decision in *Niblett* v. *Confectioners' Materials Co.*[1] that the seller may be guilty of a breach of Sect. 12 (1) (*a*) although he had the power to transfer the property in the goods. The facts of this case were as follows: the defendants, an American company, sold 3,000 tins of preserved milk to the plaintiffs, but when the goods arrived in England they were detained by the Customs authorities on the ground that their labels infringed the trade mark of a well-known English company. It was held that as this company could have obtained an injunction to restrain the sale

[1] [1921] 3 K.B. 387.

of the goods, the sellers had no right to sell them.[1] It should not be thought, however, that the mere fact that the seller has no right to sell the goods as against a third party (who may even be the true owner) means that the buyer is entitled to reject the goods or to sue for damages. In a number of cases which will be fully examined later[2] a person who is not the owner of goods and who sells them without the owner's authority is enabled by the Act to pass a good title to the buyer. In such cases it seems that while there is technically a breach of the condition implied by Sect. 12 (1) (a) the buyer has in fact suffered no damage from the breach and cannot therefore maintain an action against the seller.[3] It is true that in *Niblett* v. *Confectioners' Materials Co., Ltd.*,[4] Atkin, L.J., thought that in such a case the condition would not be broken at all, but it is submitted that the solution given here is better because there may be circumstances in which the buyer may wish to reject the goods, even though he has acquired a good legal title. In particular it seems that the legal title which is obtained under Part III of the Hire-Purchase Act, 1964, where a private purchaser buys a motor vehicle which is the subject of a hire-purchase agreement, is not in practice a very satisfactory one. The reason for this is that if the buyer later wishes to sell or trade-in the vehicle to a motor dealer, the dealer will in all probability discover the outstanding hire-purchase agreement and may well refuse to buy the vehicle. It seems, therefore, that the buyer should be entitled to reject the goods in such a case.

The Effect of a Breach of Sect. 12 (1) (a)

The normal remedies open to the innocent party where there is a breach of condition are (a) repudiation of the contract, and/or (b) a claim for damages. In addition Sect. 54 enacts that—

> Nothing in this Act shall affect the right of the buyer . . . to recover money paid where the consideration for the payment of it has failed.

In the usual case the buyer will not stand to gain financially from choosing to repudiate the contract rather than sue for damages. The reason is that he cannot retain any benefit under the contract if he wishes to repudiate it, nor does the quasi-contractual remedy preserved by Sect. 54 usually help because *ex hypothesi* there must have been a total failure of consideration, and the buyer cannot therefore have obtained any benefit under the contract. A fair summary of the

---

[1] Cf. *Sumner Permain & Co., Ltd.*, v. *Webb & Co., Ltd.*, [1922] 1 K.B. 55, the facts of which are given at pp. 84–5, where no question was raised as to the application of Sect. 12 (1), (a).

[2] Ch. 19, *post*.

[3] See the Report of the Crowther Committee on Consumer Credit (Cmnd. 4596), para. 5.7.32.

[4] [1921] 3 K.B. 387.

normal position therefore would be that the buyer cannot both have his cake and eat it.

In the case of a breach of the condition implied by Sect. 12 (1) (a), however, it appears that the buyer can do just this. The leading case is *Rowland* v. *Divall*.[1] The plaintiff bought a car from the defendant and used it for four months. He then discovered that the car had never belonged to the defendant, who had bought it in good faith from someone without title. It was held by the Court of Appeal that the buyer was entitled to recover the whole purchase price, and that the seller was not entitled to set-off anything for the four months' use of the car which the buyer had enjoyed. Atkin, L.J., observed—[2]

> The buyer has not received any part of that which he contracted to receive—namely, the property and right to possession—and, that being so, there has been a total failure of consideration.

The full implications of this decision are now fairly apparent. In *Karflex, Ltd.* v. *Poole*[3] the plaintiffs were hire-purchase dealers who bought a car from one K and hired it to the defendant with the usual option to purchase on payment of all the instalments. The defendant paid the deposit and took possession of the car, but he defaulted on the first instalment, and the plaintiffs commenced proceedings against him. It then transpired that K had never been the owner of the car at all, but the plaintiffs paid off the true owner and proceeded with their action against the defendant. It was held by a Divisional Court that the action failed because the plaintiffs were in breach of an implied condition that they had a right to sell the goods for at the date of the delivery of the car they had no such right. The defendant, therefore, who had defaulted in payment of the first instalment was held entitled to repudiate the contract, and indeed, to recover his deposit despite the fact that he had not been evicted by the true owner, and that by the time the case came on for trial there was no possibility of eviction because the original owners had been paid off. This was not actually a case of sale, but of hire-purchase, but the Court regarded the principles applicable as the same.

The second case is *Butterworth* v. *Kingsway Motors, Ltd.*,[4] where A took delivery of a car under a contract of hire-purchase. Mistakenly thinking that she had a right to sell it subject to her continuing to pay the instalments, she purported to sell it to B. B sold it to C, C sold it to the defendant, and the defendant sold it to the plaintiff. After the plaintiff had had the use of the car for no less than eleven and a half months he received a notification from the original hire-purchase dealers, who were of course still the owners of the car, claiming the delivery up to them of the vehicle. Seeing the opportunities which presented themselves the plaintiff lost no time in writing to the defendants claiming the return of the entire purchase price which he had paid. Within one week of this A paid off the balance of the hire-purchase price to the original owners. The defendant might have been forgiven for thinking that this payment removed all difficulties and closed the transaction, for the payment vested the title to the car in A and this title went to feed the defective titles of the subsequent purchasers. It was held however that the plaintiff was entitled to recover the full purchase price of £1,275 as the defendant had been guilty of a breach of Sect. 12 (1) (a). As the market had dropped in the meantime the car was worth only about £800 at the date when the plaintiff repudiated the contract. Consequently the Act enabled him to make a handsome profit of £475, a fact which no doubt explains the learned judge's view that "the plaintiff's position was somewhat lacking in merits."[1]

It is indeed possible to imagine circumstances, by no means unrealistic, which are far more extreme than those in the above cases. For example, suppose that A buys a crate of whisky from B. Suppose further that after consuming the whisky A discovers that it never belonged to B but that B had bought it in good faith from a thief. Is it to be said that A can recover the full purchase price on the ground that there has been a total failure of consideration? This suggestion is perhaps not quite so ridiculous as might appear at first sight because the consumption of the whisky lays the consumer open to an action of conversion by the true owner. There would be nothing absurd about a rule which enabled the buyer to recover the full price if he were compelled to pay the value of the goods to the true owner. But the difficulty about *Rowland* v. *Divall*[2] is that the right of the buyer to recover the full price is not made dependent on a claim by the real owner. It is quite possible, especially where stolen goods have changed hands several times, that the real owner may never be traced at all. Again, it is quite possible that the real owner may choose to sue the seller rather than the buyer for conversion. Indeed, he will probably sue the first solvent person in the chain because the damages will probably be higher. If such were to happen in the hypothetical case put above the extraordinary result would seem to follow that B would have to pay the whole price back to A on the one hand, and the whole value again to the true owner, while A on the other hand will have had a free crate of whisky. One possible way of avoiding

[1] At p. 1291. The learned judge (Pearson, J.) left open the question whether the plaintiff would have succeeded had he not claimed the return of his money before A paid off the owners. In New South Wales it has been held that if the seller obtains title (e g. by paying off the true owner) *before* the buyer seeks to repudiate the contract, it will then be too late for the buyer to recover his price: *Patten* v. *Thomas Motors Pty., Ltd.,* [1965] N.S.W.R. 1457.

[2] [1923] 2 K.B. 500.

this result might be as follows. Normally a party who claims to repudiate a contract must return any benefits received. In *Rowland* v. *Divall*[1] it was pointed out that the defendant could not complain that the car had not been returned to him for it was his very breach of condition that made this impossible. In the hypothetical case above, however, it might be argued that the plaintiff's inability to return the goods is due to the fact that he has consumed the whisky. The fact remains, of course, that even if he had not done so, the goods could still not have been returned. Moreover, if the plaintiff is to be met by this argument the injustice may well be on the other side because the true owner may yet turn up and choose to sue the buyer for conversion. In this case the buyer, having failed to recover his price from the seller may then have to pay the value of the goods to the true owner.[1]

It may be suggested with the greatest respect that the decision in *Rowland* v. *Divall*[2] rests basically on a fallacy. The object of a contract of sale is surely to transfer to the buyer the <u>use and enjoyment</u> of the goods free from any adverse third party claims. If the buyer has such use and enjoyment and no third party claim is made against him it is submitted that it is quite unrealistic to talk of a total failure of consideration. Accordingly, the Law Reform Committee recommended in their Twelfth Report[3] that the buyer should not be allowed to recover the price in full in a *Rowland* v. *Divall* situation with no allowance for the use he has had of the goods.[4] The Law Commission, while agreeing in principle with this recommendation, however, pointed out a number of practical difficulties in the proposal.[5] They concluded that no satisfactory amendment of Sect. 12 could be proposed until a study had been made of the rules relating to the law of restitution and the 1973 Act does not, therefore, deal with this question. It is worth noting that this particular problem does not seem to have arisen in other cases. It is, however, possible that a similar situation may occur where consumer goods are rejected for breach of warranty of quality. In practice this has not hitherto been a serious problem in such cases

---

[1] [1923] 2 K.B. 500.

[2] But in this event the buyer may have a remedy under Sect. 12 (1)(*b*), *post* p. 54, although it seems to strain the meaning of the words to say that a warranty of "quiet possession" can be broken in respect of goods already consumed. It has also been suggested that in the case put in the text A might be able to claim contribution from B under the Law Reform (Married Women and Tortfeasors) Act, 1935 (Treitel, *Law of Contract*, 3rd ed., p. 863). But it is doubtful if A and B can be said to be liable in respect of the "same damage," and it would be strange if, in this one case, a buyer's normal right to an indemnity from the seller for breach of Sect. 12 (1) (*a*) were to be replaced by this statutory remedy which may or may not give an indemnity as the court thinks fit.

[3] 1966 Cmnd. 2958, para. 36.

[4] See also Treitel, 30 *M.L.R.* at pp. 146–9.

[5] Law Commission and Scottish Law Commission, *Exemption Clauses in Contracts, First Report: Amendments to the Sale of Goods Act, 1893* (Law Com. No. 24 and Scot. Law Com. No. 12), paras. 15–16, hereafter referred to as Law Commission, *Exemption Clauses, First Report*.

because the buyer is usually treated as having accepted the goods after a very short period of use (see, e.g., *Long* v. *Lloyd*, [1958] 1 W.L.R. 753). No doubt if a buyer could reject for breach of warranty of quality after prolonged use a problem analogous to *Rowland* v. *Divall* could arise.

The 1973 Act has cleared up one other problem. The opening words of Sect. 12 (1)[1] originally contemplated the possibility of the parties contracting out of the implied conditions as to title. Thus a person may agree to buy goods from a bona fide possessor expressly subject to all defects in title. Goods seized and sold under a distress warrant, for instance, are sold without any warranty of title.[2] In such a case it is usual to sell merely the "title and interest" of the debtor, whatever that may be. This means, for example, that the buyer takes the risk that the goods may not belong to the tenant, but may be held by him under a hire-purchase agreement. Under the new Sect. 12 (2) the possibility of a sale of a limited interest is spelt out more clearly. The position now is that, where the parties intend only to transfer such title as the seller (or a third party) may have, there is an implied warranty that all charges or encumbrances known to the seller and not known to the buyer, have been disclosed to the buyer before the contract is made. Moreover, under the new Sect. 55 (3) the seller cannot contract out of this liability.[3]

In general this simplifies and clarifies the law, though one slightly odd result of the new Sect. 55 (3) seems to be that the seller cannot now contract out of Sect. 12 (1) (*a*) even to the extent that this extends beyond the implication of title. In *Niblett* v. *Confectioners' Materials Co.*,[4] for example (the facts of which have already been given), it appears to have been assumed by all the members of the Court that the seller would not have been liable had there been a contrary intention which negatived the implication that the sale of the tins would not constitute an infringement of a trade mark. This would seem no longer possible.

One final problem arising out of *Rowland* v. *Divall* concerns the relationship between the condition implied by Sect. 12 (1) (*a*) and Sect. 11 (1) (*c*). This latter clause, which has enough difficulties of its own, will be fully discussed later[5] but something must be said about it here. This clause states that when the buyer has accepted the goods

---

[1] " Unless the circumstances of the contract are such as to show a different intention." See on this Hudson, 20 *M.L.R.* 237, 24 *M.L.R.* 690; Reynolds, 79 *L.Q.R.* at p. 542.

[2] See *Payne* v. *Elsden* (1900), 17 T.L.R. 161, and Hudson, op. cit. See also *Warmings Used Cars, Ltd.* v. *Tucker*, [1956] S.A.S.R. 249, where it was held that in the particular circumstances of the case the condition in Sect. 12 was negatived by implication. It seems, however, that the "seller" in this case was more properly a mere agent.

[3] See *post*, p. 133, for the effect of Sect. 55 (3).

[4] [1921] 3 K.B. 387.

[5] *Post*, p. 288.

he is no longer entitled to reject them for breach of condition but is relegated to a claim for damages. In *Rowland* v. *Divall*[1] it was contended that this clause precluded the buyer from recovering his full price, but compelled him to sue for damages, but the Court rejected this argument apparently on the ground that there can be no sale at all where the seller has no right to sell the goods. This involves saying that Sect. 11 (1) (*c*) has no application at all to breaches of Sect. 12 (1) and Atkin, L.J., went the length of saying precisely that. It is, however difficult to find any warrant for this view in the Act itself.[2]

WARRANTY OF FREEDOM FROM ENCUMBRANCES AND OF QUIET POSSESSION

The new Sect. 12 (1) (*b*) which amalgamates, with amendments, the original Sects. 12 (2) and (3) provides that (except where a limited interest is sold) there is—

> An implied warranty that the goods are free, and will remain free until the time when the property is to pass, from any charge or encumbrance not disclosed or known to the buyer before the contract is made, and that the buyer will enjoy quiet possession of the goods except so far as it may be disturbed by the owner or other person entitled to the benefit of any charge or encumbrance so disclosed or known.

It is not easy to see what additional rights this confers on the buyer over and above those conferred by Sect. 12 (1) (*a*). At first sight it might appear that the first paragraph was intended to give the buyer a right to recover no more than the price of the goods, whereas a breach of the second paragraph might entitle the buyer to recover additional damages. But this explanation is untenable for, as Singleton, L.J., pointed out in *Mason* v. *Burningham*:[3] "In any event if there was a breach of the implied condition the plaintiff was entitled to treat that as a breach of warranty." In this case the plaintiff recovered damages under the old Sect. 12 (2) covering the value of repairs done to a typewriter, in addition to the price, when it appeared that the seller was not the true owner.[4]

---

[1] [1923] 2 K.B. 500.

[2] Moreover it has been said that if the buyer is aware of the seller's lack of title there can be an acceptance within Sect. 11 (1) (*c*); see *per* Devlin, J., in *Kwei Tek Chao* v. *British Traders & Shippers, Ltd.*, [1954] 2 W.L.R. 365 at p. 372, where he also points out that the contract in *Rowland* v. *Divall* was voidable and not void. These remarks are omitted from the report at [1954] 2 Q.B. 459, but presumably this does not deprive them of authority. See a note in 18 *M.L.R.* 496

[3] [1949] 2 K.B. 545. And see *Stock* v. *Urey*, [1954] N.I. 71, where the buyer of a car which was seized by the Customs authorities was held entitled to recover what he had to pay to secure the release of the car although this was more than the purchase price. Cf. *Darbishire* v. *Warran*, [1963] 1 W.L.R. 1067, a case in tort.

[4] Could it be argued on such facts that the buyer's duty to mitigate the damage requires him to retain the goods and pay damages to the real owner, since the damages would apparently not include the value of the repairs (*Greenwood* v. *Bennett*, [1972] 3 All E.R. 586)? Cf. *Blake* v. *Melrose*, [1950] N.Z.L.R. 781.

The scope of Sect. 12 (1) (b) is not entirely clear. It seems that it would protect the buyer against a wrongful disturbance of his possession by the seller himself;[1] in this situation the remedy under Sect. 12(1)(b) would overlap with a right of action in tort. Where the disturbance of the buyer's possession is by a third party the buyer can probably rely on the subsection only where the third party's act was a lawful act.[2] A seller can hardly be taken to warrant that no third party will ever tortiously interfere with the buyer's possession in the future. The analogous covenant for quiet possession on a sale of land does not protect a buyer when he is evicted by title paramount (i.e. by a party with a title superior to the seller's) but that is because of the peculiar rule that a vendor of land does not warrant that he has a good title.[3] Accordingly this qualification was thought not to apply to the old subsect. (2)[4] and this view seems clearly to be confirmed by the new version of the implied warranty in Sect. 12 (1) (b).

There are two other possible distinctions between the effects of subsect. (1) (a) and (b); first, time under the Limitation Acts would run against the buyer from the moment of sale under para. (a), while under para. (b) it is now clear that there is a continuing warranty of quiet possession. Consequently time will only run against the buyer under (b) from the time his possession is disturbed. Secondly, there are some circumstances in which a person may have a "right to sell" goods and yet may not be able to sell them free from some third party's rights. In such a case a buyer would have a remedy under Sect. 12 (1) (b) but not under Sect. 12 (1) (a). For example, a debtor who sells goods which have already been "seized" (but not physically removed) by the sheriff under a *fi. fa.* has a right to sell them (at least until they are sold by the sheriff) but he sells them subject to the sheriff's rights. If, then, the buyer has to surrender the goods he has an action for breach of Sect. 12 (1) (b).[5]

The practical operation of that part of Sect. 12 (1) (b) dealing with freedom from encumbrances is limited because the law does not generally recognise real encumbrances over chattels by a person not in possession, and even equity only does so subject to the rights of the bona fide purchaser without notice. If, therefore, the third party is not in possession of the goods he can rarely have an encumbrance which will be binding on the purchaser; on the other hand if he is in possession the buyer has no need to rely on this sub-section because the seller will simply be unable to make delivery. The buyer therefore will not be

---

[1] *Healing (Sales) Pty., Ltd.* v. *Inglis Electrix Pty., Ltd.* (1968), 42 A.L.J.R. 280.
[2] *Niblett* v. *Confectioners' Materials Co., Ltd.*, [1921] 3 K.B. at p. 403.
[3] *Bain* v. *Fothergill* (1874), L.R. 7 H.L. 158.
[4] *Mason* v. *Burningham*, [1949] 2 K.B. at p. 563.
[5] *Lloyds & Scottish Finance, Ltd.* v. *Modern Cars & Caravans (Kingston), Ltd.*, 1966] 1 Q.B. 764.

bound to pay the price, or if he has already paid it, will be entitled to recover it.[1]

The exceptional type of case where this provision may be useful would arise if, for example, a person pledged goods but obtained delivery from the pledgee for some limited purpose. An authorised sale by the pledgor would enable the buyer to invoke this part of Sect. 12 (1) (*b*) against him although he could not allege a breach of Sect. 12 (1) (*a*) because the seller had a right to sell the goods, though subject to the rights of the pledgee.[2] Another, very exceptional case is illustrated by the recent decision in *Microbeads A.C.* v. *Vinhurst Road Markings, Ltd.*[3] where the Court of Appeal awarded damages to a buyer under the old Sect. 12 (2). In this case the buyer's quiet possession had been disturbed by a patentee whose patent was only granted *after* the sale in question, so that there had been no breach of Sect. 12 (1) at the time of the sale.

[1] Sect. 28 which makes payment and delivery concurrent conditions. See p. 59, *post*.
[2] See the cases cited *post*, p. 183, n. 3.
[3] [1975] 1 All E.R. 529.

CHAPTER 9

THE DUTY TO DELIVER THE GOODS

THE DUTY TO DELIVER

UNDER Sect. 27 of the Act—

It is the duty of the seller to deliver the goods, and of the buyer to accept and pay for them, in accordance with the terms of the contract of sale.

The duty of the seller to deliver the goods is a somewhat ambiguous concept, for (leaving aside the fact that it is not generally the duty of the seller to "deliver" them in the popular sense, but the duty of the buyer to take them) it covers three entirely different possibilities.

In the first place, there may be a duty to deliver to the buyer goods in which the property has already passed. Here the duty is specific and, subject to the question of payment, it is a duty which will be broken should the seller fail to deliver those particular goods. If the property has already passed there can be no question of the seller substituting some other article without the consent of the buyer. He must deliver those particular goods and no others will do.

In the second place the seller's duty to deliver may be a duty to procure and supply to the buyer goods in accordance with the contract, but without any particular goods being designated to which the duty of delivery attaches. Thus a contract for the sale of purely generic goods does in one sense put upon the seller the duty of delivering "the goods" but there is no duty to deliver any particular lot of goods. Until such a duty arises, therefore, the seller is perfectly free to deliver any particular quantity of goods answering the contract description. If for example the seller should procure goods answering the contract description, intending to use those in performance of the contract, but later changes his mind and sells them to someone else, the buyer cannot complain that the seller has broken his duty to deliver.[1] Nor can the buyer obtain a decree of specific performance in such a case.

But there is a third possibility mid-way between the first two. It may be that the seller is under a personal duty to deliver a particular lot of goods although the property has not yet passed to the buyer. This is always so in the case of an agreement to sell specific goods, and clearly the seller cannot resell those goods without being guilty of a breach of contract. Even in the sale of unascertained goods it is

[1] See *Carlos Federspiel & Co. S.A.* v. *Charles Twigg & Co., Ltd.*, [1957] 1 Lloyd's Rep. at 255–6 *per* Pearson, J. The relevant passage is cited below, pp. 160–1.

possible for the seller's duty to deliver to attach to a particular lot of goods before the property passes. This, for example, is the effect of a notice of appropriation in a c.i.f. contract which does not pass the property, but fixes the goods to be delivered. Similarly in a f.o.b. contract where the seller ships goods but retains the bill of lading as security, the seller will come under an obligation to deliver to the buyer the actual goods shipped though the property remains in the seller for the moment.[1] These three possibilities are thus not mutually exclusive, but are rather three stages in the performance of the contract. Thus the duty to deliver may start by being unattached to any particular goods, may then become so attached, and finally the property may pass. On the other hand the three stages may be merged in one, as in the sale of specific goods, or two of them may be so merged, as where goods are appropriated to a contract fixing the duty to deliver and passing the property at the same time.

It should be noted that the legal meaning of "delivery" is very different from the popular meaning. In law delivery means "voluntary transfer of possession," which is a very different thing from the dispatch of the goods. There is in fact no general rule requiring the seller to dispatch the goods to the buyer, for under Sect. 29 (1)—

> Whether it is for the buyer to take possession of the goods or for the seller to send them to the buyer is a question depending in each case on the contract, express or implied, between the parties. Apart from any such contract, express or implied, the place of delivery is the seller's place of business, if he have one, and if not, his residence: Provided that, if the contract be for the sale of specific goods, which to the knowledge of the parties when the contract is made are in some other place, then that place is the place of delivery.

This subsection, therefore, does two things. Firstly, it creates a presumption that in a sale of specific goods the place of delivery is the place where the goods are known to be at the time of the contract. Secondly, it lays down that in all other cases, in the absence of any special agreement, the place of delivery is the seller's place of business, and failing that, his residence. Thus in the absence of a contrary intention it is the duty of the buyer to collect the goods, and not of the seller to send them. But in modern conditions of business a contrary intention will frequently be inferred from the circumstances of the case. For example, where a buyer ordered certain goods from the seller in the form "Please supply us with the following goods," an Australian Court held that it was the seller's duty to send the goods to the buyer.[2]

> Purchasers who intend to purchase goods from people whose business it is to sell them do not as a rule send in advance an order for those goods to

---

[1] See *Wait* v. *Baker* (1848), 2 Ex. 1, 8–9.
[2] *Wiskin* v. *Terdich Bros. Pty., Ltd.*, [1928] Arg. L.R. 242.

be supplied, if their intention is to go to the shop or warehouse of the sellers and there purchase them.[1]

Despite the general rule laid down in Sect. 29 (1) that it is not for the seller to send the goods to the buyer, it is his responsibility to see that the goods are in a "deliverable state." Thus Sect. 29 (5) enacts that—

Unless otherwise agreed, the expenses of and incidental to putting the goods into a deliverable state must be borne by the seller.

The meaning of this phrase is considered later.[2]

Where the seller is properly speaking under a duty to dispatch the goods to the buyer then this duty is absolute in the absence of frustrating circumstances, that is to say the seller cannot plead that he was unable to dispatch the goods through no fault of his own, or that he had taken all reasonable care in dispatching them. But a duty to deliver the goods at the buyer's premises is discharged by delivery to a respectable-looking person at these premises even though it should prove that he was not authorised to take delivery on behalf of the buyer.[3]

PAYMENT AND DELIVERY CONCURRENT CONDITIONS

Under Sect. 28 of the Act—

Unless otherwise agreed, delivery of the goods and payment of the price are concurrent conditions, that is to say, the seller must be ready and willing to give possession of the goods to the buyer in exchange for the price, and the buyer must be ready and willing to pay the price in exchange for possession of the goods.

It is not necessary for the seller actually to tender delivery before suing for the price or for damages if it is clear that the buyer would have refused to accept the goods, but it is enough that he (the seller) was ready and willing to do so.[4] And similarly a buyer need not formally tender the price before suing for non-delivery provided that he was ready and willing to do so. On the other hand the seller must have "not only the disposition but the capacity to perform the contract."[5] This dictum, however, is not easily reconciled with some *obiter dicta* of the House of Lords in the case in which it was cited, *British & Bennington, Ltd.* v. *N.W. Cachar Tea Co.*,[6] nor with the decision of the Court of Appeal in *Braithwaite* v. *Foreign Hardwood Co., Ltd.*,[7] which was not disapproved in the later case although Lord Sumner expressed some difficulty in understanding it.[8] These cases seem to establish the proposition that if the buyer wrongfully repudiates the contract the seller

---

[1] Ibid., at pp. 242–3   [2] *Post*, p. 148.
[3] *Galbraith & Grant, Ltd.* v. *Block*, [1922] 2 K.B. 155.
[4] *Levey & Co., Ltd.* v. *Goldberg*, [1922] 1 K.B. 688, 692.
[5] *Per* Lord Abinger in *De Medina* v. *Norman* (1842), 9 M. & W. 820, 827, quoted by Lord Atkinson in *British & Bennington, Ltd.* v. *N.W. Cachar Tea Co., Ltd.*, [1923] A.C. 48, 63.
[6] [1923] A.C. 48.   [7] [1905] 2 K.B. 543.
[8] [1923] A.C. at pp. 70–1; and see *Taylor* v. *Oakes* (1922), 38 T.L.R. 349, 517.

can accept the buyer's repudiation and then maintain an action even though he is unable to show that he had the capacity to perform the contract when the buyer repudiated it. On the other hand this principle must be reconciled with another equally established rule, namely that a party is not precluded from relying upon one ground for repudiation merely because at the time he gave another and unjustifiable reason for repudiating. If the buyer meets the seller's claim for damages by pleading that, notwithstanding that he previously gave an unjustified reason for repudiating, the seller was himself in breach in failing to deliver at the appointed time, these two principles appear, at first sight, to conflict.

The key to the difficulty may lie, as has recently been suggested,[1] in the fact that in *Braithwaite*'s case the contract was rescinded by the acceptance of the buyer's repudiation before delivery was ever tendered by the seller. Hence the sellers were never in breach in that case, and were entitled to damages for anticipatory repudiation by the buyers. If the contract had not been rescinded before the date on which delivery was due it seems that this would have made no difference to the question of the buyer's liability, but it would have been most material on the question of damages. Plainly, if a seller claims damages for an unjustified premature repudiation by the buyer, the fact (as subsequent events may show) that the seller would have been unable to deliver at the required time would reduce his damages, perhaps to nominal proportions.

It must also be remembered that one party may waive performance of an act which would otherwise be a condition precedent to the performance of his own obligations. In this event the other party is entitled to sue for non-performance even though he could not have fulfilled his contractual duties as a result of non-performance of that condition. In *Peter Turnbull & Co., Ltd.* v. *Mundas Trading Co. (Australasia), Ltd.*[2] the defendants contracted to sell a quantity of oats to the plaintiffs f.o.b. Sydney, to be loaded on a ship nominated by the buyers in January or February, 1951, the buyers to give fourteen days' notice of nomination. The plaintiffs informally told the defendants that they would want delivery about 14th February and intimated that they would nominate the *Afric*. The sellers later told the buyers that they could not deliver f.o.b. Sydney but offered delivery f.o.b. Melbourne instead. Negotiations followed in which the buyers sought to persuade subbuyers to accept delivery f.o.b. Melbourne but without success. On 23rd February the buyers told the sellers that they would insist on delivery f.o.b. Sydney, the sellers stated flatly that they could not make such delivery and the buyers thereupon bought in the market at an

---

[1] *Esmail* v. *J. Rosenthal & Sons, Ltd.*, [1964] 2 Lloyd's Rep. at p. 416, *per* Salmon, L.J. See further 37 *M.L.R.* 121.
[2] (1954), 90 C.L.R. 235.

increased price. The *Afric* did not in fact arrive in Sydney till March. In an action by the buyers for damages for non-delivery, the sellers pleaded that they were excused from non-delivery because the buyers had not made the required nomination and that owing to the late arrival of the *Afric* the buyers could not have taken delivery f.o.b. Sydney during the contract period. The Australian High Court held for the buyers because the sellers had "clearly intimated to the plaintiffs that it was useless to pursue the conditions of the contract applicable to shipment in Sydney and that the plaintiffs need not do so."[1]

Although the seller must normally be ready and willing to deliver before he can claim payment of the price it must be remembered that delivery has its usual legal meaning of transfer of possession in law. The meaning of this will be examined shortly but it should be said here that where goods are shipped the shipping documents represent the goods, and transfer of these transfers possession of the goods. It follows that when the seller is ready and willing to deliver the shipping documents he is entitled to demand payment of the price. A mere provision that payment shall only be due on delivery does not alter the position because delivery of the documents *is* delivery of the goods. This was clearly laid down in the dissenting judgment of Kennedy, L.J., in *Biddell Bros., Ltd.* v. *E. Clemens Horst & Co., Ltd.*,[2] which was upheld in the House of Lords.[3]

It must also be borne in mind that if the goods have perished after the risk has passed to the buyer the seller's right to receive payment ceases to depend upon his willingness to deliver the goods.[4] It is odd that Sect. 28 says nothing of this possibility.

THE MEANING OF DELIVERY

Sect. 62 defines delivery as a "voluntary transfer of possession" but it would of course be far beyond the scope of this work to examine what exactly is a voluntary transfer of possession. Suffice it to say that for present purposes delivery may take one of the following forms.

In the first place there may be a physical transfer of the actual goods themselves. This is the most obvious case, and although difficult questions of law may arise in deciding whether the physical transfer is enough to transfer legal possession we need not go into these here.

Secondly, the seller may transfer possession to the buyer by handing over to him the means of control over the goods, for example, the keys to the warehouse in which they are situated.[5]

[1] *Per* Dixon, C.J., at p. 246.
[2] [1911] 1 K.B. 934.   [3] [1912] A.C. 18.
[4] See, e.g., *McPherson, Thorn, Kettle & Co.* v. *Dench Bros.*, [1921] V.L.R. 437, at p. 445: "non-delivery was here excused by the loss of the goods which at the time were at the purchaser's risk."
[5] *Hilton* v. *Tucker* (1888), 39 Ch. D. 669; *Dublin City Distillery, Ltd.* v. *Doherty*, [1914] A.C. 823; *Wrightson* v. *Macarthur*, [1921] 2 K.B. 807.

Thirdly, Sect. 29 (3) provides that—

> Where the goods at the time of sale are in the possession of a third person, there is no delivery by seller to buyer unless and until such third person acknowledges to the buyer that he holds the goods on his behalf; provided that nothing in this section shall affect the operation of the issue or transfer of any document of title to goods.

This acknowledgement is called "attornment" and is of special importance where the goods are in the custody of warehousemen. Where the seller gives the buyer a delivery order for goods stored in a warehouse this does not transfer possession or property until the warehousekeeper attorns by accepting the warrant.[1] Mere receipt of the delivery order without any comment does not, without more, amount to an attornment.[2]

Fourthly, the goods may be delivered by the delivery of documents of title thereto. A document of title is defined by Sect. 1 (4) of the Factors Act, 1889, as—

> Any bill of lading, dock warrant, warehousekeeper's certificate, and warrant or order for the delivery of goods, and any other document used in the ordinary course of business as proof of the possession or control of goods, or authorising or purporting to authorise, either by endorsement or by delivery, the possessor of the documents to transfer or receive goods thereby represented.

The peculiar feature of documents of title is that the mere transfer or endorsement of the document, if accompanied by the necessary intention, suffices to transfer the possession and the property in the goods, even without attornment. By far the most important type of document of title is the bill of lading. When goods are shipped the shipowner or his agent delivers to the shipper a bill of lading, and this document "in law and in fact represents the goods. Possession of the bill of lading places the goods at the disposal of the purchaser."[3] There are few other kinds of documents of title today because it is not customary for warehousekeepers' receipts and similar documents to authorise or to purport to authorise the holder to claim the goods by mere endorsement or delivery of the receipt without attornment by the warehousekeeper. But it has been held that a delivery order may in certain circumstances be a document of title,[4] as also may railway receipts if suitably worded.[5] Moreover, under some private Acts of

---

[1] *Sterns, Ltd.* v. *Vickers, Ltd.*, [1923] 1 K.B. 78; *Wardar's (Import and Export) Co., Ltd.* v. *W. Norwood & Sons, Ltd.*, [1968] 2 Q.B. 663.

[2] *Laurie & Morewood* v. *John Dudin & Sons*, [1926] 1 K.B. 223; *D.F. Mount, Ltd.* v. *Jay & Jay (Provisions) Co., Ltd.*, [1960] 1 Q.B. 159.

[3] *Per* Kennedy, L.J., in *Biddell Bros., Ltd.* v. *E. Clemens Horst & Co., Ltd.*, [1911] 1 K.B. 934, at pp. 956-7. As to the time at which a bill of lading ceases to be a document of title, see *Barclays Bank, Ltd.* v. *Commissioners of Customs & Excise*, [1963] 1 Lloyd's Rep. 81.

[4] *Ant. Jurgens Margarinefabrieken* v. *Louis Dreyfus & Co., Ltd.*, [1914] 3 K.B. 40

[5] *Official Assignee of Madras* v. *Mercantile Bank of India*, [1935] A.C. 53.

Parliament certain warehousekeepers' delivery warrants are specially made documents of title, and indeed, in some cases they are fully negotiable instruments, so that an innocent transferee obtains a good title despite the transferor's lack of title.[1] Bills of lading are not, of course, fully negotiable in this sense.

Fifthly, the parties may agree that the seller should hold the goods as the buyer's agent or bailee. This suffices to transfer possession of the goods for present purposes, that is to say, it entitles the seller to demand payment of the price, although in other cases it is a question of the greatest difficulty whether or not the bailor with an immediate right to take the goods can be said to have legal possession of them.

Sixthly, delivery of the goods to the buyer's agent transfers possession to the buyer himself. Moreover, delivery to a carrier is prima facie deemed to be delivery to the buyer. Sect. 32 (1) of the Act says—

> Where, in pursuance of a contract of sale, the seller is authorised or required to send the goods to the buyer, delivery of the goods to a carrier, whether named by the buyer or not, for the purpose of transmission to the buyer is prima facie deemed to be a delivery of the goods to the buyer.

But where the carrier is an agent or servant of the seller himself delivery to him cannot constitute delivery to the buyer, for it is merely a delivery to the seller's *alter ego*.[2]

---

[1] E.g. Port of London (Consolidation) Act, 1920.
[2] *Galbraith & Grant, Ltd.* v. *Block*, [1922] 2 K.B. 155, at p. 156; *Badische Anilin und Soda Fabrik* v. *Basle Chemical Works*, [1898] A.C. 200.

CHAPTER 10

THE DUTY TO SUPPLY THE GOODS AT THE RIGHT TIME

THE TIME OF DELIVERY

SECT. 10 (1), after laying down that the time of payment is prima facie not of the essence, goes on to state that—

> Whether any other stipulation as to time is of the essence of the contract or not depends on the terms of the contract.

Although the Act thus declines to lay down any general rules the courts have done so, and it is well settled that "In ordinary commercial contracts for the sale of goods the rule clearly is that time is prima facie of the essence with respect to delivery."[1] If the time for delivery is fixed by the contract then failure to deliver at that time will thus be a breach of condition which justifies the buyer in refusing to take the goods. This rule presumably applies not only when the seller is under an obligation to dispatch the goods to the buyer but also when the buyer is bound to collect the goods from the seller.

Where the contract provides that the seller will use his best endeavours to deliver the goods by a certain date but, despite his best endeavours, he is unable to do so, he must still deliver the goods within a reasonable time after that date.[2]

Where no time has been fixed by the contract, it is provided by Sect. 29 (2) that—

> Where under the contract of sale the seller is bound to send the goods to the buyer, but no time for sending them is fixed, the seller is bound to send them within a reasonable time.

Presumably the position is the same where the seller is not bound to send the goods but is only bound to have them ready for collection. Reference should also be made here to Sect. 29 (4)—

> Demand or tender of delivery may be treated as ineffectual unless made at a reasonable hour. What is a reasonable hour is a question of fact.

Failure to deliver within a reasonable time (like failure to deliver within a specified time) may amount to a breach of condition by the seller.[3] It is important to observe that since the failure of the seller to

---

[1] *Per* McCardie, J., in *Hartley* v. *Hymans*, [1920] 3 K.B. 475, at p. 484.
[2] *McDougall* v. *Aeromarine of Emsworth, Ltd.*, [1958] 1 W.L.R. 1126.
[3] *Thomas Borthwick (Glasgow), Ltd.* v. *Bunge & Co., Ltd.*, [1969] 1 Lloyd's Rep. 17, 28.

deliver on time is a breach of condition the buyer may reject the goods although he has suffered no damage as a result of the breach. Thus in *Bowes* v. *Shand*[1] the sellers agreed to ship a quantity of Madras rice during the months of March and/or April. In fact the bulk of the rice was shipped at the end of February and only about one-eighth was shipped during March. It was held by the House of Lords that the buyers were entitled to reject the goods although it was conceded that there was no difference between the rice actually shipped and any rice which might have been shipped in March. The case has been criticised by a learned writer[2] but there can be little doubt that it conforms to the general rule in English law that a buyer can reject goods for breach of condition although he suffers no damage therefrom.[3] Whether the buyer's right to reject should be cut down in such circumstances is another matter. It will be appreciated that if no damage is suffered by the buyer he will usually only want to reject because of some external circumstance such as a fall in market prices. English courts seem fully committed to the principle that any breach of condition by the seller entitles the buyer to take advantage of a fall in the market to reject the goods.

WAIVER OF DELIVERY TIME

Although time is thus prima facie of the essence with respect to delivery there is nothing to stop the buyer waiving the condition, and if he does so the waiver will be binding on him whether made with or without consideration. It seems immaterial whether such waiver is regarded as binding under the rule in *Hughes* v. *Metropolitan Railway Co.*[4] or by virtue of Sect. 11 (1) (*a*) of the Act which states—

> Where a contract of sale is subject to any condition to be fulfilled by the seller, the buyer may waive the condition . . .

McCardie, J., in *Hartley* v. *Hymans*[5] rested his decision on Sect. 11 (1) (*a*), while Denning, L.J., in *Charles Rickards, Ltd.* v. *Oppenhaim*[6] preferred to base it on the doctrine of *Hughes* v. *Metropolitan Railway Co.*[4] In either event the buyer, after having waived the delivery date is entitled to give the seller reasonable notice that he will not accept delivery after a certain date. In *Charles Rickards, Ltd.* v. *Oppenhaim*,[6] the plaintiffs agreed to supply a Rolls Royce chassis for the defendant, to be ready at the latest on 20th March, 1948. It was not ready on this day, but the defendant continued to press for delivery, thereby impliedly waiving the condition as to the delivery date. By 29th June

---

[1] (1877), 2 App. Cas. 455.   [2] Stoljar, 71 *L.Q.R.* 533-5.
[3] See, e.g., *Arcos, Ltd.* v. *E. A. Ronaasen & Son*, [1933] A.C. 470; *Re Moore & Co., Ltd., & Landauer & Co.*, [1921] 2 K.B. 519.
[4] (1877), 2 App. Cas. 439.   [5] [1920] 3 K.B. 475.
[6] [1950] 1 K.B. 616.

the defendant had lost patience, and he wrote to the plaintiffs informing them that he would not accept delivery after 25th July. In fact the chassis was not ready until 18th October and the defendant refused to accept it. The Court of Appeal held that the defendant was entitled to reject the chassis as he had given the plaintiffs reasonable notice that delivery must be made by a certain date. If this kind of waiver is an illustration of the principle of *Hughes* v. *Metropolitan Railway Co.*[1] then *Charles Rickards, Ltd.* v. *Oppenhaim*[2] can be regarded as an illustration of the principles discussed by the House of Lords in *Tool Metal Manufacturing Co., Ltd.* v. *Tungsten Electric Co., Ltd.,*[3] as to the termination of the binding effect of an equitable estoppel by reasonable notice.

Where it is clear that the party to whom the indulgence has been granted could not in any event have performed the contract within a reasonable time, notice may not be necessary, and a mere intimation that the contract is regarded as cancelled may be sufficient.[4]

Although Sect. 11 (1) (*a*) only refers to a waiver of a condition by the buyer it is clear that the seller also may waive any condition to be performed by the buyer. So, for example, a seller who leads a buyer to suppose that a letter of credit required by the contract will not be insisted on is not thereafter entitled to plead the failure to open such a letter of credit as an answer to a claim for non-delivery.[5]

---

[1] (1877), 2 App. Cas. 439.   [2] [1950] 1 K.B. 616.
[3] [1955] 1 W.L.R. 761.
[4] *Etablissements Chainbaux S.A.R.L.* v. *Harbormaster, Ltd.,* [1955] 1 Lloyd's Rep. 303.
[5] *Panoutsas* v. *Raymond Hadley Corpn. of New York,* [1917] 2 K.B. 473; *Plastic-moda Societa* v. *Davidsons (Manchester), Ltd.,* [1952] 1 Lloyd's Rep. 527.

CHAPTER 11

THE DUTY TO SUPPLY GOODS IN THE RIGHT QUANTITY

DELIVERY OF THE RIGHT QUANTITY

WHERE the seller is required to dispatch the goods to the buyer he must send the right quantity of goods if he is not to break his contract. Similarly the seller must have the right quantity of goods available for the buyer in cases where it is the duty of the buyer to take possession and not of the seller to dispatch the goods to him. In the first place Sect. 30 (1) states—

> Where the seller delivers to the buyer a quantity of goods less than he contracted to sell, the buyer may reject them, but if the buyer accepts the goods so delivered he must pay for them at the contract rate.

Moreover the seller cannot excuse a short delivery on the ground that he will deliver the remainder in due course because Sect. 31 (1) states that—

> Unless otherwise agreed, the buyer of goods is not bound to accept delivery thereof by instalments.

The operation of these subsections is illustrated by *Behrend & Co., Ltd.* v. *Produce Brokers Co., Ltd.*[1] where the sellers agreed to sell a quantity of cotton seed ex the *Port Inglis* in London. The ship discharged a small part of the cargo in London, and then left for Hull where she discharged other goods. Fourteen days later she returned to London and discharged the remainder of the cotton seed which was the subject of the sale. It was held that the buyers were entitled to reject the later delivery while retaining the earlier one.

The counterpart of the duty not to deliver too little is the duty not to deliver too much, although this is not so obvious, for there seems at first sight no reason why the buyer should not be compelled to accept that part which should have been delivered, whether or not he accepts the rest. But this is not the law for Sect. 30 (2) lays down that—

> Where the seller delivers to the buyer a quantity of goods larger than he contracted to sell, the buyer may accept the goods included in the contract and reject the rest, or he may reject the whole. If the buyer accepts the whole of the goods so delivered he must pay for them at the contract rate.

[1] [1920] 3 K.B. 530.

67

The buyer can always accept whatever is delivered, whether too much or too little because the delivery is in effect a counter-offer which the buyer accepts by accepting the goods themselves.[1]

A slightly different position is dealt with by Sect. 30 (3)—

> Where the seller delivers to the buyer the goods he contracted to sell mixed with goods of a different description not included in the contract, the buyer may accept the goods which are in accordance with the contract and reject the rest, or he may reject the whole.

Or, presumably, he may accept the whole, paying a reasonable price for the goods not included in the contract. This subsection covers cases of a breach of the duty to supply goods in the right quantity, and cases of a breach of the duty to supply goods of the right quality. If, for example, the seller delivers the correct total quantity but only part of the goods conform to the contract, this may be regarded as a breach of either of these duties.[2]

The subsection is not confined to cases in which the seller delivers goods complying with the contract both in respect of quantity and quality, but the goods are mixed with other goods not of the contract description. It extends also to cases where an insufficient quantity of goods complying with the contract description is delivered.[3] Thus, if a person contracted to sell 100 tons of wheat the subsection would apply equally whether he delivered 100 tons of wheat and 50 tons of barley, or 50 tons of wheat and 50 tons of barley. So where sellers contracted to sell 50 tons of steel sheets divided equally into 6, 7, 8, 9 and 10 foot lengths, and delivered the whole 50 tons in 6 foot lengths, the buyers were entitled to accept one-fifth and reject the remainder.[4]

The reason why the buyer is entitled to reject the whole of the goods delivered in the circumstances dealt with by Sect. 30 is that the seller commits a breach of condition by delivering the wrong quantity. In this respect the duties of the seller are parallel to those laid down as regards sales by description. Indeed, the whole of Sect. 30 is merely an application of the duty to deliver goods conforming to the description imposed by Sect. 13, and it is one of the peculiarities of the drafting of the Act that Sect. 13 is dealt with under the heading Conditions and Warranties, while Sect. 30 is dealt with under Performance of the Contract.

The close resemblance between the duties created by Sects. 13 and 30 is brought out all the more when they are examined in detail. In both cases the slightest deviation from the terms of the contract is a breach of condition entitling the buyer to reject the goods. If the

---

[1] *Hart* v. *Mills* (1846), 15 M. & W. 85.

[2] *Re Moore & Co., Ltd., & Landauer & Co.*, [1921] 2 K.B. 519.

[3] *W. Barker & Co., Ltd.* v. *E. T. Agius, Ltd.* (1927), 33 Com. Cas. 120, at 132, where this state of the law was criticised by Salter, J. See further on this, *post*, p. 298.

[4] *Ebrahim Dawood, Ltd.* v. *Heath, Ltd.*, [1961] 2 Lloyd's Rep. 512.

seller delivers goods which fail by the slightest margin to conform to the contract description, or if he delivers a fraction too much or too little, the buyer may reject the whole. The only qualification on this is that if the deviations are "microscopic"[1] the seller may be able to plead *de minimis*.

On the meaning of a microscopic deviation two cases, one on either side of the line, may be contrasted. In *Wilensko Slaski Towarzystwo Drewno* v. *Fenwick & Co., Ltd.*,[2] the sellers sold timber of specified measurements to the buyers. There were certain permitted, but strictly defined, variations from these specifications. Slightly under 1 per cent of the timber failed to comply with the contract requirements. The buyers were held entitled to reject the goods. On the other hand in *Shipton Anderson & Co., Ltd.* v. *Weil Bros. & Co., Ltd.*,[3] the sellers contracted to sell to the buyers 4,500 tons of wheat or 10 per cent more or less. The sellers delivered 4,950 tons and 55 lb. but they did not claim payment for the 55 lb. It was held that the buyers were not entitled to reject the goods. The excess over the stipulated amount being a little over 1 lb. in 100 tons the case clearly called for the application of the maxim *de minimis*. If it had not been applied in this case the rule would have lost all commercial importance.[4] The rule *de minimis non curat lex* is a legal principle of general application, but its applicability to any particular case seems to be a question of fact which depends, *inter alia*, on how far precise accuracy can be obtained, or whether there are limits of accuracy which are commercially reasonable.[5]

The same close relationship between the duty to deliver the right quantity and the duty to deliver the right quality will be observed when we consider instalment contracts. The buyer's right to reject is the same whether the breach consists in short delivery or delivery of the wrong quality.

In the event of a breach of Sect. 30 by the seller, the buyer is entitled to recover a proportionate part of what he has paid as on a total failure of consideration, notwithstanding that he may have accepted and retained a part of the goods.[6]

---

[1] *Arcos, Ltd.* v. *E. A. Ronaasen & Son*, [1933] A.C. 470, at p. 480, *per* Lord Atkin.
[2] [1938] 3 All E.R. 429.
[3] [1912] 1 K.B. 574.
[4] See also *Arcos, Ltd.* v. *E. A. Ronaasen & Son* itself, p. 73 *post*; and *Payne and Routh* v. *Lillico & Sons* (1920), 36 T.L.R. 569, which was much relied on in *Rapalli* v. *K. L. Take, Ltd.*, [1959] 2 Lloyd's Rep. 469, a case of quality rather than quantity.
[5] *Margaronis Navigation Agency, Ltd.* v. *Henry W. Peabody & Co., Ltd.*, [1965] 1 Q.B. 300. For the effect of the *Uniform Customs and Practice for Documentary Credits* on the *de minimis* rule in contracts where the price is payable by letter of credit, see *post*, p. 236.
[6] *Behrend & Co., Ltd.*, v. *Produce Brokers, Ltd.*, [1920] 3 K.B. 530; *Biggerstaff* v. *Rowlatt's Wharf, Ltd.*, [1896] 2 Ch. 93; *Ebrahim Dawood, Ltd.* v. *Heath, Ltd.*, [1961] 2 Lloyd's Rep. 512.

CHAPTER 12

THE DUTY TO SUPPLY GOODS OF THE RIGHT QUALITY

CAVEAT EMPTOR

THE implied terms as to quality and fitness formerly laid down in Sects. 13–15 represented an important step in the abandonment of the original common law rule of *caveat emptor*. The common law had itself largely modified the rigours of this rule by 1893, but in several important respects the Act went further than the courts ever did before it was passed. But weaknesses in the drafting of the original sections gradually became apparent, and there was also growing concern at the freedom permitted to sellers to contract out of their liabilities. The Supply of Goods (Implied Terms) Act, 1973, was designed to meet these objections. This Act, largely based on the Law Commission's recommendations[1] contains the most important amendments of the Sale of Goods Act so far passed. The new Act has largely remodelled Sects. 13–15 of the original Act.

The three primary conditions laid down in the Act now appear in Sect. 13, Sect. 14 (2) and Sect. 14 (3). In one sense these three conditions, taken in that order, lay down a series of graduated duties upon the seller. In the first place, there is the implied condition that the goods must correspond with their description. This applies in far wider circumstances than those in which the two other conditions apply, but on the other hand, it does not afford a great deal of protection to the buyer, especially where the description of the goods is not a detailed one. Obviously, for example, a car may be a car, potatoes may be potatoes, a reaping machine may be a reaping machine, but in all cases the goods may be seriously defective.

The next implied condition is that the goods must be merchantable. This does not apply in all the circumstances in which the first condition applies, but, on the other hand, it affords the buyer a greater degree of protection, since goods that correspond with their description may not be merchantable. Even this, however, may not suffice to protect the buyer, since goods may correspond with their description and may be merchantable, and yet they may still be unsuitable for the buyer's purpose. Hence, in still more limited circumstances, the buyer may be able to rely on the third implied condition, namely that the goods must be fit for the purpose for which they were sold.

[1] See the Law Commission, *Exemption Clauses, First Report*.

The difficulties of exposition of this part of the law have unfortunately not been greatly reduced by the new Act though there has been some gain in simplification. As will be seen the sections frequently overlap in practice, and the same words appear several times in different places. It is, therefore, impossible to deal with this topic section by section, and it is proposed to deal with it under the following six heads—

1. Implied Conditions that Goods must Correspond with their Description;
2. Implied Conditions that the Goods are Merchantable;
3. Implied Conditions that the Goods are Fit for a Particular Purpose;
4. Implied Conditions in Sales by Sample;
5. Implied Conditions Annexed by Trade Usage;
6. Other Implied Terms.

1. IMPLIED CONDITIONS THAT THE GOODS MUST CORRESPOND WITH THEIR DESCRIPTION

Sect. 13 (1) (formerly there was no sub-section (2)) is as follows—

Where there is a contract for the sale of goods by description, there is an implied condition that the goods shall correspond with the description; and if the sale be by sample, as well as by description, it is not sufficient that the bulk of the goods corresponds with the sample if the goods do not also correspond with the description.

The Relationship between Sect. 13 and the Common Law Distinction between Representations and Contractual Terms

The first question to be examined here is the effect of Sect. 13 on the traditional common law distinction between mere representations on the one hand and terms of the contract on the other hand. At first blush it might seem that Sect. 13 does away with this distinction in the case of a sale by description since the section states that "there is an implied term that the goods shall correspond with the description." If the section applied only to those parts of the description which amounted to contractual terms in any event it would seem to be performing the somewhat odd (and redundant) function of declaring that it is an *implied* term that the seller must comply with *express* terms of the contract.

However, despite this oddity, the section does not seem, in legal theory at all events, to obliterate the distinction between mere representations and contractual terms. For instance, in *T. & J. Harrison* v. *Knowles and Foster*[1] the sellers sold two ships to the buyers each of which had been stated in particulars supplied to the buyers to have a deadweight capacity of 460 tons, but no reference was made to this in the actual memorandum of sale. In fact the capacity of each ship was

1[1918] 1 K.B. 608.

only 360 tons. In one sense these ships had been sold by description and the description certainly referred to their capacity. But the Court of Appeal held that the statements about the capacity were merely representations. So also in his very careful judgment in *Taylor* v. *Combined Buyers Ltd.*[1]—which seems to be the only case in which this question has been explicitly and fully considered—Salmond, J., held that the section does not affect the traditional distinction between mere representations and terms of contract. Similarly in the well-known case of *Oscar Chess, Ltd.* v. *Williams*,[2] where the seller sold a car which he described as a "1948 Morris," contrary to the facts, it does not seem to have occurred to anybody that the statement could have been treated as part of the description of the car and an action brought under Sect. 13, unless the buyer could first establish that the statement was a term of the contract and not a mere representation. It could, no doubt, be argued that the sale in this case was not a sale by description but a sale of a specific chattel, but it would certainly be strange if this distinction were to lead to the same statement being held a representation in one case and a condition in another.

On the other hand, more recently in *Beale* v. *Taylor*,[3] the Court of Appeal appears to have come very close to disregarding the distinction between representations and contractual terms by giving a wide application to Sect. 13 of the Act. In this case the defendant advertised his car for sale as a "Herald, convertible, white, 1961" and the car was bought by the plaintiff after examination. In fact the car was made of two parts which had been welded together, only one of which was from a 1961 model. Although the facts bore a close resemblance to those in *T. & J. Harrison* v. *Knowles and Foster* (which was not cited) the Court of Appeal here held that the words "1961 Herald" were part of the contractual description. If this case illustrates the modern trend it seems to suggest that, whatever the legal theory of the matter may be, in practice Sect. 13 makes it much easier for a buyer to argue that a descriptive statement by a seller is a contractual term and not a mere representation. But more recently still it has been suggested in the House of Lords[4] that a statement about the goods is only part of the "description" if it has been used to *identify* the goods. The implications of this are not yet clear, but it plainly could have a limiting effect on the broader interpretation placed on Sect. 13 by some of the older cases. If matters of "description" are to be strictly confined to words designed to identify the goods there is no doubt that decisions like *Beale* v. *Taylor* and many other cases referred to below must now be suspect.

The next question only arises on the assumption that the description under which the goods are sold does form a contractual term. What now has to be considered is whether Sect. 13 affects the distinction

---

[1] [1924] N.Z.L.R. 627.   [2] [1957] 1 W.L.R. 370.   [3] [1967] 1 W.L.R. 1193.
[4] *Ashington Piggeries Ltd.* v. *Christopher Hill Ltd.*, [1972] A.C. 441.

between conditions and warranties. Does every part of the contract description fall within Sect. 13 so that it is a condition of the contract that the goods should correspond with that description? Or is it open to the seller to argue that some parts of the description are in respect of minor or ancillary matters only and therefore the requirement of compliance with those parts of the description amounts merely to a warranty?

This question has never been fully considered by English courts, though once again the earlier cases tend to treat the section as having no effect on the condition/warranty distinction. Thus in *Varley* v. *Whipp*[1] Channell, J., thought that the Act had not altered the law in this respect and that it was still necessary to distinguish between conditions and warranties as part of the contract description. Similarly in *T. & J. Harrison* v. *Knowles and Foster*[2] Bailhache, J., at first instance, thought that the statement as to the capacity of the ships was intended to be a term of the contract but he held that the term was a mere warranty as the difference in capacity did not go to the root of the contract.

But in more recent cases the possibility of part of the contract description being held to amount merely to a warranty seems to have been lost sight of. In *Arcos, Ltd.* v. *E. A. Ronaasen & Son*,[3] the buyers agreed to buy a quantity of staves which they required, as the sellers knew, for making cement barrels. The contract stated that the staves were to be half an inch thick. In fact only about 5 per cent conformed to this requirement, but the rest of the staves were nearly all less than $\frac{9}{16}$ in. It was found as a fact that the goods "were commercially within and merchantable under the contract specification," and also that they were reasonably fit for the purpose for which they were sold. Despite these findings it was held by the House of Lords that the buyers were entitled to reject the goods for breach of Sect. 13. Lord Atkin said—[4]

> It was contended that in all commercial contracts the question was whether there was a "substantial" compliance with the contract: there must always be some margin: and it is for the tribunal of fact to determine whether the margin is exceeded or not. I cannot agree. If the written contract specifies conditions of weight, measurement and the like, those conditions must be complied with. A ton does not mean about a ton, or a yard about a yard. Still less when you descend to minute measurements does $\frac{1}{2}$ inch mean about $\frac{1}{2}$ inch. If the seller wants a margin he must and in my experience does stipulate for it. . . .
>
> No doubt there may be microscopic deviations which business men and therefore lawyers will ignore. . . . But apart from this consideration the right view is that the conditions of the contract must be strictly performed. If a condition is not performed the buyer has a right to reject.

[1] [1900] 1 Q.B. 513.   [2] [1917] 2 K.B. 606.
[3] [1933] A.C. 470. See also *Rapalli* v. *K. L. Take.* [1958] 2 Lloyd's Rep. 469, a very similar case.
[4] At pp. 479–80.

So also in another recent case from New Zealand—*Armaghdown Motors* v. *Gray Motors*[1]—the plaintiffs bought a car from the defendants which they were assured had not been used as a taxi. It was held that this formed part of the description of the goods and there was a breach of Sect. 13, although it would seem difficult to contend that non-use as a taxi went to the root of the contract.

Prior to the passing of the 1973 Act, it was important to consider the relation between Sect. 13 and the doctrine of the fundamental term or fundamental breach. This question will now be of very little importance because the new Sect. 55 greatly restricts the power of a seller to contract out of his liability under Sect. 13. Under Sect. 55 (4) there can be no contracting out of Sect. 13 at all in a "consumer sale" (see p. 133, as to this term). In a non-consumer sale, contracting out of Sect. 13 is only permissible to the extent that it is "fair or reasonable". For example the breach in *Arcos, Ltd.* v. *E. A. Ronaasen & Son*[2] would seem on the face of it to have been one of trivial significance; and if the contract in that case had contained an exemption clause it would have been most unreasonable to hold the seller liable for the breaches which occurred. Rules of construction, formerly widely applied to limit the operation of exemption clauses, will now be of much less importance, though doubtless they may still be used. Thus in *Robert A. Munro & Co., Ltd.* v. *Meyer*,[3] the defendant agreed to buy goods "with all faults," but it was nonetheless held by Wright, J., that this clause did not shut out the overriding requirement that the goods should answer to their description, but only served to protect the sellers from the obligation to supply merchantable goods.[4]

Meaning of "Sale by Description"[5]

With this preliminary discussion, we can now turn to consider the meaning of the phrase "sale by description." In the first place it has been held that this phrase "must apply to all cases where the purchaser has not seen the goods but is relying on the description alone."[6] Hence it follows that a sale must be by description if it is of future or unascertained goods.[7] But in addition the term applies in many cases even where the buyer has seen the goods. Early doubts as to whether an ordinary sale in a shop could be a sale by description were soon set at rest.[8] To quote from Lord Wright in *Grant* v. *Australian Knitting Mills, Ltd.*—

---

[1] [1963] N.Z.L.R. 5.   [2] [1933] A.C. 470.   [3] [1930] 2 K.B. 312.
[4] Cf. also *Pinnock Bros.* v. *Lewis & Peat, Ltd.*, [1923] 1 K.B. 690; *Vigers Bros.* v. *Sanderson Bros.*, [1901] 1 K.B. 608.
[5] See Feltham, [1969] *Journal of Business Law*, 16.
[6] *Per* Channel, J., in *Varley* v. *Whipp*, [1900] 1 Q.B., at p. 516.
[7] *Joseph Travers & Sons, Ltd.* v. *Longel, Ltd.* (1947), 64 T.L.R. 150, at 153, *per* Sellers, J.
[8] *Morelli* v. *Fitch & Gibbons*, [1928] 2 K.B. 636.

It may also be pointed out that there is a sale by description even though the buyer is buying something displayed before him on the counter: a thing is sold by description, though it is specific, so long as it is sold not merely as the specific thing, but as a thing corresponding to a description, e.g. woollen undergarments, a hot-water bottle, a second-hand reaping machine, to select a few obvious illustrations.[1]

One could add to this list beer sold in a public house, though this is hardly an obvious illustration. Moreover, it has now been made clear by the new Sect. 13 (2) that the term "sale by description" is wide enough to cover a sale even where the goods have been exposed for sale and selected by the buyer.[2] Even prior to the new Act it had been held that a sale could be by description even though the buyer had examined the goods with care[3] or even where he had himself selected them from stock offered to him by the seller.[4] In fact it is probably true to say that the only case of a sale not being by description occurs where the buyer makes it clear that he is buying a particular thing because of its unique qualities, and that no other will do.

For this reason the sale of a manufactured item will nearly always be a sale by description (except where it is second-hand) because articles made to an identical design are not generally bought as unique goods but as goods corresponding to that design. So it has even been held in Australia that the sale of an ordinary pair of "walking shoes" was a sale by description although the buyer had tried on and examined the shoes and might well have been thought to be buying the particular pair as specific goods.[5] Similarly the purchase of a second-hand car which was fully examined by the buyer was held in *Beale* v. *Taylor*[6] to be a sale by description because the buyer had relied in part on a newspaper advertisement issued by the seller.

These cases suggest that the real question at issue in deciding whether the sale should be classified as a sale by description is whether, on the true construction of the contract, the buyer has agreed to buy a specific chattel exactly as it stands to the exclusion of all liability on the part of the seller. For example, the buyer may examine a second-hand car and the seller may offer it for sale in terms which amount to saying: "There is the car; there is my offer; I guarantee nothing; take it or leave it." In this event it is thought the sale would be held to be a sale of a specific thing and not a sale by description. One of the consequences of the original Act was that if the sale was held to be a sale by description there would often be an implied condition under Sect. 14

---

[1] [1936] A.C. 85 at p. 100.
[2] See *Exemption Clauses, First Report*, para. 23.
[3] *Beale* v. *Taylor* (*supra*).
[4] *H. Beecham & Co., Pty., Ltd.* v. *Francis Howard & Co., Pty., Ltd.*, [1921] V.L.R. 428.
[5] *David Jones, Ltd.* v. *Willis* (1934), 52 C.L.R. 110.
[6] [1967] 1 W.L.R. 1193.

that the goods were merchantable. This consequence of holding a sale to be by description was so important that it seems that the courts in practice tended to interpret Sect. 13 with half an eye to Sect. 14. In other words if the court thought that on the true construction of the contract the seller should be held to warrant the merchantability of the goods it would tend to hold the sale to be a description; but under the 1973 Act the condition of merchantability is not limited to sales by description, and this may possibly lead to a tendency to a narrower construction of Sect. 13 in the future.

The Application of Sect. 13

It is to be noted that Sect. 13 (unlike Sect. 14) applies even though the goods are not sold by a person who sells "in the course of a business". Thus in *Varley* v. *Whipp*[1] the defendant agreed to buy from the plaintiff a second-hand reaping machine, which was stated to have been new the previous year and hardly used at all. This was a gross misdescription, and the defendant declined to accept it or pay for it. The defendant could not rely on Sect. 14 because the plaintiff was not a dealer in reaping machines, but as the goods did not correspond with the description it was held that there was a breach of Sect. 13. (Changes made by the 1973 Act are immaterial to this point.)

It should also be noted that the description of the goods may go beyond the mere physical state of the goods themselves. It may, for instance, include the way in which they are packed or the way in which they are marked.[2] In *Re Moore & Co., Ltd. & Landauer & Co.*[3] A agreed to buy from B 3000 tins of Australian canned fruit packed in cases of 30 tins. When the goods were delivered it was discovered that about half the cases contained only 24 tins. Despite the fact that the total number of tins was the same and that the arbitrator had found that there was no difference in value between the tins as they were packed and as they should have been packed, it was held by the Court of Appeal that the buyers were entitled to reject the whole consignment on the ground that there had been a breach of Sect. 13. This case illustrates the rule that if there has been a breach of condition the buyer is entitled to reject the goods even though he suffers no damage therefrom, whereas of course if there is only a breach of warranty the buyer's only remedy is to claim such damages as he has in fact suffered. As a general rule it is not common for a breach of condition to occur without causing some damage, but the cases show that the breach of Sect. 13 by no means invariably causes damage, and yet the buyer is always entitled to reject. It is hard to see why this indulgence should be

---

[1] [1900] 1 Q.B. 513. Note also *Beale* v. *Taylor* (*supra*) (private sale of second-hand car).
[2] *Smith Brothers* (*Hull*), *Ltd.* v. *Gosta Jacobsson & Co.*, [1961] 2 Lloyd's Rep. 522.
[3] [1921] 2 K.B. 519.

allowed the buyer in this respect, especially in view of the serious restrictions on the buyer's right of rejection in the ordinary case.

The description of the goods may also include a reference to the place where they are situated, as where goods were described as "Afloat per S.S. *Morton Bay*, due London approximately June 8."[1]

The Relationship between the Description and the Quality or Fitness of the Goods

As we shall see later, Sect. 14 deals with implied conditions as to the quality and fitness of the goods for a particular purpose. Sect. 13 does not on the face of it deal with quality or fitness for purpose. Thus, as we have seen from *Arcos, Ltd.* v. *E. A. Ronaasen & Son*,[2] it is quite possible for goods to be of merchantable quality and fit for their purpose and yet not correspond with their description.

Conversely, if the goods do correspond with their description the fact that they are unmerchantable or not fit for the purpose for which they are sold will not enable the buyer to plead a breach of Sect. 13. In this event he will frequently be able to rely on Sect. 14 (2) or (3) but these provisions are of narrower application than Sect. 13 and the question is therefore sometimes of practical importance. The point is illustrated by the recent decision of the House of Lords in *Ashington Piggeries, Ltd.* v. *Christopher Hill, Ltd.*[3] where herring meal contaminated with a substance which made it unsuitable for feeding to mink was sold to the buyers for use as mink food. It was held that the goods were still properly described as "herring meal," and it was pointed out that not every statement about the quality of fitness of the goods can be treated as a part of the "description." The Court of Appeal (whose judgment on this point was upheld in the House of Lords) went on to say of the argument that the goods should be held not to correspond with their description—

> Such a conclusion could only be reached if it were proper to take into account, in deciding whether the goods corresponded with the description, the particular and special purpose for which the particular goods were in fact used, or, perhaps, was known to the parties to be intended to be used. But if this be a relevant factor in deciding whether the goods correspond with the description, it would mean, in any case where goods are bought by description, that Sect. 14 (1)[4] of the Act is superfluous, and its result is achieved without the special conditions for the application of that subsection having to be fulfilled. The mere description of its own force would imply a condition of suitability for the particular purpose. That has never been suggested and cannot be right.
>
> The purpose for which a particular description of goods would ordinarily be used may well be an element in deciding whether or not, in the ordinary

---

[1] *Macpherson Train & Co.* v. *Howard Ross & Co.*, [1955] 1 W.L.R. 640.
[2] [1933] A.C. 470.   [3] [1972] A.C. 441.
[4] Now, the amended Sect. 14 (3).

use of language, the goods delivered correspond with the description. If goods described as oysters are not fit for human consumption, that may well be an important factor in deciding whether or not they are properly described as "oysters"; but the fact that a particular batch of oysters has some special quality which makes them harmful to a very limited category of persons with some special allergy, while they are perfectly suitable for all other oyster-eaters, can hardly prevent them from being properly described as "oysters." This is nonetheless so because the contract under which the oysters are sold may be made with the knowledge of both parties that they are intended to be eaten by a number of named persons, some or all of whom, without the knowledge of the parties, suffer from that allergy.

So, here, this Norwegian herring meal is no less properly described as "herring meal" because of the fact that, unknown to the parties, it has a quality which rendered it harmful to the particular type of animal to which, to the knowledge of the parties, it was intended to be fed.[1]

The suggestion made in the second paragraph of this quotation is well illustrated by the New Zealand case of *Cotter* v. *Luckie*.[2] In this case the buyer bought a bull described as "a pure bred polled Angus bull" from the seller. The bull had been wanted, as the seller knew, for breeding purposes but it turned out to have some physical abnormality which prevented it from breeding. The Court held that the sale was a sale by description and that the description implied that the bull was capable of breeding. The Court said—

The question—and I think the only question—for decision is whether this was or was not a sale by a description having the effect of describing the animal as a stud bull. Both parties are farmers. The respondent could have no use for the animal save for the purpose of serving his cows, and it is to be observed that it was sold not as a bull merely, but as a purebred polled Angus bull. The descriptive words appear to me to be meaningless unless intended to convey the impression that the animal might be used to get this class of stock.[3]

There is another type of case which may involve the relation between Sect. 13 and the quality or fitness of the goods. If the contract calls for goods of a certain quality this quality may itself become part of the contract description, but it seems that statements as to quality will not usually be treated as part of the contract description.

Compliance with Sect. 13

Whether goods correspond with their description will normally be a simple question of fact, but it is to be stressed that the duty of the seller is very strict indeed. We have already referred to *Arcos, Ltd.* v. *E. A. Ronaasen & Son* as an illustration of the extreme severity of the duties which the section places on the seller.

Reference has already been made to the fact that "microscopic"

---

[1] [1969] 3 All E.R. 1496, at p. 1512.   [2] [1918] N.Z.L.R. 811.   [3] At p. 813.

deviations may be disregarded in relation to the quantity of goods delivered, in accordance with the maxim, *de minimis*, and there seems no reason to doubt that the same is true of compliance with the contract description.[1] However, in *Moralice (London), Ltd.* v. *E. D. & F. Man,*[2] McNair, J., held that where the price is payable by means of a documentary credit against shipping documents, the maxim *de minimis* has no application as between the seller and the bank, and he added—

> I think it is probably true to say that when a c.i.f. contract provides that payment shall be by means of presentation of documents against an irrevocable credit, that necessarily involves, not only in the contract between the confirming bank and the seller, but in the contract between the buyer and the seller, that the documents must be such as will strictly comply with the terms of the letter of credit.[3]

In a number of more recent cases *Arcos, Ltd.* v. *E. A. Ronaasen & Son* has been distinguished by the courts. Where goods have been sold in some such terms as "fair average quality" or the like, it has been held that this phrase must be construed as businessmen would construe it and as referring only to such qualities as are normally observable by ordinary visual examination. Thus goods contaminated by some undetectable substance could still be of "fair average quality." Similarly in *Steels & Busks, Ltd.* v. *Bleecker Bik & Co., Ltd.,*[4] it was held that goods accorded with their description—which was "quality as previously delivered"—despite the presence of some new chemical, not present in the original deliveries, which rendered the goods unfit for the buyers' purposes. Sellers, J., found that "by the standard applied and accepted in the trade they complied with the description and were of the quality called for by the contract, quality not being affected by the chemical." This decision was approved by the House of Lords in the *Ashington Piggeries*[5] case on the ground that statements of this kind are not intended to be treated as part of the contract description of the goods. They are intended to indicate the quality desired, but not to identify the goods which the contract calls for. But this does not mean that the buyer is without remedy, for he may be able to claim damages under Sect. 14 (2) or (3).

But if the statement is part of the contract description it must be strictly complied with, though it does not follow that a description must always be taken literally. If goods have acquired a trade name they may

---

[1] *Arcos, Ltd.* v. *E. A. Ronaasen & Co.*, [1933] A.C. 470, *supra*; *Margaronis Navigation Agency Ltd.* v. *Henry W. Peabody & Co., Ltd.*, [1965] Q.B. 300.
[2] [1954] 2 Lloyds Rep. 526; *Soproma S.P.A.* v. *Marine & Animal By-Products Corpn.*, [1966] 1 Lloyd's Rep. 367, 390. But in practice this kind of problem would in most cases now fall to be considered under the *Uniform Customs and Practice for Documentary Credits*, see *post*, p. 236.
[3] At p. 533.
[4] [1956] 1 Lloyd's Rep. 228; *F. E. Hookway & Co., Ltd.* v. *Alfred Isaacs & Sons, Ltd.*, [1954] 1 Lloyd's Rep. 491.
[5] [1972] A.C. 441.

correspond to their description even if they are not what a literal reading of the trade name suggests they are. As Darling, J., said in *Lemy* v. *Watson*,[1] "If anybody ordered Bombay ducks and somebody supplied him with ducks from Bombay the contract to supply Bombay ducks would not be fulfilled." Thus in *Grenfell* v. *E. B. Meyrowitz, Ltd.*[2] the defendants were held not to be in breach of Sect. 13 when they supplied goggles of "safety-glass" to the plaintiff which subsequently splintered in an accident, as it was proved that "safety-glass" had acquired a technical trade meaning and the goggles in fact conformed to the normal design. Similarly in *Peter Darlington Partners, Ltd.* v. *Gosho Co., Ltd.*,[3] there was a contract for the sale of 50 tons of canary seed on a "pure basis." It was shown that there was no such thing in the trade as 100 per cent pure seed, and that the highest standard of purity was 98 per cent, and it was therefore held that the buyers were at fault in refusing to accept 98 per cent pure seed.

2. IMPLIED CONDITIONS THAT THE GOODS ARE MERCHANTABLE[4]

There are two distinct cases where the Act implies a condition of merchantability, namely Sect. 14 (2) (as amended by the 1973 Act) and Sect. 15 (2) (*c*). These are as follows—

14 (2). Where the seller sells goods in the course of a business, there is an implied condition that the goods supplied under the contract are of merchantable quality, except that there is no such condition—

(*a*) as regards defects specifically drawn to the buyer's attention before the contract is made; or

(*b*) if the buyer examines the goods before the contract is made, as regards defects which that examination ought to reveal.

15 (2). In the case of a contract for sale by sample—

(*c*) There is an implied condition that the goods shall be free from any defect, rendering them unmerchantable, which would not be apparent on reasonable examination of the sample.

Consideration of this topic falls into two parts.

(i) IN WHAT CIRCUMSTANCES DOES THE CONDITION APPLY?

"Where the seller sells goods in the course of a business"

Sect. 14 (2) in its original form applied where the goods were sold by description by a "seller who deals in goods of that description." In *Christopher Hill, Ltd.* v. *Ashington Piggeries, Ltd.*[5] a very narrow and literal construction was placed on these words by the Court of Appeal. It was there held that the words "that description" must relate

[1] [1915] 3 K.B. 731, at p. 752.
[2] [1936] 2 All E.R. 1313. As to the meaning in the motor trade of a "new" car, see *Morris Motors, Ltd.* v. *Lilley*, [1959] 1 W.L.R. 1184.
[3] [1964] 1 Lloyd's Rep. 149.
[4] See Davies (1969), 85 *L.Q.R.* 74.
[5] [1969] 3 All E.R. 1496.

back to the words "sell by description," and that therefore the sub-section did not apply unless the seller dealt in goods of precisely the same description as that under which the contract goods were sold. Where goods are sold under a broad and generic description, as e.g. "a car," or a "a pair of shoes," this interpretation caused no difficulty. But where goods are sold under a detailed description this interpretation meant that a seller would not be liable under Sect. 14 (2) unless he dealt in goods of precisely the same description. This meant that if, for example, the buyer ordered from the seller a particular brand of goods which the seller did not normally stock, e.g., an X brand mower, Sect. 14 (2) would not apply if the seller did not deal in X brand mowers even though he dealt in other mowers. This was a most unsatisfactory construction to place on the subsection[1] and the House of Lords later overruled the Court of Appeal on this point.[2] The majority of their lordships rejected this narrow interpretation of the words of "that description" and held that the words merely meant "of that kind." They made it clear, moreover, that the real question was whether the seller was selling in the course of his business, or held himself out as willing to supply the goods. The 1973 Act in effect gives statutory confirmation to this decision.

A new Sect. 14 (5) deals with the problem of a private seller who sells through an agent. This provides that the implied condition operates if the agent is selling in the course of business unless the principal is not acting in the course of business and the buyer is aware of this, or reasonable steps are taken to bring it to his notice. So, for instance, an auctioneer acting for a private seller can exclude these sections by making it clear that the principal is a private seller.

Sect. 15 (2) (c) contains no words corresponding to those in Sect. 14 (2) discussed above. This is presumably a recognition of the fact that a person who sells goods by sample is unlikely to be a private seller but will almost invariably be selling in the course of business.

Second-hand Goods

Sect. 14 (2) applies to the sale of second-hand goods[3] though it does not follow that the seller's obligations are the same in respect of new and second-hand goods. Goods may well be held to be merchantable if they are second-hand where they would not be held merchantable if new.[4] Also, the exceptions in paras. (a) and (b) are much more likely to be relevant in second-hand sales.

No Reliance on Seller Need Be Shown

The implied condition in Sect. 14 (2) normally applies even though the buyer has in no way relied on the seller's skill and judgment. For

---

[1] See Law Commission, *Exemption Clauses, First Report*, para. 31.
[2] [1972] A.C. 441.
[3] *Bartlett* v. *Sydney Marcus, Ltd.*, [1965] 1 W.L.R. 1013.   [4] See *post*, p. 86.

example if a buyer orders goods from the seller which are only made by one manufacturer so that the goods can only be obtained from that manufacturer or from someone who has bought from him, the seller will still be treated as warranting the goods to be free from latent defects.[1] The reason for this rule, which may seem hard on the seller, is that in most circumstances the seller will himself be able to obtain an indemnity from the manufacturer on the ground that the contract between them also imports the implied condition of merchantable quality. And this remains the case even though the seller cannot in the particular circumstances obtain such an indemnity, for example, because the manufacturer is insolvent or the time under the Limitation Act has run out.[2] However, if the manufacturer is only willing to supply the goods subject to some limitation on his liability and the buyer knows this fact when he orders the goods from the seller, it was held in 1969 that this would normally negative the implied condition between buyer and seller.[3] It seems, however, that this would now only be the case in non-consumer sales because the new Sect. 55 (4) prevents the exclusion of Sect. 14 (2) in consumer sales.

Similarly if the buyer orders goods which are inherently defective or unmerchantable in the sense that they would not normally be merchantable or fit for ordinary purposes, it could hardly be supposed that the buyer could sue under Sect. 14 (2). In the *Ashington Piggeries* case the Court of Appeal put the following hypothetical situation—

. . . For example, suppose that a doctor brings a prescription of his own to a pharmacist, and the pharmacist makes it up with the best possible ingredients exactly in accordance with the prescription; because the prescription is faulty, the medicine, instead of curing the doctor's cough, kills him—and would kill anyone who took it.[4]

The Court took the view that the seller would not be liable in such a case on the ground that the pharmacist would not be a seller "who deals in goods of that description." It is now clear that this is wrong, but the Court itself envisaged an alternative explanation of this result. They suggested that where the essence of the contract is the making or compounding of goods to someone else's order or prescription the seller's duty may be limited to using all reasonable skill and care in selecting materials and compounding them. But this too may be criticised for the seller's duties are traditionally thought of as warranties involving strict liability: and it could hardly be supposed that the seller would be free from liability in such a case if, despite all care and skill, he delivered goods not precisely in accordance with the specifications. It is thought that the best reason for denying liability in the hypo-

---

[1] *Young & Marten, Ltd.* v. *McManus Childs, Ltd.*, [1969] 1 A.C. 454.
[2] Ibid., at p. 467, *per* Lord Reid.
[3] *Gloucestershire C. C.* v. *Richardson*, [1969] 1 A.C. 480.
[4] [1969] 3 All E.R., at p. 1518.

thetical illustration given by the court would be that in the circum-stances given, the goods should not in law be treated as unmerchantable. As we shall see later merchantability is a somewhat flexible concept (despite the new statutory definition, *post*, p. 85) and the buyer is the best judge of what he wants. If the buyer gets exactly what he has ordered it hardly lies in his mouth to say that the goods are unmer-chantable. An alternative way of dealing with the above by hypothetical problem—namely of treating Sect. 14 (2) as excluded by implication in such circumstances—would now only be available in non-consumer sales.

Examination of the Goods

The implied condition that the goods must be merchantable is ex-cluded by the proviso to Sect. 14 (2), and, in the case of a sale by sample, by the concluding words of Sect. 15 (2) (*c*), but the effect of these provisions is slightly different. So far as a sale by description is concerned it is clear that the proviso only applies if the buyer has actually examined the goods, and the new wording of Sect. 14 (2) makes no change on this point. But the new subsection has probably altered the law on another point. In *Thornett & Fehr* v. *Beers & Son*[1] it was held that the proviso to the original Sect. 14 (2) applied where the buyer, being pressed for time, examined some barrels of glue only from the outside, although the seller offered him every facility for a more complete examination. The original section modified the com-mon law rule which was that the implied condition was excluded by the mere opportunity for examination, even if in fact the opportunity was not taken. *Thornett & Fehr* v. *Beers & Son* went some way to restore the common law position and was open to criticism on the wording of the original section. The proviso formerly said that "if the buyer has examined the goods, there shall be no implied condition as regards defects which *such* examination ought to have revealed". The crucial words were "*such* examination", i.e. the examination actually made, not a hypothetical examination which might, or ought to have been made. As there was no evidence to suggest that the defect should have been revealed by the examination actually made, the proviso should not have been relevant. This seems to be the view taken in *Frank* v. *Grosvenor Motor Auctions, Pty., Ltd.*,[2] and the new wording specifically refers to "*that* examination" which seems to put the point beyond doubt for the future.

In the case of a sale by sample, however, the effect of Sect. 15 (2) (*c*) is to exclude the implied condition that the goods are merchantable if the defect could have been discovered by reasonable examination of the sample whether or not it has in fact been examined. In a sale

[1] [1919] 1 K.B. 486.   [2] [1960] V.R. 607, 609.

by sample, the seller is entitled to assume that the buyer will examine the sample, and the latter can hardly be heard to complain of defects which he could have discovered by the simple process of examining the sample. *A fortiori* is this the case where the buyer does in fact examine the sample and discovers the defect, but decides to take the goods all the same. "If there is a defect in the sample which renders the goods unmerchantable, and the buyer, notwithstanding and with knowledge of that defect in the sample, is content to take a delivery which corresponds with the sample, and gets such a delivery, he has no ground of complaint."[1]

There are many illustrations in the reports of defects which could not have been discovered by any reasonable examination, but two will suffice here. In *Wren* v. *Holt*[2] the plaintiff recovered damages for breach of the condition of merchantability of beer which was contaminated by arsenic. The proviso was clearly inapplicable as the defect was not discoverable on reasonable examination. In *Godley* v. *Perry*[3] a child's catapult which broke in ordinary use was held to be suffering from a defect not discoverable on reasonable examination.

(ii) WHAT IS THE EXTENT OF THE SELLER'S OBLIGATION?

The extent of the seller's duty here depends largely upon the meaning to be attached to "merchantable quality" and on the new Sect. 62 (1A).

"Quality"

"Quality" is defined by Sect. 62 to include "the state or condition" of the goods and certain conclusions have been drawn from this definition. In *Niblett* v. *Confectioners' Materials Co., Ltd.*,[4] the facts of which have already been given, Bankes and Atkin, L.JJ., were of the opinion that there had been a breach of Sect. 14 (2) as well as of Sect. 12 (1). Bankes, L.J., said—

> Quality includes the state or condition of the goods. The state of this condensed milk was that it was packed in tins bearing labels. The labels were as much part of the state or condition of the goods as the tins were. The state of the packing affected the merchantable quality of the goods.[5]

On the other hand the same Court of Appeal came to a different conclusion on these facts in the case of *Sumner Permain & Co., Ltd.* v. *Webb & Co., Ltd.*:[6] The sellers sold Webb's Indian Tonic to the buyers, which they knew the buyers intended for resale in the Argentine. The

---

[1] *Houndsditch Warehouse Co., Ltd.* v. *Waltex, Ltd.*, [1944] 2 All E.R. 518, at p. 519, per Stable, J.
[2] [1903] 1 K.B. 610.   [3] [1960] 1 W.L.R. 9   [4] [1921] 3 K.B. 387.
[5] At p. 395. Similarly, it has been held in South Australia that goods may be unmerchantable by reason of bad packing: *Gilbert, Sharp & Bishop* v. *Wills & Co., Ltd.*, [1919] S.A.S.R. 114.
[6] [1922] 1 K.B. 55.

tonic contained a quantity of salicylic acid which, unknown to both parties, made its sale illegal in the Argentine. When the tonic reached the Argentine it was seized and condemned by the authorities as unfit for human consumption. It was held that there had been no breach of Sect. 14 (2) as the goods could not be said to be unmerchantable by reason of the provisions of Argentinian law. There was nothing wrong with the quality of the goods, which could have been resold by the buyers anywhere except in the Argentine. Goods are not unmerchantable merely because they are not fit for one particular purpose. The buyers' complaint was really that the goods were not fit for the purpose for which they were sold, but they also failed under Sect. 14 (1) because they had ordered them under their trade name. The case well illustrates the difference between Sect. 14 (1) (now 14 (3)) and (2).[1]

Although stress was laid on the word "quality" in *Niblett's* case that word now seems to have no significance in itself. Sect. 15 (2) (*c*) does not contain the word at all, and it would obviously have been undesirable if the requirement of merchantability had differed according to whether it was a sale by description or a sale by sample. The new Sect. 62 (1A) now makes it clear that any reference to unmerchantable goods in the Act is to be construed by reference to the new definition of merchantable quality.

"Merchantable"

The next problem is the meaning of the term merchantable, a word whose interpretation has occupied the time of the courts on many occasions. The new Sect. 62 (1A) provides—

> Goods of any kind are of merchantable quality within the meaning of this Act if they are as fit for the purpose or purposes for which goods of that kind are commonly bought as it is reasonable to expect having regard to any description applied to them, the price (if relevant) and all the other relevant circumstances.

It seems unlikely that this definition will have much impact on the former case law, most of which remains relevant and instructive.

The whole question was exhaustively discussed by the House of Lords in *Henry Kendall & Sons* v. *William Lillico & Sons Ltd.*[2] In this case the majority of their lordships adopted the definition of Farwell, L.J., in *Bristol Tramways Co., Ltd.* v. *Fiat Motors, Ltd.*[3] as amplified by Dixon, J., in the Australian High Court in the case of *Australian Knitting Mills, Ltd.* v. *Grant.*[4] According to this test, the goods

---

[1] See also *Phoenix Distributors, Ltd.* v. *L. B. Clarke*, [1967] 1 Lloyd's Rep. 518.
[2] [1969] 2 A.C. 31.
[3] [1910] 2 K.B., at p. 841.
[4] (1930), 50 C.L.R. 387, at p. 418.

should be in such a state that a buyer, fully acquainted with the facts, and therefore knowing what hidden defects exist and not being limited to their apparent condition would buy them without abatement of the price[1] obtainable for such goods if in reasonable sound order and condition and without special terms.[2]

A number of important points arising out of this definition and out of the speeches in the House of Lords require amplification. First, it is essential to remember that the question of merchantability cannot be divorced from the contract description. The question is not whether in the abstract the goods can be described as merchantable, but whether they are merchantable *under the contract description and the circumstances of the case.* This is perhaps the best explanation of the decision in *Bartlett* v. *Sydney Marcus, Ltd.,*[3] a case which might be misleading if this point were ignored. In this case the plaintiff bought a second-hand car from the defendant dealers for £950. The dealers informed the plaintiff that the clutch was defective and they offered either to put it right and sell it at £975 or to leave the buyer to put it right and sell for £950. The buyer chose the latter alternative but, when he came to have the clutch repaired, the defect was found to be more serious than anticipated and the repair cost him £84. The Court of Appeal held that the car was not unmerchantable and Lord Denning, M.R., said—

In the *Cammell Laird*[4] case, Lord Wright said the goods were unmerchantable if they were "of no use" for any purpose for which such goods would normally be used. In the *Grant*[5] case he said that merchantable meant that the article, if only meant for one particular use in the ordinary course, is "fit for that use." It seems to me that those two tests do not cover the whole ground. There is a considerable territory where on the one hand you cannot say that the article is "of no use" at all, and on the other hand, cannot say that it is entirely "fit for use". The article may be of some use though not entirely efficient use for the purpose. It may not be in perfect condition but yet it is in a usable condition. It is then, I think, merchantable.

These remarks must be read in the light of what has been said above. There can, it is thought, be no doubt that if a new car was sold with a defective clutch the car would be properly said to be unmerchantable. But in this case the car was sold as a second-hand car with a defective clutch. Under that description the car could not be said to be unmerchantable merely because the defect proved more serious than anticipated.

[1] For qualifications later made to this, see *post*, p. 87.
[2] See also the definition proposed by the Law Commission which formed the basis of the new Sect. 62 (1A)—

"Goods of any kind are of merchantable quality within the meaning of this Act if they are as fit for the purpose or purposes for which goods of that kind are commonly bought as it is reasonable to expect having regard to their price, any description applied to them and all the other circumstances."

See *Exemption Clauses, First Report*, para. 43.
[3] [1965] 1 W.L.R. 1013.   [4] [1934] A.C. 402, 430.   [5] [1936] A.C. 85, 100.

Similarly, it has often been suggested that goods are unmerchantable if they are "of no use for any purpose for which goods which complied with the description under which those goods were sold would normally be used."[1] In applying this test it must be appreciated that it is rare that goods are fitted for absolutely no use at all. For example a car which has been completely wrecked in an accident may be no use as a car but it may still be saleable as scrap or as a source of spare parts and a buyer who buys it as such could not complain that it was unmerchantable merely because it would not go. But this does not mean that a car which is sold *as a car* would be merchantable if it turned out to be so defective that it was no use as a car, though still saleable as scrap. Hence in *Kendall v. Lillico*[2] Lord Reid amended the above test so that the words "of no use for any purpose" should be read "would not have been used by a reasonable man for any purpose". Goods are then to be treated as unmerchantable if no reasonable man could use them for any purpose for which such goods would normally be used.

Secondly, the price paid by the buyer cannot be left out of account in deciding whether goods are unmerchantable. Although the goods supplied under the contract may be commercially saleable they will not be merchantable if they are only saleable at a price which was substantially lower than the contract price. In *B. S. Brown & Son, Ltd.* v. *Craiks, Ltd.*[3] buyers ordered a quantity of cloth from the seller manufacturers. The sellers of the cloth thought it was wanted for industrial purposes but the buyers wanted the cloth for making dresses for which it proved unsuitable. The buyers had not made known their purpose to the sellers and thus they failed in their claim under Sect. 14 (1) (now 14 (3)). The contract price was 36·25d. per yard which was higher than would normally have been paid for industrial cloth but not substantially higher. In fact the sellers resold some of the cloth at 30d. per yard. The buyers' claim for damages on the ground that the cloth was unmerchantable was rejected by the House of Lords. The cloth was still commercially saleable for industrial purposes although at a slightly lower price. It was held that the reference to price in the test of merchantability stated by Dixon, J., in *Grant's* case[4] was too rigidly put. Goods cannot be said to be unmerchantable merely because they are not commercially saleable at the contract price but only at a slightly lower price. They will only be unmerchantable where they can only be resold at a substantially lower price. In this case the buyers had resold some of the cloth (after they had found that it was unsuitable) for 15d. per yard but it was found that they had not obtained the best market price reasonably obtainable in so doing. Some of the judges clearly thought that if this had been the real market value of the goods

[1] *Cammell Laird & Co., Ltd.* v. *Manganese Bronze and Brass Co., Ltd.*, [1934] A.C. 402, 430, *per* Lord Wright.
[2] [1969] 2 A.C. 31, at p. 77.   [3] [1970] 1 All E.R. 823.   [4] *Supra*, p. 86.

then the difference in price would have been so great as to render them unmerchantable.

An Australian decision of 1921 illustrates a situation where the price difference was substantial enough to produce this result. In *H. Beecham & Co. Pty., Ltd.* v. *Francis Howard & Co. Pty., Ltd.*,[1] the defendants bought spruce timber for piano making from the plaintiffs. The defendants themselves selected the timber from the plaintiffs' stock but later much of it was found to be affected by dry rot, not observable on reasonable external examination. The sellers argued that the timber was merchantable because it was still saleable as timber for making boxes which was in fact one of the uses to which spruce timber was commonly put. But the buyer paid 80s. per hundred feet of timber while spruce timber for box making was only worth 30s. per hundred feet. It was held that the timber was not merchantable under the contract description because "no businessman, having a contract to buy spruce timber whether for resale or for purposes of manufacture would think for a moment of accepting this timber, its condition being known, without a very large reduction upon current market prices."

In applying the decision in *B. S. Brown* v. *Craiks*,[2] a word of caution may be desirable. It seems probable that this decision does not apply to goods which are actually defective. It has always been held that even trifling defects render goods unmerchantable[3] although they may in fact still be commercially saleable at a price not much lower than the contract price. It is not thought that the House of Lords intended to cast any doubt on this proposition; and this may explain why in this case Lord Reid suggested that "it is [not] possible to frame, except in the vaguest terms, a definition of merchantable quality which can apply to every kind of case."[4]

Thirdly, the term unmerchantable does not necessarily connote that the goods are of any specific grade or quality. As was said by Salmond, J., in *Taylor* v. *Combined Buyers, Ltd.*[5]

The term "merchantable" does not mean of good, or fair, or average quality. Goods may be of inferior or even bad quality but yet fulfil the legal requirement of merchantable quality. For goods may be in the market in any grade, good, bad, or indifferent, and yet all equally merchantable. On a sale of goods there is no implied condition that they are of any particular grade or standard. If the buyer wishes to guard himself in this respect he must expressly bargain for the particular grade or standard that he requires. If he does not do so, *caveat emptor*; and he must accept the goods, however inferior in quality, so long as they conform to the descrip-

---

[1] [1921] V.L.R. 428.   [2] [1970] 1 All E.R. 823.
[3] See, e.g., *Jackson* v. *Rotax Motor & Cycle Co., Ltd.*, [1910] 2 K.B. 937.
[4] [1970] 1 All E.R. 823, 825.
[5] [1924] N.Z.L.R. 627, 645. However, under Sect. 2–314 (2) of the Uniform Commercial Code it is provided that merchantable connotes that the goods must be of "fair average quality".

tion under which they were sold and are of merchantable quality—the term "quality" including state or condition.

Thus if the goods comply with the normal condition of goods of the quality and description under which they are sold they will not be unmerchantable merely because they are inferior to other goods of a similar type. For instance in *George Wills & Co., Ltd.* v. *Davids, Pty., Ltd.*[1] the defendants manufactured and sold canned beetroot. For some time it had been customary to can beetroots in brine but the defendants then started to can the beetroot in vinegar. Such cans had a much shorter life—about twelve months—than beetroot canned in brine, or other canned foods, which keep for at least three years, but it was held by the Australian High Court that this did not render the goods unmerchantable. The Court said—

... if the contract called for the supply of beetroot canned in vinegar, the parties were bound to deliver and accept goods of this description and, if the condition and quality of the goods were normal for goods of this description, the purchaser could have no complaint on the ground of their merchantability. It would be nothing to the point, on any such complaint, to show that beetroot canned in vinegar would not keep for as long a period as canned peas or canned beans or, indeed, beetroot canned in brine or for as long as other canned foodstuffs. Nor would it be material to show that a wholesaler, who had purchased such goods, might still have them in his store more than twelve months later. Indeed, evidence as to the keeping quality of the other goods and as to the practice in the wholesale grocery trade would not be admissible in such circumstances.[2]

A further point of some difficulty arises out of the meaning of merchantability and this gave rise to some difference of opinion in *Kendall* v. *Lillico*. It will be seen that in applying the test adopted by the majority of the House of Lords (as later modified in *Brown* v. *Craiks*) it is necessary to ask whether a buyer, fully acquainted with all hidden defects, would buy the goods without a substantial abatement of price. The problem which gave rise to some discussion in *Kendall* v. *Lillico* was illustrated by Lord Pearce as follows—

Suppose goods contain a hidden deadly poison to which there was discovered by scientists two years after delivery a simple, easy, inexpensive antidote which could render the goods harmless.[3]

It was agreed that in deciding whether the goods were merchantable it must be assumed that the buyer knew of the hidden deadly poison, but the question which divided their lordships was whether it should also be assumed that the hypothetical buyer knew of the as yet undiscovered antidote. The majority seemed to think that this was the right approach so the goods would not be unmerchantable, but the

[1] (1956–57), 98 C.L.R. 77.   [2] At pp. 89–90.   [3] [1969] 2 A.C. at p. 119

views of Lord Pearce and Lord Wilberforce to the contrary carry more conviction.

Time during Which Goods Must Be Merchantable

Some controversy has recently been aroused as to whether the seller's duty to supply merchantable goods implies that the goods must be merchantable for any particular length of time. In *Mash and Murrell* v. *Joseph I. Emmanuel*[1] sellers in Cyprus sold potatoes c. & f. Liverpool. The potatoes though sound when loaded were rotten by the time the ship arrived and it was held by Diplock, J., that the sellers were liable under Sect. 14 (2) on the ground that in such a contract the goods must be loaded in "such a state that they could endure the normal journey and be in a merchantable condition on arrival."

On the face of it this seems a reasonable decision.[2] Indeed it seems inherent in the concept of merchantability that the goods will remain in a merchantable condition for a reasonable length of time according to the circumstances of the contract and the nature of the goods. For example, if in *George Wills & Co. Ltd.* v. *David Pty., Ltd.*, cited above, the sellers had supplied beetroot canned in vinegar with a life of only a few weeks, while the normal life of such cans was twelve months, there seems no doubt that the goods would have been unmerchantable. But more recently it has been held that Diplock J.'s decision only applies to perishable goods[3] and other dicta have thrown doubt even on this.[4] The present status of the decision must therefore be in some doubt. This does not mean that a seller is not liable for defects inherent in the goods at the time of sale merely because the defect may not have become apparent or caused any difficulty till a later date. The seller is clearly liable in that situation.[5] The only doubt is whether a seller is liable where the goods are not defective when sold but have a very limited durability.[6]

Part of Goods Unmerchantable

The cases which have so far been considered were concerned with goods all of which were unmerchantable. It may happen, however, that part only of a consignment is unmerchantable and that the rest may be satisfactory. In *Jackson* v. *Rotax Motor & Cycle Co., Ltd.*,[7] the plaintiff supplied motor horns to the defendant. One consignment was rejected by the defendant as unmerchantable on the ground that

---

[1] [1961] 1 All E.R. 485, reversed on the facts, [1962] 1 All E.R. 77; *Beer* v. *Walker* (1877), 46 L.J.Q.B. 677.
[2] See the Ontario Law Reform Commission *Report on Consumer Warranties and Guarantees in the Sale of Goods* (1972, Dept. of Justice, Ontario) pp. 37–38, arguing that merchantability includes durability.
[3] *Cordova Land Corporation* v. *Victor Bros. Inc.*, [1966] 1 W.L.R. 793.
[4] *Oleificio Zucchi S.P.A.* v. *Northern Sales, Ltd.*, [1965] 2 Lloyd's Rep. 496, 518.
[5] *Guarantee Trust of Jersey, Ltd.* v. *Gardner* (1973), 117 Sol. J., 564.
[6] See also *Crowther* v. *Shannon Motor Co.*, [1975] 1 All E.R. 139.
[7] [1910] 2 K.B. 937.

about half the goods were dented and scratched owing to bad packing. The Court of Appeal held that the buyer was entitled to reject the whole consignment, as it was not possible in the circumstances of the case to invoke the *de minimis* rule.

Goods Requiring Attention to Avoid or Correct Defects

The case last mentioned also illustrates the fact that goods may be unmerchantable despite the fact that they may be put into a satisfactory condition at a trifling cost and with very little trouble. On the other hand, if it is in the contemplation of both parties that something shall be done to the goods before they are used, they must be merchantable after, but not necessarily before this is done. Thus pork which may be harmful if eaten only partly cooked is not unmerchantable if it would have been harmless when properly cooked.[1]

Flexibility of Concept of Merchantability

It will be apparent that the concept of merchantability is an extremely flexible one, and this flexibility is in no way restricted by the new statutory definition. It does not seem to be going too far to say that, in effect, the concept merely requires the goods to be of the sort of quality reasonably to be expected having regard to all the circumstances of the case. The new definition, far from being, as definitions frequently are, a straitjacket, turns out to be largely a non-definition; it delegates to the court the task of deciding what is reasonable in the circumstances of each particular case, guided no doubt by general acceptance of what reasonableness requires in various classes of cases.

3. IMPLIED CONDITIONS THAT THE GOODS ARE FIT FOR A PARTICULAR PURPOSE

The new Sect. 14 (3), replacing the original Sect. 14 (1) and now itself replaced by the Consumer Credit Act, lays down the following condition—

> Where the seller sells goods in the course of a business and the buyer, expressly or by implication, makes known—
> (*a*) to the seller, or
> (*b*) where the purchase price or part of it is payable by instalments and the goods were previously sold by a credit-broker to the seller, to that credit-broker,
> any particular purpose for which the goods are being bought, there is an implied condition that the goods supplied under the contract are reasonably fit for that purpose, whether or not that is a purpose for which such goods

---

[1] *Heil* v. *Hedges*, [1951] 1 T.L.R. 512. The pork was infected with trichinae, a distressingly common cause of infection in America where this question has given rise to much difficulty: see *Williston on Sales*, Vol. 1, § 243a (revised ed. 1948 and 1969 Supplement); contrast also *Grant* v. *Australian Knitting Mills, Ltd.*, [1936] A.C. 85.

are commonly supplied, except where the circumstances show that the buyer does not rely, or that it is unreasonable for him to rely, on the skill or judgment of that credit-broker.

(i) IN WHAT CIRCUMSTANCES IS THE CONDITION IMPLIED?

Reliance on the Seller's Skill or Judgment

Under the original Sect. 14 (1) the buyer had first to satisfy the court that he had expressly or by implication made known to the seller the particular purpose for which the goods were required so as to show that he relied on the seller's skill or judgment. In consumer sales the courts leaned heavily in favour of the buyer in this respect. For example in *Grant* v. *Australian Knitting Mills, Ltd.*,[1] Lord Wright said—

> The reliance will seldom be express: it will usually arise by implication from the circumstances; thus to take a case like that in question, of a purchase from a retailer the reliance will be in general inferred from the fact that a buyer goes to the shop in the confidence that the tradesman has selected his stock with skill and judgment.[2]

The trend of the cases was to hold that if the seller knew the purpose for which the buyer wanted the goods the buyer would be taken to have relied on the seller's skill or judgment.[3] The new Sect. 14 (3) has largely confirmed the old case law on this point. It is now clear that the onus on the buyer in the first instance is only to show that he has made known the purpose for which the goods are being bought. Reliance will then be presumed unless it is positively disproved, or if the seller can show it to have been unreasonable.

The fact that both buyers and sellers are members of the same commodity market does not of itself show that the buyer does not rely on the seller though it no doubt tends against the inference of such reliance.[4] But where one merchant has brought the goods to the attention of another and has recommended them to him such reliance may be found. When the seller is also the manufacturer the inference that the buyer has relied on him will rarely be rebutted. The fact that the buyer proposes to analyse or inspect or test the goods on delivery does not mean that he is not relying on the seller.[5] Where the seller is selling for export from the United Kingdom to some country overseas the mere fact that he knows that the buyer is buying for import into a foreign country does not show that the buyer relies on the seller's skill or judgment.[6] In such a case it is the buyer who would normally be presumed to have the necessary knowledge of the conditions in the

---

[1] [1936] A.C. 85, at p. 99.
[2] See e.g. *Godley* v. *Perry*, [1960] 1 W.L.R. 9.
[3] See Lord Guest in the *Ashington Piggeries* case, [1972] A.C. 441, at p. 477. criticising some dicta of Lord Reid in *Kendall* v. *Lillico.*
[4] *Kendall* v. *Lillico*, [1969] 2 A.C. at p. 124, *per* Lord Wilberforce.
[5] Ibid., at p. 95 (Lord Morris).
[6] *Teheran–Europe Corporation* v. *S. T. Belton, Ltd.*, [1968] 2 Q.B. 545.

country of import and reliance may thus be disproved, or alternatively may be held to be unreasonable.

The concept of "unreasonable" reliance, introduced by Sect. 14 (3), looks new, but was in fact largely inherent in the old law. Prior to the 1973 Act, a court which found that the buyer had acted unreasonably in relying on the seller, could always hold that the implied condition was excluded by a contrary intention. As a result of the new Sect. 55 this is now no longer always possible, and it was therefore necessary to give power to the court to exclude liability where "unreasonable reliance" was shown. It will, of course, be for the courts to decide what amounts to "unreasonable reliance". But a good case can be made for treating reliance as unreasonable where the seller in effect disclaims responsibility and merely proffers his advice for what it is worth.[1]

Where the buyer's complaint is that the goods do not perform as well as had been hoped rather than that they are defective in any real sense, it may be relevant that the goods have been made to a new and experimental design. In *Dixon Kerby Ltd.* v. *Robinson,*[2] the defendant agreed to buy a yacht in course of construction to an untried design by the plaintiffs. Although the plaintiffs knew that the defendant wanted the boat for sea cruising and cross-channel trips, it was held that the plaintiffs gave no warranty that the yacht would be suitable for this purpose.

It is sufficient if the buyer relies only partially on the skill or judgment of the seller. In *Cammell Laird & Co., Ltd.* v. *Manganese Bronze & Brass Co., Ltd.,*[3] the defendants agreed to construct two propellers for two ships for the plaintiffs. These were to be made according to certain specifications laid down by the plaintiffs, but certain matters, and in particular the thickness of the blades, were left to the defendants. One of the propellers proved useless owing to defects in matters not laid down in the specification. It was held by the House of Lords that the defendants were liable for breach of the condition implied by the old Sect. 14 (1) as "there was a substantial area outside the specification which was not covered by its directions and was therefore necessarily left to the skill and judgment of the seller."[4] But where the buyer has only relied partially on the skill or judgment of the seller, "the reliance in question must be such as to constitute a substantial and effective inducement which leads the buyer to agree to purchase the commodity."[5] Moreover, it must be shown that the matters of which the buyer complains were matters in respect of which he relied on the seller.[6]

[1] See *Exemption Clause: First Report*, para. 37.
[2] [1965] 2 Lloyd's Rep. 404.
[3] [1934] A.C. 402.
[4] [1934] A.C. at p. 414, *per* Lord Warrington.
[5] *Per* Lord Sumner in *Medway Oil & Storage Co., Ltd.* v. *Silica Gel Corpn.* (1928), 33 Com. Cas. 195, 196.
[6] *Christopher Hill, Ltd.* v. *Ashington Piggeries, Ltd.*, [1969] 3 All E.R. 1496, at pp. 1515–16, upheld on this point in the H.L., [1972] A.C. 441.

If, however, the buyer is well aware that the seller can only supply him with one particular brand of the goods in question it can scarcely be said that the buyer relies on the seller's skill or judgment. Thus in *Wren* v. *Holt*,[1] where the plaintiff bought beer in a public house which he knew to be tied, the Court of Appeal held that there was evidence on which the jury could find that the buyer had not relied on the seller's skill or judgment. Mere suspicion that only a certain type of goods can be supplied is not enough to exclude liability, however. In *Manchester Liners, Ltd.* v. *Rea*,[2] the defendants supplied coal to the plaintiffs for their ship the *Manchester Importer*. The coal was unsuitable for this ship, and the sellers were held liable under the section although the buyers had good ground for suspecting that the seller might have difficulty in supplying the right type of coal owing to a railway strike.

Where the buyer has invited a third party to inspect the goods on his behalf, and the third party has reported favourably to the buyer in reliance on the seller's skill and judgment, it may be a nice question whether the buyer himself can be regarded as having relied on the seller's skill and judgment or whether he has merely relied on the third party's report. If the third party is the buyer's employee acting in the course of his duty,[3] or perhaps if he actually passes on to the buyer what the seller has said, it seems that the buyer can invoke the section. But as we have seen above, the fact that the buyer proposes to have the goods inspected or tested *after* delivery does not rebut the inference that he is relying on the seller's skill or judgment.

Where sellers sold potatoes for export from Northern Ireland to Poland and it was shown that a clearance certificate was required from the Northern Ireland Ministry of Agriculture, it was held that the buyers relied on the certificate rather than on the sellers in respect of matters covered by the certificate.[4]

"Particular Purpose"

Although Sect. 14 (1) referred to "the particular purpose for which the goods are required" it was well settled that the word "particular" was used in the sense of "specified" rather than in contradistinction to "general".[5] The purpose may in fact be a very general purpose, e.g. a car to drive on the road. Moreover, the word "particular" did not exclude cases where the goods could only be used for one purpose. In *Priest* v. *Last*,[6] for example, the Court of Appeal held that a hot-water bottle was required for a particular purpose within the section although it had only one purpose in the ordinary way. To quote again from Lord Wright in *Grant* v. *Australian Knitting Mills, Ltd.*—[7]

[1] [1903] 1 K.B. 610.   [2] [1922] 2 A.C. 74.
[3] *Ashford Shire Council* v. *Dependable Motors Pty., Ltd.*, [1961] A.C. 336.
[4] *Phoenix Distributors, Ltd.* v. *L. B. Clarke, Ltd.*, [1967] 1 Lloyd's Rep. 518.
[5] *Kendall* v. *Lillico*, [1969] 2 A.C. at p. 123, *per* Lord Wilberforce.
[6] [1903] 2 K.B. 148.   [7] [1936] A.C. 85 at p. 99.

There is no need to specify in terms the particular purpose for which the buyer requires the goods, which is nonetheless the particular purpose within the meaning of the section, because it is the only purpose for which anyone would ordinarily want the goods.

These decisions appear to be largely confirmed by the new provisions which have substituted the words "any particular purpose" for "the particular purpose".

Some difficulty has arisen where the purpose for which the buyer wants the goods is made known to the seller but there is some peculiarity about the purpose of which the seller is unaware. In *Griffiths* v. *Peter Conway, Ltd.*,[1] the plaintiff contracted dermatitis from a Harris Tweed coat which she had bought from the defendants. It was found as a fact that the plaintiff had an unusually sensitive skin, and that the coat would not have harmed a normal person. It was argued for the plaintiff that the case fell within the precise words of the section as the coat was not fit for the purpose for which it was required, viz., her personal use. This argument was rejected by the Court of Appeal.[2]

In reaching this decision the Court was obliged to distinguish *Manchester Liners* v. *Rea*,[3] which has been referred to above, and in which it was held that coal supplied by sellers for a particular ship was required by the section to be suitable for that ship. Lord Greene pointed out that ships differed in their types and requirements and that coal merchants knew this well enough; hence if a merchant undertook to supply coal for a particular ship he was bound to supply coal suitable for that ship. There was no normal or standard type of ship from which the plaintiff's ship differed. But in *Griffiths* v. *Peter Conway Ltd.*[4] this was the position. A normal person would have been unaffected by the coat. This does not mean that persons who are, in one sense, "abnormal", are never protected by the section, because there are clearly degrees of abnormality. For instance, a drug unfit for use by pregnant women would seem clearly to be unfit for their purpose if sold to a woman who is in fact pregnant.

In the *Ashington Piggeries* case,[5] herring meal was sold for compounding into animal feeding stuffs, and the meal was contaminated with some toxic element. This rendered the meal toxic to most animals though it was only seriously dangerous to mink. It was held that the case differed from *Griffiths* v. *Peter Conway, Ltd.*, which was a "highly special case" because, although mink were peculiarly susceptible to the toxic element, there was evidence that this element was also harmful to other animals.

---

[1] [1939] 1 All E.R. 685.
[2] See also *Ingham* v. *Emes*, [1955] 2 Q.B. 366, a case of skill and labour. It is also instructive in this connection to compare *Sumner Permain & Co., Ltd.* v. *Webb & Co., Ltd.*, [1922] 1 K.B. 55, *supra*, p. 80 and *Mash & Murrell* v. *Joseph I. Emmanuel, Ltd.*, [1961] 1 All E.R. 485.
[3] [1922] 2 A.C. 74.   [4] [1939] 1 All E.R. 685.   [5] [1972] A.C. 441.

Moreover, it was held that the burden of proof was on the seller to establish that the toxic element was harmless to other animals.

Resale may be a particular purpose within the meaning of the section where it is clear enough for what purposes the goods will ultimately be used. But where a buyer buys goods which have a wide variety of possible uses, the responsibility placed on the seller may be heavy indeed. In *Kendall* v. *Lillico*,[1] Brazilian ground-nut extraction was sold for the purpose of compounding it into feeding-stuff for cattle and poultry, and it was held that there was a breach of the section because the extraction proved fatal to turkeys, though it was not dangerous to cattle. In the *Ashington Piggeries* case (*supra*) the original suppliers were merely selling herring-meal for compounding into animal feeding-stuffs and this proved fatal to mink. Again the suppliers were held liable. It will be seen that in cases of this nature the "particular purpose" may be very wide indeed, and although the goods may be quite satisfactory for a wide range of uses, the seller will be liable if the goods are in fact unsuitable for any one of those uses to which the buyer puts the goods. The only qualification on this seems to be that it must be shown that the particular use to which the buyer put the goods was not unforeseeable or abnormal. It is unnecessary to show that this particular use was actually contemplated by the parties. Nor, under the new Sect. 14 (3) is it necessary that the goods are commonly supplied for the purpose in question. Thus in the *Ashington Piggeries* case it was enough to render the ultimate suppliers liable that herring-meal was commonly used in feeding-stuffs for mink; it was not necessary to go further and show that this was the particular purpose for which the feeding-stuff would be likely to be used.

Status of seller irrelevant

Since the subsection formerly stated that the seller was liable "whether he be the manufacturer or not" it might have been thought that it only applied to manufactured goods, but it was well settled that it also applied to non-manufactured goods, such as foodstuffs.[2] The new Sect. 14 (3) has now dropped these words altogether.

"Where the seller sells goods in the course of a business"

The original Sect. 14 (1) only applied where the goods were of a description "which it is in the course of the seller's business to supply". The Court of Appeal in *Christopher Hill, Ltd.* v. *Ashington Piggeries, Ltd.*,[3] placed a narrow interpretation on this part of the old Sect. 14 (1) similar to (but rather wider than) the interpretation they had placed on the corresponding words in the original Sect. 14 (2). But here again the

---

[1] [1969] 2 A.C. 31.
[2] *Frost* v. *Aylesbury Dairy Co., Ltd.*, [1905] 1 K.B. 608 (typhoid infected milk). *Wallis* v. *Russell*, [1902] 2 I.R. 585 (infected crabs).
[3] [1969] 3 All E.R. 1496.

House of Lords took a much broader approach[1] and the new Act now makes it clear that so long as the seller is selling in the course of business this requirement is satisfied.

Whatever interpretation is given to these words it is clear that they exclude from the operation of Sect. 14 (3) all cases of private sales of second-hand goods, and that in practice only manufacturers, wholesalers, retailers and dealers will be caught by this implied condition. Since the implied condition that the goods are merchantable is limited in the same way, as has been seen, it follows that there is still fairly wide scope for the application of the maxim *caveat emptor* in private sales.

The former Proviso to Sect. 14 (1)

Sect. 14 (1) originally had a proviso which excluded liability where goods were sold under a "patent or other trade name", but once again the courts leaned heavily in favour of the buyer in interpreting the words of the Act. There were two leading cases on the interpretation of the proviso, *Bristol Tramway Co., Ltd.* v. *Fiat Motors, Ltd.*[2] and *Baldry* v. *Marshall.*[3]

The second case virtually interpreted the proviso out of existence, since it was plain that the only circumstances in which the proviso applied were circumstances in which the buyer had not relied on the skill or judgment of the seller. It is clear from *Baldry* v. *Marshall* that the fact that goods were ordered under a patent or trade name was not enough to exclude the seller's liability unless the circumstances showed that the buyer was not relying on the seller's skill or judgment. Although normally a person who buys goods in a shop is relying impliedly on the seller's skill and judgment it is reasonably clear that where he orders the goods under a trade name he is relying on the reputation of the maker rather than on the shopkeeper. "If a person goes in [sc. a shop] and asks for a bottle of R. White's lemonade, or somebody's particular brand of beer, he is not relying on the skill and judgement of the person who serves it to him."[4] Consequently the Law Commission felt that the proviso had ceased to serve any purpose and it disappeared in the 1973 Act.

(ii) What is the Extent of the Seller's Obligation?

The second question which arises under this subsection is, What is the extent of the seller's obligation? Three points arise here.

Goods to Which Sect. 14 (3) Extends

In the first place, to what goods does the implied condition extend? The section refers to goods "supplied under a contract of sale," and in *Geddling* v. *Marsh*[5] it was held that this covered not only goods

---

[1] [1972] A.C. 441.   [2] [1910] 2 K.B. 831.   [3] [1925] 1 K.B. 260.
[4] *Per* Lewis, J., in *Daniels* v. *White*, [1938] 4 All E.R. 258 at 263.
[5] [1920] 1 K.B. 668.

which were the actual subject matter of the sale, viz. mineral waters, but also the bottles in which the waters were contained, even though these remained the property of the seller.[1] Consequently the plaintiff was able to recover damages for injuries received when a defective bottle burst.

The point arose again in *Wilson* v. *Rickett Cockerell & Co., Ltd.*,[2] where the plaintiff ordered a consignment of Coalite from the defendants. Unknown to either party the Coalite contained an explosive substance which blew up in the plaintiff's fireplace causing considerable damage. In actual fact the plaintiff did not succeed under the old Sect. 14 (1) because she had ordered the goods under their trade name, but she succeeded under Sect. 14 (2) on the grounds that the goods were not of merchantable quality. However, for present purposes the reasoning of the Court of Appeal is as relevant to the old Sect. 14 (1) as to Sect. 14 (2). Referring to the words "goods supplied under a contract of sale" Denning, L.J., observed—

> In my opinion that means the goods delivered in purported pursuance of the contract. The section applies to all goods so delivered whether they conform to the contract or not: that is, in this case, to the whole consignment, including the offending piece, and not merely to the Coalite alone.[3]

Dealing with the defendants' argument that there was nothing wrong with the Coalite as such, and that it was only the presence of the piece of explosive that made the goods dangerous the same learned lord justice remarked—

> Coal is not bought by the lump. It is bought by the sack or by the hundredweight or by the ton. The consignment is delivered as a whole and must be considered as a whole, not in bits. A sack of coal, which contains hidden in it a detonator, is not fit for burning and no sophistry should lead us to believe that it is fit.[4]

One would have thought the contrary was unarguable, and indeed, the Court of Appeal seemed to think so too, had it not been for the decision of the Court of Session in *Duke* v. *Jackson*[5] where on the same facts the coal merchant was held not liable as there was nothing wrong with the coal itself. The Court of Appeal in refusing to follow this case, pointed to *Chapronière* v. *Mason*[6] where the defendant sold a bun containing a stone on which the plaintiff broke a tooth, and a verdict for the defendant was set aside by the Court of Appeal. These cases have received implicit statutory confirmation by the new Act, because the new Sect. 14 (3) expressly extends the implied condition to the "goods supplied under the contract".

---

[1] Cf. *Beecham Foods, Ltd.*, v. *North Supplies* (*Edmonton*), *Ltd.*, [1959] 1 W.L.R. 643.
[2] [1954] 1 Q.B. 598.   [3] [1954] 1 Q.B. 598, at p. 607.
[4] [1954] 1 Q.B. 598, at p. 606.   [5] [1921] S.C. 362.   [6] (1905), 21 T.L.R. 633.

Strictness of Seller's Liability

In the second place, it is now beyond doubt that the defendant's obligations extend under Sect. 14 (3) to latent defects not discoverable by any amount of diligence or care. In *Frost* v. *Aylesbury Dairy Co., Ltd.*,[1] the argument was pressed that the buyer "could not be said to rely on the skill or judgment of the sellers in a case in which no skill or judgment would enable them to find out the defect" in the goods supplied. This contention, however logical, was rejected, and it has never found favour since.

This point now seems to have been put beyond doubt by *Kendall* v. *Lillico*[2] where Lord Reid said—

> If the law were always logical one would suppose that a buyer who has obtained a right to rely on the seller's skill and judgment, would only obtain thereby an assurance that proper skill and judgment had been exercised, and would only be entitled to a remedy if a defect in the goods was due to failure to exercise such skill and judgment. But the law has always gone further than that. By getting the seller to undertake to use his skill and judgment the buyer gets under Sect. 14 (1) [now 14 (3)] an assurance that the goods will be reasonably fit for his purpose and that covers not only defects which the seller ought to have detected but also defects which are latent in the sense that even the utmost skill and judgment on the part of the seller would not have detected them.

But the seller's duty is only to supply goods which are "reasonably" fit, not which are absolutely fit. This is likely to be of special importance where the relevant "particular purpose" is very broadly stated. For if the goods are suitable for most subdivisions within a broad "purpose" the fact that they may not be reasonably fit for some rare and improbable subdivision will not necessarily involve a breach of Sect. 14 (3). This point was discussed by Lord Pearce in *Kendall* v. *Lillico*:[3]

> I would expect a tribunal of fact to decide that a car sold in this country was reasonably fit for touring even though it was not well adapted for conditions in a heat-wave: but not, if it could not cope adequately with rain. If, however, it developed some lethal or dangerous trick in very hot weather, I would expect it to be found unfit. In deciding the question of fact the rarity of the unsuitability would be weighed against the gravity of its consequences. Again, if food was merely unpalatable or useless on rare occasions, it might well be reasonably suitable for food. But I should certainly not expect it to be held reasonably suitable if even on very rare occasions it killed the consumer. The question for the tribunal of fact is simply "were these goods reasonably fit for the specified purpose?"

In the *Ashington Piggeries* case[4] sellers sold herring meal to buyers which was suitable for inclusion in foodstuffs for most animals but was contaminated with some substance which rendered it poisonous to mink. The buyers used the meal in preparing foodstuffs which were sold to

---

[1] [1905] 1 K.B. 608.   [2] [1969] 2 A.C. at p. 84.
[3] [1969] 2 A.C. at p. 115.   [4] [1972] A.C. 441.

mink companies; the companies used the foodstuffs as mink food and suffered serious losses in consequence. They sued the buyers who claimed in turn against the sellers. The buyers argued that the meal was required to be reasonably fit for inclusion in animal foodstuffs generally; the sellers argued that the meal was only required to be reasonably fit for inclusion in feeding stuffs for pigs, poultry and cattle. It was held, in effect, that the meal was required to be fit for inclusion in feeding stuffs for any animals to which the sellers ought to have contemplated that it might be fed.

A very similar approach was adopted by Rees, J., in the earlier case of *Vacwell Engineering Co. Ltd.* v. *B.D.H. Chemicals.*[1] In this case the defendants sold glass ampoules containing a chemical known as boron tribromide to the buyers who required it for use in certain manufacturing processes. The chemical, in itself, was perfectly fit for the plaintiff's purposes but it was liable to react with great violence on contact with water though this was unknown to the plaintiffs. The plaintiff's process required the labels to be washed off the ampoules and while this was being done one of them broke causing a reaction which shattered all the others and as a result a very violent explosion occurred. It was held that the goods were not reasonably fit for the purpose for which they were sold and the defendants were liable because they ought to have foreseen the possibility of the chemical coming into contact with water. Both in this case and in the *Ashington Piggeries* case the issue under the old Sect. 14 (1) was very similar to a general argument that the damage which occurred was too remote in accordance with the ordinary principles of contract law discussed recently by the House of Lords in the *Heron II.*[2] In this type of situation it seems that the application of these principles is in effect identical with the question whether the goods are reasonably fit for their purpose under Sect. 14 (3).

Time for Which Goods Must Be Reasonably Fit

The third point concerns the length of time during which the goods must remain reasonably fit for their purpose. Similar questions arise in dealing with the implied condition that the goods must be merchantable (see *ante*, p. 90). The principle is the same here, and is illustrated by the recent case of Crowther v. Shannon Motor Co.[3]

Comparison Between Sect. 13, Sect. 14 (2) and (3) and Sect. 15 (2) (c)

It is clear by now that the conditions implied by Sect. 13, Sect. 14 (2), Sect. 14 (3) and Sect. 15 (2) (c) must frequently overlap in practice, and in fact it has often happened that a plaintiff has succeeded under several of the corresponding sections of the original Act. It may therefore be useful to complete this examination of these implied conditions by comparing and contrasting the provisions of the three subsections.

[1] [1969] 3 All E.R. 1681.   [2] [1969] 1 A.C. 350.   [3] [1975] 1 All E.R. 139.

Firstly, both subsections of Sect. 14 only apply where the goods are supplied by a seller who sells in the course of business, and it is clear under the new Act that this qualification means the same in the two cases. In sales by sample this restriction does not apply. Nor does it apply to the requirements of Sect. 13.

Secondly, in all cases, the provisions apply to manufactured and to non-manufactured goods alike.

Thirdly, Sect. 14 (3) only applies where the buyer relies on the skill or judgment of the seller, whereas Sects. 14 (2) and 15 (2) (c) apply even where this is not the case. This distinction may be more apparent than real because the most obvious way in which the buyer can show that he is not relying on the seller is to examine the goods himself, and if he does so Sect. 14 (2) excludes liability for defects which ought to have been revealed by that examination. Sect. 15 (2) (c) also excludes liability for defects discoverable by reasonable examination of the sample whether it is in fact examined or not. In one respect, however, Sect. 14 (3) is clearly wider than the other two subsections because a person may examine the goods and still rely partly on the seller's skill or judgment. In another respect it is narrower than the other two, because if the examination is taken to indicate a lack of reliance on the seller's skill or judgment it will exclude Sect. 14 (3) altogether, whereas it will only exclude liability under Sect. 14 (2) in respect of defects which could have been discovered by the examination, and the same is true of Sect. 15 (2) (c). There are also other situations in which it is plain that the buyer is not relying on the seller's skill and judgment (as where he orders goods only obtainable from one source) and yet Sect. 14 (2) applies. Examination appears at first sight to be irrelevant to Sect. 13, and there is no doubt that the condition in Sect. 13 can apply even though the buyer has examined the goods. But it is also clear that examination of the goods may be a relevant factor in deciding whether the sale is a sale by description or not. Moreover it seems unlikely that a buyer could rely on non-conformity with description where he is aware of such non-conformity from his examination of the goods.

Fourthly, Sect. 14 (3) is wider than the other subsections in that goods may be perfectly merchantable although not fit for the purpose for which they were bought. On the other hand the wider liability only attaches if the purpose is expressly or impliedly made known to the seller, while the condition as to merchantability applies in any event. Sect. 13, as we have seen, deals with description and not quality or fitness, but in some circumstances the description includes matters of quality or fitness. Goods may comply with their description but be unmerchantable or unfit for their purpose, but the converse is also true.

Fifthly, Sect. 14 (2) and Sect. 14 (3) applies to all sales whether by description or by sample, or in any other way, whereas Sect. 13 only applies to sales by description, and Sect. 15 (2) (c) only applies to sales by sample.

4. IMPLIED CONDITIONS IN SALES BY SAMPLE

The meaning of a sale by sample has been left for treatment here, where it can be most conveniently dealt with. Sect. 15 (1) says somewhat unhelpfully—

A contract of sale is a contract for sale by sample where there is a term in the contract, express or implied, to that effect.

This subsection means that the mere fact that a sample is provided for the buyer's inspection does not make the sale a sale by sample. It is only a sale by sample if there is evidence of an intention that it should be such. In this connection the parol evidence rule has given rise to some difficulty; it has been held in a number of cases[1] that, if the contract is reduced to writing, and the writing contains no reference to a sample, parol evidence is not normally admissible to show that a sample was produced to the buyer and that the sale is a sale by sample. But where the description of the goods has no common or definite trade meaning, such evidence may be admissible to identify the description with a sample. So, for instance, where sellers sold "matchless No. 2475 39/40 white voile" under a written contract it was held open to the buyers to identify this product by reference to a sample though no mention of the sample was contained in the contract.[2] It has also been held in Australia that a parol collateral contract may be proved under which the goods are warranted equal to sample, even where the contract is in writing and contains no reference to a sample.[3]

The classic exposition of the effect of a sale by sample is that of Lord Macnaghten in *Drummond* v. *Van Ingen*—

The office of a sample is to present to the eye the real meaning and intention of the parties with regard to the subject matter of the contract which, owing to the imperfections of language, it may be difficult or impossible to express in words. The sample speaks for itself. But it cannot be treated as saying more than such a sample would tell a merchant of the class to which the buyer belongs, using due care and diligence, and appealing to it in the ordinary way and with the knowledge possessed by merchants of that class at the time. No doubt the sample might be made to say a great deal more. Pulled to pieces and examined by unusual tests which curiosity or suspicion might suggest, it would doubtless reveal

---

[1] *Meyer* v. *Everth* (1814), 4 Camp. 22; *Gardiner* v. *Gray* (1815), 4 Camp. 144; *Ginner* v. *King* (1890), 7 T.L.R. 140.

[2] *Cameron & Co.* v. *Slutzkin Pty., Ltd.* (1923), 32 C.L.R. 81.

[3] *L. G. Thorne & Co. Pty., Ltd.* v. *Thomas Borthwick & Sons, Ltd.* (1956), 56 S.R. (N.S.W.) 81.

every secret of its construction. But that is not the way in which business is done in this country.[1]

It follows from this, as was held by the House of Lords in this case, and as Sect. 15 (2) (c) of the Act lays down, that the use of a sample does not protect the seller from liability in respect of defects not reasonably discoverable on examination of the sample, although the bulk may in fact correspond perfectly with the sample. This is the requirement of merchantability which has been discussed above.[2]

The other provisions of the Act in respect of sales by sample are—

15 (2). In the case of a contract for sale by sample—

(a) There is an implied condition that the bulk shall correspond with the sample in quality:

(b) There is an implied condition that the buyer shall have a reasonable opportunity of comparing the bulk with the sample:

The first of these subsections lays down the obvious requirement that the bulk must correspond with the sample. It has been held that "it is no compliance with a contractual obligation for an article to be delivered which is not in accordance with the sample but which can by some simple process, no matter how simple, be turned into an article which is in accordance with the sample."[3] It should be noted, however, that where, according to the normal usages of trade, the sample is intended merely for visual examination, the buyer cannot complain that the bulk does not correspond with the sample, so long as, on a normal visual examination, it would appear to correspond, even though there are in fact differences, even material differences. The point is that, if the sample is only intended for a simple visual examination, the buyer has in no way been misled by a sample being different from the bulk if the difference could only have been discovered by microscopic examination.[4]

The second subsection dealing with the buyer's right to inspect the goods is in effect a special instance of the general right of examination conferred by Sect. 34. The subsection is not very happily expressed, however, because it is difficult to see how there can be a breach of the condition which it implies without a breach of the more fundamental duty of delivering the goods. What it really means, and what Sect. 34 says, is that the buyer is not to be deemed to have accepted the goods until he has had an opportunity of examining them. The effect of the acceptance is that the buyer can no longer reject for breach of condition, but is relegated to his right to claim damages.[5]

[1](1887), 12 App. Cas. 284, at p. 297. See also *Godley* v. *Perry*, [1960] 1 W.L.R. 9.
[2] P. 80 *et seq., ante.*
[3] *E. & S. Ruben, Ltd.* v. *Faire Bros., Ltd.*, [1949] 1 K.B. 254, at p. 260, *per* Hilbery, J.
[4] *Hookway & Co.* v. *Alfred Isaacs*, [1954] 1 Lloyd's Rep. 491; *Steels & Busks* v. *Bleecker Bik & Co.*, [1956] 1 Lloyd's Rep. 228.
[5] P. 288, *post.*

It may finally be remarked here that in a sale by sample and description the combined effect of Sects. 13 and 15 is that the goods must correspond with the sample, *and* with the description, *and* (if the seller is selling in the course of business) be merchantable. But Sect. 15 (2) (*c*) still operates so as to exclude liability in respect of defects which should have been discovered on reasonable inspection of the sample.

5. IMPLIED CONDITIONS ANNEXED BY TRADE USAGE

Sect. 14 (4), replacing and slightly altering the original Sect. 14 (3), lays down that—

> An implied warranty or condition as to quality or fitness for a particular purpose may be annexed to a contract of sale by usage.

This subsection merely illustrates the general rule applicable to all contracts that the intention of the parties must be ascertained in the light of all the surrounding circumstances. Where the transaction is connected with a particular trade, the custom and usage of that trade must be considered as a part of the background against which the parties contracted. In the words of Parke, B., in a leading case—

> It has long been settled, that, in commercial transactions, extrinsic evidence of custom and usage is admissible to annex incidents to written contracts, in matters with respect to which they are silent.[1]

A simple modern illustration is provided by *Peter Darlington Partners Ltd.* v. *Gosho Co., Ltd.*[2] which has already been referred to. The case was concerned with a sale of canary seed, and according to the custom of the trade the buyer was not entitled to reject the goods for impurities in the seed, but was entitled to a rebate on the price, proportionate to the percentage of admixture in the seed. It was held that the contract was governed by this trade custom.

6. OTHER IMPLIED TERMS

Sect. 14 (1) is now as follows—

> Except as provided by this section, and section 15 of this Act and subject to the provisions of any other enactment, there is no implied condition or warranty as to the quality or fitness for any particular purpose of goods supplied under a contract of sale.

Now that the provisions of Sect. 14 have been overhauled by the 1973 Act this residual exclusion of additional implied terms is unobjectionable and indeed inevitable. What is perhaps surprising is that the draftsman did not see fit to relegate this clause to the end of the section rather than leave it at the head.

---

[1] *Hutton* v. *Warren* (1836), 1 M. & W. 466, at p. 475.
[2] [1964] 1 Lloyd's Rep. 149.

MISTAKE AS TO QUALITY

It is traditional to treat the problem of mistake as to subject-matter in general, and mistake as to quality in particular, in isolation from the conditions implied by the Sale of Goods Act,[1] but now that it is becoming increasingly accepted that a mistake of this kind is merely a relevant factor to be considered in the construction of the contract, this approach has become inappropriate. If the correct view is that a mistake as to quality only renders a contract inoperative (or, as it is usually put, void) where this is the true construction of the contract, it is plain that it is impossible to consider the question of mistake without first examining the implied terms as to quality laid down in the Act.

As I have sought to show elsewhere,[2] where there is a contract for the sale of goods which turns out to be defective the courts are faced with three possible solutions to the case. (1) It may be held that the responsibility is on the seller, because of an express or implied term or misrepresentation. (2) It may be held that the buyer has taken the risk of the goods being defective, i.e. that it is a case of *caveat emptor*. (3) It may be held that neither seller nor buyer has taken the risk or may reasonably be held to have taken the risk or responsibility of the goods being defective. Although academic lawyers have frequently discussed cases of the third sort as being part of some "doctrine" of mistake (often drawing analogies with Roman law) the courts have rarely adopted this approach.

Claim by Buyer that Contract Void for Mistake

In practice a party who alleges that a contract of sale is "void" owing to a mistake as to the quality of the goods does so for the very reason that the terms implied by the Sale of Goods Act do not protect him, or alternatively, because he wishes to reject the goods and he cannot do so for breach of condition owing to the strict limitations imposed on the right of rejection by the Act.[3] For this reason it will be found that it is nearly always a buyer, rarely a seller, who claims a contract to be "void" on such a ground. Confusion has also arisen from some cases, because in holding that a buyer is entitled to reject goods for breach of condition, the courts have sometimes used language which is capable of being interpreted to mean that the contract is itself void.

In practice the courts have nearly always dealt with cases of this sort by asking "Has the seller not delivered what he contracted to sell?" (i.e. "Has there been a breach of Sect. 13?") and "Has there been any express or implied condition or warranty relating to the quality of the goods?" (i.e. "Has there been a breach of Sect. 14 (2) or (3)?"). If the answer to either of these questions is "Yes," the buyer has his remedy,

---

[1] A tradition followed in the first edition of this book.
[2] See "Mistake in the Construction of Contracts," 24 *M.L.R.* 421.
[3] See *post*, p. 287.

whereas if the answer to both questions is in the negative the buyer has no remedy: it is a case of *caveat emptor*. To argue that the contract is void for mistake in such circumstances is an attempt to add new terms to those implied by the Act, or to evade the restrictions on the right of rejection imposed by Sects. 11 and 35. It has already been seen that Sect. 14 (1) prevents the implication of terms, other than those there set out, which would impose additional responsibilities on the seller in respect of the quality or fitness of the goods.[1] Nevertheless, it is possible that these words would not prevent the implication, in suitable cases, of genuine conditions in the offer or acceptance, subject to which the buyer is prepared to contract. Such a condition would not impose a liability on the seller, but would, if unsatisfied, prevent a contract coming into existence, or from operating where it has already come into existence. *Financings, Ltd.* v. *Stimson*,[2] could be regarded as an illustration of a contract "void by mistake", but the courts simply do not adopt this analysis. In that case, where the goods, unknown to the parties, were damaged between the offer and the acceptance, the court treated the question as one of construction of the offer.

While it is not possible in a book of this nature to examine in detail all the cases on this subject, it is necessary to glance at a few of them.

For many years *Smith* v. *Hughes*[3] has been a leading, if puzzling, case on this point. In this famous case the defendant agreed to buy a specific quantity of oats from the seller after the seller had given the buyer a sample. The buyer declined to accept the goods on the ground that they were new oats and not, as he thought, old oats. In such circumstances the approach of the courts today would simply be to ask if the seller had contracted to deliver old oats or the specific parcel of oats sold, old or not. As the buyer had seen a sample of the oats it is hard to see how the buyer (absent any express warranty) could today get such a case on its feet. Any attempt to rely on mistake is simply to fudge the issue.

In *Leaf* v. *International Galleries*[4] the plaintiff bought a painting from the defendants which was believed by both parties to be, and was stated by the defendants to be, a Constable. Some years later the plaintiff discovered that the picture was a copy, and he brought an action claiming rescission of the contract. Now it is possible that the buyer could have obtained damages for breach of condition, but he did not want damages—he wanted to rescind the contract. Unfortunately for him his claim to reject the goods for breach of condition was plainly barred by the Act, and he accordingly attempted to argue that he could rescind for innocent misrepresentation instead. This claim was rejected by the Court on the ground that he was too late. It will be seen that no suggestion was made that the contract was void for mistake, but

---

[1] P. 104, above.
[2] [1962] 1 W.L.R. 1184
[3] [1871] L.R. 6 Q.B. 597, *ante*, pp. 24–5.
[4] [1950] 2 K.B. 86.

Denning, L.J., discussed the possibility in his judgment and rejected it because—

> Such a mistake does not avoid the contract: there was no mistake at all about the subject matter of the sale. It was a specific picture "Salisbury Cathedral". The parties were agreed in the same terms on the same subject matter, and that is sufficient to make a contract.[1]

Denning, L.J., might also have added that if the sellers had expressly stated that the picture was a Constable the risk of its not being a Constable was plainly on them, and accordingly any construction of the contract which would have placed the risk on neither party was ruled out. There was thus no room for any holding that the contract was void for mistake.

The most recent case on this topic also seems to bear out the above views. This is *Harrison & Jones* v. *Bunten & Lancaster*,[2] where the appellants (from arbitration) agreed to buy from the respondents a quantity of Calcutta Kapok "Sree" brand. Both parties were under the impression that this was a brand of pure Kapok but in fact it contained a proportion of cotton, which rendered it unsuitable for the buyers' purposes, and they claimed to reject it. Pilcher, J., held that the contract was not void for mistake. He said—[3]

> When goods, whether specific or unascertained, are sold under a known trade description without misrepresentation, innocent or guilty, and without breach of warranty, the fact that both parties are unaware that goods of that known trade description lack any particular quality is, in my view, completely irrelevant; the parties are bound by their contract, and there is no room for the doctrine that the contract can be treated as a nullity on the ground of mutual mistake, even though the mistake from the point of view of the purchaser may turn out to be of a fundamental character.

It is true that elsewhere in his judgment[4] Pilcher, J., said that "there are, no doubt, many cases in which proof of a mutual mistake[5] as to a quality of a fundamental character will serve to avoid a contract of sale," but the fact remains that there is no case in our reports to illustrate such a rule with the single exception of the doubtful case of *Nicholson & Venn* v. *Smith Marriott.*[6] The plaintiffs here bought a set of table linen described as Caroline whereas it was in fact discovered to be Georgian. The plaintiffs sued for and obtained damages for breach of warranty, but the learned judge went on to say that in his opinion the contract was void for mistake. His remarks on this point

---

[1] At p. 89.
[3] At p. 658.
[5] I.e. common mistake.
[2] [1953] 1 Q.B. 646.
[4] At p. 656.
[6] (1947), 177 L.T. 189.

were therefore *obiter*, and they were disapproved by Denning, L.J., in *Solle* v. *Butcher*.[1]

It remains to consider whether the position in equity differs from the position at law. Before the decision in *Solle* v. *Butcher* there was no ground for thinking that equity recognised a wider doctrine of common mistake than law. The only difference was that equity treated contracts affected by common mistake as voidable and not void. The reason for this was that most of these cases involved title to land, and in such cases the parties went to the Chancery because they wished to have documents delivered up for cancellation. Once within the jurisdiction of equity they had of course to accept such terms as the court wished to impose. Hence the impression arose that such contracts were not void but voidable.

Solle v. *Butcher* is not a case of sale of goods, and whatever the *ratio decidendi* of the case it would appear that the profession has not yet been convinced that there is an independent doctrine of mistake in equity which entitles a court to set aside contracts owing to a mistake as to the subject matter of the contract.[2] Even if the views of Denning, L.J., are eventually accepted it is unlikely that they will be applied to purely commercial contracts such as the sale of goods, and it is submitted that it would be unfortunate if this were ever done. The law applicable to the sale of goods is on the whole both well-known and reasonably definite. It might create considerable uncertainty in business relations if a vague and discretionary doctrine of mistake in equity were to be applied to the sale of goods. An argument based on mistake in equity was also pressed in *Harrison & Jones* v. *Bunten & Lancaster* but Pilcher, J., said—[3]

> On the facts of the case . . . neither party was at fault. . . . I am well satisfied that it would not be right on the facts of this case to say that the contracts were voidable on equitable grounds, and I do not propose to say any more about that.

It is submitted that this dictum is applicable to all cases of sale of goods, if not, indeed, to all commercial transactions, and it is proposed to follow the learned judge's example, and not to "say any more about that."[4]

Claim by Seller that Contract Void for Mistake

We have mentioned above that a claim that a contract is void for mistake is more usually made by the buyer and not by the seller.

[1] [1950] 1 K.B. 671 at p. 692. The learned judge (Hallett, J.) did not explain how he was able to award damages for breach of warranty if the contract was void.
[2] It was followed in *Grist* v. *Bailey*, [1967] Ch. 532, but seriously doubted by the High Court of Australia in *Svonosio* v. *McNamara* (1956), 96 C.L.R. 186.
[3] [1953] 1 Q.B. 646 at p. 654.
[4] For a full discussion of *Solle* v. *Butcher* see 24 *M.L.R.* at pp. 440–2, and for comment on *Grist* v. *Bailey* see the present writer's article in (1968), 2 *Ottawa Law Rev.* 337 at pp. 350–2.

Buyers are now well protected by the law, at least in respect of mistakes as to the quality of the goods they buy, and for this reason, it has been suggested, there has been increasing reluctance to recognise additional buyer rights by holding a contract void for mistake at the suit of a buyer. The converse situation is somewhat different. There are no implied terms to protect the seller or to ensure that he receives fair value for his goods. Doubtless this difference has arisen for a variety of reasons, but the main one would seem to be that buyers are more likely to be private individuals than sellers. Of course, in the commercial sphere, where goods are bought and sold in bulk, buyers and sellers are businessmen alike, but in the consumer sphere, the consumer is usually the buyer, and less commonly the seller. However, this is not invariably the case. Individuals sometimes sell goods to dealers, for example, second-hand cars, antiques or farm produce. In such situations the law still offers no real protection to the individual seller against the danger of being over-reached. Of course, in extreme cases there may be the possibility of relying on fraud, misrepresentation or undue influence, but there are no implied terms to protect the seller. It is in precisely this sort of case that courts may be found willing to protect a seller by invoking mistake doctrines. The most famous such case is undoubtedly the American decision in *Sherwood* v. *Walker*,[1] in which Mrs. Sherwood sold a cow, believed by both parties to be barren, for $80. In fact the cow was with calf and her true value was between $750 and $1,000. The majority of the court held the contract to be void for mistake on the ground that the parties were mistaken as to the substance of the thing sold. There is a sense in which the goods here were *more* than fit for the purpose for which they were sold; the court's holding goes some way to saying that this excess fitness may be so gross that it would be unfair to hold the seller to the bargain. The protection thus accorded the seller still falls far short of that given to the buyer, of course. He is entitled to complain of *any* deficiency in the fitness of the goods. By conventional modern English standards, *Sherwood* v. *Walker* is probably wrong; certainly it is difficult to believe that the case would be followed if the contract were between two business parties. But the decision seems more acceptable if it is recognised as a consumer protection case; this would involve a recognition that an individual seller selling to a buyer who buys in the course of business requires greater protection that other sellers, just as the individual buyer buying from the seller who sells in the course of business has long been recognised to have greater rights than other buyers.

[1] (1887) 33 N.W. 919.

CHAPTER 13

CONSUMER PROTECTION

In recent years the problem of consumer protection has received a good deal of publicity and (although this problem extends well beyond the law of sale of goods) recent legislative changes have justified the decision in the fourth edition to collect together a number of questions for discussion in this chapter. The most important of these questions relate to the quality and fitness of goods sold under consumer sales and therefore this seems a convenient place in which to consider them.

THIRD PARTIES AND PRODUCTS' LIABILITY

We have seen that in general a seller who is sued under Sect. 14 (2) or (3) is liable irrespective of all due care and skill; and we have also referred to many cases which illustrate that the seller's strict liability extends to consequential loss caused by the defective goods, and is not limited to losses arising under the contract itself. Thus if the buyer suffers personal injury through use of defective goods he can claim damages from the seller under the implied terms in the Sale of Goods Act despite the fact that the seller has not been guilty of any negligence. In this respect the buyer is in a privileged position compared to most persons who suffer personal injury. Normally claims for damages for personal injury must be made in tort and generally speaking, of course, such claims require proof of negligence on the part of the defendant.

But it will also be seen that the doctrine of privity of contract imposes serious limitations on this form of liability—conveniently called "products' liability" in America. Firstly, the buyer's remedy is only available against the actual seller. If the buyer wishes to sue the manufacturers he cannot prima facie invoke the strict liability involved in a breach of warranty, but must still base his case on negligence as, for instance, in the famous case of *Donoghue* v. *Stevenson*.[1] However, there are a number of qualifications to be made to this prima facie situation. Firstly, strict liability can often be effectively imposed on the manufacturer through third and (if necessary) fourth party proceedings. If the buyer sues the seller for breach of warranty, the seller may claim an indemnity from his own supplier, and that supplier (if not himself the manufacturer) may in turn claim an indemnity from the manufacturer. As between each pair of parties the relationship will be contractual and liability for breach of warranty can be established. For instance,

[1] [1932] A.C. 562.

in *Dodd* v. *Wilson*[1] the plaintiff farmer employed a veterinary surgeon to inoculate his cattle with some serum; it proved to be defective and many of the cattle died or became diseased. The plaintiff recovered damages from the surgeon as on an implied warranty; the surgeon brought in his suppliers as third parties, and the suppliers brought in the manufacturers as fourth parties. The surgeon obtained an indemnity from the third parties, and they in turn obtained an indemnity from the fourth parties. In this way the plaintiff effectively obtained damages for breach of implied warranty from the manufacturer through the intermediaries. More recently, the House of Lords has given the existence of rights of indemnity as itself a good ground for imposing strict liability on a supplier in contracts for work and materials.[2] This is, however, a somewhat clumsy and costly expedient. Why should not the plaintiff have a direct remedy against the manufacturer for breach of warranty? Moreover the expedient may not always work, for example if one of the intermediaries is insolvent, cannot be found, only carries on business overseas or has gone out of business.

A second possible expedient whereby a buyer may be able to hold a manufacturer strictly liable despite the apparent absence of privity is the collateral contract. For instance in *Wells* v. *Buckland Sand*[3] the plaintiff bought sand for growing chrysanthemums in reliance on an express assurance that the sand was suitable for this purpose. This assurance was not given by the seller but by the manufacturer. It was held that there was a collateral contract and the buyer was entitled to damages. This was a case in which a specific and personal assurance was given to the buyer by the manufacturer. What is not clear is whether such a claim could be based on statements made in a manufacturer's advertisements. Apart from the famous case of *Carlill* v. *Carbolic Smoke Ball Co.*[4] there are hardly any illustrations of this possibility in English law. But in America it has been held that a person who buys a car in reliance on an advertisement that the car has "shatterproof" windscreens can sue the manufacturers for breach of warranty if the windscreen is not in fact shatterproof.[5]

The collateral contract, however, has serious limitations as a device for holding a manufacturer strictly liable for defective products. In particular, it only helps a buyer where he can find some *express* statement or assurance that can be construed as a warranty. There is, as yet, no authority which goes so far as to hold that a manufacturer could be liable for breach of *implied* warranties on the basis of a collateral contract. The step from express to implied warranties would be a momentous one in practice; but in legal theory it seems a small extension.

---

[1] [1946] 2 All E.R. 691.
[2] *Young & Marten, Ltd.* v. *McManus Childs*, [1969] 1 A.C. 454.
[3] [1965] 2 Q.B. 170.   [4] [1893] 1 Q.B. 256.
[5] *Baxter* v. *Ford* (1932), 12 P. 2d. 409; 15 P. 2d. 1118; 35 P. 2d. 1090.

A manufacturer markets his products through retailers; he advertises directly to the public inviting them to buy his products. It does not seem unreasonable to hold that he is impliedly offering a warranty of reasonable fitness for ordinary use to a member of the public who buys the product.

The doctrine of privity of contract is also very material in the law of products' liability in another major respect. Not only does the doctrine normally restrict liability to the seller; it also normally confines the remedy to the buyer. A sub-buyer, a donee, a member of the buyer's family, an employee of the buyer, a mere bystander—none of these can sue the seller (nor, *a fortiori*, the manufacturer) for breach of warranty, but only for negligence. Indeed the position of the non-buyer plaintiff is even more perilous where he wants to complain of defects in the article purchased and not sue for consequential damage caused by a defective article. In the latter case, at least, there is no doubt that he can sue the manufacturer if negligence can be proved. But in the former event it is very doubtful if an action for negligence lies at all.[1] Sometimes, again, the liability may be passed on to the original seller through a chain of intermediaries, but this would not always be possible. For instance, if a person buys a new car and shortly afterwards sells it privately to a sub-buyer and the car turns out to have some defect which has to be put right at the sub-buyer's expense, he would appear to have no remedy against anyone. The sale, being a private sale, would not attract the conditions in Sect. 14 of the Sale of Goods Act. The sub-buyer would probably not be able to sue the original seller nor the manufacturer even if negligence could be shown.

In some situations the courts have struggled against the logical results of the doctrine of privity. For instance in *Lockett* v. *A. M. Charles, Ltd.*[2] a husband and wife went into a hotel for a meal and the wife was made ill by being served infected food. Negligence on the part of the hotel was not made out so the claim had to be made in contract as on a breach of warranty. The hotel argued that the only contract was with the husband as it was a reasonable presumption that he would pay the bill. This argument was rejected by Tucker, J., who held that in the absence of evidence to the contrary both husband and wife were in contractual relationship with the hotel. He held that the normal inference where a person orders food in a hotel or restaurant is that he makes himself liable to pay for it, whatever the position may be as between the person ordering the food and his companions. But it would be difficult to apply this reasoning (say) where a person ordered a meal for a child. Similarly if somebody books a private room at a hotel to

---

[1] See the discussion of this point in the author's article in 83 *L.Q.R.*, pp. 263–4; *The Diamentis Pateras*, [1966] 1 Lloyd's Rep. 179; *Young & Marten, Ltd.* v. *McManus Childs*, [1969] 1 A.C. 454, at p. 469; *Dutton* v. *Bognor Regis U.D.C.*, [1972] 1 Q.B. 373, at 396; *Rivtow Marine* v. *Washington Ironworks* [1973], 6 W.W.R. 692, see 37 *M.L.R.* 320.   [2] [1938] 4 All E.R. 170.

entertain a large party it would be clear that only he was in a contractual relationship with the hotel. Or again, where it is plain from the circumstances that the meal is to be paid for by a man and that a lady companion is only his guest, the lady will have no claim for breach of warranty.[1]

There is no doubt that the doctrine of privity can lead to some very anomalous results in these cases. A man buys a bottle of perfume (say) and gives it to his wife as a present. If the bottle explodes and injures her she cannot sue the seller for breach of warranty. If, however, he has bought the bottle at his wife's request, and therefore as her agent, the position is different. This difference seems indefensible.

It seems appropriate here to draw attention to recent developments in the United States in this area.[2] Starting with tinned and packaged foodstuffs, American courts began, some fifty years ago, to allow the non-buying consumer to sue for breach of implied warranties. Later this exception was extended to cover all products, and the Uniform Commercial Code, Sect. 2–318 (now enacted almost throughout the United States), gives a right of action on a seller's warranty to any member of the buyer's family or household. At the same time American courts have begun to allow actions against manufacturers on implied warranties despite the absence of privity. In some cases this double-barrelled attack on privity has enabled a plaintiff to sue the manufacturer even where the plaintiff was not the buyer and the manufacturer was not the immediate seller. In *Henningsen* v. *Bloomfield Motors*[3] the plaintiff was given a car by her husband as a present. The car had a steering defect which caused an accident in which the plaintiff was injured. She was held entitled to recover against the retailer and the manufacturers on implied warranties without proof of negligence.

These developments, while achieving satisfactory results in most cases, sometimes fell short of the ideal. For instance, there seemed no reason to confine the remedy to consumers or users of the goods. The plaintiff might be a mere bystander injured (say) by a defective car. Moreover the contractual approach caused difficulties with exemption clauses. Eventually some American courts abandoned the fictitious contract approach and decided to impose a direct and strict liability in tort on manufacturers. This approach was foreshadowed by Traynor, C.J., in *Escola* v. *Coca-Cola Bottling Co.*;[4] it was taken up in *Greenman* v. *Yuba Power Products*[5] and rapidly attracted considerable support. In 1965 the American Law Institute adopted a new section 402A in its *Restatement* of Tort Law imposing strict liability in tort on manufacturers for defective consumer products if they are "unreasonably

---

[1] *Buckley* v. *La Reserve* (1955), Cr. Law. Rev. 451.
[2] See Legh-Jones, [1969] *Camb. L.J.* 54; Prosser, "The Assault Upon the Citadel" (1960), 69 *Yale L.J.* 1099; "The Fall of the Citadel," 50 *Minn. L.R.* 791 (1966)—the "citadel" is of course the doctrine of privity.
[3] (1960), 161 A. 2d. 165. [4] (1944), 150 P. 2d. 436. [5] (1962), 377 P. 2d. 897.

dangerous." In effect, therefore , American law has reverted to the tort approach exemplified in *Donoghue* v. *Stevenson*, while upgrading the liability from negligence to strict liability.

It only needs to be added that English law lags a long way behind American law in these respects. The Law Commission briefly examined the issues involved but decided that fundamental changes of this nature could not be made within the context of a proposal to reform Sects. 13 to 15 of the Sale of Goods Act. They took the view that further intensive studies of products' liability as a whole were needed[1] and they have now embarked upon that task.

Indeed, full study of "products' liability" would plainly lead on to the wider implications of reforming or abolishing all personal injury claims and replacing them by some form of social insurance. However, even within the context of the present law there is plainly a serious need for reform here. It has been suggested that the real mistake of English law has been to impose liability for defective goods on a retail seller and that this is a liability which should be placed firmly on the manufacturer.[2] There is certainly much to be said in favour of this course but it is also arguable that retailers should continue to bear a secondary liability.

EXEMPTION CLAUSES AND MANUFACTURERS' GUARANTEES

There appears to be virtually no English authority on the legal effect of manufacturers' guarantees. But the use of such guarantees is today so widespread, and they are so closely linked with the problem of exemption clauses in consumer sales, that it seems desirable to devote some attention to them here.

The manufacturers' guarantee is now a document well known to the public. It is very common practice for the purchaser of consumer goods costing more than a few pounds to be supplied with a printed document by the retailer from whom he buys the goods. The document is issued by the manufacturer, and is normally attached to the goods themselves when sold. The typical guarantee contains undertakings by the manufacturer as to defects in the goods sold. Almost invariably the manufacturer undertakes to repair or replace defective parts or equipment free of charge during a specified time, such as six months or one year. In the case of vehicles the time limit is supplemented by a mileage limit as well. Frequently the buyer is required to dispatch the defective goods or parts at his own cost for repair or replacement. Some guarantees also limit the liability of the manufacturer so that he is not responsible for labour costs. Frequently the guarantee is expressed to be given in lieu of the statutory implied conditions and warranties. Almost invariably, it excludes all liability for consequential damage.

---

[1] *Exemption Clauses, First Report*, paras. 60–3.
[2] Jolowicz (1969), 32 *M.L.R.* 1.

These undertakings differ from the statutory conditions and warranties in several important respects. In particular the manufacturer does not *warrant* the goods free from defects; he is not liable in damages for defects, still less is he liable for consequential damage done by defective goods. His warranty is to repair or replace.

Many difficult legal issues arise out of these guarantees; in particular, it is often uncertain whether the guarantee is enforceable against the manufacturer, and the effect of a guarantee on the statutory implied terms is also unclear. In order to examine these issues it is necessary to distinguish between the buyer's relationship with the retailer on the one hand, and his relationship with the manufacturer on the other.

Buyer and Retailer

As between the buyer and the retailer it would seem that the terms of the guarantee can have no legal effect. Prima facie, if the guarantee is an effective legal document at all it can only be effective as a contract between the buyer and the manufacturer. And it is well settled law that the presence of an exemption clause in a contract between X and Y cannot affect the legal relationship between X and Z. The doctrine of privity of contract prevents the third party from relying on the exemption clause.[1] In view of the well-known hostility of the courts to exemption clauses, particularly where these purport to deprive a consumer of his normal statutory rights, it would not be surprising if a court was content to apply existing authorities to achieve this result.

Nevertheless it is possible for a retail seller to argue that the existing case law does not entirely cover the position under discussion. A retailer who sells goods with a manufacturer's guarantee attached which purports to protect him from liability could argue that he offers to sell the goods only on the understanding that the buyer accepts the guarantee. On this view, the terms of the guarantee, in so far as they purport to protect the retailer, would be imported into the contract of sale itself. This argument undoubtedly has commercial reality to support it. The average retailer who sells goods under a manufacturer's guarantee, and the average buyer who buys such goods, probably both assume that the responsibility for defects in the goods is on the manufacturer and not the retailer. But it seems very unlikely that a court would accept this argument. At the least a court would probably demand proof that the buyer knew of the exclusion terms in the guarantee when he bought the goods if these are relied on by the retailer. More probably a court would apply the doctrine of privity of contract and hold that terms in the guarantee could not affect the contract of sale itself. In any event the point has very little practical importance since the 1973 Act. Under

[1] *Adler* v. *Dickson*, [1955] 1 Q.B. 158; *Scruttons* v. *Midland Silicones*, [1962] A.C. 446; cf. *N.Z. Shipping Co.* v. *Satterthwaite*, [1974] 1 All E.R. 1015.

this Act exemption clauses in a consumer sale are void anyhow[1] so the point could only arise in relation to a retail sale of goods which is not a consumer sale as defined by Sect. 55 (7).

It should be added, however, that whatever the *legal* efficacy of these exclusions may be, there is a strong probability that they have a practical efficacy. The ordinary buyer may well be misled by the terms of most manufacturers' guarantees into thinking that he has bargained away any rights against the retailer. Consideration is now being given to prohibiting the use of such void clauses.

Buyer and Manufacturer

In considering the relationship between the buyer and the manufacturer the first question to be answered is whether a guarantee can constitute an enforceable contract at all. But in order to answer this question it may be necessary to ask which party is relying on the guarantee. The buyer may rely on it by simply suing for breach of the undertakings contained in it; but another possibility is that the buyer sues the manufacturer in tort under the rule in *Donoghue* v. *Stevenson*,[2] and the manufacturer seeks to protect himself by setting up the terms of the guarantee as a defence.

If it is the manufacturer who wishes to rely on the guarantee he would, of course, have to prove a bilateral contract with acceptance by the buyer, and an agreement by the buyer to waive some or all of his common law rights. What is strange about most guarantees is that they purport to exclude the statutory implied terms although these terms do not avail against the manufacturer. Since the buyer does not buy from the manufacturer there is no sale and no implied terms as between buyer and manufacturer. But there is, of course, the *Donoghue* v. *Stevenson* liability (which extends to consequential loss) and a guarantee which is accepted by the buyer may well involve surrender of these rights by the buyer in return for the undertakings in the guarantee itself. This is not precluded by the 1973 Act (because the contract between him and the manufacturer is not a sale of goods) but in view of the strict construction placed on exemption clauses it would doubtless be necessary for the guarantee to make it plain that it is given in lieu of *all* legal liabilities if it is to have this effect. A guarantee which merely referred to "conditions and warranties, whether express or implied by common law or statute" would not (it is thought) be clear enough to exclude the manufacturer's liability for negligence.

If it is the buyer who sues on the guarantee it is thought that prima facie the guarantee would be enforceable by him as a collateral contract. The mere purchase of the goods by the buyer would normally be a sufficient consideration for this purpose.[3] If the guarantee merely

---

[1] *Post*, p. 131.   [2] [1932] A.C. 562.

[3] But there might be problems if the buyer only became aware of the guarantee after completing the purchase.

contains undertakings by the manufacturer it could amount to a unilateral contract and no intimation of acceptance to the manufacturer would be necessary. But if the guarantee involves the giving up by the buyer of some rights which he would otherwise enjoy (such as his rights under *Donoghue* v. *Stevenson*) the agreement would be *bilateral* (promise for promise) and an acceptance by the buyer would then be required, and communication would be necessary. Failure to communicate an acceptance would then presumably render the whole guarantee (including the manufacturer's undertakings) legally ineffective even though no communication of acceptance is requested.

STATUTORY DUTIES

A great deal of consumer protection is today provided for by particular statutes. Some of these, like the Food and Drugs Act, 1955, are concerned, to some extent, with the quality and fitness of goods supplied for public consumption. Some, like the Weights and Measures Act, 1963, are (in part) designed to see that the consumer is not supplied with short measure. More recently, Parliament has passed the very comprehensive Trade Descriptions Act, 1968, which is mainly designed to prohibit false or misleading statements or advertisements by retail sellers.

These statutes all rely on the criminal law for their enforcement. It is generally assumed by Parliament and public alike that, when the consumer feels aggrieved, his reaction is to complain to a public authority rather than to take legal proceedings. Hence few of these modern statutes provide any form of civil remedy to the aggrieved consumer though there is at least one notable exception. For instance, under the Consumer Protection Act, 1961, power is given to the Home Secretary to make regulations for the purpose of imposing standards on the manufacturers of goods for the protection of the public.[1] By Sect. 2 of the Act it is an offence to sell goods not complying with any such regulations, and by Sect. 3 (1) any obligation imposed by Sect. 2 is a duty owed to any person who may be affected by a contravention. A person who buys goods not complying with any regulations made under the Act would, therefore, have an action for breach of statutory duty against the seller. Such an action would be quite independent of negligence. Furthermore, an exemption clause would not protect the seller from such an action because it is not possible for a person to contract out of a statutory duty cast directly on him.[2] Moreover, the action would also be available at the suit of the non-buyer plaintiff, for example a child who is injured by an oil heater purchased by his parent. This provision is, in some respects, a statutory innovation

---

[1] See, e.g., Oil Heaters Regulations, 1962 (No. 884).
[2] *I.C.I., Ltd.* v. *Shatwell*, [1965] A.C. 656.

which appears to have been prompted by the appeal made by Lord du Parcq in *Cutler* v. *Wandsworth Stadium, Ltd.*[1] that Parliament should make its intention clear where it intends penal legislation to confer civil rights.

There is no similar provision in other consumer protection legislation such as the Food and Drugs Act, 1955, and it has been held that breach of these Acts gives no civil remedy.[2] It is not easy to understand why this should be so. The traditional argument that such statutory provisions are intended for the benefit of the public as a whole seems pure sophistry. Statutes laying down requirements as to the purity of food or drink supplied to the public would seem obviously to be for the benefit of every consumer likely to consume the food and drink. To say that these are intended for the benefit of the public as a whole seems merely to beg the question. For this seems to assert rather than to demonstrate that no individual should have a remedy for breach of such provisions.

Parliament's own policy on these questions also seems hard to understand. While the Consumer Protection Act expressly allows for the action for breach of statutory duty (as mentioned above) some recent legislation expressly disallows the possibility of civil remedies. For instance the Trade Descriptions Act, 1968, Sect. 35, expressly provides that failure to comply with that Act does not render any contract void or unenforceable. And Sect. 17 of the Merchandise Marks Act, 1887, which gave a civil remedy for breach of that Act is repealed and not reproduced by the Trade Descriptions Act. It is not easy to understand why Parliament does not make greater use of the action for breach of statutory duty as a consumer remedy. It sometimes has the great advantage from the public point of view that statutory regulations become to some degree self-enforcing. If the aggrieved party can himself take proceedings, no public expenditure is required to enforce the statute. But in any event it seems strange that a seller can, in a civil court, hold a buyer to a contract on terms imposed by him in contravention of clear statutory provisions.

CONSUMER REMEDIES

The above discussion of statutory regulations relating to contracts of sale leads directly on to another point. The law of sale of goods appears on the face of it to confer satisfactory civil remedies to a buyer who has bought goods which prove defective or otherwise unsatisfactory. But in practice there is a good deal of evidence that the expense and trouble of civil litigation are so great that the average

---

[1] [1949] A.C. 398, at p. 410.
[2] *Square* v. *Model Farm Dairies* (*Bournemouth*) *Ltd.*, [1939] 2 K.B. 365. Cf. *Read* v. *Croydon Corporation*, [1938] 4 All E.R. 631 (statutory duty to supply wholesome water).

consumer gets no real protection from them in minor cases. In 1969 the Consumer Council conducted a sample survey of a number of County Court Cases involving "small" claims, these being defined as mainly in the £20 to £100 area.[1] Out of a total of 1,104 cases investigated not a single one was an action brought by a consumer. While business firms and tradesmen frequently launched claims for £10 or even £5, consumers were invariably advised by solicitors not to sue unless a claim was for at least £30. The only cases in which consumer claims were regularly put forward appeared to be those in which consumers were sued for the price of goods and then set up breach of warranty as a defence. The Consumer Council also addressed a questionnaire to a large number of solicitors about consumer claims. The almost unanimous response was that consumer claims were unsatisfactory for plaintiff and solicitor alike. Some solicitors took the attitude that it was pointless even to write letters of complaint because of the cost. All advised against legal proceedings by the consumer. The Consumer Council concluded that it was doubtful whether the County Courts are suitable forum for consumer claims.

Since October 1973 an amendment to the County Court Rules has come into force which may make some contribution to solving these problems. Where no more than £75 is involved, arbitration instead of trial can now be ordered (usually before the Registrar of the County Court). The hope is that the greater informality and lower cost involved in an arbitration may make it easier and more worth while for minor claims to be made. This may to some extent be assisted by the now fashionable "Do-it-Yourself" advice schemes for would-be litigants, such as the Consumers' Association publication, *How to sue in the County Court*.

It is not easy to know what the ultimate solution of these problems is likely to be. It seems clear that the trend towards use of the criminal law as the main method of consumer protection is likely to increase. Moreover, compensation orders are now being made under the Criminal Justice Act, 1972, in large numbers of prosecutions brought under the Trade Descriptions Act. But some method must be found of enabling the consumer to enforce the legal rights given to him by the Sale of Goods Act without paying out more in legal costs than the claim is worth and it remains to be seen whether the new arbitration procedure proves a success. At present it must be admitted that in many circumstances the most effective remedy of the aggrieved consumer is to write a letter of complaint to a daily newspaper rather than to resort to litigation in the courts.[2] This is no credit to the legal system.

[1] See *Focus* (the Consumer Council journal), July 1969, p. 2.
[2] The *Daily Express* regularly publishes letters of complaint from consumers together with an account of the newspaper's efforts to secure redress. There seems little doubt that fear of adverse publicity is a most effective stimulus to the redress of consumer complaints.

FAIR TRADING ACT

Intensification of interest in consumer protection has recently led to the enactment of the Fair Trading Act, 1973. Much of this comprehensive Act is designed to replace the existing legislation on monopolies and restrictive practices, and has little direct relevance to consumer protection or the law of sale. But the Act also contains a number of wholly new concepts and procedures which may eventually come to play an important role in consumer protection, though there will be little immediate impact.

The Act creates the new post of Director General of Fair Trading. The Director has the general duty of keeping under review commercial activities affecting consumers, and in particular, commercial practices which may adversely affect the interests of consumers in the United Kingdom (Sect. 2). A Consumer Protection Advisory Committee is also constituted by the Act (Sect. 3). Various "consumer trade practices" may be referred to this Committee to report on whether they adversely affect the economic interests of consumers (Sect. 13). These "practices" include practices affecting the terms and conditions on which goods or services are supplied, advertising of those terms and conditions, promotion of goods and services, methods of salesmanship, packaging and "get-up" of goods and methods of demanding or securing payment. The Director General of Fair Trading may also refer to the Advisory Committee proposed recommendations to prohibit or regulate certain practices, e.g., where he is of the opinion that the practice has the effect of misleading consumers as to their rights and obligations or subjecting them to undue pressure or of causing inequitable terms or conditions to be imposed in consumer transactions (Sect. 17). Following the Report of the Advisory Committee an Order may be made in accordance with specified procedure, by the Secretary of State, subject to approval by both Houses of Parliament. Such an Order may contain such provisions as the Secretary of State considers appropriate for giving effect to the proposals referred to the Advisory Committee, subject to any modifications proposed in the Report. Under Sect. 26 of the Act a contract is not rendered void or unenforceable only as a result of a contravention of an Order and an Order does not in principle confer civil rights. However, the Director may include in his recommendations to the Advisory Committee proposals relating to any matters mentioned in Schedule 6 of the Act. These include the prohibition of exclusion terms and also envisage the imposition of a requirement that specified terms should be included. These prohibitions or requirements may be incorporated in the Secretary of State's Order subject to compliance with the specified statutory procedures. In this way the civil law may ultimately be affected by the prohibition of some terms and the compulsory incorporation of other terms in certain classes of transaction. It seems probable that Advisory Committee Reports and Orders consequent thereon will, in the first instance, relate to particular classes of goods or services.

Additional functions are conferred on the Director by Part III of the Act which enables the Director to investigate business practices detrimental or unfair to consumers which have been persisted in by a supplier. The Director may require satisfactory written assurances that the practice will be discontinued, failing which he may take proceedings before the Restrictive Practices Court, or in less important cases, other lower courts. The court may make suitable Orders to restrain the practice in question.

The first Report of the Advisory Committee has proposed that an Order should be made prohibiting the use of advertisements or written clauses which contain void exemption clauses, and which may mislead consumers who do not appreciate that the clauses are indeed void.[1]

[1] See 1974/5 H.C. 6.

CHAPTER 14

EXCLUSION OF SELLER'S LIABILITY

EXEMPTION CLAUSES

MANY contracts, especially "standard-form contracts," contain exemption clauses whose purpose is to negative the terms which would normally be implied in favour of a buyer. At first there was nothing legally objectionable in this course in contracts of sale of goods because Sect. 55 of the Act (now Sect. 55 (1))[1] originally enabled the parties to negative or vary, by express agreement, any of the terms which were implied by the Act. Similarly, in hire-purchase agreements which did not fall within the ambit of the Hire-Purchase Act, 1965, all implied conditions and warranties could be, and almost invariably were, excluded by the terms of the agreement. In cases governed by the Hire-Purchase Acts, however, the right to contract out of the implied terms was always severely restricted.[2]

Although the courts did what they could to control the more extreme forms of abuse of this power of contracting out, the position became more and more unsatisfactory, as will be seen below. Eventually, it became clear that the task of controlling unreasonable exemption clauses was beyond the power of the courts and the position was radically altered by the Supply of Goods (Implied Terms) Act, 1973. This Act greatly restricts the power of the seller to contract out of his liability for defective goods and also extends the restrictions formerly applicable to hire-purchase contracts. In practice this Act will render the common law rules concerning exemption clauses of much less importance, but there will no doubt still be cases in which it may be necessary to decide whether an exemption clause has been made part of the contract and what its effect would be, before the impact of the new Act can be examined. Accordingly, a brief statement of the common law follows and then the new Act is closely examined.

If a seller relies on an exemption clause he will first have to show that the clause was incorporated in the contract, i.e. that it was part of his offer which was accepted by the buyer. He can do this in one of two ways, namely by showing that the buyer has actually signed a contract incorporating the clause in question, or by showing that the clause was brought to the notice of the buyer.

In the first case, the fact that the buyer has not understood, or even read, the contract or the clause in question is immaterial.[3] Even in this

---

[1] *Ante*, p. 43. [2] See *post*, p. 336.
[3] *L'Estrange* v. *Graucob*, [1934] 2 K.B. 394.

122

case, however, there are some circumstances in which the seller may be disentitled from relying on the exemption clause. For example, if the seller has misrepresented the effect of the clause, whether fraudulently or innocently, he will not be able to rely on it.[1] So also, an express oral statement made by the seller may in some circumstances be treated as a warranty or condition which overrides the terms of the written agreement.[2] Finally, there are some, though admittedly rare, circumstances in which a party may plead that the contract was wholly void because he was mistaken as to the very nature of the transaction.[3] In the absence of fraud this plea is unlikely to arise in practice in cases of sale of goods because it must be rare indeed that a buyer (or seller) is unaware of the nature of such a transaction.

Secondly, a party to a written contract can rely on an exemption clause even where the other party has not signed it, if he has given reasonable notice of the existence of the clause. This is a general principle of the law of contract which is not of such great importance in the law of sale of goods as it is in relation to certain other types of contract, and it would be outside the scope of this subject to discuss the cases in detail.[4]

CONSTRUCTION OF EXEMPTION CLAUSES

Where it is held that an exemption clause is incorporated in a contract, important and difficult questions of construction may arise. The general principle is that embodied in the *contra proferentem* maxim, namely that exemption clauses will be construed strictly against the parties relying on them. At least three general propositions may be deduced from the great mass of authorities on the subject.

In the first place the courts will interpret exemption clauses strictly, and in particular they will attribute precise legal meaning to technical terms. For example, in *Wallis, Son & Wells* v. *Pratt*,[5] the plaintiff bought from the defendant seeds described as "common English sainfoin," which were, as it transpired, a different and inferior variety known as giant sainfoin. The contract contained a term excluding all warranties express or implied. The plaintiff had accepted the goods and was therefore precluded by Sect. 11 (1) (c) from rejecting them, and was compelled to treat the breach of condition as a breach of

---

[1] *Curtis* v. *Chemical Cleaning & Dyeing Co., Ltd.*, [1951] 1 K.B. 805.
[2] *Couchman* v. *Hill*, [1947] K.B. 554; *Harling* v. *Eddy*, [1951] 2 K.B. 739
[3] This is the plea of *non est factum*, as to which see Cheshire & Fifoot, *Law of Contract*, 8th ed., pp. 234–40; Treitel, *Law of Contract*, 3rd ed., pp. 264–70; *Saunders* v. *Anglia Building Society*, [1971] A.C. 1004.
[4] The leading cases are *Parker* v. *S.E. Railway* (1877), 2 C.P.D. 416; *Thompson* v. *L.M.S.R.*, [1930] 1 K.B. 41; *Chapelton* v. *Barry U.D.C.*, [1940] 1 K.B. 532. See Cheshire & Fifoot, *Law of Contract*, 8th ed., pp. 123–41; Treitel, *Law of Contract*, 3rd ed., pp. 173–8.
[5] [1911] A.C. 394, upholding dissent of Fletcher Moulton, L.J., in [1910] 2 K.B. 1003.

warranty. Despite this it was held by the House of Lords that the exemption clause did not protect the sellers. The term in question was a condition and not a warranty, and its nature was not altered by the fact that the plaintiff was compelled to fall back on his remedy in damages. So also in *Baldry* v. *Marshall*[1] the defendants' obligation to deliver a car suited to the plaintiff's requirements was held to be a condition and was therefore not excluded by a clause which referred only to guarantees and warranties.

One of the most striking cases on the construction of exemption clauses is the decision of the House of Lords in *Beck & Co., Ltd.* v. *Szymanowski & Co., Ltd.*,[2] where the defendants had sold to the plaintiffs 2,000 gross 6-cord sewing cotton thread reels, the length on each reel stated to be 200 yards. The contract provided that: "The goods delivered shall be deemed to be in all respects in accordance with the contract, and the buyers shall be bound to accept and pay for the same accordingly, unless the sellers shall within fourteen days after the arrival of the goods at their destination receive from the buyers notice of any matter or thing by reason whereof they may allege that the goods are not in accordance with the contract." The reels only had 188 yards of cotton instead of 200 but this fact was not discovered by the buyers until 18 months later. The buyers claimed damages. It was held that the above clause provided no defence to the sellers, and the ingenious reason given by their lordships for their decision was well summarised by Lord Shaw—[3]

> The damages are claimed not in respect of the goods delivered but in respect of goods which were not delivered.

Again in *Minister of Materials* v. *Steel Bros. & Co., Ltd.*,[4] a contract for the sale of goods contained a term limiting the right to complain of defects of quality to a period of sixty days after the discharge of the goods at their destination. The goods were damaged as a result of defective packing. The Court of Appeal held that the ground of complaint was not the quality of the goods within the meaning of the exemption clause. Yet in the converse position it has been held that the "quality" of the goods within the meaning of Sect. 14 (3) includes the state of the packing, and that if this is unsatisfactory the goods are not of merchantable quality.[5]

In the second place, it is a general principle of construction of exemption clauses that, where a party would, apart from the particular provisions of the contract in question, be liable in the absence of negligence,

---

[1] [1925] 1 K.B. 260   [2] [1924] A.C. 43.
[3] At p. 50. Two of the law lords (Lords Wrenbury and Atkinson) agreed with the C.A. that even if the exemption clause did apply it only served to exclude the right to reject and not to claim damages: see [1923] 1 K.B. 457.
[4] [1952] 1 T.L.R. 499.
[5] *Niblett* v. *Confectioners' Materials Co., Ltd.*, [1921] 3 K.B. 387, p. 48, *ante*.

an exemption clause in general terms does not protect him from liability for negligence.[1] Since a seller is liable on the implied conditions under the Sale of Goods Act irrespective of negligence, an exemption clause in general terms would not exclude the liability of the seller for negligence. Again, however, this principle is not of great importance in consumer sales since in these days of manufactured pre-packaged products, the circumstances in which a retail seller will be guilty of negligence will be few. But commercial sellers of goods which are potentially hazardous or dangerous may sometimes be liable both in negligence and under the Sale of Goods Act, and in such cases this principle of construction could be important.[2]

Finally, mention must be made of two particular provisions in the Act bearing on the general question of construction. First, reference should be made to Sect. 55 (2), formerly (with verbal alterations only) Sect. 14 (4) which says—

> An express condition or warranty does not negative a condition or warranty implied by this Act unless inconsistent herewith.

Secondly, in addition to exclusion or variation of implied terms by express agreement Sect. 55 (1) says that "the course of dealing between the parties" or "usage, if the usage is such as to bind both parties to the contract" may have the same effect. So far as usage is concerned nothing need be added to the observations made above dealing with the implication of terms by usage,[3] for they are equally applicable here. With regard to the expression "course of dealing between the parties" this has been judicially explained to mean that previous dealings between the parties may raise an implication that certain terms are or are not to be included in the contract, if these have or have not been implied on previous occasions.[4] "If two parties have made a series of similar contracts each containing certain conditions, and then they make another without expressly referring to those conditions it may be that those conditions ought to be implied."[5] But in order to justify the implication of terms—and more particularly, it would seem, the implication of terms contrary to those normally implied—by reference to a course of dealing it must be shown that in fact there has been a consistent course of dealing in which the same terms have been regularly if not invariably incorporated in the past.[6] Thus, where over a period of years parties have regularly contracted on the basis of certain written terms

---

[1] *Rutter* v. *Palmer*, [1922] 2 K.B. 87.

[2] See, e.g., *Vacwell Engineering Co., Ltd.* v. *B.D.H. Chemicals, Ltd.*, [1969] 3 All E.R 1681 (though there was no exemption clause in this case).

[3] P. 104, *ante*.

[4] *Pocahontas Fuel Co., Ltd.* v. *Ambatielos* (1922), 27 Com. Cas. 148, at p. 152, per McCardie, J.

[5] *Per* Lord Reid in *McCutcheon* v. *David MacBrayne, Ltd.*, [1964] 1 W.L.R. 125 at p. 128. See *British Crane Hire Corporation* v. *Ipswich Plant Hire*, [1974] 1 All E.R. 1059.   [6] Ibid.

for the supply of goods, the terms may be held to be incorporated in oral contracts for the supply of the same goods between the same parties.[1]

FUNDAMENTAL BREACH AND FUNDAMENTAL TERMS

For some fifteen or twenty years in the 1950s and 1960s the courts attempted to achieve some measure of protection for consumers in dealing with harsh or oppressive exemption clauses. In retrospect it is now easy to see this judicial activity as a response to a particular social situation. With the great post-war consumer boom well under way, with the huge increase in ownership of consumer durables and above all vehicles, and with inflation rapidly making nonsense of the early Hire-Purchase Acts,[2] the courts began to see a steady stream of really hard cases. Most of these cases involved contracts of hire-purchase for second-hand cars or other vehicles. Invariably all liability for defects was excluded and frequently real hardship to the consumer was the probable result of strict adherence to the law. The courts' answer to this was the invention of the doctrines of fundamental breach and fundamental terms. Over a period of years a number of Court of Appeal decisions laid it down that there was a general principle of the law of contract, applicable to contracts of sale and hire-purchase, as to all other contracts, that a party could not rely on an exemption clause, however widely drawn, if he was guilty of a fundamental breach of contract. It was never wholly clear whether this was the same as the proposition that a party who was guilty of a breach of a fundamental term could not rely on an exemption clause. The language of the courts was somewhat ambiguous, breach of fundamental term, and fundamental breach being used indiscriminately as though they meant the same thing. This "doctrine" appeared to be firmly established but it was destined to be short-lived. Much of the steam was taken out of the area by the Hire-Purchase Act, 1964, which dealt with the most frequent and pressing cases of injustices by restricting the owner's ability to exclude liability for defects in contracts up to £2,000.

Then in 1966 the House of Lords decided the case of *Suisse Atlantique Société d'Armement Maritime, S.A.* v. *N.V. Rotterdamsche Kolen Centrale.*[3] This was not in all respects an easy decision to understand but the principal point to emerge from the *Suisse Atlantique* case was the firm and unanimous holding that the "doctrine" of fundamental

---

[1] *Kendall* v. *Lillico*, [1969] 2 A.C. 31. Dicta of Lord Devlin in *McCutcheon* v. *David MacBrayne, Ltd. (supra)* to the effect that actual knowledge of the terms was required before they could be incorporated into an oral contract, were disapproved in *Kendall* v. *Lillico*.

[2] The first Hire-Purchase Act, of 1938, only applied where the total purchase price did not exceed £50 and this was only increased to £300 in 1951 where the figure remained till 1964.

[3] [1967] 1 A.C. 361.

breach is not a rule of law but merely a rule of construction. Parties are free to make whatever provision they desire in their contracts, but it is a rule of construction that an exemption clause does not protect a party from liability for fundamental breach. It follows that if the contract by express provision does protect a party from such a result and the court thinks that the provision was intended to operate in the circumstances which have occurred, the provision must be given full effect.

In this state of things the Court of Appeal's decision in *Harbutt's Plasticine, Ltd.* v. *Wayne Tank & Pump Co.*.[1] merely served to confuse matters rather than to clarify them. Seizing on some dicta in the *Suisse Atlantique* case the court here laid it down that the doctrine of fundamental breach operates as a rule of construction only where the contract continues in existence after the breach. But where the contract comes to an end as a result of the breach the exemption clause can no longer be relied upon by the guilty party; it seems that in saying this the Court took the view that these consequences follow as a matter of law and not as a matter of construction. The Court went on to hold (and this seems wholly new law) that in some cases a contract is terminated automatically as a result of a fundamental breach and once again an exemption clause can no longer operate. All this seems as confusing as it is unsound. Why should the parties not make provision for what is to happen after a fundamental breach has occurred? To say that the contract is "at an end" is to use abstract language for a dubious purpose; when the question concerns the application of a provision of the contract to the events which have occurred, the whole question is whether the contract still applies, and to assert that it is "at an end" merely begs the question. It omits, moreover, to explain how and why the contract should be at an end if the parties have declared that it is not to be at an end. It is submitted that this decision is wrong; it is inconsistent with the whole tenor of the speeches in the *Suisse Atlantique* case although the Court purported to follow that decision.

At all events, it was clear that the law could not long be left in the state in which it had been left by the *Suisse Atlantique* decision. Indeed, several of the Law Lords in that case recognised the need for legislative reform, but the problem which they felt to be incapable of solution by the courts was that of drawing a line between consumer and business contracts. While it was generally agreed that some protection was required for consumers, it was also beginning to be more widely appreciated that a common solution for all types of contract was not necessarily acceptable. The first major legislative development was the Misrepresentation Act, 1967, although this was actually based on the Tenth Report of the Law Reform Committee which pre-dated the

---

[1] [1970] 1 Q.B. 447; criticised by Legh-Jones and Pickering in (1970) 86 L.Q.R. 513. See also *Kenyon, Son & Craven, Ltd.* v. *Baxter, Hoare & Co., Ltd.*, [1971] 1 W.L.R. 519.

Suisse Atlantique case. Further inquiries and statutes followed which are discussed in the following pages.

MISREPRESENTATION ACT, 1967, SECT. 3

We have already referred briefly to Sect. 3 of the Misrepresentation Act, 1967, and it is now necessary to consider its effect more fully.[1] The section is as follows:

3. If any agreement (whether made before or after the commencement of this Act) contains a provision which would exclude or restrict—
  (*a*) any liability to which a party to a contract may be subject by reason of any misrepresentation made by him before the contract was made; or
  (*b*) any remedy available to another party to the contract by reason of such a misrepresentation;
that provision shall be of no effect except to the extent (if any) that, in any proceedings arising out of the contract, the court or arbitrator may allow reliance on it as being fair and reasonable in the circumstances of the case.

This section is an attempt to deal with provisions which exclude or restrict liabilities or remedies which would otherwise arise from a misrepresentation. Its origin is to be found in the Tenth Report of the Law Reform Committee but it is completely different in character and scope from the clause which was recommended by the Law Reform Committee and which was part of the abortive 1965 Bill. This would have totally avoided all clauses excluding or restricting any liability or remedy arising from a fraudulent or negligent misrepresentation, but would not have affected innocent misrepresentations in this particular respect. When the 1966 Bill was introduced, clause 3 was still confined to fraudulent and negligent misrepresentations, but, instead of providing for a total ban on exclusion clauses, the Bill now provided that such clauses would be valid where the terms of a contract had been "arrived at in negotiations between the parties." In the House of Lords this provision was attacked as being unworkable,[2] and the clause was amended in two major respects. First, its scope was broadened to cover all misrepresentations; and, secondly, instead of simply avoiding an exclusion provision, the section now lays down that such a provision "shall be of no effect except to the extent (if any) that . . . , the court or arbitrator may allow reliance on it as being fair and reasonable in the circumstances of the case."

The scope of Sect. 3 centres round the words "a provision which would exclude or restrict any liability . . . or any remedy" which would otherwise arise from the misrepresentation. These words seem comprehensive enough, although they are not perhaps wholly appropriate to the case of a misrepresentee who simply sets up the misrepresentation

[1] The following account is an abbreviated version of the article by the present writer and G. H. Treitel in 30 *M.L.R.* 369, pp. 379–84.
[2] 274 H.L. 936–7.

as a defence to an action by the misrepresentor. However, it seems reasonable to treat this as, in a broad sense, a "remedy available" to the misrepresentee. Apart from this, it seems clear that Sect. 3 applies to any provision which would exclude or restrict, first, a claim for damages by the misrepresentee, either for fraud, or for negligence under Sect. 2 (1) and, secondly, the right to rescind the contract (or to get damages in lieu), and consequential claims for the recovery of money or property by the misrepresentee.

The width of the section is enormous. For example, it would apply to a "no-cancellation clause," i.e. one excluding the right to repudiate while preserving the misrepresentee's claim for damages, if any. But presumably in a straightforward commercial contract between parties at arm's length, the court would exercise its discretion, either under Sect. 3 itself so as to allow reliance on such a provision, or under Sect. 2 (2) so as to award damages in lieu of rescission. On the face of it, the section also appears to apply to clauses excluding liability for misdescriptions, however trivial. But normal commercial stipulations for a margin relating, for example, to the description of goods being sold would presumably not be within the section, either on the ground that there would in fact be no misrepresentation if the misdescription falls within the stipulated margin, or on the ground that such a provision does not exclude or restrict a liability or remedy, but merely prevents the liability or remedy arising in the first place.

This last point does, however, throw up another difficulty, for the distinction between a provision which excludes or restricts a liability or remedy which would otherwise arise, and a clause which prevents such a liability or remedy from arising at all, is indeed a fine one. What would a court make, for instance, of an agreed damages clause? On a literal construction of the section there can be little doubt that such a clause does fall within its scope, but such a clause differs from the typical exempting provision in that it is normally intended for the benefit of both parties, though in the actual result it can, of course, benefit only one party or the other. It has recently been held that an arrangement whereby a principal limits the authority of his agent to commit him by representations is not a clause which limits or excludes the liability of the seller.[1] Such a clause is not caught by Sect. 3, therefore. Another type of case where there may be difficulty in saying whether the provision restricts or excludes a liability or remedy which would otherwise arise may occur where the representor tries to evade the normal consequences of a misrepresentation by stipulating that the representation should not be relied on. For example, if a dealer sells a second-hand car with an inaccurate mileage reading, what is the effect of an express statement by the seller that the correctness of the reading is not vouched

---

[1] *Overbrooke Estate, Ltd.* v. *Glencombe Properties, Ltd.*, [1974] 1 W.L.R. 1335.

for? On one view its effect would be to prevent the mileage reading being treated as a misrepresentation at all; on another view the case would fall within Sect. 3. Doubtless in a case of this kind (though others can be envisaged), the court would uphold the provision in its discretion even if the section did apply to it, but it might be argued that the section has no application at all to this sort of case on the ground that the representor does not expect or intend that the representation will be acted on by the representee.

On the other hand the section does not apply to exclusion provisions of the kind in question in the *Hedley Byrne* case,[1] for even though the misrepresentee may subsequently enter into a contract on the strength of the misrepresentation in that sort of situation, the exclusion provision does not exclude or restrict any liability of "a party to a contract" by reason of "a misrepresentation made by him," nor does it exclude or restrict a remedy available to a party to the contract by reason of "such a misrepresentation." Nor would it apply to provisions excluding liability for negligent advice given during the performance of contractual duties arising, for example, from professional relationships, because (even if such advice could be equated with "misrepresentation") it would not be made *before* the contract, but during its existence.

If a provision of the agreement purports to exclude or limit the misrepresentor's liability in respect of such misrepresentations, the misrepresentee is presumably entitled to disregard the effect of the misrepresentation as a contractual term, and seek rescission or, if the circumstances warrant, damages under Sect. 2 (1). Thus, whatever the effect of Sect. 3 may be on the misrepresentation as a contractual term (and this is discussed below) it seems reasonably clear that Sect. 3 will not operate the less on the misrepresentation as a misrepresentation merely because it has also become a contractual term.

But the question may also arise whether Sect. 3 does in fact have any effect on a misrepresentation as a contractual term, if it subsequently becomes such a term. It seems probable that provisions dealing solely with liabilities and remedies arising from contractual terms are unaffected by the section because of the wording of paragraph (*a*) which refers to any liability to which a party may be subject "by reason of any misrepresentation made by him before the contract was made." On the other hand, read literally the section would invalidate (subject to the court's discretion) any provision which excludes or restricts liabilities or remedies and which deals *both* with misrepresentations and with contractual terms. The point is that the section does not invalidate a provision only *to the extent* that it excludes or restricts a liability or remedy arising from a misrepresentation; it invalidates the whole provision, though subject to the discretion of the court. In practice exclusion provisions of this nature are unlikely to be drafted in two

[1] [1964] A.C. 465.

separate clauses, one dealing with misrepresentations, and one dealing with contractual terms; and it may therefore be a moot question in some cases whether the exclusion provision is really one provision only (in which case it would seem wholly void, subject to the court's discretion) or whether it could be construed as two provisions, in which case it would remain valid in so far as it dealt with contractual terms. So far as contracts of sale of goods are concerned this point is largely academic, because the new statutory controls now extend to implied terms as well as misrepresentations.

The operation of the section is entrusted entirely to the discretion of the court. This discretion is an exceptionally wide one, for it enables the court not merely to uphold or reject the exclusion clause, but to uphold it "to the extent (if any) that the court finds fair and reasonable in the circumstances." On the face of it, this confers a quite remarkable power of remoulding the clause on the court with absolutely no guidance as to the factors to be considered by the court in exercising its discretion. It seems that the court could even rewrite an exclusion clause which precludes an award of damages by limiting the damages to a figure which the court thinks reasonable. It could rewrite a comprehensive exclusion clause by upholding it in so far as it precludes rescission, but condemning it in so far as it precludes an award of damages.[1] It could rewrite the clause so as to leave the misrepresentor protected in respect of some of the matters covered by the misrepresentation, while leaving him liable in respect of other matters. It could, in short, do more or less anything it felt like doing.

SUPPLY OF GOODS (IMPLIED TERMS) ACT, 1973

We have discussed in the preceding sections the extent to which the courts have been able to regulate the use of exemption clauses by strict construction of such clauses and by use of the principle of fundamental breach and other similar methods. It is, nevertheless, clear that the power of the courts to protect consumers and other buyers against oppressive exemption clauses was severely limited. Two inquiries were conducted into this question, the first by the Molony Committee on Consumer Protection[2] and the second by the Law Commissions.[3] Both inquiries found that freedom of contract was being abused by certain commercial concerns which consistently limited their liability in respect of goods sold. Frequently, consumers did not even appreciate the extent to which they were signing away or otherwise waiving their

---

[1] But the court may well be reluctant to take this course where the misrepresentation was wholly innocent, because this would leave the misrepresentee remediless, and in any event the additional discretion of the court under Sect. 2 (2) could be exercised so as to refuse rescission.

[2] Final Report, Cmnd. 1781, 1962.

[3] *Exemption Clauses, First Report*, paras. 17–19 and Part V.

normal contractual rights when they bought goods from such sellers. But even where the consumer was alive to the true situation he was usually powerless to negotiate or ask for special treatment. Organised consumer bodies have lately been able to bring pressure on manufacturers with encouraging results in some areas but the general position remained unsatisfactory.

Both the Molony Committee and the Law Commissions concluded that legislation was called for and this legislation has now appeared in the form of the Supply of Goods (Implied Terms) Act, 1973. Apart from restating, with substantial amendments, the whole of Sects. 12–15 of the Sale of Goods Act, the new Act contains a greatly expanded Sect. 55. Subsect. (1), with immaterial variations, corresponds to the original Sect. 55;[1] subsect. (2) replaces the old Sect. 14 (4).[2] The remainder of the section, which is entirely new, is as follows—

(3) In the case of a contract of sale of goods, any term of that or any other contract exempting from all or any of the provision of section 12 of this Act shall be void.

(4) In the case of a contract of sale of goods, any term of that or any other contract exempting from all or any of the provisions of section 13, 14 or 15 of this Act shall be void in the case of a consumer sale and shall, in any other case, not be enforceable to the extent that it is shown that it would not be fair or reasonable to allow reliance on the term.

(5) In determining for the purposes of subsection (4) above whether or not reliance on any such term would be fair or reasonable regard shall be had to all the circumstances of the case and in particular to the following matters—

(a) the strength of the bargaining positions of the seller and buyer relative to each other, taking into account, among other things, the availability of suitable alternative products and sources of supply;

(b) whether the buyer received an inducement to agree to the term or in accepting it had an opportunity of buying the goods or suitable alternatives without it from any source of supply;

(c) whether the buyer knew or ought reasonably to have known of the existence and extent of the term (having regard, among other things, to any custom of the trade and any previous course of dealing between the parties);

(d) where the term exempts from all or any of the provisions of section 13, 14 or 15 of this Act if some condition is not complied with, whether it was reasonable at the time of the contract to expect that compliance with that condition would be practicable;

(e) whether the goods were manufactured, processed, or adapted to the special order of the buyer.

(6) Subsection (5) above shall not prevent the court from holding, in accordance with any rule of law, that a term which purports to exclude or restrict any of the provisions of section 13, 14 or 15 of this Act is not a term of the contract.

(7) In this section "consumer sale" means a sale of goods (other than a sale by auction or by competitive tender) by a seller in the course of a business where the goods—

    (*a*) are of a type ordinarily bought for private use or consumption; and

    (*b*) are sold to a person who does not buy or hold himself out as buying them in the course of a business.

(8) The onus of proving that a sale falls to be treated for the purposes of this section as not being a consumer sale shall lie on the party so contending.

(9) Any reference in this section to a term exempting from all or any of the provisions of any section of this Act is a reference to a term which purports to exclude or restrict, or has the effect of excluding or restricting, the operation of all or any of the provisions of that section, or the exercise of a right conferred by any provision of that section, or any liability of the seller for breach of a condition or warranty implied by any provision of that section.

(10) It is hereby declared that any reference in this section to a term of a contract includes a reference to a term which although not contained in a contract is incorporated in the contract by another term of the contract.

(11) This section is subject to section 61 (6) of this Act.

It will be seen that under subsect. (3) there can now be no contracting out of Sect. 12 at all. This is, however, slightly misleading because Sect. 12 itself envisages a limited form of contracting out in that it now clearly recognises the possibility of a sale of a limited interest in goods. The Commissions did not think that there was any reason why a seller should not make it plain that he is only selling such title as he may have, or where he acts only as agent, such title as some third party may have. But the Commissions proposed that even in such a case the seller should be held liable if there should turn out to be some charge or encumbrance on the goods known to the seller but not known to the buyer or disclosed by the seller. Thus a seller who (for example) knows that the goods he sells are held under some hire-purchase agreement should not be allowed to conceal this fact and protect himself merely by purporting to sell only the hirer's interest in the goods. Sect. 55 (3) of the Act now gives effect to these recommendations.

The effect of the new Sect. 55 on contracting-out of Sects. 13–15 is, of course, much more dramatic and more radical. Under Sect. 55 (4) no exclusion of the seller's duties under Sects. 13–15 is permissible at all in a "consumer sale" and is only permissible subject to a test of reasonableness in other cases. In evaluating the significance of these provisions there are two obvious matters to be considered, first the meaning of a "consumer sale", and secondly the extent to which some limited forms of contracting-out may still be possible through the inherent operation of Sects. 13–15 themselves.

As to the first point, a "consumer sale" is defined by the new Sect. 55 (7) and the onus of showing that a sale is not a consumer sale is on

the seller (Subsect. (8)). The definition in Subsect. (7) has certain difficulties but some points are clear enough. First, a sale by auction or
competitive tender is not a consumer sale. Secondly, a sale by a seller
not selling in the course of business is not a consumer sale. And thirdly,
a sale of goods of a type not ordinarily bought for private use or consumption is not a consumer sale. The more difficult question concerns
goods which are of a type ordinarily bought for private use or consumption, but which are sold to a person who does not buy for private
use or consumption, or which are sold to a person who buys or holds himself out as buying them "in the course of business". The term "business"
is defined in Sect. 7 (1) of the new Act to include a profession and also
the activities of any government department, local authority or statutory
undertaker. The concept of a sale "in the course of business" is familiar
enough, but the concept of buying goods "in the course of business" is
more difficult. Clearly a sale is not a consumer sale where the buyer
buys for resale or where the goods are raw materials to be used by the
buyer in his own manufacturing process. What is less clear is whether
goods will be treated as bought "in the course of business" merely
because they are bought by a business for use (of some kind) *in* a
business. Or, to put the point differently, must it be shown that the
buyer *makes a business of buying* goods of the relevant type? To take
a simple hypothetical example, suppose a firm of solicitors buys
carpets for use in its offices, and there is nothing to distinguish the
carpets from ordinary domestic carpeting. It is clear that Sect. 55 (7) (*a*)
is satisfied. But what of para. (*b*)? Are the goods bought "in the course
of a business"? Although the point is not free from difficulty, it is
thought that the answer is No. The Act does not exclude a sale from the
category of a consumer sale merely because the goods are bought *by* a
business; they must be bought *in the course of a business*, or at least the
buyer must hold himself out as so buying. This would seem to imply,
either that the buyer buys for processing or resale, or at least that the
goods are to be put to some distinctive business use. If the goods are
to be used by the business in the same way that they would be used by
consumers it seems that the buyer is not buying "in the course of a
business".

As to the second point, it must be observed that both Sects. 14 (2)
and (3) will still enable the intention of the parties to operate so as to
modify the seller's duties despite Sect. 55. For example, if the seller
makes it clear that the buyer should not rely on any opinion the seller
offers as to the suitability of the goods for a particular purpose, it may
be held that the buyer has acted unreasonably in relying on the seller
under Sect. 14 (3). Similarly, under Sect. 14 (2) the seller may escape
liability for unmerchantable goods by pointing out defects in the goods
even without any attempt to incorporate an exemption clause. It is to
be expected that some sellers may attempt to take advantage of these

provisions by incorporating written clauses into their conditions of sale declaring (for example) that "all defects have been drawn to the attention of the buyer and the buyer acknowledges this fact", or that "the seller offers no opinion as to the suitability of the goods for any particular purpose and the buyer acknowledges that he does not rely on the seller's skill or judgment". It is likely that such clauses would be void as attempts to exclude the liability of the seller by agreement under Sect. 55. Under Sects. 14 (2) and (3) it is the *facts* which matter, and not the agreement. The question under these sections will be: Were the defects in fact drawn to the buyer's attention? Did the buyer in fact rely or reasonably rely on the seller's skill or judgment?

PART III

THE DUTIES OF THE BUYER

CHAPTER 15

THE DUTY TO PAY THE PRICE

PAYMENT OF THE PRICE

IT is the duty of the buyer to pay the price of the goods he has bought, and in the absence of a contrary agreement he is not entitled to claim possession of the goods unless he is ready and willing to pay the price in accordance with the contract. Whether it is necessary that the buyer should actually have tendered the price before he can insist on delivery is a doubtful point which will be discussed later.

If no time is fixed for payment, the price is due immediately on the conclusion of the contract, provided that the seller is ready and willing to deliver the goods. Unless otherwise agreed the seller is not bound to accept payment in anything but cash, and if he does accept payment by bill of exchange he is entitled to retain the goods until the bill is met. But if the seller accepts payment by a bill not maturing immediately he must be taken to have agreed to allow the buyer credit, and cannot claim to retain the goods.

Where the seller accepts payment by cheque or other negotiable instrument, it is normally deemed to be a conditional payment only and if it is not honoured the seller may sue either on the instrument, or he may sue for the price of the goods. It is theoretically possible for a cheque or other instrument to be accepted as absolute payment but an intention to accept in absolute payment must be strictly shown.[1] Similarly, agreement to furnish a letter of credit in payment for goods sold would not normally be treated as depriving the seller of his right to sue for the price if, in exceptional circumstances, the goods are delivered to the buyer but payment is not made under the credit.[2] Where payment is made by cheque and the cheque is later met the payment relates back to the time when it was handed over.[3] Consequently if the cheque reaches the seller on the date agreed he cannot

---

[1] *Maillard* v. *Argyle* (1843), 6 M. & G. 40.

[2] *W. J. Alan & Co., Ltd.* v. *El Nasr Export & Import Co.*, [1972] 2 Q.B. 179; *Saffron* v. *Société Minière Cafrika* (1958), 100 C.L.R. 231; see *post*, pp. 237–8.

[3] *Marreco* v. *Richardson*, [1908] 2 K.B. 584. But as between a trustee in bankruptcy and the payee the payment is only deemed to be made when the cheque is met: *In re Hone A Bankrupt, Ex parte The Trustee* v. *Kensington Borough Council*, [1951] Ch. 85. Cf. *Bolt & Nut Co. (Tipton), Ltd.* v. *Rowlands, Nicholls & Co., Ltd.* [1964] 2 Q.B. 10.

complain that there has been delay in payment, provided that it is met in due course. If the seller agrees that the price shall only be due on request he is bound to afford a reasonable time to the buyer for payment after making his request,[1] and if he writes to the buyer asking him for his cheque the mere posting is a sufficient payment, even if the cheque is stolen *en route* and cashed by the thief.[2]

Sect. 10 of the Act says—

(1) Unless a different intention appears from the terms of the contract, stipulations as to time of payment are not deemed to be of the essence of a contract of sale. . . .

(2) In a contract of sale "month" means prima facie calendar month.

It has been said that this section is "seriously at odds" with Sects. 27 and 28,[3] but it is submitted that this is not in fact the case. Although it is obviously the duty of the buyer to pay the price agreed at the appointed time, the effect of Sect. 10 is to create a presumption that this duty is only a warranty and not a condition. In other words a buyer who fails to pay the price on the day fixed is guilty of a breach of warranty for which the seller can recover damages if he has in fact suffered any, but he is not entitled to treat the contract as repudiated and resell the goods elsewhere.[4] Although this rule has been criticised on the ground that it extends compulsive credit to the buyer,[5] there seems no reason why the seller should be entitled to repudiate the contract merely because the buyer is late in paying the price, perhaps by only a day or two. Indeed, even repeated failure by the buyer to pay on time (e.g. in an instalment contract) may not justify repudiation by the seller, at least where there is no serious fear that the buyer will not pay at all.[6] It can make little difference to the seller in the usual way whether he is paid one day earlier or later, and if it does make a difference he should stipulate for a right of immediate resale on default in payment by the buyer. Moreover, damages may be obtained for the late payment where additional costs have been imposed on the seller,[6] and anyhow interest may be awarded to the seller by a court where he has been kept out of his money.[7]

In any event the compulsive credit which the seller has to extend to the buyer is severely limited, for Sect. 48 (3) provides that—

Where the goods are of a perishable nature, or where the unpaid seller gives notice to the buyer of his intention to re-sell, and the buyer does

[1] *Brighty* v. *Norton* (1862), 3 B. & S. 305.

[2] *Norman* v. *Ricketts* (1886), 3 T.L.R. 182; cf. *Comber* v. *Leyland*, [1898] A.C. 524.

[3] Stoljar, "Untimely Performance in the Law of Contract," 71 *L.Q.R.*, 527, 539.

[4] *Payzu, Ltd.* v. *Saunders*, [1919] 2 K.B. 581. Where the price is to be paid by means of a banker's confirmed credit, however, it seems that failure to open the credit at the right time justifies repudiation (see Chapter 22).

[5] Stoljar, loc. cit., p. 540.

[6] *Decro-Wall International, S.A.* v. *Practitioners in Marketing, Ltd.*, [1971] 1 W.L.R. 361.

[7] Under Sect. 3 of the Law Reform (Miscellaneous Provisions) Act, 1934.

not within a reasonable time pay or tender the price, the unpaid seller may re-sell the goods and recover from the original buyer damages for any loss occasioned by his breach of contract.

The indirect result of this subsection is to create an exception to Sect. 10 in the case of perishable goods, for in such a case the seller may resell the goods without notice to the buyer as soon as there is default in payment. As regards non-perishable goods the period of compulsive credit can be brought to an end by the seller giving notice to the buyer of his intention to resell. Although failure to pay the price at the appointed time is only a breach of warranty, if the delay is of inordinate length it may be possible to infer an intention to abandon the contract, and the seller may thus be justified in reselling even without notice. Thus in *Pearl Mill Co., Ltd.* v. *Ivy Tannery Co., Ltd.*,[1] the defendant sold goods to the plaintiffs, "delivery as required," in September 1913. Part of the goods were supplied between then and September 1914. From then until 1917 the buyers made no requests for further deliveries, although the sellers several times inquired when they would require the remainder of the goods. In July 1917 the buyers claimed delivery of the remainder of the goods, and on the sellers refusing to deliver them, they brought an action for breach of contract. It was held by a Divisional Court that there was evidence of an intention on the part of the buyers to abandon the contract, and the sellers were under no obligation to give notice to the buyers that they regarded the contract as terminated.

[1] [1919] 1 K.B. 78.

CHAPTER 16

THE DUTY TO TAKE DELIVERY

WE have seen that the general rule is that it is for the buyer to take delivery of the goods from the seller's place of business, and not for the seller to send the goods to the buyer. We have also seen that the time of delivery of the goods by the seller, or the time at which he is to have the goods ready for collection is prima facie of the essence, but that the time for payment is prima facie not of the essence. The question now has to be answered whether the buyer's duty to take delivery at a particular time is of the essence.

The general rule seems to be that this is no more of the essence than the time of payment,[1] and consequently the buyer's failure to take delivery of the goods at the time agreed does not justify the seller in forthwith disposing of them to someone else. But as we have seen, if the delay is of such an inordinate length as to justify the seller in assuming that the buyer has abandoned the contract, he may treat the delay as a repudiation.

Moreover if the contract is for the sale of goods of a perishable nature[2] the buyer's duty to take delivery at the right time is of the essence, and default by the buyer justifies the seller in reselling immediately.[3] In this respect the position is also the same in regard to payment for as we have seen Sect. 48 (3) enables the seller to resell perishable goods without notice to the buyer if the price is not paid when due.

It also seems that in a spot contract, i.e. a contract for almost immediate delivery and payment, there will be a breach of condition if the buyer fails to take delivery at the time agreed.[4] It may well be that in such a case there will be a contrary intention which makes the time of payment also of the essence. It is important that the rules as to the time of payment and the time for taking delivery should be the same, because otherwise difficulties would arise if the seller refused to allow the buyer to take delivery on the ground of non-payment. If the seller could transform a breach of the warranty as to payment into a breach of condition as to taking delivery by the simple expedient of exercising his lien, this would in effect turn every agreement

---

[1] *Woolfe* v. *Horn* (1877), 2 Q.B.D. 355; *Saint* v. *Pilley* (1875), L.R. 10 Ex. 137; *Kidston* v. *Monceau Iron Works Co., Ltd.* (1902), 7 Com. Cas. 82.

[2] This rule probably also applies to a sale of livestock: *Harrington* v. *Browne* (1917), 23 C.L.R. 297.

[3] *Sharp* v. *Christmas* (1892), 8 T.L.R. 687.

[4] *Thames Sack & Bag Co., Ltd.* v. *Knowles* (1918), 88 L.J.K.B. 585.

for time of payment into a condition. If the time of payment is not of the essence, therefore, it is submitted that it cannot be held that the time for taking delivery is of the essence. But there is nothing to prevent an express agreement that the time for taking delivery shall not be of the essence, but that the time for payment shall be.

It must be borne in mind that even where the time of delivery is not of the essence Sect. 20 casts on the buyer, where there is delay in taking delivery, the risk of accidental destruction of, or damage to, the goods which might not have occurred but for the delay.

Where a buyer contracts to take delivery of goods as speedily as possible although no time limit is actually imposed, he is under an obligation to remove the goods within a reasonable time.[1] And in such circumstances the measure of damages for breach may, in an appropriate case, be the benefit to the buyer rather than the loss to the seller.[2] If the contract provides for the delivery of the goods in instalments, and the buyer wrongfully refuses to accept one or more instalments, the question whether the seller may treat the whole contract as repudiated is dealt with by Sect. 31 (2). As will be seen later,[3] this merely provides that the answer to this question depends on the terms of the contract and all the circumstances of the case. In practice the issue usually involves breach by the seller rather than the buyer, and it has been held that the question to be considered is the gravity of the breach in relation to the whole contract, and the probability of its recurrence.[4]

Where the contract does not provide for delivery by instalments there is nothing in the Act corresponding to Sect. 30 (1) entitling the seller to repudiate the contract if the buyer refuses to accept some part of the goods only. Whether such refusal amounts to repudiation, therefore, depends on general principles of contract law, i.e. on whether the breach goes to the root of the contract. Where a buyer refused to take 728 sheep out of a total contract quantity of over 6,000, and he was entitled to refuse 448 sheep, it was held that the seller could not repudiate the whole contract.[5]

It should be noted that in some contracts, especially f.o.b. contracts, the buyer's duty to take delivery often involves many incidental obligations, e.g. the duty to nominate a ship for the transport of the goods, etc. Breach of these duties usually discharges the seller as a necessary consequence.[6]

---

[1] *Penarth Dock Engineering Co., Ltd.* v. *Pounds*, [1963] 1 Lloyd's Rep. 359.
[2] Ibid.   [3] See *post*, p. 284.
[4] *Maple Flock Co., Ltd.* v. *Universal Furniture Products* (*Wembley*), *Ltd.*, [1934] 1 K.B. 148, *post*, p. 286.
[5] *Francis* v. *Lyon* (1907), 4 C.L.R. 1023.
[6] As to f.o.b. contracts, see *post*, p. 220.

PART IV

THE EFFECTS OF THE CONTRACT

CHAPTER 17

THE TRANSFER OF PROPERTY

THE MEANING OF "PROPERTY"

PART II of the Act is divided into two sections, headed "Transfer of Property as Between Seller and Buyer," and "Transfer of Title." It must be said at once that there is something very curious about this terminology. The term "property" defined by Sect. 62 as "the general property in goods," is commonly used by lawyers to signify title or ownership, and in every day usage this terminology is also applied to the sale of goods. Yet the Act talks of a transfer of property as between seller and buyer, and contrasts this with the transfer of title. It is trite learning, however, that the distinguishing feature of property rights is that they bind not merely the immediate parties to the transaction, but also all third parties. How, then, can there be such a legal phenomenon as a transfer of property *as between seller and buyer*?[1] Either there is a mere transfer of rights and duties from seller to buyer, or there is a transfer of property which affects the whole world. Nor is it possible to adopt the solution of saying that "property" is used in its medieval sense of "right to possession," when at least it would make sense to talk of a transfer as between seller and buyer. The Act itself precludes the adoption of this view because it lays down the clear rule that the buyer's right to possession depends either on payment of the price or the granting of credit, and not on the passing of the property. In other words the mere fact that the property in the goods has passed to the buyer does not confer on him a title good against third parties, nor does it confer on him the right to possession as against the seller. What then is this peculiar legal conception which the Act calls "the property in the goods"? The answer can only be given by considering the consequences which flow from the mere passing of property, and contrasting these with the consequences which follow when the buyer has acquired a full title binding upon third parties.

In the first place, then, what is the position of the buyer if he wishes to obtain possession from the seller? The answer which has already been intimated, is that he can only do so if he pays the price, or if

---

[1] See Lawson in 65 *L.Q.R.* 362, especially at pp. 359–60. Cf. for a different view, Battersby & Preston (1972) 35 *M.L.R.* 268.

the seller sees fit to grant him credit. Nor can the buyer avoid this consequence by framing his action in tort and suing for conversion or detinue, for these actions will only lie at the hands of someone with an immediate right to possession, and this the buyer has not got until he tenders the price. For the same reason the buyer cannot sue a third party who interferes with the goods while still in the seller's hands, unless he has paid or tendered the price, or the seller has granted him credit.[1] Again, if the buyer resells the goods the sub-buyer can only obtain possession on the same terms as the original buyer, that is to say by payment of the price, unless the original seller has assented to the second sale.[2] The same applies if the buyer pledges the goods instead of selling them. In all these cases the buyer's so-called property avails him nothing, for the position would be precisely the same even if no property had passed.

The same is true if the buyer goes bankrupt before payment of the price. The seller cannot be compelled to deliver up the goods to the trustee in bankruptcy, and relegated to his right to prove in the bankruptcy for the price, even though the property in the goods has passed to the buyer. Indeed, quite the contrary, the law goes out of its way to protect the seller from the bankruptcy of the buyer by conferring on him the right of stoppage *in transitu* should the buyer go bankrupt after the seller has dispatched the goods to him, but before the buyer has received them.

Suppose, next, that the buyer has actually obtained the possession of the goods. Once again the passing of the property has little practical effect because Sect. 25 (2) of the Act enables the buyer in possession to pass a good title to a third party, binding on the first seller, whether or not the property had already passed to the original buyer. Moreover it is arguable that Sect. 25 (2) has the strange result that the buyer, even if in possession, and even if he has the property, cannot pass a good title to a mala fide transferee.[3] No doubt it is true that if the goods are delivered to the buyer with a stipulation that the property is only to pass on payment the seller may be able to recover the goods in the event of the buyer's bankruptcy. But even here the seller may be defeated by the reputed ownership clause of the Bankruptcy Act, 1914.

What then is the position if the seller, being still in possession of the goods, resells them to a third party? Yet again the answer is that the transfer of property has little effect, for Sect. 25 (1) enables the seller in possession to pass a good title to a bona fide transferee, whether or not the transfer is wrongful as against the first buyer. And since the

[1] *Lord* v. *Price* (1874), L.R. 9 Ex. 54. But in some circumstances an action in negligence may lie: *Lee Cooper, Ltd.* v. *C. H. Jeakins & Sons, Ltd.*, [1967] 2 Q.B. 1; cf. *Margarine Union G.m.b.H.* v. *Cambay Prince S.S. Co.*, [1969] 1 Q.B. 219.

[2] Sect. 47. But if the buyer has passed the documents of title to the third party the seller's rights are defeated.

[3] But as to this see pp. 205–6, *post*.

Privy Council's decision in *Pacific Motor Auctions Pty., Ltd.* v. *Motor Credits (Hire Finance), Ltd.*,[1] it is immaterial in what capacity the seller retains possession. Of course if the goods are actually delivered to the buyer and then returned to the seller to hold as bailee he will not be able to pass a good title to a third party, but once again the same result would follow if property passed on delivery instead of by mere agreement.

At first sight the bankruptcy of the seller might seem to have substantial results when connected with the passing of property, for it might be thought that the buyer's rights would be unaffected because of his property. There are certainly cases where this is so but their frequency is greatly reduced by the "reputed ownership" clause of the Bankruptcy Act, 1914,[2] which enacts that all goods "in the possession order or disposition of the bankrupt in his trade or business by the consent or permission of the true owner under such circumstances that he is the reputed owner thereof" vest in the trustee in bankruptcy for the benefit of all the creditors. In other words the buyer's property will once again be defeated if the seller has possession of the goods in his trade or business. This itself indicates that where the seller is in possession but not in his trade or business, the buyer's property will at last come into its own and protect him from the claims of the seller's trustee in bankruptcy. More important in modern times is the fact that the reputed ownership clause does not apply to companies and therefore the buyer's property will generally protect him should a seller company go into liquidation while the goods are still in its hands.[3]

Finally reference must be made to two important results which generally follow from the passing of property. The first of these is that the risk in the goods prima facie passes with the property. The second[4] consequence is that generally speaking the seller is not entitled to sue for the price of the goods unless the property has passed. If the buyer repudiates the contract before this happens the seller's remedy is prima facie an action for damages for non-acceptance. Yet even here one cannot say that these consequences follow naturally or logically from the passing of the property. Roman law had much the same rules as English law so far as risk is concerned, yet it refused to recognise the conveyancing effect of a contract of sale. Nor is there any necessary or logical connection between the right to sue for the price and the

---

[1] [1965] A.C., *post*, p. 203.   [2] Sect. 38 (*c*).

[3] Even here the buyer's property may have to be registered under Sect. 95 of the Companies Act, 1948, as "a charge created or evidenced by an instrument which, if executed by an individual, would require registration as a bill of sale." Cf. *Stoneleigh Finance, Ltd.* v. *Phillips*, [1965] 2 Q.B. 537.

[4] Formerly a third consequence was that, when the property in specific goods passed to the buyer, he could no longer reject them for breach of condition. The law on this point was altered by the Misrepresentation Act, 1967, Sect. 4, see *post*, p. 290.

passing of property. Indeed, it will be suggested later[1] that a number of unfortunate consequences follow from the present rules on this subject.

To sum up, it may be said that the most important practical consequences which flow from the mere passing of the property may be reduced to three—[2]

1. If the seller is a company, the buyer will generally have a good title against the liquidator in the event of the company being wound up while the goods are still in its possession.

2. The risk passes prima facie when the property passes.

3. Generally speaking the seller can only sue for the price if the property has passed.

It will be observed that only the first of these consequences affects third parties, and that although, therefore, the passing of the property may have important results as between buyer and seller, its effect on third parties is minimal.[3]

It would not be an unfair or inaccurate summary of the position to to say that the Act, having once adopted the rule that property may pass by the mere contract, then has to make the most elaborate provisions which substantially reverse this rule in practical result though not in name. One cannot but reflect how much simpler the position would have been had the common law and the Sale of Goods Act adopted the rule of Roman law that the property in the goods passes on and not before delivery. Had this been done, all the special rights of the unpaid seller might have been unnecessary,[4] as also would much of Sect. 25. Then also the term "property" would have retained its usual meaning instead of being debased to signify scarcely anything more than the personal rights of the buyer against the seller which arise from the mere contract. Alternatively, the law might well have abandoned the "conceptual" approach altogether and adopted the "specific issue" approach, i.e. have dealt with each specific question, such as the buyer's ability to pass title, passing of risk, liability for the price, etc., without reference to the passing of property. This is the approach of the Uniform Commercial Code which is now in force throughout nearly all of the United States.

Many of the above points will have to be considered at greater length in more appropriate places, but it was thought necessary to refer to them here in order that the significance of the passing of the property might be kept in its true perspective. We can now pass on

---

[1] *Post*, p. 273.

[2] Another important result is that in war time the ownership of a cargo for prize purposes depends upon the property. But this is obviously of limited application.

[3] Lawson, 65 *L.Q.R.* 352 at p. 359, goes so far as to say: "If we look at the other effects [than passing of risk] of the transfer of property as between seller and buyer in the common law systems, we shall see that they are for the most part, if not entirely, illusory." As we have seen this is a slight exaggeration.

[4] I.e. the whole of Part IV of the Act.

to examine the circumstances in which this peculiar concept, the property, passes under the contract.

THE PASSING OF PROPERTY: I. SPECIFIC GOODS

The exact moment at which the property passes depends upon whether the goods are specific or unascertained, and this cleavage is so fundamental that the subject will be dealt with under two separate sections.

Sect. 17 of the Act is as follows—

(1) Where there is a contract for the sale of specific or ascertained goods the property in them is transferred to the buyer at such time as the parties to the contract intend it to be transferred.

(2) For the purpose of ascertaining the intention of the parties regard shall be had to the terms of the contract, the conduct of the parties, and the circumstances of the case.

Although this section only applies to specific or ascertained goods, it is well settled that, as a matter of general principle, the same holds true for unascertained goods.[1]

Sect. 18 (which applies to both specific and unascertained goods) goes on to state—

Unless a different intention appears, the following are rules for ascertaining the intention of the parties as to the time at which the property in the goods is to pass to the buyer.

And the section then sets out five Rules for ascertaining the intention of the parties.

In practice these Rules are of the greatest importance, for the parties do not usually have any clear intention, still less express any, as to the passing of the property.[2] Moreover, it appears that even if the parties do express such an intention it will have no effect if the property has already passed in accordance with the rules laid down in Sect. 18. In *Dennant* v. *Skinner and Collom*,[3] the plaintiff sold a car to X by auction. X, who was a swindler, gave a false name and address, and asked to be allowed to take the car away in return for his cheque. The plaintiff allowed X to do this on obtaining his signature to a document which stated that the title to the vehicle would not pass until the cheque was met. X sold the car which was ultimately resold to the defendant. Hallett, J., held that the intention of the parties as expressed in this document was too late to prevent the property from

[1] *Ginzberg* v. *Barrow Haematite Steel Co.*, [1966] 1 Lloyd's Rep. 343. But this is subject to the qualification laid down in Sect. 16, see *post*, p. 155.

[2] *Smyth & Co., Ltd.* v. *Bailey Son & Co., Ltd.*, [1940] 3 All E.R. 60, at p. 67, *per* Lord Wright.

[3] [1948] 2 K.B. 164. It is odd that the defendant did not rely on Sect. 25 (2) which would appear to have been decisive of this part of the case.

passing since it had already done so on the fall of the hammer,[1] in accordance with Rule 1 of Sect. 18.

RULE 1

This Rule is as follows—

> Where there is an unconditional contract for the sale of specific goods, in a deliverable state, the property in the goods passes to the buyer when the contract is made, and it is immaterial whether the time of payment or the time of delivery, or both, be postponed.

This Rule gives rise to a number of perplexing questions.

"Unconditional Contract"

In the first place, what is an unconditional contract within the meaning of this Rule? This may mean either (a) a contract not subject to a condition precedent or subsequent, or (b) a contract not containing any conditions in the sense of essential stipulations, the breach of which gives the buyer the right to treat the contract as repudiated. At first sight it seems too clear for argument that the former of these interpretations is the correct one. Throughout the Act the term "conditional contract" is used in this sense. Thus Sect. 1 (2) says: "A contract of sale may be absolute or conditional," which clearly means subject to a condition precedent, for otherwise there would be no point in the contrast. Again, Rules 2, 3 and 4 of Sect. 18 all deal with contracts subject to a condition precedent, so that the natural inference is that Rule 1, by contrast, deals with contracts not subject to such conditions. Furthermore, and this is surely conclusive, it is difficult to see how there can be any such thing as an unconditional contract if condition means essential stipulation. Every contract must contain at least one essential stipulation, and most contracts contain a great many more. In every contract of sale there must be one fundamental condition or obligation, namely that of having goods ready for delivery to the buyer, and if this makes all contracts of sale conditional within Rule 1 it is deprived of all effect.

Yet despite these arguments the question has not been free from difficulty though it is thought that these difficulties have now been set at rest in England at least. The trouble arose largely from Sect. 11 (1) (c) of the Act which, in its original form, deprived the buyer of the right to reject goods for breach of condition "where the contract is for specific goods, the property in which has passed to the buyer." If the term "unconditional contract" in Rule 1 was given its natural meaning the result appeared to be that in the vast majority of sales of specific

---

[1] It may be that this case turned on the fact that the sale was by auction. In a sale in a shop it seems that no contract is made (and hence no property passes) until the parties have agreed on the mode of payment (see *Ingram* v. *Little*, [1961] 1 Q.B. 31, at p. 49), and in a supermarket no contract is made until the price is actually paid *Lacis* v. *Cashmarts*, [1969] 2 Q.B. 400, at p. 407).

goods there was no real right to reject for breach of condition at all. The property passed when the contract was made and at that very same time the right to reject was lost under Sect. 11 (1) (c). This was such a startling result that the judges, consciously or unconsciously, strove to avoid it by giving a forced interpretation to the words "unconditional contract" in Rule 1. Thus in *Varley* v. *Whipp*[1] to which reference has already been made, it was held that the sale of a reaping machine was not an unconditional sale despite the fact that it was clearly not subject to any conditions precedent, but no reasons were given for this part of the decision. Similarly in *Ollett* v. *Jordan*,[2] a case dealing with the meaning of "unconditionally appropriated" within Rule 5, it was held that the property in fish did not pass to the buyer owing to the fact that there was a breach of the implied condition that the fish was fit for human consumption, although there was no condition precedent. Finally in *Leaf* v. *International Galleries*,[3] and again in *Long* v. *Lloyd*,[4] there were dicta which supported the conclusion reached in *Varley* v. *Whipp*.[5] Fortunately these difficulties now seem to be a matter of past history. The Misrepresentation Act, 1967, Sect. 4, has repealed the words "where the contract is for specific goods the property in which has passed to the buyer." As a result, there will be no need for judges to give an unnatural construction to the words "unconditional contract" in Sect. 18, Rule 1, in order to avoid depriving a buyer of his right to reject goods.

Specific goods

The next question which arises under Rule 1 is as to the meaning of "specific goods." It has already been observed that this term does not necessarily mean the same thing wherever it appears in the Act, despite the single definition by Sect. 62 of specific goods as goods "identified and agreed upon at the time a contract of sale is made." At any rate, so far as the passing of property is concerned it seems settled that future goods can never be specific, although they may possibly be sufficiently specific to come within the doctrine of frustration. The meaning of "identified" still remains to be examined. In *Kursell* v. *Timber Operators & Contractors, Ltd.*,[6] the plaintiff sold to the defendants all the trees in a Latvian forest which conformed to certain measurements on a particular date, the buyers to have fifteen years in which to cut and remove the timber. Almost immediately afterwards the Latvian Assembly passed a law confiscating the forest. The Court of Appeal held that the property in the trees had not passed to the defendants as the goods were not sufficiently identified, since not all the trees were to pass but only those conforming to the stipu-

---

[1] [1900] 1 Q.B. 513.   [2] [1918] 2 K.B. 41.   [3] [1950] 2 K.B. 86.
[4] [1958] 1 W.L.R. 753.   [5] [1900] 1 Q.B. 513.
[6] [1927] 1 K.B. 298. Cf. *Lord Eldon* v. *Hedley Bros.*, [1935] 2 K.B. 1—sale of haystacks held to be of specific goods though buyer not obliged to take mouldy or unmerchantable hay.

lated measurements. An Australian decision provides an interesting contrast to this case. In *Joseph Reid Pty., Ltd.* v. *Schultz*[1] a sale of *all* the millable or marketable hardwood timber on a certain site was held to be a sale of specific goods.

Deliverable state

The third question arising out of Sect. 18, Rule 1, is the meaning of "deliverable state." Under Sect. 62 (4)—

> Goods are in a "deliverable state" within the meaning of this Act when they are in such a state that the buyer would under the contract be bound to take delivery of them.

It is to be noted that Sect. 62 (4) does not purport to give a comprehensive definition of "deliverable state." In particular it does not say that, if the buyer would *not* be bound to take delivery of the goods, then the goods are *not* in a deliverable state. The buyer is not bound to take delivery of defective goods, but it does not follow that *all* defective goods are not in a deliverable state within the meaning of this provision. If this were so, property would never pass in defective goods[2] but it seems to be generally accepted that defects do not prevent property passing. (If the buyer rejects the goods property revests in the seller.) Sect. 62 (4) was probably intended to cover the case where the goods could not be said to be in a deliverable state physically, yet the buyer had agreed to take delivery as they stood. This means that the words "deliverable state" cannot be construed by reference to the definition of delivery in Sect. 62 as "a voluntary transfer of possession." The possession of goods can probably always be transferred in law, if the parties intend to transfer it, no matter what the physical condition of the goods may be. If this was what "deliverable state" meant, therefore, goods would probably always be in a deliverable state.

The authorities on this point are not of great assistance. In *Underwood Ltd.* v. *Burgh Castle Brick & Cement Syndicate*[3] the plaintiffs sold a condensing engine to the defendants f.o.b. The engine weighed over 30 tons and was cemented to the floor. The engine had to be dismantled after being detached from the floor, a task which of course fell on the sellers under the f.o.b. contract, and which was expected to take about two weeks and to cost about £100. It was held that the engine was not in a deliverable state, and that the property had not passed when the contract was made. *Philip Head & Sons Ltd.* v. *Showfronts, Ltd.*[4] was a case under Sect. 18, Rule 5 (1), which also contains the phrase "in a deliverable state." Here the plaintiffs sold carpeting to the defendants which they were required to lay. The carpet was delivered to the

---

[1] (1949), S.R. (N.S.W.) 231.

[2] In the first edition I argued that this was indeed so. But this argument was largely a response to the difficulties created by Sect. 11 (1) (c) of the Act which have now been removed by Sect. 4 of the Misrepresentation Act, 1967, see *post*, p. 290.

[3] [1922] 1 K.B. 343.   [4] [1970] 1 Lloyd's Rep. 140.

defendants' premises but was stolen before it could be laid. It was held that the carpet was not in a deliverable state, apparently because it was a heavy bundle and difficult to move. But importance was attached to the fact that the carpet had to be laid. This seems a better ground for holding that the property had not passed.

Factors indicating a contrary intention

There is no doubt that the rule that property passes when the contract is made does not fit easily into the pattern of consumer sale.[1] It is therefore not surprising to see the suggestion being made that in modern times very little is needed to rebut the inference that property passes on the making of the contract.[2] It seems that in an ordinary sale in a shop property does not pass at least until the parties have agreed on the mode of payment,[3] and on a sale in a supermarket property does not pass until the price is paid.[4]

Despite the fact that Rule 1 states that it is immaterial for purposes of passing of property whether the time of payment, or the time of delivery, or both, be postponed, it is not possible to ignore such postponement completely. For, if payment or delivery or both be postponed, this may be some indication of a contrary intention which excludes the operation of Rule 1 altogether. Yet in a recent Irish case[5] where the plaintiff had agreed to trade-in his old car with the defendants in part-exchange for a new one, and was allowed to retain and use the old one pending delivery of the new one, it was held that property and risk had both passed to the defendants. The decision seems a border-line one, and it is thought that on such facts a court would be fully justified in finding a contrary intention which would negative an intention to pass property before delivery.[6] It certainly seems quite wrong that the risk should be held to be on the buyer while the seller still has the use of the car.

Another factor which may point to a contrary intention is any specific agreement on the transfer of risk. As will be seen the risk in the goods prima facie passes with the property. If the risk has passed, therefore, this may be some indication that the property has also passed.[7] Conversely where the risk is still on the seller this may be evidence

---

[1] See *post*, p. 168.

[2] *R. V. Ward, Ltd.*, v. *Bignall*, [1967] 1 Q.B. 534, at p. 545, *per* Diplock, L.J.

[3] *Ingram* v. *Little*, [1961] 1 Q.B. 31, at p. 49.

[4] *Lacis* v. *Cashmarts*, [1969] 2 W.L.R. 329, at pp. 333-4; cf. *Watts* v. *Seymour*, [1967] 2 Q.B. 647.

[5] *Clarke* v. *Michael Reilly & Sons* (1962), 96 I.L.T.R. 96.

[6] The decision seems to have been influenced by an admission by the defendants that they would have regarded it as a breach of contract had the plaintiff sold his old car to a third party. This may well have been correct but it does not follow that property had passed.

[7] *The Parchim*, [1918] A.C. 157, 168.

that the property has not passed.[1] On the other hand in *Re Anchor Line, Ltd.*,[2] the Court of Appeal inferred that the property in goods had not passed because there was a specific clause in the contract placing the risk upon the buyer, and if the property had passed such a clause would not have been necessary. One can only say, therefore, that the proper inference to be drawn from an agreement placing the risk on the buyer must depend on all the circumstances of the case.[3]

An obligation to insure placed upon one party by the contract is also an indication that he bears the risk,[4] and it has been said that this is an indication that he also has the property. But again it is possible to draw a contrary inference from this fact, for why should a party who has not got the property in the goods concern himself whether they are insured or not? Once again, therefore, the proper inference to be drawn must depend on all the circumstances of the case.

In trying to determine what is the correct inference to draw from a contractual provision about the transfer of risk, or the obligation to insure, the following appear to be relevant factors to bear in mind. Firstly, it seems that, where the seller simply *advises* the buyer to insure, this is some indication that risk and property have passed to the buyer.[5] Such advice does not suggest that the seller retains any property in the goods, as might be argued if he actually stipulated for insurance. Secondly, there may be cases in which a seller may retain some interest in the goods even where the property has passed, e.g. he may still have a lien or some sort of charge on the goods.[6] In such circumstances the seller may very well wish to require the buyer to insure the goods in order to protect his own interest; and this would be no indication that property and risk had not passed. Conversely, where the contract requires the buyer to insure the goods and the seller has on the face of it no interest in the goods once the property and risk have passed from him, the correct inference may well be that property and risk have not passed.

Another kind of case in which the presumption contained in Rule 1 would normally be rebutted is a contract for the sale of goods and land together. For example, where a person contracts to sell a house, together with some furnishings, the presumption that property passes on the

---

[1] *Carlos Federspiel & Co., S.A.* v. *Charles Twigg & Co., Ltd.*, [1957] 1 Lloyd's Rep. 240, at 255; *President of India* v. *Metcalfe Shipping Co.*, [1969] 2 W.L.R. 125.
[2] [1937] Ch. 1.
[3] For a review of some earlier conflicting cases on the inference to be drawn from such a stipulation, see *McPherson, Thorn, Kettle & Co.* v. *Dench Bros.*, [1921] V.L.R. 437.
[4] *Allison* v. *Bristol Marine Ins. Co., Ltd.* (1876), 1 App. Cas. 209, 229 *per* Blackburn, J.
[5] See, e.g. *Donaghy's Rope and Twine Co. Ltd.* v. *Wright, Stephenson & Co.* (1906), 25 N.Z.L.R. 641.
[6] As, e.g., in a hire-purchase contract. In the case of motor vehicles, such contracts always require the hirer to insure but this is certainly no indication that the risk has not passed to the hirer.

making of the contract would be rebutted. The normal inference in such a case would be that the property is only to pass on conveyance.[1] Indeed, where (contrary to the normal English practice) the vendor is not fully paid on conveyance and the price is to be paid by instalments, the property may not even pass on delivery of possession.[2]

Where goods are to be supplied *and installed or fitted* by the seller in a building or construction so that the goods will become fixtures in the technical sense, the property does not normally pass until the work of installation has been completed.[3] This is normally explained by saying that the contract is for work and materials in such a case, rather than a sale of goods. Hence if the contract is clearly intended to be for the sale of goods to be afterwards installed,[4] even by the seller, Rule 1 will ordinarily apply. It seems best, however, to explain these differences as resting on the intention of the parties and the nature of the transaction rather than on its technical classification. Whether it is a contract for the sale of goods or for work and materials is itself immaterial.[5]

RULES 2 AND 3

In contrast to Rule 1 which deals with the unconditional sale of specific goods, Rules 2, 3 and 4 deal with the conditional sale of specific goods. But unlike Rule 1 which deals with *all* unconditional contracts, Rules 2 and 3 deal only with certain types of conditional contract. Rules 2 and 3 are as follows—

> Rule 2. Where there is a contract for the sale of specific goods and the seller is bound to do something to the goods, for the purpose of putting them into a deliverable state, the property does not pass until such thing be done, and the buyer has notice thereof.
>
> Rule 3. Where there is a contract for the sale of specific goods in a deliverable state, but the seller is bound to weigh, measure, test, or do some other act or thing with reference to the goods for the purpose of ascertaining the price, the property does not pass until such act or thing be done, and the buyer has notice thereof.

It is a little difficult to see why Rule 2 should be confined to cases where the seller is bound to do something to put the goods "into a deliverable state." Thus it seems that the Rule would not, for example, apply where the seller has agreed to repair the goods, e.g. to overhaul a second-hand car. On the other hand such a sale may well be a conditional sale, in which case none of the Rules in Sect. 18 would apply to

---

[1] *Commissioner of Stamps* v. *Queensland Meat Export Co., Ltd.*, [1917] A.C. 624. The same result could be arrived at by holding that the sale is conditional on conveyance and so not within Rule 1.

[2] *Warren* v. *Forbes*, [1959] V.R. 14.

[3] *Clark* v. *Bulmer* (1843), 11 M. & W. 243; *Aristoc Industries Pty., Ltd.* v. *R. A. Wenham (Builders) Pty., Ltd.*, [1965] N.S.W.R. 581.

[4] *Pritchett and Gold and Electrical Power Storage Co.* v. *Currie*, [1916] 2 Ch. 515.

[5] See *Young & Marten, Ltd.* v. *McManus Childs*, [1969] 1 A.C. 454.

it at all. In such a case the court may simply fall back on Sect. 17 and hold that property is not to pass until the repairs have been done as this is the presumed intention of the parties.[1]

Rule 3 requires little comment. It clearly deals with cases where the passing of the property is conditional upon the performance of some act with reference to the goods. The presumption embodied in this rule is probably somewhat weaker than those in Rules 1 and 2, because it is easy to imagine circumstances in which the parties intend the property to pass at once, especially if the price has been paid. So, for instance, where a seller sold haystacks for delivery at the buyer's convenience, and the price was paid at once, though liable to adjustment when the hay was weighed on delivery, it was held that the property passed at once.[2] Similarly, it is probable that the property would be field to have passed if the goods have been delivered, although the seller has still to do something to ascertain the price, e.g. to look up the list price in a catalogue.

At all events Rule 3 only applies to acts to be done by the seller. in *Nanka Bruce* v. *Commonwealth Trust, Ltd.*,[3] A sold cocoa to B at an agreed price per 60 lb., it being arranged that B would resell the goods, and that the cocoa would then be weighed in order to ascertain the total amount due from B to A. It was held that the weighing did not make the contract conditional, and that the property passed to B before the price was ascertained.

RULE 4

Rule 4 deals with a different type of transaction altogether although it is very similar to a conditional sale, and may become a sale in due course—

> When goods are delivered to the buyer on approval or "on sale or return" or other similar terms the property therein passes to the buyer.

The Rule then proceeds to give two instances in which the property passes to the buyer—

> (a) When he signifies his approval or acceptance to the seller or does any other act adopting the transaction.

It has been held that any action by the buyer inconsistent with his free power to return the goods is an act adopting the transaction within the meaning of the Rule. Thus where a person obtains goods on sale or return or similar terms, and then resells or pledges them, this is an act adopting the transaction, and the third party is therefore protected against the seller. Nor is it material that the first buyer is guilty of a criminal offence.[4]

---

[1] *Anderson* v. *Ryan*, [1967] I.R. 34, at p. 37.
[2] *Lord Eldon* v. *Hedley Bros.*, [1935] 2 K.B. 1.   [3] [1926] A.C. 77.
[4] *Kirkham* v. *Attenborough*, [1897] 1 Q.B. 201; *London Jewellers, Ltd.* v. *Attenborough*, [1934] 2 K.B. 206; *Genn* v. *Winkel* (1911), 28 T.L.R. 483.

An express stipulation that the property is not to pass until the goods are paid for is effective to protect the seller, because this is evidence of a contrary intention which overrides Rule 4.[1] Even in such a case, however, the seller may be caught by the doctrine of estoppel,[2] or by the provisions of Sect. 2 of the Factors Act, 1889.[3] In *Weiner* v. *Harris*,[4] the plaintiff sent jewellery to F, a retailer, under a standing contract whereby the property was to remain in the plaintiff until the goods were sold or paid for. F pledged the jewels in question with the defendant. Cozens-Hardy, M.R., posed the following question: "Was the transaction the ordinary well-known transaction of goods taken on sale or return, or was it a transaction under which F was constituted agent for sale, with authority to sell, and bound to account to his principal for the proceeds of such sale?" In the former case Sect. 18, Rule 4, would be overridden by a contrary intention, and the seller would be protected. In the latter case F would be a mercantile agent enabled by Sect. 2 of the Factors Act to pass a good title to a buyer or pledgee. The Court of Appeal had no doubt that in this case F was a mercantile agent, and the defendants were protected.

It has been held that a person who has obtained goods on sale or return cannot pass a good title to a third party under Sect. 25 (2) of the Act, if there is a contrary intention which excludes the operation of Rule 4.[5] The reason for this is not very clear but it seems to depend on the view that such a person is not, within the meaning of Sect. 25 (2), a person who has bought or agreed to buy goods. He has an option to purchase, but that is all; until he exercises his option, by accepting the goods or adopting the transaction, there is no sale. But there is one difficulty about this analysis, and that is that the buyer can "adopt" the transaction without communicating his intention to the seller. If this were really a mere option it would seem that the buyer would have to communicate his acceptance to the seller.

The second alternative given by Rule 4 is—

> (b) If he does not signify his approval or acceptance to the seller but retains the goods without giving notice of rejection, then, if a time has been fixed for the return of the goods, on the expiration of such time, and, if no time has been fixed, on the expiration of a reasonable time. What is a reasonable time is a question of fact.[6]

Thus if a time has been fixed for the return of the goods the buyer is deemed to have exercised his option to buy them if he retains them after this time. Here again, therefore, the transaction may be completed without a communication of acceptance. It is clear that an *unsolicited*

---

[1] *Weiner* v. *Gill*, [1906] 2 K.B. 574; *R.* v. *Eaton* (1966), 50 Cr. App. Rep. 189.
[2] On estoppel, see *post*, p. 184.   [3] On the Factors Act, see p. 193, *post*.
[4] [1910] 1 K.B. 285.   [5] *Edwards* v. *Vaughan* (1910), 26 T.L.R. 545.
[6] See *Poole* v. *Smith's Car Sales (Balham), Ltd.*, [1962] 2 All E.R. 482.

delivery of goods with an offer to sell them does not have this effect,[1] and it is therefore arguable that delivery on sale or return must be more than a mere option or offer to sell. The buyer may, of course, waive the time limit and accept the goods at once by so informing the seller, or by doing some act which adopts the transaction.

The sub-rule only applies if it is the buyer who retains the goods. Thus where goods were delivered to X on sale or return within one week, and two days later they were seized by execution creditors of X who retained them until after the week was over, it was held that the property had not passed under Rule 4 (*b*).[2]

Other conditional contracts

Other types of conditional contracts of sale of specific goods are considered in Sect. 19, the first subsection of which is as follows—

> Where there is a contract for the sale of specific goods or where goods are subsequently appropriated to the contract, the seller may, by the terms of the contract or appropriation, reserve the right of disposal of the goods until certain conditions are fulfilled. In such case, notwithstanding the delivery of the goods to the buyer, or to a carrier or other bailee . . . for the purpose of transmission to the buyer, the property in the goods does not pass to the buyer until the conditions imposed by the seller are fulfilled.

Even if the property does not pass to the buyer because of the operation of this subsection, yet if he has actually obtained possession of the goods the position is almost the same as if the property had passed. In particular he can pass a good title to a third party under Sect. 25 (2).

The courts have been very ready to find that the seller has reserved the right of disposal and that the buyer does not acquire property in the goods, before actual delivery. In *Re Shipton Anderson & Co., Ltd., and Harrison Bros. & Co., Ltd.*,[3] the owner of a specific parcel of wheat in a warehouse sold it on the terms "payment cash within seven days against transfer order." The goods were requisitioned by the government under Emergency Powers before delivery to the buyer. It was held by the Court of Appeal that the express term quoted above was in effect a right of disposal reserved by the seller, as he was not bound to hand over a delivery order until payment. Consequently the property had not yet passed and the contract was frustrated by the seizure of the goods. The result is perhaps a little surprising because, in the absence of a contrary intention, every seller is entitled to retain possession until payment by exercising his lien, and, subject to certain conditions, he may eventually resell the goods

---

[1] Indeed the goods may become the property of the buyer without payment under the Unsolicited Goods and Services Act, 1971.
[2] *In re Ferrier*, [1944] Ch. 295.   [3] [1915] 3 K.B. 676.

if the price is not paid.[1] Surely this does not mean that the seller always reserves the right of disposal within the meaning of the section.

Sect. 19 (1) is only a generalisation of the specific case dealt with by Sect. 19 (2) which is concerned with goods sent by sea. As this is by far the most important illustration of the reservation of the right of disposal, more detailed consideration of this question will be postponed until later.[2]

Yet another type of conditional contract is dealt with by Sect. 19 (3)—

> Where the seller of goods draws on the buyer for the price, and transmits the bill of exchange and bill of lading to the buyer together to secure acceptance or payment of the bill of exchange, the buyer is bound to return the bill of lading if he does not honour the bill of exchange, and if he wrongfully retains the bill of lading the property in the goods does not pass to him.

In other words the transfer of the property by the bill of lading in such a case is conditional upon the bill of exchange being honoured, and if, for example, the buyer should become bankrupt with the bill of lading still in his possession, not having accepted the bill of exchange, the seller will be able to claim the goods.

It should be noted, however, that this subsection does not protect the seller if the buyer should transfer the bill of lading to a sub-buyer who takes in good faith and for value. In this event the sub-buyer gets a good title under Sect. 25 (2), the proviso to Sect. 47, and Sect. 10 of the Factors Act, 1889.[3]

THE PASSING OF PROPERTY: II. UNASCERTAINED GOODS

The meaning of unascertained goods has already been discussed and it has been seen to cover three possibilities. Firstly, goods to be manufactured or grown by the seller. Secondly, purely generic goods, and thirdly an unidentified portion of a specified whole. Although the Act does not distinguish between these three types of unascertained goods, the rules as to the passing of property and risk may well differ in the three cases. In particular it will be seen that the passing of risk in an unidentified portion of a specified whole may well take place at a different time from the usual. And secondly it will be seen that what amounts to an unconditional appropriation in one type of sale may not be so in another.

The fundamental rule is laid down by Sect. 16 that—

> Where there is a contract for the sale of unascertained goods no property in the goods is transferred to the buyer unless and until the goods are ascertained.

[1] See p. 267, *post.*　　　　[2] Pp. 224–5, *post.*
[3] *Cahn* v. *Pockett's Bristol Channel Co., Ltd.,* [1899] 1 Q.B. 643.

Sect. 18, Rule 5, then says that, subject to a contrary intention—

> (1) Where there is a contract for the sale of unascertained or future goods by description, and goods of that description and in a deliverable state are unconditionally appropriated to the contract, either by the seller with the assent of the buyer, or by the buyer with the assent of the seller, the property in the goods thereupon passes to the buyer. Such assent may be express or implied, and may be given either before or after the appropriation is made.

The first and most difficult question that arises under this rule is the meaning to be attributed to "unconditionally appropriated." Rule 5 (2) gives one illustration of an unconditional appropriation—

> Where, in pursuance of the contract, the seller delivers the goods to the buyer or to a carrier or other bailee . . . (whether named by the buyer or not) for the purpose of transmission to the buyer, and does not reserve the right of disposal, he is deemed to have unconditionally appropriated the goods to the contract.

This sub-rule must be read subject to Sect. 16 because it is clear that if the seller delivers the goods to a carrier still mixed with other goods no property can pass. Thus in *Healey* v. *Howlett & Sons*,[1] the defendant ordered twenty boxes of mackerel from the plaintiff, a fish exporter carrying on business in Ireland. The plaintiff dispatched 190 boxes and instructed the railway officials to earmark twenty boxes for the defendant and the remaining boxes for two other consignees. The train was delayed before the defendant's boxes were earmarked, and by the time this was done the fish had deteriorated. It was held that the property in the fish had not passed to the defendant before the boxes were earmarked, and that they were therefore still at the seller's risk when they deteriorated.

Apart from the particular instance given in Rule 5 (2) the meaning of the term "unconditional appropriation" has been discussed on many occasions by the courts. As to the meaning of "unconditional" it appears that the appropriation is not unconditional if the seller only means to let the buyer have the goods on payment.[2]

Reference has already been made to Rule 3 under which, in a sale of specific goods, the passing of the property is postponed if the seller is bound to weigh, measure, test or do some other act for the purpose of ascertaining the price. Although this Rule is confined to sales of specific goods it seems that the position is the same in a sale of unascertained

---

[1] [1917] 1 K.B. 337. Conversely, if the seller delivers goods to the buyer with the intention that the goods will lose their identity by being mixed with other similar goods, it is almost impossible to hold that the property has *not* passed: *Chapman Bros.* v. *Verco Bros. & Co., Ltd.* (1933), 49 C.L.R. 306; *South Australian Insurance Co.* v. *Randell* (1869), L.R. 3 P.C. 101.

[2] *Stein, Forbes & Co., Ltd.* v. *County Tailoring Co., Ltd.* (1916), 86 L.J.K.B. 448 per Atkin, J., and see *Cheetham & Co., Ltd.* v. *Thornham Spinning Co., Ltd.*, [1964] 2 Lloyd's Rep. 17, which could perhaps have been decided on this ground.

goods. In *National Coal Board* v. *Gamble*[1] the appellants supplied coal as part of a bulk sale to a purchaser by loading it on to the buyer's lorry at a colliery. The coal was loaded by means of a hopper and subsequently driven to a weighbridge where the weight of the coal was ascertained, and the statutory weight-ticket supplied. It was held that the property did not pass until the coal had been weighed and the ticket given to and accepted by the buyer. The Court had no doubt that if too much had been loaded on to the lorry the seller could have insisted on the excess being unloaded. It seems (although this was not stated in the judgments) that the correct analysis of the facts was that, although the coal was appropriated to the contract by being loaded on to the lorry, the appropriation was not unconditional until it was weighed and the weight-ticket accepted by the buyer.

Despite the fact that the word "appropriated" has been said to be "a term of legal art [which] has a certain definite meaning,"[2] it is extremely difficult to define it with precision. One thing at least is clear, that where an unidentified part of a bulk is sold there can be no appropriation until there is a severance of the part sold from the rest. *Healey* v. *Howlett & Sons*[3] is one authority for this. Another is *Laurie & Morewood* v. *John Dudin & Sons.*[4] The defendants were warehousemen who were in possession of some maize belonging to A. A sold part of it to B and B resold it to the plaintiffs, who obtained a delivery order and lodged it with the defendants. A, not having been paid by B, stopped delivery, and the plaintiffs then brought an action of detinue against the defendants. The Court of Appeal disposed of the case on the short ground that without severance no property could have passed to the plaintiffs.

But where an unidentified part of a specified bulk is sold, it seems that the property can pass in some exceptional cases even without an unconditional appropriation. In *Wait and James* v. *Midland Bank,*[5] sellers sold on credit 1,250 quarters of wheat from a particular cargo lying in a certain warehouse. The buyers were given delivery orders which were accepted by the warehousekeepers, and they pledged the wheat to a bank. At this stage no property could pass because no severance had taken place. Later the sellers sold and delivered the remainder of the cargo to other buyers. It was held by Roche, J., that the property thereupon passed to the buyers and the pledge was therefore good against the sellers. He seems to have assumed that what was required to pass the property was that the goods should become ascertained, rather than that they should be unconditionally appropriated.

[1] [1959] 1 Q.B. 11.
[2] *Re Blyth Shipbuilding Co., Ltd.*, [1926] Ch. 494, at 518, *per* Sargant, L.J.
[3] [1917] 1 K.B. 337.
[4] [1926] 1 K.B. 223. See also *Wardar's* (*Import & Export*) *Co., Ltd.* v. *W. Norwood & Sons, Ltd.*, [1968] 2 Q.B. 663.
[5] (1926), 31 Comm. Cas. 172.

The question of appropriation has arisen in a number of shipbuilding cases. In such cases, as in the case of all goods to be manufactured by the seller, the general presumption is that no property is to pass until the article is completed.[1] This is still the case even if the price is to be paid by instalments during the construction of the ship.[2] But it was said "there is no doubt that a contract might be so framed as to give the purchaser power to claim the property in those parts which, when they are put together, make the complete ship."[3] And since then it has become customary for shipbuilding contracts to do precisely this where the price is payable by instalments as the work proceeds. Thus in *Re Blyth Shipbuilding Co.*,[4] A agreed to build a ship for B, the price to be paid by instalments as the work proceeded. The contract provided that on the payment of the first instalment "the vessel and all materials and things appropriated for her should thenceforth . . . become and remain the absolute property of the purchaser."[5] A went bankrupt before the ship was complete. A certain amount of worked and unworked material was lying about the yard at the relevant time. It was held by the Court of Appeal that the property in the incomplete ship had passed to the buyers. The worked and unworked material gave rise to more difficulty, but in the result it was held that neither had been sufficiently appropriated to pass the property.

It may well be that what is necessary to constitute an unconditional appropriation will vary according to the type of goods in question and the general circumstances of the case. In particular where goods are being manufactured by the seller the courts will not too readily infer that the materials have been appropriated since this might hamper the freedom of the seller to manufacture the goods as he thinks best. This consideration does not apply in the case of goods to be grown by the seller, and here it might well be held that the property in the goods, if sufficiently designated, passes as soon as they come into existence. So also where an unidentified part of a specified bulk is sold, the only thing necessary for appropriation is the separation of the part sold from the rest, with the assent of the parties. Thus in *Aldridge* v. *Johnson*[6] the plaintiff agreed to buy one hundred quarters of barley out of a particular parcel of two hundred quarters which he had inspected. It was held that, as soon as the seller filled some sacks sent by the buyer with the barley, the property passed.

Before the Sale of Goods Act was passed there was some divergence between the requirements of common law as to appropriation of un-

---

[1] *Reid* v. *Macbeth*, [1904] A.C. 223.
[2] *Laing & Sons* v. *Barclay, Curle & Co.*, [1908] A.C 35.
[3] Ibid, *per* Lord Halsbury, at p. 43.   [4] [1926] Ch. 494.
[5] A clause of this kind does not deprive the buyer of any right of rejection he may have when the vessel is completed: *McDougall* v. *Aeromarine of Emsworth Ltd.*, [1958] 1 W.L.R. 1126.
[6] (1857), 7 E. & B. 885.

ascertained goods to a contract of sale, and the requirements of equity as to the transfer of an equitable interest in future property sold or assigned by one party to another. While common law insisted on identification of the particular thing sold, equity was not so stringent.[1] In *Tailby* v. *Official Receiver*[2] Lord Watson stated the single requirement of equity "which must be fulfilled in order to make the assignee's right attach to a future chose in action, which is that on its coming into existence it shall answer the description in the assignment, or, in other words, that it shall be capable of being identified as the thing, or as one of the very things assigned." In other words no unconditional appropriation was required in equity so long as identification was possible of what was assigned. If the contract was one which a court of equity would enforce by a decree of specific performance it was held that an equitable interest in the property passed as soon as the property came into existence and was identifiable as such.

It was never entirely clear whether (and, if so, to what extent) this equitable doctrine applied to an ordinary sale of unascertained goods. It certainly applied to the assignment of a future chose in action and to a covenant to convey or mortgage real estate. In these cases the equitable doctrine meant that once the property came into the hands of the seller, or the chose in action became currently due, the assignee or buyer was entitled to the property or chose in preference to judgment creditors or a trustee in bankruptcy of the seller or assignor. But an ordinary contract of sale of goods has never been specifically enforceable in equity though there are dicta in *Holroyd* v. *Marshall*[3] suggesting that a contract for the sale of specific goods or of an unspecified part of a specified bulk may be so enforceable.

For some years after the passing of the Act it was an open question whether this equitable rule was applicable to contracts of sale of goods but the question seems to have been settled by *Re Wait*.[4] Wait bought 1,000 tons of wheat *ex Challenger* on 20th November, 1925. The following day he contracted to sell 500 tons of this to X. X paid Wait on 5th February, and Wait went bankrupt on 24th February. The ship arrived on 28th February. Wait's trustee claimed the whole 1,000 tons as assets in the bankruptcy, while X claimed either that he had an equitable assignment or charge on the 500 tons, or that he was entitled to specific performance of the contract under Sect. 52. A majority of the Court of Appeal decided against X on both grounds.[5] There had clearly been insufficient appropriation at law to pass the property and Lord Hanworth, M.R., was of the opinion that even if the equitable doctrine of *Tailby* v. *Official Receiver* survived the Sale of Goods Act, the goods were not sufficiently identified even in equity.

---

[1] *Holroyd* v. *Marshall* (1862), 10 H.L.C. 191.
[2] (1888), 13 App. Cas. 523 at p. 533.
[3] *Supra.*   [4] [1927] 1 Ch. 606
[5] As to the second ground, see p. 319, *post.*

But Lord Atkin went much further than Lord Hanworth. He denied that equity would ever have applied its doctrines to an ordinary sale of future goods. He went on to say that even if equity would ever have applied its doctrine to such a case, it could not do so now having regard to the Sale of Goods Act. He said—[1]

> The Code was passed at a time when the principles of equity and equitable remedies were recognised and given effect to in all our courts, and the particular equitable remedy of specific performance is specially referred to in Sect. 52. The total sum of legal relations (meaning by the word "legal" existing in equity as well as in common law) arising out of the contract for the sale of goods may well be regarded as defined by the Code. It would have been futile in a Code intended for commercial men to have created an elaborate structure of rules dealing with rights at law, if at the same time it was intended to leave, subsisting with the legal rights equitable rights inconsistent with, more extensive, and coming into existence earlier than the rights so carefully set out in the various sections of the Code.
>
> The rules for transfer of property as between seller and buyer, performance of the contract, rights of the unpaid seller against the goods, unpaid seller's lien, remedies of the seller, remedies of the buyer, appear to be complete and exclusive statements of the legal relations both in law and equity.

These are powerful arguments and although they only depend on the authority of one member of the Court of Appeal they have not been challenged since. Ever since *Re Wait* it seems to have been assumed that the only issue in cases of this kind is whether the goods have been unconditionally appropriated to the contract under Rule 5. For instance, in *Carlos Federspiel & Co. S.A.* v. *Charles Twigg & Co., Ltd.*,[2] sellers manufactured bicycles to the buyers' orders. The bicycles were made and packed in containers with the buyers' name and address on them. Before the goods could be shipped the sellers became insolvent. It was held that the property had not passed to the buyers. After a comprehensive review of the authorities, old and new, Pearson, J., summed up the law relating to appropriation in the following passage—

> First, Rule 5 of Sect. 18 of the Act is one of the Rules for ascertaining the intention of the parties as to the time at which the property in the goods is to pass to the buyer unless a different intention appears. Therefore the element of common intention has always to be borne in mind. A mere setting apart or selection by the seller of the goods which he expects to use in performance of the contract is not enough. If that is all, he can change his mind and use those goods in performance of some other contract and use some other goods in performance of this contract. To constitute an appropriation of the goods to the contract the parties must have had, or be reasonably supposed to have had, an intention to attach the contract

---

[1] At pp. 635-6.   [2] [1975] Lloyd's, Rep. at pp. 255-6.

irrevocably to those goods, so that those goods and no others are the subject of the sale and become the property of the buyer.

Secondly, it is by agreement of the parties that the appropriation, involving a change of ownership, is made, although in some cases the buyer's assent to an appropriation is conferred in advance by the contract itself or otherwise.

Thirdly, an appropriation by the seller with the assent of the buyer may be said always to involve an actual or constructive delivery. If the seller retains possession, he does so as bailee for the buyer. There is a passage in Chalmers' *Sale of Goods Act*, 12th. ed., at p. 75 where it is said—

In the second place, if the decisions be carefully examined, it will be found that in every case where the property has been held to pass, there has been an actual or constructive delivery of the goods to the buyer.

I think that is right, subject only to this possible qualification, that there may be after such constructive delivery an actual delivery still to be made by the seller under the contract. Of course, that is quite possible, because delivery is the transfer of possession, whereas appropriation transfers ownership. So there may be first an appropriation, constructive delivery, whereby the seller becomes bailee for the buyer, and then a subsequent actual delivery involving actual possession, and when I say that I have in mind in particular the cases cited, namely, *Aldridge* v. *Johnson*[1] and *Langton* v. *Higgins*.[2]

Fourthly, one has to remember Sect. 20 of the Sale of Goods Act, whereby the ownership and the risk are normally associated. Therefore, as it appears that there is reason for thinking, on the construction of the relevant documents, that the goods were, at all material times, still at the seller's risk, that is prima facie an indication that the property had not passed to the buyer.

Fifthly, usually, but not necessarily, the appropriating act is the last act to be performed by the seller. For instance, if delivery is to be taken at the seller's premises and the seller has appropriated the goods when he has made the goods ready and identified them and placed them in position to be taken by the buyer and has so informed the buyer, and if the buyer agrees to come and take them, that is the assent to the appropriation. But if there is a further act, an important and decisive act, to be done by the seller, then there is prima facie evidence that probably the property does not pass until the final act is done.

Probably the decisive fact in this case was that the sellers were responsible for arranging shipment of the goods. By contrast, where sellers made rope for buyers' order, and stored the rope in a warehouse from which deliveries were made as requested, it was held that there was an unconditional appropriation.[3] This case is also authority for saying that, even if the goods are stored with other similar goods, they are sufficiently earmarked if the sellers can identify the particular goods set aside for the buyers. It is immaterial that nobody else could tell

[1] (1857), 7 E. & B. 885.   [2] (1859), 4 H. & N. 402.
[3] *Donaghey's Rope and Twine Co., Ltd.* v. *Wright Stephenson & Co.* (1906), 25 N.Z.L.R. 641.

which goods were meant for which buyer. However, it is doubtful whether this would be an acceptable rule where the only "appropriation" is in the seller's mind, and there is no independent objective evidence of the "appropriation", e.g., in the seller's books or records.

Where goods are in the possession of a third party, such as a warehousekeeper, and the third party sets the goods aside for delivery to the buyer, the goods are unconditionally appropriated at the latest when a delivery order is accepted.[1]

The assent which Rule 5 requires for the appropriation may be express or implied. Where, therefore, the defendant sold some rice to the plaintiff from a specified parcel at a particular place, and sent the plaintiff a note of appropriation, his assent was implied from his failure to reply for a whole month.[2] Consequently, although Rules 2 and 3 only required notice to be given to the buyer of the fulfilment of conditions in a sale of specific goods, while Rule 5 requires the buyer's assent, there seems to be little difference in practice.

Rule 5 also says that the assent may be given before or after the appropriation is made, and this gives rise to some difficulty. Suppose, for example, that a person orders goods by post, and that the seller dispatches goods answering that description to the buyer, when does the property pass? Rule 5 (2) which has been set out above,[3] states that in such circumstances the goods are deemed to be unconditionally appropriated to the contract, but the rule does not say that the buyer's assent is deemed to have been given. It must be remembered that the buyer must assent to the appropriation and not merely to the dispatch of the goods.

But it is nevertheless clear that, where the seller is required to ship the goods to the buyer, the customary course of business rests on the assumption that shipment is an unconditional appropriation with the assent of the buyer.[4] The buyer's assent is to be inferred from the nature of the transaction itself. It does not follow that property is always transferred on shipment; whether it is transferred then or later depends on the nature and terms of the contract. These questions are discussed in a later chapter. Here it is merely desired to stress that the apparent absence of a prior assent to the appropriation does not prevent property passing on shipment. Unfortunately, this appears to be one of those areas in which a rule suitable for commercial contracts is not necessarily suitable for consumer contracts. When a consumer orders goods by post the dispatch of the goods to him by the seller should not pass the property, for if it does the goods will be at buyer's risk in course of post. But it is doubtful whether it is open to the courts to take this

---

[1] *Wardar's (Import & Export) Co., Ltd.* v. *W. Norwood & Sons, Ltd.*, [1968] 2 Q.B. 663.

[2] *Pignataro* v. *Gilroy & Son*, [1919] 1 K.B. 459.   [3] P. 156. *ante.*

[4] See *James* v. *Commonwealth* (1939), 62 C.L.R. 339, at p. 377; *Saffron* v. *Société Minière Cafrika* (1958), 100 C.L.R. 231, at p. 242.

view having regard to the House of Lords decision in *Badische Anilin und Soda Fabrik v. Basle Chemical Works*,[1] where it appears to have been held that the posting of ordered goods vested the property in the buyer. However, this case is perhaps not decisive because this point was not disputed and the case really turned on the special provisions of patent law. Moreover, there are other cases which tend to support the view here put, although it cannot be said that any of them are directly in point.[2]

[1] [1898] A.C. 200.
[2] See *Noblett* v. *Hopkinson*, [1905] 2 K.B. 214; *Pletts* v. *Campbell*, [1895] 2 Q.B. 229; *Pletts* v. *Beattie*, [1896] 1 Q.B. 519 and cf. *Preston* v. *Albuery*, [1964] 2 Q.B. 796, *per* Ashworth, J., at p. 805.

CHAPTER 18

RISK AND FRUSTRATION

RISK AND FRUSTRATION DISTINGUISHED

WHEN a person is bound to bear the accidental loss of, or damage to, the goods they are said to be at his risk. The doctrine of frustration is sometimes said to be merely an aspect of the general rules as to risk, but this is not entirely accurate. If an executory contract is frustrated neither party is under any liability to the other. On the other hand, if the goods are at the seller's risk and they perish or deteriorate, although the buyer is not liable to the seller for the price, it by no means follows that the seller is not liable to the buyer for non-delivery, if the buyer can prove that he has suffered loss therefrom. The rules as to risk have nothing to say in such a case, and if the seller is to be exempted from liability it must be by the doctrine of frustration. Conversely, if the goods are at the buyer's risk he is clearly liable for the price even though the goods have perished or deteriorated. But it does not follow that he may not also be liable for damages for non-acceptance if the seller can prove that he has suffered any.[1] Only frustration can discharge the buyer from the liability for non-acceptance.

Nonetheless the doctrines of risk and frustration are undoubtedly connected and it is convenient to consider them in the same chapter. The next three sections will be devoted to an examination of the Transfer of Risk, Frustration, and Effects of Frustration. As the following pages will demonstrate the whole subject of risk and frustration is bedevilled by the distinction between specific and unascertained goods, and by the failure of the Act to draw any distinction between the different types of unascertained goods. Indeed, it is difficult at times to avoid the conclusion that the draftsmen of both the Sale of Goods Act and the Law Reform (Frustrated Contracts) Act, 1943, forgot that there were sales of unascertained goods other than purely generic goods.

TRANSFER OF RISK

The general rule laid down by Sect. 20 is that prima facie the risk passes with the property—

> Unless otherwise agreed, the goods remain at the seller's risk until the property therein is transferred to the buyer, but when the property therein is transferred to the buyer, the goods are at the buyer's risk whether delivery has been made or not.

[1] E.g. storage charges; see Sect. 37.

164

If there is an express agreement that one party is to bear the risk even though he has no property (as, for example, there always is in hire-purchase contracts), effect must no doubt be given to the agreement, but in the absence of such an express contract, "the rule *res perit domino* is generally an unbending rule of law arising from the very nature of property".[1] While this is no doubt largely true in a static situation where property remains with one person throughout, it is not necessarily true of the dynamic situation where property is being transferred from one party to another. In this situation there is nothing peculiar about separating the transfer of risk from the transfer of property and this commonly happens where goods are shipped under a c.i.f. or an f.o.b. contract.[2] Apart from these cases, two other exceptional cases seem to be established by the authorities, in one of which the risk passes before the property, and in the other, the risk passes after the property. The best example of the former exception is *Sterns, Ltd.* v. *Vickers, Ltd.*[3] The defendants sold to the plaintiffs 120,000 gallons of spirit which was part of a total quantity of 200,000 gallons in a storage tank belonging to a third party. The plaintiffs obtained a delivery order which the third party accepted, but the plaintiffs decided to leave the spirit in the tank for the time being for their own convenience. The spirit deteriorated in quality between the time of sale, and the time when the plaintiffs eventually took delivery of the 120,000 gallons. Despite the fact that the property clearly had not passed because there had been no appropriation, the Court of Appeal held that the risk had passed to the buyers.

Although the decision in *Sterns, Ltd.* v. *Vickers, Ltd.*[3] appears to have been approved by the House of Lords, and must therefore be accepted as correct on its particular facts, it may well give rise to difficulty. Suppose, for example, that the spirit had been stored in two separate tanks each containing 100,000 gallons, and that the contents of one tank only had deteriorated, would the buyer have been compelled to take all the deteriorated spirit, or would he have been able to claim all the spirit from the other tank? Or should the good and bad spirit be divided between the parties in proportion to their respective interests? This latter solution appears to be the logical conclusion from *Sterns, Ltd.* v. *Vickers, Ltd.*, since it gives effect to the holding that the risk is on the buyer, and at the same time it offers a fair solution to the problem.

At all events the exceptional nature of this case was emphasised by the House of Lords in *Comptoir D'Achat et de Vente du Boerenbond Belge S.A.* v. *Luis de Ridder Limitada*,[4] where Lord Porter said—

---

[1] *Hausen* v. *Craig & Rose* (1859), 21 D. 432, at p. 438, *per* Lord President Inglis, quoted by Lord Normand in *Comptoir D'Achat et de Vente* v. *Luis de Ridder Limitada*, [1949] A.C. 293, at 319.
[2] See Chapter 20.   [3] [1923] 1 K.B. 78.   [4] [1949] A.C. 293.

It is difficult to see how a parcel is at the buyer's risk when he has neither property nor possession except in such cases as *Inglis* v. *Stock*[1] and *Sterns, Ltd.* v. *Vickers, Ltd.*[2] where the purchaser had an interest in an undivided part of a bulk parcel on board a ship, or elsewhere, obtained by attornment of the bailee to him.[3]

And Lord Normand observed—

In those cases in which it has been held that the risk without the property has passed to the buyer it has been because the buyer rather than the seller was seen to have an immediate and practical interest in the goods,[4] as for instance when he has an immediate right under the storekeeper's delivery warrant to the delivery of a portion of an undivided bulk in store, or an immediate right under several contracts with different persons to the whole of a bulk not yet appropriated to the several contracts.[5]

It can be seen, therefore, that the acceptance of the delivery warrant in *Sterns, Ltd.* v. *Vickers, Ltd.*[6] was regarded as the crucial factor in the case, since it was this which gave the buyer an immediate right to possession. This may serve to distinguish *Healey* v. *Howlett & Sons*[7] which is not otherwise easy to reconcile with *Sterns, Ltd.* v. *Vickers, Ltd.* Here it was held that the risk in twenty boxes of fish, which were dispatched to the buyer as part of a total of 190 boxes, none of which had been earmarked for him, was still on the seller. The Court pointed out the difficulties which would have arisen if some only of the boxes had deteriorated or perished.

It should, moreover, be remembered that it is only in the sale of an unidentified part of a specific whole that it can ever be held that the risk passes before the property in a sale of unascertained goods. It clearly cannot do so in the case of goods not owned or possessed by the seller, except in the sense that the buyer may conceivably have contracted to pay the price whether or not the goods are delivered.

It is not easy to imagine circumstances in which the risk remains with the seller after the property has passed, in the absence of express agreement to this effect, but if the decision in *Head* v. *Tattersall*[8] has survived the Act, it may provide an illustration of such a case. The

---

[1] (1885), 10 App. Cas. 263, an f.o.b. case in which risk was held to have passed on shipment before the goods were specifically appropriated to the contract.
[2] [1923] 1 K.B. 78
[3] At p. 312.
[4] But this is not really so as regards c.i.f. contracts, for the seller retains the general property and the buyer has not even an immediate right to possession. See the remarks of Lord Wright in *Smyth & Co., Ltd.* v. *Bailey & Co., Ltd.*, [1940] 3 All E.R. 60, at p. 67, quoted p. 225, *post.*
[5] At p. 319.
[6] [1923] 1 K.B. 78. Where the goods are in the possession of the seller himself, it seems the risk may pass on the making of the contract, or at least when delivery falls due, see *Donaghy's Rope & Twine Co., Ltd.* v. *Wright, Stephenson & Co.* (1906), 25 N.Z.L.R. 641, at pp. 651-2.
[7] [1917] 1 K.B. 337.   [8] (1870), L.R. 7 Ex. 7.

plaintiff bought a horse from the defendant, warranted to have been hunted with the Bicester hounds, and the plaintiff was given a week in which to return the horse if it did not answer the description. The horse was accidentally injured before the week was up, and the plaintiff claimed to return it, having discovered that it had not been hunted with the Bicester hounds. It was held that the plaintiff was entitled to return the horse and recover the price. The risk was thus held to be on the seller although the property had probably passed to the buyer, subject to the possibility of being divested. There is no reason to think that the case would not be decided in the same way today, but in most such cases, of course, the property does not pass until the expiry of the time fixed in accordance with Sect. 18, Rule 4 (b). However, the decision may well illustrate a broader principle of some importance, namely that the risk always remains on the seller when the buyer has a right of rejection. Thus if the seller delivers defective goods which the buyer is entitled to reject it seems that the risk remains on the seller unless and until the buyer accepts the goods. Although this rule is not actually spelt out in the Act,[1] it seems to follow from the rules as to acceptance.[2] As will be seen later there is nothing in these rules to prevent rejection merely because the goods have been accidentally lost or damaged and by exercising his right to reject the buyer can thus effectively throw the risk on the seller.

A fairly common instance of an express agreement, under which the property passes before the risk, occurs where the seller agrees to dispatch specific goods at his own risk to the buyer. In this event the seller is only liable for deterioration or destruction not necessarily incident to the course of transit, for Sect. 33 provides—

> Where the seller of goods agrees to deliver them at his own risk at a place other than that where they are when sold, the buyer must, nevertheless, unless otherwise agreed, take any risk of deterioration in the goods necessarily incident to the course of transit.

It seems that the words "any risk . . . necessarily incident to the course of transit" must be confined to risks which would have arisen with any goods answering the contract description.[3] Thus, a risk of deterioration which is only incidental to the course of transit because of the defective condition of the goods at the commencement of the transit is not covered by this provision. Reference has already been made to *Mash & Murrell* v. *Joseph I. Emmanuel, Ltd.*,[4] where it was held that the seller's warranty that the goods are of merchantable quality continues for a reasonable time after shipment in a c.i.f. con-

---

[1] Cf. Sect. 2–510 of the U.C.C.
[2] See *post*, p. 287.
[3] See 28 *M.L.R.* 180 at p. 189 and [1962] *Journal of Business Law* 352.
[4] [1961] 1 All E.R. 485, *supra*, p. 85.

tract, and to subsequent cases throwing some doubt on this decision.
These cases prompt the question whether there is any need for a
doctrine of risk in English law, at least so far as deterioration of the
goods is concerned. It seems to accord more with the techniques of the
English law of sale to approach such questions by asking whether the
seller has continuously warranted the condition of the goods. If so,
then clearly the seller remains liable for the deterioration in their condition. If not, then indeed the risk is the buyer's, but it is perhaps misleading to think of the risk of deterioration in almost tangible terms as
something which "passes" from seller to buyer. There is no distinction
in principle between the risk of deterioration which is treated by Sect.
20 as passing with the property, and the ordinary risk which every
buyer takes in respect of matters not covered by conditions and warranties imposed on the seller.

It may, indeed, be that a similar analysis could be made of the risk
of accidental destruction of the goods. The real question which arises
in such circumstances is whether the buyer remains liable to pay the
price or whether the seller's inability to deliver the goods discharges
the buyer. Prima facie, one would have thought that the latter should be
the case because payment and delivery are, under Sect. 28 of the Act,
concurrent conditions. This is not, of course, the law, but it is far from
obvious why the risk of accidental destruction should be on the buyer
prior to delivery. Indeed, in retail sales the technical legal position is so
grotesque that it is difficult to believe that a seller would ever take
advantage of it. If, for example, a person buys an article in a shop for
later delivery, and the shop is burned down with its stock overnight,
the buyer would probably be astonished to learn that he remains liable
for the price.[1] In point of fact the goods would almost certainly be insured, and if the buyer were required to pay the price it is thought that
the seller would be a constructive trustee of the proceeds of the insurance policy for the buyer.[2]

The question of who should bear the risk of accidental destruction
therefore boils down, in modern conditions, to who should be required
to insure them. It is surely very doubtful whether the present rule which
lays the obligation to insure (or more strictly, the risk of not insuring)
on the party who has the property, is in most circumstances the right
solution. Certainly in retail sales and similar transactions a powerful
case could be made for saying that the most appropriate person to
insure would nearly always be the party with physical possession, if
only because in practice this is what would normally happen. To take
a simple example, in a hire-purchase agreement the person who ought

[1] Perhaps a court would today hold that property in such a case does not pass on
the making of the contract: see the dictum of Diplock, L.J., in *R. V. Ward* v. *Bignall*,
[1967] 1 Q.B. 534, at p. 545.
[2] See Sect. 47, Law of Property Act, 1925, and *Maurice* v. *Goldsbrough Mort &
Co., Ltd.*, [1939] A.C. 452 and cases therein cited.

to insure the goods is clearly the person in possession, and of course all hire-purchase agreements of vehicles impose an obligation to insure on the hirer.

Even in commercial or bulk sales it seems doubtful whether the present rule is the most appropriate one. Here again it seems probable that the right person to insure normally is the person in physical possession, although it may be that special provision would be necessary in relation to insurance while the goods are in the hands of a carrier for transmission to the buyer. And it may well be that commercial practice would, in many circumstances, rebut the prima facie presumption that the person in possession should insure.

At all events the concept of "risk" is concerned only with accidental destruction or deterioration, and does not cover damage to the goods caused by the fault of either party. Sect. 20 therefore has the following two provisos—

> Provided that where delivery has been delayed through the fault of either buyer or seller the goods are at the risk of the party in fault as regards any loss which might not have occurred but for such fault.
> Provided also that nothing in this section shall affect the duties or liabilities of either seller or buyer as a bailee . . . of the goods of the other party.

The first proviso was applied in *Demby Hamilton & Co., Ltd.* v. *Barden*.[1] X contracted to sell 30 tons of apple juice to be delivered to Y in weekly loads. X crushed the apples, and put the juice in casks pending delivery. The buyer was late in taking delivery and some of the juice went bad. Applying the first proviso the learned judge held that the buyer was liable. It is important to note that the party in fault is not liable for all risks, but only for those which "might not have occurred but for such fault."

The second proviso means that the mere fact that one party is in fault does not discharge the other from his obligations to take due care as a bailee. In particular, the fact that the buyer is late in taking delivery does not mean that the seller is not still bound to take all reasonable care of the goods.[2] If he also is in fault interesting questions might arise as to the possibility of applying the Law Reform (Contributory Negligence) Act, 1945. Consideration of these problems, however, would take us too far afield, and we must be content with a reference to a discussion of the matter elsewhere.[3]

---

[1] [1949] 1 All E.R. 435.
[2] In the Tasmanian case of *Sharp* v. *Batt* (1930), 25 Tas. L.R. 33, at p. 56, it was held that the buyer remained liable in the absence of gross negligence by the seller. It is doubtful if an English court would require the negligence to be gross.
[3] See Glanville Williams, *Joint Torts and Contributory Negligence*, pp. 382–32; *Belous* v. *Willetts*, [1970] V.R. 45; Treitel, *op. cit.*, pp. 829–32.

FRUSTRATION

It has already been suggested that the doctrine of frustration covers a wider field than the rules as to risk. The drafting of Sect. 7 supports this view—

> Where there is an agreement to sell specific goods, and subsequently the goods, without any fault on the part of the seller or buyer, perish before the risk passes to the buyer, the agreement is thereby avoided.

The doctrine of risk simply lays down that prima facie if the goods perish before the property passes, the seller must bear the loss and cannot claim the price. Were the doctrine of frustration merely an aspect of the rules as to risk, this section would be an absurdity, for it would, in effect, be saying that where the risk is on the seller he must bear the risk of the goods perishing. But Sect. 7 does more than this, for it enacts that in the circumstances there mentioned the contract is avoided. This means that both parties are discharged from their obligations, in other words, not only is the buyer not liable for the price, but the seller is not liable for non-delivery.

The scope of Sect. 7 is comparatively narrow. It only applies to a contract for the sale of specific goods in which neither the property nor the risk[1] has passed, but as we have seen, the general presumption is that a contract for the sale of specific goods passes both the property and the risk at once. Sect. 7 therefore only applies where Sect. 18, Rule 1, does not apply for some reason, or where, if it does apply, Sect. 20 does not. It will prima facie apply wherever there is a case of a conditional sale of specific goods under Sect. 18, Rules 2 and 3.

The meaning of the word "perish" in Sect. 7 is presumably the same as in Sect. 6 and the discussion there may be referred to. Destruction of part only of specific goods also raises similar questions in the two sections. If a person agrees to sell specific goods, part only of which perish before the risk passes to the buyer, does Sect. 7 operate to frustrate the contract and discharge the seller? *Barrow, Lane & Ballard, Ltd.* v. *Phillip Phillips & Co., Ltd.*,[2] suggests that if the contract is unseverable it is frustrated by the perishing of part of the goods, whereas if it is severable it is frustrated only as to the part which has perished. But this conclusion seems suspect in the light of *H. R. & S. Sainsbury* v. *Street.*[3] This case, although not itself falling under Sect. 7, suggests that where part only of the goods perish, the seller may well be obliged to offer the remaining goods to the buyer. The buyer, however, may not be obliged to take them.

It is submitted that the perishing of the goods cannot frustrate a

[1] *Horn* v. *Minister of Food*, [1948] 2 All E.R. 1036.
[2] [1929] 1 K.B. 574.
[3] [1972] 1 W.L.R. 834, *supra*, p. 45.

contract otherwise than under Sect. 7. If the property and the risk have both passed it surely cannot be said that the subsequent destruction of the goods can frustrate the contract. Frustration cannot apply to a fully executed contract.[1] Nor is it easy to see how the result can be different if the property has passed but the risk has not. If the property has passed it can hardly be said that the object of the contract can be defeated by supervening events. There remains the possibility that the risk may have passed before the property, and the goods may have perished after the one and before the other. Here, again, it is submitted there cannot be frustration for this would discharge the buyer's obligation to pay the price, or enable him to recover it if already paid, and this would mean that the risk was on the seller and not the buyer.[2]

Perishing of specific goods is the only instance of frustration provided for by the Act, but there is no doubt that at common law a contract for the sale of specific goods may be frustrated by any event which destroys the whole basis of the contract, provided that the event occurs before the property and risk have passed to the buyer.[3] The question remains whether a contract for the sale of unascertained goods can be frustrated by perishing of the goods or otherwise. The answer depends upon the type of unascertained goods in question. In the first place it is probable that an agreement to sell purely generic goods cannot be frustrated by the destruction of the goods, because *genus numquam perit*. It is no concern of the buyer that the seller had a particular stock in mind which is accidentally destroyed after the making of the contract.

> Suppose A has contracted to sell to B unascertained goods by description—for example, "a" Bentley Mark VI (not "this" Bentley Mark VI) and suppose, further, that the seller expects to acquire the goods from a particular source, which may, indeed, be the only source available, the bare fact, without more, that when the time for delivery comes, that source has dried up and that the seller cannot draw on it, does not absolve the seller. He is still, in the absence of some contractual term excusing him, liable for non-delivery.[4]

It does not follow from this that a contract for the sale of unascertained goods of the other two types discussed above cannot be frustrated by the perishing of the goods. For example, if a person agrees to sell a crop to be grown on a particular field, the contract may be

[1] See *Re Shipton Anderson & Co., Ltd., and Harrison Bros. & Co., Ltd.*, [1915] 3 K.B. 676, where the C.A. clearly thought there could be no frustration if property and risk had both passed.

[2] *Horn* v. *Minister of Food, supra.* Certainly in c.i.f. contracts where the risk usually passes before the property, the perishing of the goods between these two events does not frustrate the contract.

[3] E.g. *Re Shipton Anderson & Co., Ltd., and Harrison Bros. & Co., Ltd.*, [1915] 3 K.B. 676.

[4] *Monkland* v. *Jack Barclay, Ltd.*, [1951] 2 K.B. 252, at p. 258, *per* Asquith, L.J.

frustrated by the failure of the crop;[1] or, if a person agrees to construct machinery in a building owned by another, and the whole building with the machinery is accidentally destroyed before it is completed, the contract may be frustrated.[2]

There seems to be no reason why, in an appropriate case, a contract for the sale of any type of unascertained goods may not be frustrated by some event other than the perishing of the goods. It may, of course, be more difficult to persuade the Court that the event which has occurred has destroyed the basis of the contract where the goods are unascertained, and indeed in *Blackburn Bobbin Co., Ltd.* v. *Allen & Sons*,[3] McCardie, J., went so far as to say—

> In the absence of any question as to trading with the enemy, and in the absence also of any administrative intervention by the British Government authorities, a bare and unqualified contract for the sale of unascertained goods will not (unless most special facts compel an opposite implication) be dissolved by the operation of [the doctrine of frustration].

But although this case was affirmed in the Court of Appeal[4] none of the lords justices was as cautious as McCardie, J. On the contrary they all treated the case as though the doctrine of frustration might have applied, but that it did not do so because the alleged frustrating event only affected the way in which the seller was going to perform the contract. Such being the case, as Pickford, L.J., observed—

> Why should a purchaser of goods, not specific goods, be deemed to concern himself with the way in which the seller is going to fulfil his contract by providing the goods he has agreed to sell?[5]

A striking instance of the application (in effect) of this principle is to be found in the Suez Canal cases,[6] where the House of Lords held that the closure of the canal did not frustrate c.i.f. contracts for the sale of Sudanese groundnuts to European buyers, despite the fact that the only alternative route was via the Cape of Good Hope, several thousand miles longer. The decisive point was that these were contracts for the sale of goods c.i.f. in which the buyers were only concerned with the ultimate arrival of the goods at their destination. Precisely how the sellers got the goods to the buyers was their own business.

Similarly, the contract is not frustrated merely because the buyer is unable to export the goods for resale as he had intended.[7] But in

---

[1] *Howell* v. *Coupland* (1876), L.R. 1 Q.B.D. 258.
[2] *Appleby* v. *Myers* (1867). L.R. 2 C.P. 651.
[3] [1918] 1 K.B. 540, at p. 550.   [4] [1918] 2 K.B. 467.
[5] At p. 469. Cf. *Re Thornett & Fehr & Yuills, Ltd.*, [1921] 1 K.B. 219.
[6] *Tsakirogolou & Co., Ltd.* v. *Noble & Thorl G.m.b.H.*, [1962] A.C. 93, overruling *Carapanayoti & Co., Ltd.* v. *E. T. Green, Ltd.*, [1959] 1 Q.B. 131.
[7] *McMaster & Co., Ltd.* v. *McEuen & Co., Ltd.*, [1921] S.C. (H.L.) 24. But where an English company orders goods from a foreign company, both parties being aware that an export licence is necessary, the failure to obtain the licence may frustrate the contract: Cf. *A. V. Pound & Co., Ltd.* v. *M. W. Hardy & Co., Inc.*, [1956] A.C. 588. See *post*, pp. 230–1.

Re Badische Co., Ltd.,[1] Russell, J., held that a contract to supply unascertained goods which both parties knew could only be obtained from Germany was frustrated by the outbreak of war. He said—[2]

> Speaking for myself, I can see no reason why, given the necessary circumstances to exist, the doctrine should not apply equally to the case of unascertained goods. It is, of course, obvious from the nature of the contract that the necessary circumstances can only very rarely arise in the case of unascertained goods. That they may arise appears to me to be undoubted.

More recently it has been affirmed that there is no legal principle excluding the doctrine of frustration in the case of a c.i.f. contract, though also confirming that the doctrine would only apply rarely in practice.[3] In this case a seller carrying on business in Malta agreed to sell potatoes c.i.f. London, shipment between 14th and 24th April. In fact only one vessel called at Malta during this period and the seller was unable to obtain space on it. It was held that the seller took the risk of being unable to get shipping space and was liable.

Whatever the true basis of the doctrine of frustration it would appear that Sect. 7 is only a prima facie rule of construction and nothing more, so that it does not necessarily apply merely because the facts fall within its purview. Once again there are at least three possible constructions similar to those which were discussed in connection with *Couturier* v. *Hastie*[4] and *Howell* v. *Coupland*[5] (and again, yet further possible constructions may be possible where part only of the goods perish).

1. There may be an implied condition that if the goods perish the contract will be discharged, and neither party will be liable, i.e. the contract may be frustrated.

2. The seller may contract that the goods will not perish, in which case the seller will not only have to bear the loss of the goods, i.e. will be unable to claim the price, but he may also be liable for damages for non-delivery.

3. The buyer may contract that he will take the consequences of the goods perishing, in which case he will have to pay the price whatever happens to the goods, and he may also be liable for damages for non-acceptance.

EFFECTS OF FRUSTRATION[6]

The consequences of frustration of a contract for the sale of goods depend upon whether the Law Reform (Frustrated Contracts) Act, 1943,[7] applies or not.

[1] [1921] 2 Ch. 331.   [2] At p. 382.
[3] *Lewis Emmanuel & Son, Ltd.* v. *Sammut*, [1959] 2 Lloyd's Rep. 629.
[4] (1856), 5 H.L.C. 673, pp. 40–44, *ante.*   [5] (1876), 1 Q.B.D. 258, p. 44, *ante.*
[6] See Glanville Williams, *Law Reform (Frustrated Contracts) Act, 1943*, pp. 81–90.
[7] Hereafter called the Frustrated Contracts Act.

(i) Cases to which the Frustrated Contracts Act does not apply

Sect. 2 (5) (c) of the Frustrated Contracts Act excludes from its operation—

> Any contract to which section seven of the Sale of Goods Act, 1893 . . . applies, or [to] any other contract for the sale, or for the sale and delivery, of specific goods, where the contract is frustrated by reason of the fact that the goods have perished.

With regard to contracts to which Sect. 7 of the Sale of Goods Act applies this is clear enough, but the interpretation of the second part of this clause is a matter of serious difficulty. As we have seen it is probable that no contract for the sale of specific goods is frustrated "by reason of the fact that the goods have perished" otherwise than in accordance with Sect. 7. Yet if this is so there is no room at all for the application of the second half of Sect. 2 (5) (c) of the Frustrated Contracts Act. Moreover, even if, contrary to the above contention, a contract may be frustrated in such circumstances, it is still not easy to understand the object of this clause. Three cases may be considered.

Firstly, where there is a contract for the sale of specific goods in which the property and the risk have both passed to the buyer. Even if such a contract could be frustrated by the perishing of the goods, which seems highly improbable, the Frustrated Contracts Act does not apply. It may be that this was intended to avoid any possible doubt that in such an event the buyer is still liable to pay the whole price and cannot ask the court for any relief under the Act of 1943.

Secondly, where there is a contract for the sale of specific goods in which the property has not yet passed, but in which the risk has passed to the buyer. Once again it seems inconceivable that such a contract could be frustrated at all, because this would render meaningless the statement that the risk is on the buyer, but if such a contract can be frustrated the Act does not apply. The intention here may have been to avoid all difficulty in c.i.f. contracts should the goods perish after the risk has passed but before the bill of lading is transferred. In this event the buyer is still bound to pay the whole price and cannot invoke the Act of 1943.

Thirdly, where the property has passed but the goods are still at the seller's risk. If such a contract is frustrated by the perishing of the goods, which again seems unlikely, the Frustrated Contracts Act does not apply. Presumably this is to avoid any doubt that the seller must bear the whole loss and cannot transfer any of it to the buyer.

In considering the cases to which the Frustrated Contracts Act does not apply, therefore, it may be permissible to concentrate on cases under Sect. 7 of the Sale of Goods Act, that is to say where there is a sale[1] of specific goods in which neither property nor risk has passed to the buyer, and the contract is frustrated by the perishing of the goods. To such a case the ordinary common law rules of frustration apply. The most important of these are as follows—

1. In the first place both parties are discharged from all obligations not yet accrued before the destruction of the goods. In other words, the seller is not liable for non-delivery of the goods, and the buyer is not liable for non-payment of the price.

2. Secondly, if the price, or any part of it, has been paid it can be recovered if there is a total failure of consideration. This was the law even before the decision in the *Fibrosa* case[2] because the rule in *Chandler* v. *Webster*,[3] which was overruled in that case, was never applied to contracts for the sale of goods.[4]

3. If there is a total failure of consideration and the buyer can recover the price, the seller is not entitled to set off anything for expenses which he may have incurred before the frustrating event. For example, suppose that A agrees to buy some goods from B and pays the price, or part of it in advance, but B is to do something to the goods to put them into a deliverable state. Suppose further, that the goods are accidentally destroyed after B has done some of the work. This is a case to which Sect. 18, Rule 2, applies, and therefore prima facie the property and the risk do not pass until the work is completed and the buyer has notice thereof. The case, therefore, falls within the clear wording of Sect. 7 of the Sale of Goods Act, and the Frustrated Contracts Act does not apply. The common law rule therefore enables the buyer to recover the whole amount which he has paid in advance, and the seller is not entitled to retain any of it on account of the expenses incurred. It is difficult to see why this should be so, for as a matter of justice there seems no material distinction between such a case, and the *Fibrosa* case[5] to which the Frustrated Contracts Act clearly would apply. Moreover, the arbitrary results of Sect. 2 (5) (c) of the Frustrated Contracts Act are brought out all the more when it is remembered that Sect. 7 of the Sale of Goods Act only deals with frustration through perishing of the goods. If the contract is frustrated by some other event, e.g. the outbreak of war or the like, Sect. 7 has no application, and the Frustrated Contracts Act can be invoked. It is submitted that this is quite unjustifiable, and it is hard to see why Sect. 2 (5) (c) of the Act of 1943 was thought necessary at all, especially as the workings of the Act are left to the discretion of the court.

4. The fourth rule at common law is that payments made under a contract which is subsequently frustrated cannot be recovered if there

---

[1] It must also be remembered that, if the contract is one for skill and labour, or exchange, or hire-purchase, the Frustrated Contracts Act can always apply.
[2] [1943] A.C. 32.   [3] [1904] 1 K.B. 493.
[4] *Logan* v *Le Mesurier* (1847), 6 Moo. P.C.C. 116.
[5] [1943] A.C. 32.

is only a partial failure of consideration. Suppose, for example, A agrees to buy a specific parcel of 100 tons of wheat now in a warehouse, the price to be paid in advance, but the goods to remain the property of the seller, B, until delivery, and delivery to be by instalments of 10 tons each. One instalment is delivered, and the rest of the wheat is then accidentally destroyed by fire. Prima facie the risk remains with the seller until the property has passed, so that this is a case within Sect. 7 of the Sale of Goods Act. The question whether the goods have perished within the meaning of that section probably depends upon the construction of the contract. Prima facie it would appear that the destruction of the undelivered part of the goods avoids the whole contract. To this case the Frustrated Contracts Act does not apply, and the position at common law remains. These common law rules, however, are by no means easy to apply to a case of this kind. At first sight it might be thought that nothing can be recovered because there is only a partial failure of consideration, but in fact it is submitted that the buyer can recover the amount of the price which is to be attributed to the goods which have perished. The reason for this is that the risk in respect of those goods was on the seller when they perished. The same result will follow if the buyer has not paid the price in advance.

In these cases, therefore, the Frustrated Contracts Act is not needed and does not apply, because the common law can achieve a satisfactory result through the rules as to risk. Yet, illogically, if the contract is frustrated by some event other than the perishing of the goods, the Frustrated Contracts Act does apply.

5. Finally, the usual common law rule is that if a contract is frustrated it is not possible to compel one party to pay for a benefit received where the contract was to perform one indivisible thing, and nothing has been paid in advance. So that if one party has partly performed his contract and finds that he cannot complete it as a result of frustration he is not entitled at common law to any part of the agreed price.[1]

But although this is the general rule at common law, it can hardly be applied without qualification to contracts of sale of goods. Even if the party who has received the benefit before the frustrating event cannot be made to pay for that benefit under the contract, he may be sued upon an implied new contract which arises from his acceptance of the benefit, and his refusal to disgorge it. So, for example, if part of the goods under a contract of sale have been delivered, and then frustration prevents the seller from delivering the remainder, the buyer may be liable on a new implied promise to pay for the goods delivered, which arises from his refusal to return the goods. But it seems to be established law that the new promise must be capable of

---

[1] *Cutter* v. *Powell* (1795), 6 T.R. 320; *Appleby* v. *Myers* (1867), L.R. 2 C.P. 651.

being implied in fact.[1] If, therefore, the buyer still has the goods in his possession when the contract is frustrated, no doubt such a new promise can be implied, but if he has already disposed of them it appears that he cannot be made liable to pay a proportionate part of the price for them.[2] This seems a harsh and unreasonable result which could be mitigated by development of restitutionary remedies. Once again, the position is different under the Frustrated Contracts Act, and it is hard to see why sales of specific goods should be distinguished from sales of unascertained goods, nor is it easy to see why the result should differ according to the nature of the frustrating event. Yet such is the effect of Sect. 2 (5) (c) of the Frustrated Contracts Act, 1943.

(ii) Cases to which the Frustrated Contracts Act does apply

The Frustrated Contracts Act applies *inter alia* to all contracts for the sale of unascertained goods, and to contracts for the sale of specific goods which are frustrated by some event other than the perishing of the goods. The Act effects three main changes in the law.

1. Firstly, it enables a person to recover any payments made under a contract which has since been frustrated even though there has only been a partial failure of consideration. This is the effect of Sect. 1 (2) of the Frustrated Contracts Act—

> All sums paid or payable to any party in pursuance of the contract before the time when the parties were so discharged . . . shall, in the case of sums so paid, be recoverable from him as money received by him for the use of the party by whom the sums were paid, and, in the case of sums so payable, cease to be so payable:

So, for example, if a person agrees to buy 1,000 tons of wheat, payment in advance and delivery by instalments, and the contract is frustrated after only one instalment is delivered, this subsection applies. The payee is therefore bound to repay the price paid in advance even though there is no total failure of consideration. The same result could be reached by applying Sect. 2 (4) of the Act of 1943—

> Where it appears to the Court that a part of any contract to which this Act applies can properly be severed from the remainder of the contract, being a part wholly performed before the time of discharge, or so performed except for the payment in respect of that part of the contract of sums which are or can be ascertained under the contract, the Court shall treat that part of the contract as if it were a separate contract and had not been frustrated and shall treat the foregoing section of this Act as only applicable to the remainder of that contract.

[1] *Sumpter* v. *Hedges*, [1898] 1 Q.B. 673.
[2] Sect. 30 (1) (p. 67, *ante*), it is submitted, has no application to such a case, because it postulates circumstances in which the delivery of only part of the goods is a breach of contract, and in which the buyer may reject that part at once. The case put here is one in which the delivery of part of the goods is not a breach of contract and the buyer cannot therefore reject them when delivered.

By severing the executed from the frustrated part of the contract, the court can in effect turn a partial failure of consideration in respect of the whole contract, into a total failure of consideration in respect of the frustrated part, and in this way enable the payer to recover his payment.

2. The second main change made by the Act is to enable the payee to retain part or all of a sum which would otherwise be recoverable as on a total (or now, a partial) failure of consideration, if he has incurred expenses in or for the purpose of the performance of the contract. Thus Sect. 1 (2) continues—

> Provided that, if the party to whom the sums were so paid or payable incurred expenses before the time of discharge in, or for the purpose of, the performance of the contract, the Court may, if it considers it just to do so having regard to all the circumstances of the case, allow him to retain or, as the case may be, recover the whole or any part of the sums so paid or payable, not being an amount in excess of the expenses so incurred.

The Act leaves the whole question to the discretion of the court, and the probable consequence of this is that the payee will not be allowed to retain a sum equivalent to the whole of the expenses which he has incurred. The object of the Act was to avoid the injustices which followed at common law of throwing the whole loss on to one party or the other, and it is not likely that the Act merely contemplated shifting this loss from one party to the other. Probably, therefore, the court would, in a suitable case, divide the loss between the two parties, and permit the payer to recover accordingly.

3. The third main change in the law effected by the Act is the creation of a special exception to the rule commonly known as the rule in *Cutter* v. *Powell*.[1] This case laid down that, where there is a contract to perform a complete action, and nothing is payable in advance, no part of the agreed amount can be recovered if the contract is not completely performed as a result of frustration or any other cause. The position is now regulated by Sect. 1 (3) of the Frustrated Contracts Act—

> Where any party to the contract has, by reason of anything done by any other party thereto in, or for the purpose of, the performance of the contract, obtained a valuable benefit (other than a payment of money to which the last foregoing subsection applies) before the time of discharge, there shall be recoverable from him by the said other party such sum (if any), not exceeding the value of the said benefit to the party obtaining it, as the Court considers just, having regard to all the circumstances of the case . . .

Thus where part only of the goods has been delivered, and the contract is then frustrated, we have seen that at common law the seller

---

[1] (1795), 6 T.R. 320.

may be unable to recover anything if the circumstances are such that it is not possible to imply a new promise to pay. Where the Frustrated Contracts Act applies, however, Sect. 1 (3) thus enables the court to compel the buyer to pay for the part which he has received although it would not have been possible to imply the existence of a promise to pay at common law.

Despite the fact that the Frustrated Contracts Act was passed to mitigate the harshness of the common law rules, it still leaves a substantial area for their operation. The Act only alters the common law where something has been paid in advance, or where one party has received a valuable benefit under the contract before the frustrating event. But in contracts for the sale of goods to be manufactured by the seller there is rarely any benefit obtained before the contract is fully executed, so the Frustrated Contracts Act does nothing unless there has been some prepayment. Suppose, for example, A orders machinery from B, nothing to be paid until delivery. After B has incurred considerable expense in the construction of the machinery the contract is frustrated by the outbreak of war or the like. Although this is not a case within Sect. 7 of the Sale of Goods Act, and the Frustrated Contracts Act could apply, it provides no remedy to the seller. Yet surely his position is no less meritorious because he has not insisted on being paid in advance. The same result follows where there is a payment in advance, but the seller has incurred expense in excess of this amount.[1] If, for example, in the *Fibrosa* case[2] the sellers had spent well over £1,000 on the machinery before the frustrating event, they would not, even under the Frustrated Contracts Act, have been able to recover anything from the buyers over and above the amount of the advance payment. Here again, therefore, the seller's rights depend on the purely fortuitous question of how much has been paid in advance.[3]

It is submitted, therefore, that although the Frustrated Contracts Act is a very valuable measure of reform, it still leaves much to be desired. In particular it is submitted that Sect. 2 (5) (c) could safely be repealed, and provision should be made for the case where the seller has incurred expenditure before the frustrating event, but where nothing has been paid in advance, and where the buyer has had no valuable benefit.

It is, however, possible that the whole question is a somewhat

[1] Unless the seller has incurred expense at least twice as great as the prepayment the problem will probably not arise, because, as has been submitted, the court would probably divide the loss, and not permit the seller to throw the whole of it on to the buyer.

[2] [1943] A.C. 32.

[3] But if the sum is *payable* before the frustrating event the mere fact that it has not been *paid* will not deprive the payee of his right to sue, subject to appropriate deductions, of course.

academic one. The strangest aspect of the law relating to the Frustrated Contracts Act is that there is still no reported case in which it has been applied. The reason for this is not entirely clear, but it is possible that businessmen are less attracted than lawyers by the justice of dividing a loss between the contracting parties.

CHAPTER 19

TRANSFER OF TITLE BY A NON-OWNER

NEMO DAT QUOD NON HABET

THE second half of Part II of the Act is entitled "Transfer of Title," and it deals with those cases in which a seller with no right to the goods may nonetheless pass a good title to a third party. In most of these cases the question which arises is which of two innocent people is to suffer for the fraud of a third. A thief steals goods and sells them to someone who buys in good faith and for value; a person hands goods to an agent to obtain offers and the agent sells them without authority and disposes of the proceeds; a swindler buys goods, induces the seller to let him have them on credit, and promptly resells or pledges them for whatever he can get; a person sells goods, but retains possession of them and fraudulently resells them to a third party. In all these cases the law has to choose between rigorously upholding the rights of the owner to his property on the one hand, and protecting the interests of the purchaser who buys in good faith and for value on the other hand.

> In the development of our law, two principles have striven for mastery. The first is for the protection of property: no one can give a better title than he himself possesses. The second is for the protection of commercial transactions: the person who takes in good faith and for value without notice should get a better title. The first principle has held sway for a long time, but it has been modified by the common law itself and by statute so as to meet the needs of our times.[1]

The first of these principles is of course still the general rule, and is affirmed by the Act in Sect. 21 (1):

> Subject to the provisions of this Act, where goods are sold by a person who is not the owner thereof, and who does not sell them under the authority or with the consent of the owner, the buyer acquires no better title to the goods than the seller had, unless the owner of the goods is by his conduct precluded from denying the seller's authority to sell.

This rule is frequently dignified by the use of Latin in the tag, *nemo dat quod non habet*, or more shortly, *nemo dat*. It may be that the words "where goods are sold" must be given their strict significance and do not cover cases of an agreement to sell. So where a car dealer agreed to sell a car to which he had no title, but before the car was delivered he had

---

[1] *Bishopsgate Motor Finance Corpn.* v. *Transport Brakes, Ltd.,* [1949] 1 K.B. 332, 336-7, *per* Denning, L.J.

obtained title, it was held that Sect. 21 (1) did not apply.[1] The original agreement was not a sale but only an agreement to sell.

Where the goods are sold with the express authority of the owner the ordinary rules of principal and agent apply and no special difficulty arises. But Sect. 21 (1) also refers to the "consent" of the owner, and reference should also be made to Sect. 47—

> Subject to the provisions of this Act, the unpaid seller's right of lien . . . or stoppage *in transitu* is not affected by any sale, or other disposition of the goods which the buyer may have made, unless the seller has assented thereto.

If, therefore, the buyer, not being in possession, resells the goods and the seller assents to such sale, the sub-buyer obtains a good title free from the first seller's lien or right of stoppage *in transitu*. The effect of such assent on the part of the seller is very similar to that of estoppel, but the difference seems to be that whereas estoppel can only operate if the assent is communicated to the sub-buyer, the seller may assent to the resale within the meaning of Sect. 47 even though he only communicates his assent to the buyer. But the mere fact that the seller has been informed of a resale and has not objected thereto does not amount to an assent within Sect. 47. In *Mordaunt Bros.* v. *British Oil & Cake Mills, Ltd.*,[2] the defendants sold oil to X who resold part of it to the plaintiffs and gave them delivery orders in respect of that part. The plaintiffs paid X for the oil and sent the delivery orders to the defendants who accepted them without comment. The defendants delivered instalments of the oil direct to the plaintiffs as and when they were paid by X, but on X's falling into arrears with the payments, they refused to deliver any more. Pickford, J., held that the defendants had not assented to the resale within Sect. 47. "In my opinion," he said,[3] "the assent which affects the unpaid seller's right of lien must be such an assent as in the circumstances shews that the seller intends to renounce his rights against the goods. It is not enough to shew that the fact of a sub-contract has been brought to his notice and that he has assented to it merely in the sense of acknowledging receipt of the information."[4]

On the other hand in *D. F. Mount, Ltd.* v. *Jay & Jay Co., Ltd.*[5] Salmon, J., came to a different conclusion on the following facts. The

---

[1] *Anderson* v. *Ryan*, [1967] I.R. 34. But it seems that, even if the seller had purported to sell the car before he had obtained title, his subsequent acquisition of the title would have gone to "feed" the contract—see above, p. 51.

[2] [1910] 2 K.B. 502.   [3] At p. 507.

[4] The case might well be different if the goods were specific because in that case the acceptance of the delivery order would have been an attornment which would have passed property, but no property can pass in unascertained goods. Cf. *Laurie & Morewood* v. *John Dudin & Sons*, [1926] 1 K.B. 223. And if the delivery order was a document of title the result would be different: *Ant. Jurgens Margarinefabrieken* v. *Louis Dreyfus & Co.*, [1914] 3 K.B. 40.

[5] [1960] 1 Q.B. 159.

defendants were owners of 500 cartons of tinned peaches lying at the wharf of D. The defendants were approached by M at a time when the market was falling, and M told them that he had a customer for 250 cartons. He made it clear that he, M, would pay the defendants out of the price he obtained from the sub-purchaser. The defendants agreed to sell the cartons to M and gave him a delivery order. M sent the order to D who received it without acknowledgement. Later M sold the cartons to the plaintiffs who paid M. The defendants, never having received the price from M, subsequently claimed to be still entitled to the cartons. Salmon, J., held that the defendants had assented to the sale within the meaning of Sect. 47—

> In the present case the defendants were anxious to get rid of the goods on a falling market. They knew that M could only pay for them out of the money he obtained from his customers, and that he could only obtain the money from his customers against delivery orders in favour of those customers. In my view the true inference is that the defendants assented to M reselling the goods, in the sense that they intended to renounce their rights against the goods and to take the risk of M's honesty.[1]

The maxim *nemo dat* has a wider application than Sect. 21 of the Sale of Goods Act, because the latter only applies to a sale of goods by a non-owner, while the maxim also covers those cases where an owner sells goods, but is unable to sell them free from some encumbrance or charge existing in favour of a third party. In point of fact this is an unusual situation for the law generally sets its face against the recognition of encumbrances which run with chattels into the hands of third parties,[2] and of course equitable rights are always subject to those of a purchaser for value in good faith without notice. There is one not uncommon situation, however, where the law does recognise such encumbrances as binding on third parties. Where a person pledges goods, or the documents of title to goods, and subsequently the pledgee returns the goods or the documents to the pledgor for a limited purpose, for example, to obtain clearance of the goods from the warehouseman, any unauthorised disposition by the pledgor will not prejudice the rights of the pledgee.[3] In other words, the seller, although owner of the goods, cannot sell them free from the pledgee's right. It may be that technically, this result depends upon the pledgee's retention of possession, but since the courts are prepared to hold that the return of the custody of the goods or documents of title does not transfer possession back to the pledgor, this is not much consolation to the innocent third party. It might well be

[1] At p. 167.

[2] *McGruther* v. *Pitcher*, [1904] 2 Ch. 306; *Dunlop Pneumatic Tyre Co., Ltd.* v. *Selfridge & Co., Ltd.*, [1915] A.C. 847.

[3] *N.W. Bank* v. *Poynter*, [1895] A.C. 56; *Reeves* v. *Capper* (1838), 5 Bing. N.C. 136; *Official Assignee of Madras* v. *Mercantile Bank of India, Ltd.*, [1935] A.C. 53; *Mercantile Bank of India, Ltd.* v. *Central Bank of India, Ltd.*, [1938] A.C. 287.

thought that the extension of the rule *nemo dat* to these cases is unjustifiable, for it seems extraordinary that an owner who is in actual possession of his goods with the consent of the pledgee, cannot transfer a good title free from the pledge to an innocent third party. The hardship on the third party who buys goods from the admitted owner in actual possession is so obvious as to need no stressing. At all events there are two limitations on the rule *nemo dat* in this connection.

In the first place, if the pledgee returns the goods to the pledgor with authority to sell them, an innocent buyer from the pledgor obtains a good title free from the pledge, even though the pledgor fraudulently absconds with the purchase money.[1] And in the second place, if the pledgor is a mercantile agent, the return of the goods to him by the pledgee will enable the third party to plead that the pledgor was in possession of them with the consent of the owner and consequently that he is protected by Sect. 2 (1) of the Factors Act, 1889.[2]

As the opening words of Sect. 21 indicate there are a number of exceptions to the general rule *nemo dat*, which are of considerable importance, though they do not, of course, swamp the main rule itself, at any rate so far as the sale of goods is concerned.

ESTOPPEL

The first exception is provided by the doctrine of estoppel, which is embodied, in this connection, in the concluding words of Sect. 21 (1) itself, which may be repeated here—

. . . unless the owner of the goods is by his conduct precluded from denying the seller's authority to sell.

This provision merely throws us back on the common law doctrine of estoppel for it gives no indication when the owner is by his conduct precluded from denying the seller's authority to sell. It seems that there are two distinct cases where the owner is so precluded. The first is where he has by his words or conduct represented to the buyer that the seller is the true owner, or has the owner's authority to sell, and the second is where the owner, by his negligent failure to act allows the seller to appear as the owner, or as having the owner's authority to sell. These are generally called estoppel by representation and estoppel by negligence respectively. The terminology of the subject is, however, somewhat confusing. On the one hand, estoppel by representation is sometimes sub-divided into estoppel by words and estoppel by conduct, while the wording of the Act suggests that estoppel by words is merely a species of estoppel by conduct. On the other hand there is also much

---

[1] *Babcock* v. *Lawson* (1880), 5 Q.B.D. 284.
[2] *Lloyds Bank* v. *Bank of America*, [1938] 2 K.B. 147. On the Factors Act, see p. 193, *post*.

controversy about the propriety of the term "estoppel by negligence". Strictly speaking it seems there is no such thing as estoppel by negligence.[1] All these estoppels rest in the last resort on a representation of some kind. A person may make a representation by words or by conduct, but how does a person make a representation by negligence? The answer appears to be that this is really a representation through an omission to correct a misrepresentation made by a third party. Thus if A stands by while B makes a representation to C which A knows to be incorrect, A may be said, loosely, to be guilty of misrepresentation by negligence. In truth what has happened is that A, by his negligence, has allowed B to mislead C by a misrepresentation. Thus, the correct approach is that this kind of estoppel rests in every case on a representation. The representation may be (1) by words, or (2) by conduct, or (3) by a negligent omission. Although the point is not free from doubt it seems that in the first two cases it is unnecessary to show fraud or an intent to deceive or negligence as a foundation for the estoppel.[2] The only requirements are those common to all estoppels, viz., that the representation must be one of fact, that it must be unambiguous and that it must be acted upon. In the third class of case, however, it seems that negligence, in the sense of a breach of a duty of care (or of course, fraud) must be proved.

Estoppel by words

A good example of estoppel by words is the decision of the Court of Appeal in *Henderson & Co.* v. *Williams*.[3] G & Co. were induced by the fraud of one, F, to sell him goods lying in certain warehouses of which the defendants were warehousemen. The circumstances were such that the contract between G & Co. and F was void for mistake. On the instructions of G & Co. the defendants transferred the goods in their books to the order of F. F sold the goods to the plaintiffs, who being suspicious of the bona fides of the seller, made inquiries of the defendants. The latter supplied the plaintiffs with a written statement that they held the goods to the order of F, and when this did not satisfy them, they endorsed it with a further statement, that they now held the goods to the plaintiffs' order. G & Co., not having been paid by F, instructed the defendants not to deliver the goods to the plaintiffs, but to themselves, and they gave them an indemnity against so doing. It was held that both G & Co. and the defendants were estopped

---

[1] See *Saunders* v. *Anglia Building Society*, [1971] A.C. 1004 at p. 1038 *per* Lord Pearson, and the author's article in 9 *Alberta Law Rev.* (1971), 347.

[2] A good example of the confusion in this branch of the law is provided by *Seton, Laing & Co.* v. *Lafone* (1887) 19 Q.B.D. 68 where the whole discussion was in terms of estoppel by negligence and yet the only representation was that of the defendant himself. This was a simple example of estoppel by representation and negligence ought not to have been relevant. (In the last edition I was misled into treating the case as an example of estoppel by negligence.)

[3] [1895] 1 Q.B. 521.

from denying the plaintiffs' right to the goods, the former because they had represented that F was the owner by ordering the defendants to transfer the goods into his name in their books, and the latter because they had attorned to the plaintiffs, i.e. represented to them that they held the goods to their order.[1]

Estoppel by conduct

An early leading case is *Farquharson Bros.* v. *J. King & Co., Ltd.*[2] The plaintiffs were timber merchants who owned timber housed with a dock company. The plaintiffs' clerk had authority to send delivery orders to the dock company, and the latter were instructed to act on the clerk's delivery orders, but the clerk had no authority to sell the timber himself. The clerk fraudulently transferred some of the timber to himself under an assumed name, and gave the dock company instructions accordingly. He then sold the timber to the defendants under his assumed name, and instructed the dock company to deliver the goods to their order. The plaintiffs, having discovered the clerk's fraud, brought an action for conversion. The House of Lords held that the defence of estoppel failed because the defendants had not acted on any representation made by the plaintiffs concerning the authority of the clerk. Even the dock company would not have needed, or been able to plead estoppel. As Lord Halsbury pointed out they would not have been liable simply because they had done nothing more than obey their principal's instructions. Despite the vigorous judgments of Lord Halsbury[3] and Lord Macnaghten in this case, and the expressions of astonishment that the defence should ever have been set up, let alone accepted (as it was, by the Court of Appeal) it is by no means easy to lay down what sort of conduct is sufficient to invoke the doctrine of estoppel. One thing, at any rate, is clear, that merely allowing another person to have possession of goods which he does not own is not by itself enough to bring into operation the doctrine of estoppel. There are so many different circumstances in which an owner of goods may allow another to have possession of them, that it cannot be claimed that such conduct amounts to an unambiguous representation that the party in possession is the owner or has the owner's authority to sell. Although the Privy Council accepted a proposition of almost this width in *Commonwealth Trust, Ltd.* v. *Akotey*[4] this case was virtually overruled by the Privy Council

---

[1] The position of the warehouseman in this sort of case is unenviable, for if he had delivered the goods to the plaintiffs he would have been liable to G & Co. for disobeying their instructions: *Rogers* v. *Lambert*, [1891] 1 Q.B. 318. His proper course is to take interpleader proceedings.

[2] [1902] A.C. 325.

[3] Lord Halsbury's judgment was a little too vigorous for he thought the clerk was guilty of larceny: see the note by Pollock, [1902] A.C. at p. 329.

[4] [1926] A.C. 72.

itself in *Mercantile Bank of India, Ltd.* v. *Central Bank of India, Ltd.*[1] In the latter case X pledged railway receipts, which in this case were documents of title, with the Central Bank in return for an advance. In accordance with the usual practice the Bank then returned them to X to enable him to obtain clearance of the goods, but X fraudulently pledged them with the Mercantile Bank in return for an advance from them. It was held that there was no estoppel because the possession of the railway receipts "no more conveyed a representation that the merchants (X) were entitled to dispose of the property than the actual possession of the goods themselves would have done."[2] If estoppel by conduct is to be invoked there must be some act which positively misleads the third party beyond merely allowing a non-owner to have possession of the goods.[3]

In *Central Newbury Car Auctions, Ltd.* v. *Unity Finance, Ltd.*[4] a swindler called on the plaintiffs and offered to buy a Morris car on hire-purchase terms, leaving with the plaintiffs in part exchange a Hillman car which, as it transpired, was also let on hire-purchase. The swindler signed hire-purchase forms whereby the Morris was to be sold to a finance company and then let to him, and he was thereupon given the registration book and permitted to drive the Morris away. The finance company refused the hire-purchase proposal, and the car was later discovered in the possession of the defendants, who had bought it in good faith from an unknown person, who was presumed to be the swindler. The Court of Appeal (Denning, L.J., dissenting) held that there was no estoppel, and that the plaintiffs were entitled to recover the car. The registration book of a car is not a document of title[5] and in fact it contains a warning that the person in whose name the car is registered may or may not be the owner. Hence it was not possible to say that the plaintiffs had in any way represented the swindler to be the owner, or to have the owner's authority to sell. The case for invoking estoppel was based entirely on the fact that the owner had entrusted possession of the goods to another party; and this (as we have seen) is normally insufficient to raise an estoppel.

On the other hand, in *Eastern Distributors, Ltd.* v. *Goldring,*[6] where, in pursuance of a plan to deceive a finance company, one M signed and delivered forms to C which enabled C to represent that he had M's authority to sell a car belonging to him, it was held by the Court of Appeal that M was estopped from setting up his title against the plaintiffs who had bought the car from C. It was also held that the estoppel in fact operated to pass a good title to the plaintiffs not only against M

---

[1] [1938] A.C. 287. But Denning, L.J., in *Central Newbury Car Auctions, Ltd.* v. *Unity Finance, Ltd.,* [1957] 1 Q.B. 371, seemed to think that it was rightly decided.
[2] At 303, *per* Lord Wright. [3] *Jerome* v. *Bentley,* [1952] 2 All E.R.114.
[4] [1957] 1 Q.B. 371.
[5] *Joblin* v. *Watkin & Roseveare (Motors), Ltd.* (1948), 64 T.L.R. 464.
[6] [1957] 2 Q.B. 600.

himself, but also against a buyer in good faith from M. It is, however, not entirely clear why the case was not disposed of on the simpler ground that C had M's apparent authority to sell, although in fact he exceeded that authority.[1]

So also, if the owner of goods entrusts the possession of them to a dealer with authority to sell, or to obtain offers or something of that kind, the owner would normally be estopped if the dealer sold without authority, or in excess of his authority. But this form of estoppel is now of little practical importance because it has been largely overtaken by the statutory protection conferred on innocent purchasers by the Factors Act, 1889.[2]

Ostensible Ownership and Ostensible Agency

There is an important distinction between a representation (or conduct equivalent to a representation) that the seller has authority to sell the goods as agent, on the one hand, and a representation that the seller is himself the owner, on the other hand. Where the true owner represents or enables the seller to represent himself as owner, and knows that the seller will or may sell as an owner, it is immaterial that the seller sells outside the ordinary course of business unless this demonstrates lack of good faith on the buyer's part. In *Lloyds and Scottish Finance Ltd.* v. *Williamson*[3] the plaintiff entrusted his car to a dealer and authorised him to sell at or above a certain price. The dealer sold the car above this price but the price was not paid in cash but set-off against a debt owed by the dealer to a friend of the buyer. For this reason the sale was outside the ordinary course of business but it was held that this was immaterial. Since the owner knew that the seller might very well sell as a principal and not as an agent and had authorised him to do so, it made no difference how he sold the goods.

But if the case is one of ostensible agency the position is different. For it is reasonably implicit that an agent is only authorised to sell in the ordinary course of business and if he does not do so there will be no estoppel. Ostensible agency may arise in one of two ways; it may arise where the owner authorises an agent to sell as agent only, or it may arise where the buyer knows that the agent is not himself the owner and acts on the assumption that he is an agent only. This latter possibility is illustrated by *Motor Credits (Hire Finance) Ltd.* v. *Pacific Motor Auctions Pty., Ltd.*[4] In this case M Ltd., who were dealers in vehicles, sold a number of vehicles to the plaintiffs under a "display agreement" whereby M Ltd. remained in possession of the cars for display in their showrooms. They were paid 90 per cent of the price and were authorised to sell the vehicles as agents for the plaintiffs. M Ltd. got into financial difficulties and the plaintiffs revoked their

---

[1] See *per* Devlin, L.J., at p. 606.   [2] See below, p. 193.
[3] [1965] 1 W.L.R. 404.   [4] (1963), 109 C.L.R. 87.

authority to sell the vehicles, but M Ltd. nevertheless sold a number of them to the defendants who were bona fide purchasers for value. The sale was outside the ordinary course of business partly because it took place after business hours and partly because the defendants agreed to sell the cars back to M Ltd. in certain events (in fact it is clear that the defendants really wanted the vehicles as security for pre-existing debts owed to them). The defendants knew all about the display plan agreement and could not therefore have supposed that M Ltd. were owners though they did suppose M Ltd. to have authority to sell. On these facts the Australian High Court held that the defendants were not protected; as this was a case of ostensible agency and not ostensible ownership the defendants would only have been protected if the sale had been in the ordinary course of business. This decision was reversed on appeal to the Privy Council,[1] without consideration of this point, on the ground that the defendants were protected by Sect. 25 (1) of the Act. This aspect of the case is considered later.[2]

Estoppel by Negligence

As we have already seen, estoppel by negligence may be established where the owner of goods has, by his negligence, allowed a third party to represent himself as owner or as having the owner's authority to sell. But the application of the principle of estoppel by negligence is severely restricted by the fact that, as in the law of tort, there can be no negligence unless there is a duty to take care. It is for this reason, that—

> If I lose a valuable dog and find it afterwards in the possession of a gentleman who bought it from somebody whom he believed to be the owner, it is no answer to me to say that he would never have been cheated into buying the dog if I had chained it up or put a collar on it, or kept it under proper control. If a person leaves a watch or a ring on a seat in the park or on a table at a café and it ultimately gets into the hands of a bona fide purchaser, it is no answer to the true owner to say that it was his carelessness and nothing else that enabled the finder to pass it off as his own.[3]

Since there is no duty of care on an owner of property to see that it does not get lost or stolen it is comparatively rare to find a clear case of estoppel by negligence in this connection. The dictum of Ashurst, J., in *Lickbarrow* v. *Mason*[4] which is frequently quoted in this connection by despairing counsel, that "wherever one of two innocent persons must suffer by the acts of a third, he who has enabled such third person to occasion the loss must sustain it," has been more

---

[1] [1965] A.C. 867. [2] *Post*, p. 203.
[3] *Farquharson Bros.* v. *C. King & Co., Ltd., per* Lord Macnaghten, [1902] A.C. at 335-6. [4] (1787), 2 T.R. 63.

qualified than any other case in the books, and has been dissented from more often than it has been followed.[1]

The necessity for establishing a duty of care often precludes the operation of the doctrine of estoppel in those cases where an owner is induced to part with goods to a buyer under a contract void for "mistake." In those cases the owner can claim the goods even from a bona fide purchaser from the fraudulent buyer, and it is no defence to say that it was the owner's negligence, however gross, which enabled the buyer to obtain the goods unless a duty to take care can be established.[2] Similarly just as entrusting goods to another has been held not to amount to a representation that he is the owner or has authority to sell, so also if that party represents himself to be owner or to have authority to sell, the owner will not normally be defeated by the plea of estoppel by negligence. Once again the reason given is that there is no duty of care on the owner of goods to protect the possible interests of third parties.[3] On the other hand estoppel by negligence was applied in *Coventry Shepherd & Co.* v. *Great Eastern Rly. Co.*[4] where the defendants negligently issued two delivery orders relating to the same load of goods. The person to whom they were issued was thereby able to represent to the plaintiffs (to whom he pledged the goods) that the goods were in fact available.

A more recent case where a duty to take care was established, although on the facts it was held not to be broken, is *Mercantile Credit Co., Ltd.* v. *Hamblin*[5] in which the facts were these. The defendant wished to borrow some money on the security of her car. She consulted a dealer who was apparently solvent and respectable and he gave her some hire-purchase forms to sign in blank. She signed the forms thinking they were some sort of mortgage transaction, but retained possession of her car throughout. The dealer told her that he would find out what sum he could arrange for her to raise and would let her know. He also gave her a blank cheque which she was to fill in for the agreed figure on the scheme being completed. In fact the dealer completed the hire-purchase forms so as to constitute an offer by himself to sell the car to the plaintiffs, a finance company, and an offer by the defendant to take the car on hire-purchase terms from the plaintiffs. Without further reference to the defendant he sent the forms to the plaintiffs who purported to accept both offers. The defendant repudiated the alleged agreement and it was held by the Court of Appeal that

---

[1] See, e.g., *Farquharson Bros.* v. *C. King & Co.* at p. 342, *per* Lord Lindley, "Such a doctrine is far too wide"; *London Joint Stock Bank* v. *MacMillan*, [1918] A.C. 777, at p. 836, *per* Lord Parmoor; *Jones* v. *Waring & Gillow, Ltd.*, [1926] A.C. 670, at p. 693, *per* Lord Sumner; *Wilson & Meeson* v. *Pickering*, [1946] 1 K.B. 422, at p. 425, *per* Lord Greene.

[2] See, e.g., *Cundy* v. *Lindsay* (1878), 3 App. Cas. 459; *Ingram* v. *Little*, [1961] 1 Q.B. 31.

[3] See the *Mercantile Bank of India* case [1938] A.C. 287, *ante*, p. 187.

[4] [1883], 11 Q.B.D. 776.   [5] [1965] 2 Q.B. 242.

she was not bound by it because she had not in fact authorised the dealer to make any offer to the plaintiffs and was not estopped from denying that she had done so. Although the Court held that the defendant did owe a duty of care sufficient to raise an estoppel they held that she had not in fact failed to take care. In the particular circumstances of the case it was not unreasonable for her to have trusted the dealer.

The importance of the case lies in the fact that the Court treated the existence and the nature of the duty to take care in such circumstances as the same as those which arise in the ordinary law of negligence. Thus, Pearson, L.J., found a "sufficient relationship or proximity" between the defendant and the plaintiffs from the fact that the defendant intended that the documents which she signed should constitute an offer to contract subject to certain conditions being fulfilled, and that she had entrusted the documents to the dealer and was thereby arming him with "the means to make a contract ostensibly on her behalf."[1]

It should finally be added that if estoppel does operate it will do so whether the transaction is a sale, pledge or other disposition, but that it will not bind anyone who does not claim under the person estopped. A person claiming under title paramount cannot be bound by an estoppel to which he was not privy.

Somewhat akin to the doctrine of estoppel in this connection are cases in which a person who sells goods without title subsequently acquires the title, e.g. by paying off the true owner. In such circumstances it has been suggested[2] that the seller's subsequent acquisition of title "goes to feed" the defective title of the buyer and any person deriving title through the buyer. This concept has not, however, been fully worked out and may give rise to some interesting questions, e.g.: Can a title be acquired and "fed" in goods which have already been consumed?

Relationship between Estoppel and Other Principles

It will be apparent that the doctrine of estoppel is closely connected with other legal principles. The ostensible authority of an agent to transfer the title of goods in excess of his actual authority is based on principles similar to, if not identical with, those in the doctrine of estoppel. It must be admitted that legal theory in these areas is in a state of some confusion and it is not always easy to understand the basis for a decision. Estoppel, in particular, sometimes appears to be invoked to justify decisions which can be explained more simply. For instance in *Snook* v. *London West Riding Investments, Ltd.*[3] the plaintiff was held

---

[1] [1965] 2 Q.B. at p. 275. But it is to be noted that in these estoppel cases the court is in effect recognising a duty to take care to prevent financial loss. It is still doubtful how far such a duty is recognised in tort law.

[2] *Butterworth* v. *Kingsway Motors, Ltd.*, [1954] 1 W.L.R. 1286.

[3] [1967] 2 Q.B. 786.

estopped from denying the title of the defendant's predecessors to a car although he had intended to transfer the property to them.

The use of estoppel in such cases seems merely confusing. The whole purpose of the doctrine is to prevent the plaintiff from denying his real intentions when he has misled other parties as to those intentions. Where in fact his real intention was to transfer title it is surely unnecessary to invoke estoppel.

SALE BY AGENT

This exception may be quickly disposed of. Sect. 21 (1) says, *inter alia*, that if the goods are not sold with the authority or consent of the owner, the buyer acquires no title. But this section is subject to the provisions of the Act, and Sect. 61 preserves the rules of common law regarding principal and agent. It follows that, according to the ordinary principles of common law, a sale within the apparent or usual authority of an agent, even though outside his actual authority, will bind the owner. It is not of course every agent who has an apparent authority. Unless the agent belongs to a certain class of agent who usually have a certain authority it cannot be said that the agent has any apparent authority wider than his actual authority.[1]

It is not within the scope of this work to analyse in detail the circumstances in which an agent can pass a title to a third party where he acts beyond his actual authority. It seems, however, that in addition to cases in which the agent acts within his "usual" or "ostensible" authority, there is an independent principle which, at least in some circumstances, enables an agent to pass a title beyond his actual authority. If, for example, an agent is authorised to sell at a certain price, and sells below this price to a bona fide purchaser it seems that the purchaser gets a good title, irrespective of whether the agent has any usual or ostensible authority, or indeed, whether he is known to be an agent at all. In such circumstances it seems that the courts draw a distinction not unlike that drawn in vicarious liability in the law of tort.[2] If the agent has acted within the course of his employment as an agent he binds the principal even though he exceeds his actual authority; if, on the other hand, he acts right outside the course of his employment, he does not bind his principal.[3] Another view, however, is that this line of authorities is an anomaly and should not be extended.[4] On this view the third party will only be protected if the agent had apparent or usual authority beyond his actual authority.

[1] *Jerome* v. *Bentley*, [1952] 2 All E.R. 114.
[2] Treitel, *Law of Contract*, 3rd ed., p. 627.
[3] See e.g., *Brocklesby* v. *Temperance Building Society*, [1895] A.C. 173; *Fry* v. *Smellie*, [1912] 3 K.B. 282, and cf. *France* v. *Clark* (1884), 26 Ch. D. 257. Despite some rather loose dicta in *Mercantile Credit Co., Ltd.* v. *Hamblin*, [1965] 2 Q.B. 242, it is thought that negligence is not an essential feature of this type of liability.
[4] See *Chitty on Contracts*, 23rd ed., Vol. II, §65.

See pg 185.

SECT. 2 OF THE FACTORS ACT, 1889

The next exception to the rule *nemo dat* is provided by Sect. 2 of the Factors Act, 1889. Sect. 21 (2) of the Sale of Goods Act runs—

Provided also that nothing in this Act shall affect—

(a) The provisions of the Factors Acts, or any enactment[1] enabling the apparent owner of goods to dispose of them as if he were the true owner thereof;

At common law the doctrine of estoppel (or apparent authority) would normally have protected a third party who bought goods from a dealer in the ordinary course of business, where the goods had been entrusted to the dealer by the true owner.[2] But the common law did not protect a *pledgee*; the courts took the view that a "factor" was acting outside the normal course of business if he pledged goods rather than resold them.[3] This was a somewhat unreal approach when applied to the commercial agents of import merchants who regularly pledged imported goods (or documents of title thereto) to banks or other financial institutions in order to provide finance pending the arrival and resale of the goods.[4] Accordingly, Parliament took a hand and passed a series of Factors Acts, beginning in 1823 and culminating in the present Act of 1889. The Acts were partly declaratory of the common law and partly an extension of it;[5] but the present Act specifically declares that it is not to be construed in derogation of the common law,[6] and it now appears that there may be circumstances in which the common law is wider than the Act. Thus (as seen above) a sale by an agent *outside* the ordinary course of business is protected at common law if the true owner has authorised the agent to sell as an owner, and not merely as an agent.[7]

By a somewhat strange twist, the provisions of the Factors Act are now usually applied to situations quite different from those for which they were enacted. The typical Factors Act case envisaged by Parliament was that of the commercial agent who pledged or resold goods consigned by foreign merchants to English ports; the typical case to which the Act is applied today concerns a motor vehicle entrusted to a motor dealer for sale or to obtain offers.

---

[1] The words "any enactment" apparently refer to the reputed ownership clause of the Bankruptcy Act, 1914.

[2] The leading case was *Pickering* v. *Busk* (1812), 15 East 38, but there is no doubt the principle itself was older than this.

[3] *Paterson* v. *Task* (1743), 2 Str. 1178, was the first of a long line of decisions to this effect.

[4] See Holdsworth, *History of English Law*, Vol. XIII, pp. 380–1.

[5] See *Cole* v. *North Western Bank* (1875), L.R. 10 C.P. 354, at p. 362.

[6] Sect. 13.

[7] *Lloyds and Scottish Finance, Ltd.* v. *Williamson*, [1965] 1 W.L.R. 404.

Sect. 2 (1) of the Factors Act is as follows—

> Where a mercantile agent is, with the consent of the owner, in possession of goods or of the documents of title to goods, any sale, pledge, or other disposition of the goods, made by him when acting in the ordinary course of business of a mercantile agent, shall, subject to the provisions of this Act, be as valid as if he were expressly authorised by the owner of the goods to make the same; provided that the person taking under the disposition acts in good faith, and has not at the time of the disposition notice that the person making the disposition has not authority to make the same.

The meaning of this subsection requires the most careful consideration, clause by clause.

Mercantile Agent

A mercantile agent means "a mercantile agent having in the customary course of his business as such agent authority either to sell goods or to consign goods for the purpose of sale, or to buy goods, or to raise money on the security of goods."[1] Whether a person is a mercantile agent or has merely obtained goods on sale or return is sometimes a difficult question. In the ordinary way it makes no difference to the result, because a sale or other disposition by the party entrusted with the goods will be valid in either event. If the party entrusted with the goods is a mercantile agent, a sale by him will be validated by the Factors Act, while if he is held to have the goods on sale or return, a sale by him will normally be treated, under Sect. 18, Rule 4, as an act "adopting the transaction" which passes property to him and through him to the sub-buyer. But in some cases it does make a difference whether the party with the goods is a mercantile agent or has the goods on sale or return because it is possible to contract out of Sect. 18 Rule 4, while it is not possible to contract out of the provisions of Sect. 2 of the Factors Act, 1889.[2]

A person may be a mercantile agent although he is only acting for a single principal,[3] but he must be more than a mere servant. A person who induces another to let him have goods on a representation that he knows a third party who will buy them is not, without more, a mercantile agent.[4] But a person may be a mercantile agent without carrying on the business of being a mercantile agent.[5] And as every business must have a beginning, a man may be held to be a mercantile agent in respect of the transaction in question even though he has never acted as one before.[6] If the person who obtains the goods is not a mercantile

---

[1] Sect. 1 (1).
[2] See *Weiner* v. *Harris*, [1910] 1 K.B. 285, discussed on p. 153, *ante*.
[3] *Lowther* v. *Harris*, [1927] 1 K.B. 393.
[4] *Jerome* v. *Bentley*, [1952] 2 All E.R. 114.
[5] *Weiner* v. *Harris*, *supra*.
[6] *Mortgage Loan & Finance Co. of Australia* v. *Richards* (1932), S.R. (N.S.W.) 50, at p. 58.

agent at the time he obtains them, the fact that he becomes such later while the goods are still in his possession will not bring the case within the Factors Act,[1] unless presumably, the owner later consents to his possession as mercantile agent.

The Consent of the Owner

The next requirement of the subsection is that the mercantile agent must be in possession of the goods *with the consent of* the owner. The meaning of these last words, which also appear in Sect. 25 (2),[2] gave rise to considerable difficulty where a person was induced to part with goods as a result of fraud, and in particular, where he parted with the goods in circumstances amounting to larceny by a trick under the old law of theft. It was at one time thought that in such a case the goods could not be said to be in the possession of the agent with the consent of the owner,[3] but it is probably safe to say that this view would not be accepted since the decision in *Pearson* v. *Rose & Young*.[4] The plaintiff delivered his car to X, a mercantile agent, in order to obtain offers, but with no authority to sell it. The agent obtained possession of the registration book by a trick in such circumstances that the owner had clearly not consented to parting with the possession of it, and then promptly sold the car, as he had intended to do from the first. The Court of Appeal held that the question whether the agent had committed larceny by a trick was quite immaterial, and that in each case the only question was whether the goods were in his possession with the consent of the owner. In this case the mercantile agent had possession of the car with the consent of the owner, but not of the registration book. The Court further held that a sale without a registration book would not have been a sale in the ordinary course of business, and that the defendants were therefore not protected by the Factors Act.[5]

The dicta in *Pearson* v. *Rose & Young*[6] were applied by Sellers, J., in *Du Jardin* v. *Beadman*,[7] a case under Sect. 25 (2) of the Sale of Goods Act where the learned judge held that although the goods were obtained by larceny by a trick, they were nonetheless in the possession of the buyer with the consent of the seller. Since the coming into force of the Theft Act, 1968, the offence of larceny by a trick has disappeared from English law, and there can be no doubt that these cases represent the modern law on the subject.

It has been suggested that a purchaser cannot rely on the owner's consent to the mercantile agent's possession if that consent was given

---

[1] *Heap* v. *Motorists' Advisory Agency, Ltd.*, [1923] 1 K.B. 577.

[2] P 205, *post*.

[3] Dicta in *Oppenheimer* v. *Frazer*, [1907] 2 K.B. 50.

[4] [1951] 1 K.B. 275. See also *Folkes* v. *King*, [1923] 1 K.B. 282.

[5] On this aspect of the case see the criticism in 67 *L.Q.R.* 3, which appears to be well founded. See also *Stadium Finance, Ltd.* v. *Robbins*, [1962] 2 Q.B. 664.

[6] [1951] 1 K.B. 275.   [7] [1952] 2 Q.B. 712.

under an illegal contract.[1] But this would produce the strange result that the owner of the goods could rely on his own illegal agreement with the agent to defeat the claims of an innocent third party. Moreover, the suggestion bears some resemblance to cases prior to *Pearson* v. *Rose & Young* (*supra*) which gave an artificial meaning to the word "consent" in Sect. 2 of the Factors Act. It is submitted that this suggestion is wrong.

Not only the requirement of consent, but also the word "owner" has given rise to difficulty in this section. In *Lloyds Bank* v. *Bank of America*[2] the plaintiffs lent money to X, a mercantile agent, on the security of documents which were pledged with them. The documents were then returned to X under a "trust receipt"[3] to enable him to sell the goods as trustee for the plaintiffs, but X fraudulently pledged them with the defendants for an advance. The defendants pleaded that they were protected by Sect. 2 of the Factors Act, 1889, but the plaintiffs argued that as X, the mercantile agent, was himself the owner of the goods, it could not be said that he was in possession with the consent of the owner, within the meaning of the Act. The Court of Appeal rejected these arguments, however. In the words of Lord Greene, M.R.—

> Where the right of ownership has become divided among two or more persons in such a way that the acts which the section is contemplating could never be authorised save by both or all of them, these persons together constitute the owner.[4]

In this case the plaintiffs were the legal pledgees, and, in equity, beneficiaries of the proceeds of sale, while X was the legal owner, and beneficial owner, subject to the prior claim of the plaintiffs. Consequently, these two persons together constituted the owner within the Act, and the goods were nonetheless in the possession of X with the consent of the owner, because he was himself one of those two persons.

Goods Entrusted to the Mercantile Agent as Such

The purchaser from the mercantile agent will not be protected if the goods were entrusted to him for some purpose quite unconnected with his business as a mercantile agent—

> The owner must consent to the agent having them for a purpose which is in some way or other connected with his business as a mercantile agent. It may not actually be for sale. It may be for display, or to get offers, or

---

[1] *Belvoir Finance Co., Ltd.* v. *Harold G. Cole & Co., Ltd.*, [1969] 1 W.L.R. 1877.
[2] [1938] 2 K.B. 147.
[3] A "trust receipt" is obtained by a banker who has advanced money against documents in respect of imported goods when the documents are released to the buyer before the advance is paid off. See Gutteridge & Megrah, *Law of Bankers' Commercial Credits*, 4th ed., 1968, pp. 170–6.
[4] At p. 162.

merely to put in his showroom; but there must be a consent to something of that kind before the owner can be deprived of his goods.[1]

Subsects. (2), (3) and (4) of Sect. 2 are also concerned with the meaning of the consent referred to in Sect. 2 (1). Sect. 2 (2) lays down that, if the agent obtains the goods with the consent of the owner, the subsequent withdrawal of the consent will not affect the rights of a purchaser who had no notice of the withdrawal. Sect. 2 (3) enacts that, if the agent is in possession of the goods with the consent of the owner, and he obtains possession of the documents of title by virtue of his possession of the goods, he shall be deemed to have such possession also with the consent of the owner. Finally, Sect. 2 (4) enacts that "For the purposes of this Act the consent of the owner shall be presumed in the absence of evidence to the contrary."

Sale in Ordinary Course of Business

The purchaser claiming the protection of Sect. 2 must next prove that the mercantile agent acted in the ordinary course of business. This cannot be read literally, because obviously in one sense a sale without the authority of the owner can rarely, if ever, be in the ordinary course of business, and it is only in this event that the Factors Act is needed at all. Consequently this should probably be taken as meaning "appearing to act in the ordinary course of business".[2] Alternatively it may mean that the mercantile agent must act in the ordinary course of business except for the fact that he does not have the owner's authority.

It is immaterial that the third party dealt with the mercantile agent as a principal and did not know him to be an agent; and it is also immaterial that the agent entered into a transaction not normally sanctioned by the custom of the trade, unless, perhaps, the custom is so notorious that the third party would normally be taken to have knowledge of it as, e.g., if an auctioneer were to pledge goods entrusted to him for sale. In other words the phrase, "acting in the ordinary course of business of a mercantile agent" means "acting in such a way as a mercantile agent in the ordinary course of business as a mercantile agent would act, that is to say, within business hours, at a proper place of business, and in other respects in the ordinary way in which a mercantile agent would act, so that there is nothing to lead the pledgee to suppose that anything is done wrong, or to give notice that the disposition is one which the mercantile agent had not authority for."[3]

---

[1] *Pearson* v. *Rose & Young*, [1951] 1 K.B. at p. 288 *per* Denning, L.J. There is a long line of authority supporting this viewpoint, dating back to *Cole* v. *North Western Bank* (1875), L.R. 10 C.P. 354. It has also been recently held that the decision in the *Pacific Motor Auctions* case, [1965] A.C. 867 *post*, p. 203), has not affected the law on this point: *Astley Industrial Trust* v. *Miller*, [1968] 2 All E.R. 36.

[2] See 67 *L.Q.R.* 6. Cf. *Oppenheimer* v. *Attenborough*, [1908] 1 K.B. 221.

[3] *Per* Buckley, L.J., in *Oppenheimer* v. *Attenborough*, [1908] 1 K.B., at pp. 230-1.

So also, if a mercantile agent sells goods on the terms that the price is not to be paid directly to him but to one of his creditors, this may well be outside the ordinary course of business.[1] But a sale is not necessarily outside the ordinary course of business because the price is not paid in cash.[2] Whether the mercantile agent has acted in the ordinary way in which a mercantile agent would act in any particular case is of course a question of fact.[3]

It seems that the requirement, that the agent must act in the ordinary course of business, is distinct from the requirement, that the buyer must take in good faith and without notice.[4] A buyer may be in good faith even though the sale is outside the ordinary course of business. To this extent the dictum above, from Buckley, L.J.'s judgment in *Oppenheimer* v. *Attenborough*, must be modified. For if the agent is only held to act outside the ordinary course of business in circumstances in which the buyer would have notice of his lack of authority, it would seem that the buyer would necessarily fail on the second requirement in any event.[5]

These decisions give rise to the question whether the requirement that the agent must act in the ordinary course of business serves any useful purpose. It would seem that the owner is already adequately protected by the requirement that the buyer must act in good faith and without notice, and this additional requirement could well be dropped in any future reform of the law.[6]

Sale, pledge or other disposition

What sort of transaction amounts to a "disposition" has been discussed in relation to Sect. 25 (1) of the Sale of Goods Act. The point is dealt with later.[7]

Good faith

The next requirement of Sect. 2 is that the buyer must prove that he took in good faith and without notice that the sale was made without the owner's authority, and the burden of proof is apparently on him

---

[1] *Lloyds & Scottish Finance, Ltd.* v. *Williamson*, [1965] 1 W.L.R. 404, at p. 408.
[2] *Tingey & Co.* v. *John Chambers*, [1967] N.Z. L.R. 785.
[3] *Biggs* v. *Evans*, [1894] 1 Q.B. 88.
[4] *Lloyds & Scottish Finance, Ltd.* v. *Williamson, supra; Pacific Motor Auctions Pty., Ltd.* v. *Motor Credits (Hire Finance), Ltd.*, [1965] A.C. 867.
[5] In both the cases cited in the last note sales were made outside the ordinary course of business, but the buyers acted in good faith and were both held to be protected, though for different reasons.
[6] The U.C.C. retains the requirement that the sale must be in the ordinary course of business on the ground that purchasers (in the U.S.A.) were frequently held to be in good faith in cases where the result outraged common sense. See the Commentary to Sect. 2–403 (2).
[7] See *post*, p. 204.

in this respect,[1] although under Sect. 23 lack of good faith must be proved by the original owner.[2]

Pledges

Although a pledge is included within the protection of this section, Sect. 4 of the same Act excludes a pledge made for an antecedent debt. Thus if a mercantile agent pledges goods in his possession with the consent of the owner, the pledgee will have to prove that the pledge was made in return for a loan given at the same time, and not before the pledge was made.

SPECIAL POWERS OF SALE

Sect. 21 (2) says that—

> Nothing in this Act shall affect—
> (b) The validity of any contract of sale under any special common law or statutory power of sale, or under the order of a court of competent jurisdiction.

This provision covers a large number of miscellaneous cases where a non-owner may pass a good title to goods, the most important of which are—

Common Law Powers

The most important of these is the power of sale of a pledgee, but if the pledge is made under a "regulated agreement", i.e. is taken by a provider of credit from a consumer, the power must be exercised under the Consumer Credit Act, 1974 (see below).

Statutory Powers

There are a large number of these; the most important include the power of a sheriff to sell goods seized under a writ of execution;[3] the power of an innkeeper to sell goods upon which he has a lien under Sect. 1 of the Innkeepers Act, 1878; the powers conferred by the Disposal of Uncollected Goods Act, 1952; and the new powers relating to pawns under the Consumer Credit Act, 1974. Under Sect. 120 of this Act a pawn for under £15 can be forfeited at the end of the redemption period, but a pawn for a sum exceeding £15 can only be realised in accordance with the procedures laid down in Sect. 121.

---

[1] *Heap* v. *Motorists Advisory Agency, Ltd.*, [1923] 1 K.B. 577; although the reasons given are not convincing the result seems sensible. It is not difficult for the buyer to prove his good faith, but it would be very hard for the owner to disprove it. Hence the Law Reform Committee recommended the endorsement of this case: Cmnd. 2958, para. 25.

[2] *Whitehorn Bros.* v. *Davison*, [1911] 1 K.B. 463. The Law Reform Committee recommends reversal of this decision—see previous note.

[3] Sect. 15, Bankruptcy and Deeds of Arrangement Act, 1913. The buyer acquires a good title even if the goods did not belong to the person against whom execution issued and even if he knew of the rights of the true owner. *Curtis* v. *Maloney*, [1951] 1 K.B. 736; *Dyal Singh* v. *Kenyan Insurance, Ltd.*, [1954] 1 All E.R. 847.

Sale by Order of the Court

The Court has a wide jurisdiction under the Rules of the Supreme Court to order the sale of goods which "for any just and sufficient reason it may be desirable to have sold at once," e.g. because they are of a perishable nature, or because the market is falling. The Court has power to insist on a sale despite the objections of the owner, where such a course seems necessary or desirable.[1]

SALE IN MARKET OVERT[2]

The fifth exception to the *nemo dat* rule is the case of a sale in market overt, retained by Sect. 22 of the Act—

(1) Where goods are sold in market overt, according to the usage of the market, the buyer acquires a good title to the goods, provided he buys them in good faith and without notice of any defect or want of title on the part of the seller.

This exception can be explained, but scarcely justified, on historical grounds only, and it may be regretted that the Sale of Goods Act did not abolish it as was at one time proposed.[3]

"Market overt" means "an open public and legally constituted market."[4] Such a market may be held under a charter or a statute, and by long standing custom, every shop within the City of London is market overt for the purposes of this rule.[5] The sale need not be by a trader in the market, nor need it be by auction if sales by private treaty are according to the usage of the market. On the other hand the goods must be such as are usually sold in the market and the sale must be open and between the hours of sunrise and sunset.[6] The rule apparently only applies to a sale and not to a pledge.

The sale of horses in market overt was formerly governed by the Sale of Horses Act, 1555, and the Sale of Horses Act, 1588, which laid down elaborate regulations to be followed on such a sale, and the effect of these Acts was preserved by Sect. 22 (2) of the Sale of Goods Act. All these provisions were repealed by the Criminal Law Act, 1967, as a consequence of the abolition of the distinction between felonies and misdemeanours. Horses therefore now fall within the ordinary rule.

Formerly, the title acquired by a purchaser in market overt was a somewhat precarious one for it was liable to be defeated if the party responsible for the loss of the goods was later convicted of false pretences or larceny. The law as to the former possibility was altered by

---

[1] *Larner* v. *Fawcett*, [1950] 2 All E.R. 727.
[2] See (1956), 9 *Current Legal Problems*, 113.
[3] See Chalmers, *Sale of Goods Act*, 15th ed., p. 100.
[4] *Lee* v. *Bayes* (1856), 18 C.B. 599, 601, *per* Jervis, J.
[5] *Case of Market Overt* (1596), 5 Co. Rep. 83b., discussed exhaustively by Scrutton, J., in *Clayton* v. *Leroy*, [1911] 2 K.B. 1031.
[6] *Reid* v. *Commissioner of Metropolitan Police*, [1973] Q.B. 551.

Sect. 24 (2) of the Sale of Goods Act. Sect. 24 (1) which provided for revesting on conviction for larceny remained law until 1969 when the Theft Act, 1968, came into force. This Act completely repeals Sect. 24 of the Sale of Goods Act. There is, therefore, no longer any question of revesting of the title once acquired in market overt.[1]

SALE UNDER A VOIDABLE TITLE

Sect. 23 confirms the common law rule that a person cannot avoid a voidable contract to the prejudice of third party rights acquired in good faith and for value—

> When the seller of goods has a voidable title thereto, but his title has not been avoided at the time of the sale, the buyer acquires a good title to the goods, provided he buys them in good faith and without notice of the seller's defect of title.

The great practical importance of this rule is that, if a person buys goods by fraud, and disposes of them before the other party avoids the contract, a buyer in good faith[2] from the fraudulent party acquires a good title. Where, however, the fraud is such as to nullify the offer or acceptance and prevent any real contract from coming into existence, the buyer acquires no title at all and cannot therefore pass anything on to the innocent third party.[3] Consequently, this section does not protect such a buyer and unless he can invoke one of the other exceptions to the *nemo dat* rule, such as estoppel, or Sect. 2 of the Factors Act, 1889, he will have no defence to an action of conversion by the owner.

In general the defrauded party can only rescind the contract by communicating with the other party to the contract, and notifying him of the rescission. But in *Car & Universal Finance, Ltd.* v. *Caldwell*[4] the Court of Appeal held that the seller can rescind the contract by evincing an intention to do so and taking all steps open to him (such as informing the police) where he is unable to communicate with the fraudulent party, at least where this is because the fraudulent party is deliberately keeping out of the way. The Court left open the question whether the law would be the same where the innocent party's inability to communicate with the other is not due to the fact that the latter is deliberately keeping out of the way. At first sight it seems as though this decision has fundamentally affected the protection afforded to the

---

[1] Sect. 28 of the Theft Act gives jurisdiction to a criminal court to make a restitution order in favour of the owner of stolen goods. This power can be exercised when the goods are in the possession of a third party, but it clearly does not authorise a criminal court to deprive a bona fide purchaser of a title which he may have obtained. In fact it has been said that restriction orders should only be made in clear cases and not where there may be serious disputes as to ownership, etc.: *R.* v. *Church* (1970), 53 Cr. App. R. 65.

[2] The onus of proof of lack of good faith is on the original owner: *Whitehorn Bros.* v. *Davison*, [1911] 1 K.B. 463.

[3] As, e.g., in *Cundy* v. *Lindsay* (1878), 3 App. Cas. 459 and similar cases.

[4] [1965] 1 Q.B. 525.

innocent third party by the Act because it had previously been assumed that a contract could not be rescinded without communication. Where the contract is fraudulently induced it was generally thought that in practice there was little that the innocent party could do to defeat a bona fide purchaser. This view of the law was, moreover, adopted in Scotland in *McLeod* v. *Kerr*[1] which was decided in the same year as *Caldwell's* case. The facts in this case were substantially identical with those in *Caldwell's* case and the Court of Session held that "by no stretch of imagination" could the seller's conduct amount to rescission of the contract. However, as will be seen later, the decision in *Caldwell's* case will be of limited application in practice because in circumstances to which it applies the third party will often get a good title under Sect. 25 (2) of the Act.[2]

Although Sect. 23 only refers to the possibility of a sale, the common law rule is the same and presumably still applies to pledges, and a person with a voidable title to goods who pledges them before the other party avoids the title, can pass a good title to the pledgee.[3] But a trustee in bankruptcy takes no better title than the bankrupt had, and if the bankrupt had a voidable title, the seller can still avoid that title and retake the goods even after they have vested in the trustee.[4]

SELLER IN POSSESSION

The last two exceptions to the *nemo dat* rule are contained in Sects. 8 and 9 of the Factors Act, 1889, which are reproduced with the omission of a few words in Sect. 25 (1) and (2) of the Sale of Goods Act. Sect. 8 of the Factors Act is as follows— S 24

> Where a person, having sold goods, continues, or is, in possession of the goods or of the documents of title to the goods, the delivery or transfer by that person, or by a mercantile agent acting for him, of the goods or documents of title under any sale, pledge or other disposition thereof, (or under any agreement for sale, pledge or other disposition thereof), to any person receiving the same in good faith and without notice of the previous sale, shall have the same effect as if the person making the delivery or transfer were expressly authorised by the owner of the goods to make the same.

The words in brackets are omitted in Sect. 25 (1) of the Sale of Goods Act.[5]

There was for some years a continuous stream of authority holding

---

[1] [1965] S.C. 253.   [2] *Post,* p. 205.
[3] See, e.g., *Phillips* v. *Brooks,* [1919] 2 K.B. 243.
[4] *In re Eastgate,* [1905] 1 K.B. 465.
[5] This section is hereafter referred to as Sect. 8. The omitted words in Sect. 25 are one of the oddities of the Sale of Goods Act. If Parliament, in 1892, thought that Sects. 8 and 9 of the Factors Act were too wide, why did it not repeal them, and if it did not think they were too wide, why did it leave out these few words?

that it was not enough that the seller was simply in possession of the goods when he resold them, but that the third party claiming under this section must go further and show that the seller was in possession as seller, and not in some other capacity, e.g., as bailee.[1]

However, the authority of these decisions was severely shaken by the decision of the Privy Council in *Pacific Motor Auctions Pty., Ltd.* v. *Motor Credits (Hire Finance), Ltd.*,[2] the facts of which have already been given.[3] The Privy Council held that the defendants obtained a good title under a section of the New South Wales Sale of Goods Act identical with Sect. 25(1) of the English Act. In delivering the opinion of the Board, Lord Pearce rejected the earlier English decisions as wrongly decided. The Privy Council held that the words "continues . . . in possession" in the section were intended to refer to the continuity of physical possession, regardless of any private transaction between the seller and the first buyer which might alter the legal title under which the possession was held. Accordingly, unless there is an actual transfer of physical possession the seller is to be treated as continuing in possession and as able to pass a good title under the section.[4] The Privy Council approved the New Zealand case of *Mitchell* v. *Jones*[5] where the seller sold and delivered a horse to the buyer, but later borrowed it back and wrongfully sold it again. In such a case the second buyer is not protected; the seller is "in possession" in a literal sense but the fact that he was a seller originally is no longer relevant. He is a bailee, not a seller.[6]

This decision has now been followed by the Court of Appeal[7] and is much to be welcomed. It has rid the law of an unnecessary complication for it has replaced the previous imprecise criteria for determining whether a seller was in possession "as seller" by the simple criterion of whether he has remained in physical possession throughout. It is also thought that the result is more equitable than that reached in the earlier cases, since, if a purchaser chooses to leave the seller in possession, the risk of the seller proving dishonest should rest on him rather than on a bona fide purchaser.

In the application of this provision it must be borne in mind that there

---

[1] *Staffs Motor Guarantee, Ltd.* v. *British Wagon Co., Ltd.*, [1934] 2 K.B. 305; *Eastern Distributors* v. *Coldring*, [1957] 2 Q.B. 600; *Dore* v. *Dore, The Times*, 18th March 1953; *Halfway Garage (Nottingham), Ltd.* v. *Lepley, Guardian*, 8th February 1964.

[2] [1965] A.C. 867.   [3] *Supra*, p. 188.

[4] Prima facie, a dealer in possession under such an agreement would be able to pass a title under Sect. 2 of the Factors Act. (See, e.g., the C.A. decision in *St. Margaret's Trust, Ltd.* v. *Castle*, 28th July, 1964, (1964), 10 *Current Law*, 175a.) But the transaction in this case was not "in the ordinary course of business."

[5] (1905), 24 N.Z.L.R. 932.

[6] The words "or is in possession" give rise to some difficulty, but have been explained as covering the case where the seller did not originally have possession o.' the goods but only acquired possession later.

[7] *Worcester Works Finance, Ltd.* v. *Cooden Engineering Co., Ltd.*, [1972] 1 Q.B. 210.

is nothing in the section to alter the usual commercial meaning of the word possession. Consequently it has been held that goods which were at the seller's disposal though physically in the custody of warehousemen were in the possession of the seller within Sect. 8 of the Factors Act.[1]

In most cases, the party claiming the protection of this section will rely on a sale or pledge, but the section also refers to other "disposition". In *Worcester Works Finance, Ltd.* v. *Cooden Engineering Co., Ltd.*,[2] the Court of Appeal held that this was a very wide word, but that it did not cover a mere transfer of possession; there must be some transfer of an interest in the goods to constitute a disposition. In this case one G, bought a car from the defendants, paying the price with a cheque which was not met. He then sold the car to another finance company—the plaintiffs—but retained the possession of the car as he had induced the plaintiffs to accept a hire-purchase proposal for the benefit of an accomplice. Subsequently the defendants, with the consent of G, retook the car from him. It was held that the defendants were protected as against the plaintiffs. So far as the plaintiffs were concerned, G was a seller who remained in possession. Moreover, the retaking of the car by the defendants was a "disposition" by G to them inasmuch as it amounted to a rescission of the contract between them, and therefore it revested the property in the defendants.

This case is also authority for the proposition that a party relying on Sect. 8 of the Factors Act need not prove that the seller remained in possession with the consent of the buyer. The difference in wording between Sects. 2 and 8 in this respect clearly shows that Sect. 8 was intended to apply even where the seller wrongfully retains possession after the sale.

It should be noted that Sect. 8 does not go so far as the doctrine of estoppel, nor so far as Sect. 22 or 23 of the Sale of Goods Act, nor so far as Sect. 2 (1) of the Factors Act, in one important respect. Sect. 8 only protects the third party if the goods or documents of title are delivered or transferred to him. Thus if a person sells and transfers the property in goods to A, retaining possession, and then proceeds to sell them to B, still retaining possession, A has the better right. Sect. 8 only protects B against A when the goods or documents of title have been delivered or transferred to him, and until this happens the rule *nemo dat* must apply. Under the doctrine of estoppel or Sect. 2 of the Factors Act, however, the second buyer is protected as from the moment of sale. On the other hand, if the second buyer has acquired possession he is protected although he has only agreed to buy the goods, and the property has not yet passed to him.[3] But in another respect, Sect. 8

---

[1] *City Fur Co., Ltd.* v. *Fureenbond*, [1937] 1 All E.R. 799.
[2] [1972] 1 Q.B. 210. See Preston, (1972) 88 L.Q.R. 239.
[3] This is the effect of Sect. 8, differing in this respect from Sect. 25 (1).

goes further than Sect. 2 of the Factors Act since it applies even where the sale is not in the ordinary course of business.

As is to be expected, Sect. 8 only applies when the property in the goods has passed to the buyer under the contract of sale, for if the property has not so passed obviously the seller sells by virtue of his property in the goods and no statutory exception to the *nemo dat* rule is needed. Hence Sect. 8 only applies where the seller has "sold" (not "agreed to sell") the goods.

BUYER IN POSSESSION

Sect. 9 of the Factors Act and Sect. 25 (2) of the Sale of Goods Act contain provisions parallel to those of Sect. 8 and Sect. 25 (1). Sect. 9 is as follows—

> Where a person, having bought or agreed to buy goods, obtains with the consent of the seller possession of the goods or the documents of title to the goods, the delivery or transfer, by that person or by a mercantile agent acting for him, of the goods or the documents of title under any sale, pledge or other disposition thereof (or under any agreement for sale, pledge or other disposition thereof) to any person receiving the same in good faith and without notice of any lien or other right of the original seller in respect of the goods, shall have the same effect as if the person making the delivery or transfer were a mercantile agent in possession of the goods or documents of title with the consent of the owner.

The words in brackets are omitted in Sect. 25 (2) of the Sale of Goods Act.[1] Sect. 25 (3) then goes on to say that—

> In this section the term "mercantile agent" has the same meaning as in the Factors Acts.

The meaning of this term is explained by Sect. 1 (1) of the Factors Act, 1889, which has already been set out above.[2]

A person "having bought or agreed to buy goods"

It has already been seen that Sect. 8 only applies where the property has passed to the first buyer before the second sale, because otherwise the special provision is not necessary. But Sect. 9 applies where the first buyer has "bought or agreed to buy goods," that is to say, it applies whether or not the property has passed to the first buyer. This is a curious provision for it is not easy to see why there should be any special enactment to protect a person who has bought goods from a buyer in possession when the property has already passed to this buyer. Prima facie the buyer can sell the goods in these circumstances and pass a good title by virtue of his own property. It is to be hoped that a court would dismiss as mere surplusage the words "bought or" in Sect. 9 even though the section imposes certain restrictions on the buyer's ability to pass a good title to a third party; in fact (as appears

[1] Hereafter referred to as Sect. 9.   [2] P. 194, *ante.*

below) it is not easy to envisage circumstances in which these restrictions would become applicable. But possibly they do not matter anyhow because it is arguable that a buyer can always pass property even at common law if it has already passed to him, and therefore Sect. 9 could be ignored in such a case.

The fact that Sect. 9 only applies where a person has bought or agreed to buy goods means that there must be a contract of sale within the meaning of the Act. In other words there must be a contract under which the seller transfers or agrees to transfer the property in goods to the buyer, so that a mere option to purchase is not a contract of sale until the option is exercised. It is for this reason, as we have seen, that the ordinary hire-purchase agreement is drafted in the form of a bailment with an option to purchase. A person in possession of goods under such an agreement is not a person who has "bought or agreed to buy goods" within the meaning of Sect. 9 of the Factors Act.[1] On the other hand "A contract of sale may be absolute or conditional,"[2] and a person in possession of goods under a contract in which the transfer of the property is conditional, whether on payment,[3] or on the occurrence of some other event,[4] is a person who has agreed to buy goods within Sect. 9.

However, the law on this point was profoundly affected by the Hire-Purchase Act, 1965. In accordance with the general assimilation of conditional sale agreements to hire-purchase agreements, that Act provided that, for the purposes of Sect. 9 of the Factors Act (and Sect. 25 (2) of the Sale of Goods Act), "the buyer under a conditional sale agreement shall be deemed not to be a person who has bought or agreed to buy goods."[5] A conditional sale agreement for the purposes of this provision is an agreement for the sale of goods under which—

the purchase price or part of it is payable by instalments, and the property in the goods is to remain in the seller (notwithstanding that the buyer is to be in possession of the goods) until such conditions as to the payment of the instalments or otherwise as may be specified in the agreement are fulfilled.

An agreement in which the price is not payable by instalments is not, therefore, a conditional sale agreement for this purpose and remains within the protection of Sect. 9 of the Factors Act.[6]

It is important to observe that the provisions of the new law relating to conditional sales mentioned above are confined to agreements which

---

[1] *Helby* v. *Matthews*, [1895] A.C. 471; *Belsize Motor Supply Co., Ltd.* v. *Cox* [1914] 1 K.B. 244.

[2] Sect. 1 (2).   [3] *Lee* v. *Butler*, [1893] 2 Q.B. 318.

[4] *Marten* v. *Whale*, [1917] 2 K.B. 480.

[5] Sect. 54 of the 1965 Act. The Consumer Credit Act, 1974, replaces these provisions without altering the quoted words. See Schedule 4, para. 2.

[6] So, for instance, *Marten* v. *Whale* (*supra*) would still be decided in the same way today.

are generally within the protection of the Consumer Credit Act, 1974. In other words a buyer in possession under a conditional sale agreement can still pass a good title under Sect. 9 of the Factors Act if the total credit provided exceeds £5,000, or if the buyer is a corporation.[1]

It is apparent, then, that these Acts have, to a large extent, done away with the distinction between conditional sale agreements and hire-purchase agreements which has existed ever since the celebrated cases of *Lee* v. *Butler*[2] and *Helby* v. *Matthews*.[3] In view of the fact that the tendency over the last century has been to widen the circumstances in which a non-owner can transfer a good title this particular move may seem a retrograde step. The justification for it appears to be that in practice conditional sale agreements of this kind have not been commonly used as a method of consumer finance, and that it is desirable to assimilate the law relating to conditional sale and hire-purchase, partly in order to prevent evasion of the Acts and partly in the interests of simplicity. Moreover, the practical effect of this statutory modification of *Lee* v. *Butler* is much qualified by the special provisions relating to motor vehicles. As will be seen later, Part III of the Hire-Purchase Act, 1964, protects a bona fide purchaser of a motor vehicle from a person in possession under a hire-purchase *or* a conditional sale agreement.[4]

A person who obtains goods on "sale or return" has also been said to be outside the provisions of Sect. 9 because he also is not a person who has agreed to buy goods, although in a certain sense he has made a conditional contract of sale.[5] We have already seen that in many cases it makes no difference whether a person who has taken goods on sale or return comes within Sect. 9, or not, because if he sells or pledges the goods he does an act adopting the transaction within Sect. 18, Rule 4 (b) and the property passes to him, with the result that the sub-buyer or pledgee is protected. We have also seen that it is possible to contract out of Sect. 18,[6] but it is not possible to contract out of Sect. 9 of the Factors Act, so that in this event it is of vital importance to decide whether the case comes within Sect. 9 or not.

The Consent of the Seller

The protection afforded to a third party by Sect. 9 is only available if the goods were in the possession of the buyer with the consent of the seller. This is similar to the requirement which appears in Sect. 2 and the law is the same. Consequently, it is not material that the buyer obtained the goods by a criminal offence, the only question being whether the seller in fact consented to the buyer having possession.[7]

---

[1] Sect. 8 of the 1974 Act.   [2] [1893] 2 Q.B. 318.
[3] [1895] A.C. 471.   [4] See *post*, p. 213.
[5] *Edwards* v. *Vaughan* (1910), 26 T.L.R. 545. See the doubts expressed about this case at p. 153, *supra*.
[6] *Weiner* v. *Gill*, [1906] 2 K.B. 574, p. 153, *ante*.
  Du Jardin v. *Beadman*, [1952] 2 Q.B. 712, p. 195, *ante*.

Nor is it material that the seller has revoked his consent to the buyer having possession. As we have seen, Sect. 2 (2) of the Factors Act specifically states that the subsequent withdrawal of his consent by the seller does not prevent the operation of the Act. This means that the decision in *Car & Universal Finance Co.* v. *Caldwell*[1] is of little practical importance. In that case, as we have seen, it was held that a contract of sale induced by fraud could be rescinded without communicating with the fraudulent party. But it is now clear that the only result of this is to force the third party to rely on Sect. 9 of the Factors Act instead of Sect. 23 of the Sale of Goods Act.[2]

Possession of the Goods

As under Sect. 8, the third party is only protected if he has actually obtained possession of the goods, and not if he has merely bought or agreed to buy them. It is, however, uncertain if the section will apply whatever the nature of the buyer's possession. For instance, would the section apply if a person agrees to sell a car, but insists on a cash price, and then allows the buyer to take the car to a garage for an emergency repair?[3] Despite some doubts expressed in Australia,[4] it is thought that the section would apply. In *Marten* v. *Whale*[5] it was applied even though the goods were temporarily loaned to the buyer, and the analogy of the *Pacific Motor Auctions*[6] case appears conclusive.

Documents of Title

Where the buyer has obtained the documents of title to the goods with the consent of the seller, the position is a little more complicated as a result of the seller's right of lien and of stoppage *in transitu*, if he is still unpaid. Sect. 47 of the Sale of Goods Act reproduces in almost identical terms Sect. 10 of the Factors Act, 1889, although the latter is not repealed. The proviso to Sect. 47 is as follows—

> Provided that where a document of title to goods has been lawfully transferred to any person as buyer or owner of the goods, and that person transfers the document to a person who takes the document in good faith and for valuable consideration, then, if such last-mentioned transfer was by way of sale the unpaid seller's right of lien . . . or stoppage *in transitu* is defeated, and if such last-mentioned transfer was made by way of pledge or other disposition for value, the unpaid seller's right of lien . . . or stoppage *in transitu* can only be exercised subject to the rights of the transferee.

It is sometimes said[7] that this section is more favourable to the third party than Sect. 9 of the Factors Act because it says nothing about

---

[1] [1965] 1 Q.B. 525, p. 201, *ante*.
[2] But there is one important respect in which Sect. 9 may be narrower than Sect. 23, see *post*, p. 211.
[3] See *Langmead* v. *Thyer Rubber Co., Ltd.* (1947), S.R. (S.A.) 29, at p. 34.
[4] Ibid.   [5] [1917] 2 K.B. 480.   [6] [1965] A.C. 867, *ante*, p. 203.
[7] E.g. Schmitthoff, *Sale of Goods*, 2nd. ed., p. 168.

the requirement that he must not have notice of the rights of the original seller, but it may be doubted whether this really adds anything to the requirement of good faith.

It must be added that Sect. 19 (3) of the Sale of Goods Act[1] is subject to these sections. In *Cahn* v. *Pockett's Bristol Channel Steam Packet Co., Ltd.*,[2] the sellers shipped copper on the defendants' ship, and sent bills of lading together with a draft to the buyers. The buyers being insolvent did not accept the draft, but they transferred the bills of lading to the plaintiffs in pursuance of a contract previously made. The sellers, learning of the buyers' bankruptcy, stopped the goods *in transitu*. The Court of Appeal held that, although the buyers had acted wrongfully in transferring the bills of lading when they did not accept the draft, this breach of Sect. 19 (3) did not deprive the plaintiffs of the protection afforded by Sect. 47 of the Sale of Goods Act.[3]

Although Sect. 47 only talks of a transfer of a document of title, it has been held that it applies also where the documents are issued by the seller to the buyer and transferred by the latter to a third party taking in good faith and for value.[4] On the other hand the proviso apparently applies only where it is the same document which is transferred (or issued) to the buyer, and by the buyer to the third party.[5] In contrast, Sect. 9 applies even where there are two separate documents.[6]

Good Faith and Notice

The third party must take the goods "in good faith and without notice of any lien or other right of the original seller in respect of the goods." Where the buyer is in possession of the goods with the consent of the seller it is difficult to see how the seller can have any lien or other right in respect of the goods. Under Sect. 43 (1) the unpaid seller loses his lien—

(b) When the buyer or his agent lawfully obtains possession of the goods.

If the buyer has obtained possession with the consent of the seller it seems to follow of necessity that he has lawfully obtained possession, and it is submitted that this is still the case if the buyer has obtained possession by a criminal offence. This question was discussed in the New Zealand Court of Appeal in *Jeffcott* v. *Andrews Motors, Ltd.*[7] where, however, the Court by-passed the issue. It was there held unnecessary to decide whether the seller's lien could survive where the buyer obtained possession of the goods by criminal fraud, on the ground that in any event the third party was protected by the terms of Sect. 9.

---

[1] P. 155, *ante*.   [2] [1899] 1 Q.B. 643.
[3] And Sect. 25 (2), and Sects. 9 and 10 of the Factors Act, an extraordinary duplication of statutory provisions.
[4] *Ant. Jurgens & Margarinefabrieken* v. *Louis Dreyfus & Co., Ltd.*, [1914] 3 K.B. 40.
[5] *D. F. Mount, Ltd.* v. *Jay & Jay Co., Ltd.*, [1960] 1 Q.B. 159, at 168.
[6] Ibid.   [7] [1960] N.Z.L.R. 721.

If the lien survives in such circumstances the survival must be purely academic and, it seems, quite meaningless as it gives the seller no right to obtain the possession of the goods from the third party. It is therefore submitted that in whatever capacity the buyer obtains control of the goods, provided it is with the consent of the owner, Sect. 9 applies, and the buyer can pass a good title to an innocent third party free from the seller's claims.

However, if the buyer merely obtains possession of the documents of title to the goods and not of the goods themselves, it may be that in some circumstances the seller could still have a lien on the goods themselves, and effect could then be given to the section by holding that a purchaser with notice of the lien would take subject to the lien, whether or not the property had passed to the original buyer. This is an unlikely eventuality, however, for possession of the documents of title normally carries with it possession of the goods themselves—this is certainly the case with bills of lading—and it could only be in the most extraordinary circumstances that the seller could transfer the documents to the buyer while retaining a lien on the goods themselves.

Apart from the possibility of the seller retaining his lien the section also requires that the third party should take without notice of any "other right of the original seller in respect of the goods." But where the buyer has already bought the goods so that the property has passed to him it is again not easy to see of what "other right of the original seller" the third party can have notice. The mere fact that the price has not been paid to the knowledge of the third party surely cannot bring this clause into operation because it is a common business occurrence for a seller to be paid for goods before he himself has paid for them and knowledge of these circumstances can scarcely be held to put the buyers upon inquiry. In any event this would not seem to be a right "in respect of the goods" but a personal right in respect of the contract of sale. Moreover if the property has passed to the buyer it is hard to see how there can be any question of bad faith on the part of the sub-buyer. Even if he is aware that the buyer has not paid the seller and cannot do so because he has become insolvent, it is clear that the original seller cannot impugn the sub-buyer's title on the ground of bad faith, otherwise a person could never safely buy goods which he knew had not been paid for. It is, therefore, submitted that the requirement that the third party must receive the goods "in good faith and without notice of any lien or other right of the original seller in respect of the goods" can generally only be applicable where the property has not passed to the buyer, and even then it is difficult to see how any question of lien can arise.[1]

[1] On the whole of this difficult question see a review of the second edition of this book by J. C. Smith in the *Journal of the S.P.T.L.*, Vol. VII, pp. 226–7, to which I am indebted.

Effect of Sect. 9

There is one curious but important difference in the wording of Sects. 8 and 9. The former says that a sale by a seller in possession shall, subject to the conditions laid down, "have the same effect as if the person making the delivery or transfer were expressly authorised by the owner of the goods to make the same." On the other hand, Sect. 9 says that a sale by a buyer in possession shall, subject to the conditions already discussed, have the same effect "as if the person making the delivery or transfer were a mercantile agent in possession of the goods or documents of title with the consent of the owner." What exactly is the significance of these last words? If read literally they would appear to create a serious difficulty because, it may be recalled, an unauthorised sale by a mercantile agent in possession of goods with the consent of the owner is only made effective to pass a title by Sect. 2 (1) of the Factors Act, 1889, if the mercantile agent is *acting in the ordinary course of business.* If a person is not a mercantile agent how can he be said to act in the ordinary course of business of a mercantile agent? As Pearson, L.J., said in *Newtons of Wembley, Ltd.* v. *Williams*,[1] "It seems on the face of it to be an impossible position." Nevertheless the Court of Appeal thought that the buyer must somehow be treated as a notional mercantile agent, and the Court has to ask whether the sale would have been in the ordinary course of business had he been a mercantile agent. In this case the Court decided that the sale would have been in the ordinary course, so it may be that the Court's view on the main issue could be regarded as *obiter.* But this cannot be said of the earlier and unreported case of *Lambert* v. *G. & C. Finance Corporation, Ltd.*[2] In this case the plaintiff sold his car to X who offered him a cheque for the price. The plaintiff reluctantly accepted the cheque but insisted on keeping the log book until the cheque was met. In fact the cheque was worthless and X sold the car to a dealer who disposed of it to the defendants. The learned judge held that the retention of the log book showed an intention that the property was not to pass until the cheque was met, and that the defendants did not obtain a title under Sect. 9 of the Factors Act. Since X had sold the car without the log book the learned judge had no difficulty in holding that the sale was not in the ordinary course of business, or rather would not have been in the ordinary course of X's business had he been a mercantile agent.

In the *Lambert* case and the *Newtons of Wembley* case it may well be that substantial justice was done. But if the dicta in the latter case are followed this may not always be possible. For example, a sale by a mercantile agent outside business premises would not generally be in the ordinary course of business.[3] But if a private individual who is not a mercantile agent were, e.g., to sell a second hand car, the sale would

[1] [1965] 1 Q.B. 560, at p. 578.   [2] See (1963), *Sol. Jo.* 666.
[3] *Oppenheimer* v. *Attenborough & Sons, supra.*

almost certainly take place outside business premises, and a strict application of the *Newtons of Wembley* case would take the case outside Sect. 9. In the circumstances it is unfortunate that the Court was not referred to dicta in Australia[1] and New Zealand[2] which take a contrary view. On this view the effect of a sale by a buyer in possession is the same "as if" the buyer were a mercantile agent and the sale was in the ordinary course of his business. "The section operates to validate a sale as if the buyer in possession were a mercantile agent; it does not require that he should act as though he were a mercantile agent."[3] There is no doubt that this was thought to be the law in *Lee* v. *Butler*[4] and has been assumed to be the law ever since. The Law Reform Committee has recommended that the law be amended to restore the position to what it was formerly thought to be.[5]

Effect of Sect. 9 Where Seller is Not the Owner

One difficult point remains to be mentioned. What is the effect of Sect. 9 where the seller was not himself the owner of the goods? For instance, if a thief steals a car and sells it to a car dealer who resells it, does Sect. 9 apply to the resale? Davies, L.J., who decided the *Newtons of Wembley* case at first instance, distinguished *Car & Universal Finance, Ltd.* v. *Caldwell*[6] on the ground that in that case the first purchaser from the defrauded owner was a purchaser in bad faith, "so that the the provisions of Sect. 25 (2) of the Sale of Goods Act, 1893, and of Sect. 9 of the Factors Act, 1889, could not apply"[7] that is, to a resale by him. It has, however, been suggested by a learned writer[8] that if Sect. 9 is read literally then it is at least arguable that the section covers the subsequent sale even-where the first purchaser is not in good faith. Indeed, this argument goes even further, for it would lead to the result that, if goods are stolen and then disposed of to a first purchaser who himself disposes of them to a second purchaser, although the first clearly obtains no title, the second does. This is a startling conclusion which at first sight seems so contrary to everything one knows about the law that it cannot be right. If this is indeed the law there can be little doubt that a large number of cases have been wrongly decided, and many innocent buyers of motor vehicles have been wrongfully deprived of their vehicles, because it never seems to have occurred to anybody that a buyer from a thief has a greater power to pass title than the thief himself has.[9]

Yet the argument in favour of this view is not easy to refute. It is

---

[1] *Langmead* v. *Thyer Rubber Co., Ltd.* (1947), S.R. (S.A.) 29, at p. 39.
[2] *Jeffcott* v. *Andrew Motors Ltd.*, [1960] N.Z.L.R. 721, at p. 729, *per* Gresson, P.
[3] Ibid.   [4] [1893] 2 Q.B. 318.
[5] Twelfth Report, Cmnd. 2958, 1966, para. 23.   [6] [1965] 1 Q.B. 525, *supra*.
[7] [1964] 2 All E.R. at 138.   [8] W. L. Cornish in 27 *M.L.R.* 472.
[9] One such case is *Butterworth* v. *Kingsway Motors, Ltd.*, [1954] 1 W.L.R. 1286, *supra*, p. 50.

based on the fact that, in the example put, the car dealer is undoubtedly a person who has agreed to buy the goods and who has obtained possession of them with the consent of the seller (the thief). This being so, the disposition by him to the second buyer (who is assumed to be in good faith) is, by Sect. 9, to have the same effect as if the first buyer were a mercantile agent in possession of the goods with the consent of the *owner*. Thus, the strange result appears to be that the consent of the seller (the thief) is to be treated as equivalent to the consent of the owner. If the dicta in the *Newtons of Wembley* case are followed it would, of course, be necessary to show that the sale by the first buyer to the second buyer was in the ordinary course of business.

The only way to avoid this conclusion appears to be to read the reference to the consent of the "owner" at the conclusion of Sect. 9 as a reference to the consent of the "seller."[1] This, it is thought, is the construction most likely to appeal to a court (which would surely be reluctant to give effect to such a novel argument), but it does almost as much violence to the section as would be done if the requirement of a sale in the ordinary course of business were confined to the case of a person who is in fact a mercantile agent—and this, as has been seen, the courts have so far refused to do. On ordinary principles of construction it is difficult in a section which uses both words "owner" and "seller" to read them as meaning the same thing. Nevertheless, this argument has been accepted in New Zealand, and the attempt to read the section in this novel and extended form has been rejected.[2]

PART III OF THE HIRE-PURCHASE ACT, 1964

Part III of the Hire-Purchase Act, 1964 (as re-enacted by The Consumer Credit Act, 1974) provides, in essence, that a bona fide purchaser for value of a motor vehicle from a person in possession under a hire-purchase agreement or a conditional sale agreement obtains a good title. The simplicity of result contrasts starkly with the complexity of the statutory language which occupies four full pages in the Queen's printer's copy of the Act. Sect. 27 (1) and (2) are as follows—

(1) This section applies where a motor vehicle has been bailed or (in Scotland) hired under a hire-purchase agreement, or has been agreed to be sold under a conditional sale agreement, and before the property in the vehicle has become vested in the debtor, he disposes of the vehicle to another person.

(2) Where the disposition referred to in subsection (1) is to a private purchaser, and he is a purchaser of the motor vehicle in good faith without

---

[1] In 27 *M.L.R.* 472, it is also suggested that it could be argued that a buyer from a thief has not agreed to buy at all. With respect, this seems untenable. An agreement to sell may be made even where the seller has no title.

[2] *Elwin* v. *O'Regan & Maxwell*, [1971] N.Z.L.R. 1124, at pp. 1130–2. See also for some Canadian cases, 37 *M.L.R.* 213 and 38 *M.L.R.* 77.

notice of the hire-purchase agreement or conditional sale agreement (the "relevant agreement"), that disposition shall have effect as if the creditor's title to the vehicle had been vested in the debtor immediately before that disposition.

Thus, the power of a person in possession under a conditional sale agreement to pass a title which was taken away by the sections already discussed, is, so far as concerns motor vehicles, in effect restored by this section. There is, however, one important limitation on this new power to pass title, and that is that a "trade or finance purchaser" is not protected. The "private purchaser" referred to in Sect. 27 (2) is any purchaser other than a trade or finance purchaser, and this term is defined by Sect. 29 (2) to mean a person who carries on a business which consists wholly or partly—

(a) of purchasing motor vehicles for the purpose of offering or exposing them for sale, or

(b) of providing finance by purchasing motor vehicles for the purpose of bailing or (in Scotland) hiring them under hire-purchase agreements or agreeing to sell them under conditional sale agreements.

Thus, the car dealer and the finance company are outside the protection of these sections. If, however, such a purchaser, having acquired a vehicle from a hirer in possession under a hire-purchase agreement, proceeds to dispose of it to a third party, the third party will be protected by Sect. 27 (3). The section also deals with the possibility that a vehicle which has been disposed of by a hirer to a finance company is then relet under a new hire-purchase agreement to a new hirer. In this event the new agreement is itself a disposition by virtue of the definition in Sect. 29 (1) and the new hirer is protected. Moreover, his protection is not displaced by the fact that, before he exercises his option to purchase, the true facts may have come to light. Sect. 27 (4) provides, in effect, that in such circumstances the time for determining whether the new hirer is in good faith or not is when he enters into the hire-purchase agreement and not when he exercises his option to purchase. It may be noted that the trade or finance purchaser will not itself be better off as a result of the subsequent disposition because it will remain liable in conversion to the original owner under Sect. 27 (6).

The first requirement of these provisions, then, is that the vehicle must have been let under a hire-purchase agreement or been agreed to be sold under a conditional sale agreement. The Act does not, therefore, apply where the vehicle has been let under a simple hiring agreement. Nor does the Act have any bearing on the situation which arose in *Central Newbury Car Auctions, Ltd.* v. *Unity Finance, Ltd.*,[1] where a dealer allowed a swindler to have possession of a vehicle on his signing hire-purchase proposal forms which were later rejected by the finance

[1] [1957] 1 Q.B. 371, *supra*, p. 187.

company. It seems anomalous that the dealer is not at risk in this sort of case for he clearly takes a much greater chance than a dealer who actually enters into a hire-purchase agreement himself. If the finance company accepts the hirer's proposals in this sort of case, then presumably his power to pass title becomes effective as from the moment when the contract is completed, i.e. in most cases, when the acceptance is posted to him.

It is important to note that the Act does not require the hirer to be in possession *under* the hire-purchase agreement. It merely requires that the vehicle "has been bailed under a hire-purchase agreement" and that the hirer should have disposed of it before the property has passed to him. And the definition of "debtor" in Sect. 29 (4) makes it clear that even if the agreement has already been determined the former hirer is still the debtor for the purposes of Sect. 27. So also is a hirer who is in possession under a time order made under Sect. 130 (4) of the 1974 Act.[1]

The next requirement of these provisions is that there must have been a "disposition" by the hirer or buyer. This is defined by Sect. 29 (1) from which it appears that a disposition includes a sale, a contract of sale, and a letting under a hire-purchase agreement. These provisions are wider than Sect. 9 of the Factors Act in that they protect a purchaser even though the vehicle has not yet been delivered to him, whereas under the Factors Act the purchaser is only protected after delivery. On the other hand they are narrower in that the definition of "disposition" is exhaustive, whereas under the Factors Act any disposition is protected. This is, however, largely an academic point for vehicles are unlikely to be pledged, and the only other type of disposition which is likely to be encountered, viz. the creation of a lien, would almost inevitably be in favour of a trade or finance purchaser who would not be protected anyhow.[2]

Finally, the purchaser must buy in good faith and without notice of the hire-purchase or conditional sale agreement. For this purpose it is immaterial that the buyer may know that the vehicle was the subject of a hire-purchase agreement if he believes that the finance company has been paid off.[3]

Sect. 28 of the 1964 Act contains a number of elaborate presumptions to meet the not uncommon situation where a person in possession of a vehicle which was once the subject of an unfulfilled hire-purchase agreement does not know precisely what has happened to the vehicle before he acquired it. The net effect of these presumptions appears to be as follows. The onus of proof that the defendant (or an earlier

---

[1] *Post*, p. 342.

[2] Similarly, the unusual transaction held to be a disposition in *Worcester Works Finance, Ltd.* v. *Cooden Engineering Co., Ltd.*, [1972] 1 Q.B. 210 (*supra*, p. 204) is unlikely to occur except in favour of a trade or finance purchaser.

[3] *Barker* v. *Bell*, [1971] 1 W.L.R. 983.

purchaser) was himself a purchaser in good faith and without notice lies on the defendant. But once this has been proved, there appear to be only two ways in which the finance company will be able to establish its title against the defendant. One will be to show that the first private purchaser to acquire the vehicle was not a purchaser in good faith. If this can be established then no subsequent purchaser can acquire a title under Sect. 27 even if he is himself in good faith. Secondly, the finance company may be able to establish that the vehicle was not in fact disposed of by the hirer at all, but was, e.g., stolen from him, or was disposed of by someone who had obtained temporary control of the car with the hirer's consent.

WRITS OF EXECUTION

Sect. 26 of the Act enacts that a writ of execution against goods binds them from the time when the sheriff receives the writ, but that a purchaser for value in good faith without notice of the writ acquires a good title to the property. The section reads—

(1) A writ of *fieri facias* or other writ of execution against goods shall bind the property in the goods of the execution debtor as from the time when the writ is delivered to the sheriff to be executed;[1] and, for the better manifestation of such time, it shall be the duty of the sheriff, without fee, upon the receipt of any such writ to endorse upon the back thereof the hour, day, month and year when he received the same.

Provided that no such writ shall prejudice the title to such goods acquired by any person in good faith and for valuable consideration, unless such person had at the time when he acquired his title notice that such writ or any other writ by virtue of which the goods of the execution debtor might be seized or attached had been delivered to and remained unexecuted in the hands of the sheriff.

(2) In this section the term "sheriff" includes any officer charged with the enforcement of a writ of execution.

Under this section "the title or right given by virtue of the writ remains effective not only against the goods in the hands of the original debtor, but also against any transferee other than a purchaser in good faith for value."[2] It is therefore effective against a trustee in bankruptcy. Where the execution is not completed before the date of the receiving order, however, the trustee in bankruptcy takes priority over the execution creditor, subject to the payment of the costs of the uncompleted execution.[3]

There is no doubt that a debtor whose goods have been seized under a writ of *fi. fa.* is able to sell them and pass title thereto at any time

[1] Under Sect. 22 of the Administration of Justice Act, 1965, this provision has effect in certain cases as if, for the time when the writ is delivered to the sheriff there were substituted references to the time when it is received by the registrar of the County Court.

[2] *Per* Danckwerts, J., in *Re Cooper*, [1958] Ch. 922, at 928–9.

[3] Bankruptcy Act, 1914, Sect. 40 (1).

until they have actually been sold by the sheriff.[1] From the buyer's point of view, however, the important thing is not so much whether he obtains the title, but whether he does so free from the sheriff's right of seizure. The answer given by this section is that he does so provided that he has acquired the title before the writ has been executed. In *Lloyds & Scottish Finance, Ltd.* v. *Modern Cars & Caravans (Kingston), Ltd.*,[2] a judgment creditor issued a writ of *fi. fa.* which was delivered to the sheriff. The sheriff's officer seized the debtor's caravan (in which the debtor was living) but temporarily left the debtor in possession after telling him that he must not move the caravan. The officer made a number of visits to the caravan while the debtor negotiated with the creditor, and third party claims were disposed of, but eventually the debtor sold the caravan to a purchaser who took it in good faith and for value. The purchaser claimed that he obtained a good title under the proviso to Sect. 26 (1) on the ground that until the caravan was sold the writ of *fi. fa.* "remained unexecuted in the hands of the sheriff." In rejecting this contention Edmund Davies, J., said—

> When by the opening words of the section it is provided that, "A writ of *fieri facias* . . . shall bind the property in the goods of the execution debtor . . .," this simply means that on delivery of the writ the sheriff acquires a legal right to seize sufficient of the debtor's goods to satisfy the amount specified in the writ (*Samuel* v. *Duke*).[3] The proviso, accordingly, does no more than protect a purchaser of the goods against that right of seizure if the stated conditions are fulfilled. It has no scope for operation where an actual seizure of the debtor's goods has already been effected; and where this has occurred it is immaterial whether or not the purchaser from the debtor had notice of the seizure or even of the writ.[4]

PROPOSALS FOR REFORM

There can be no doubt, after the above discussion that the law relating to the transfer of title to chattels is in a complex and confused state. It has been complained that "statutory protection for the *bona fide* purchaser has developed in a piecemeal and haphazard fashion; and some of the relevant provisions have been so drafted and interpreted as to make their application depend not on principles of equity or justice but on fine technicalities which have little rhyme and less reason".[5] In his judgment in *Ingram* v. *Little*[6] Devlin, L.J., as he then was, suggested that it might be possible to apportion the loss which occurs when an innocent owner and an equally innocent bona fide purchaser are left to dispute over the title to goods after some dishonest middle party has quit the scene. The result of this suggestion was that the whole topic was referred to the Law Reform Committee.[7] The Com-

---

[1] *Re Davies, Ex parte Williams* (1872), 7 Ch. App. 314.
[2] [1966] 1 Q.B. 764.   [3] (1838), 3 M. & W. 622.   [4] At pp. 780–1.
[5] See the Report of the Crowther Committee on Consumer Credit (1971, Cmnd. 4596) para. 4.2.8.
[6] [1961] 1 Q.B. 31.   [7] Twelfth Report, Cmnd. 2958, 1966.

mittee in fact rejected Lord Devlin's suggestion as impractical, largely because of the complications which would ensue where the goods pass through several hands. For example, a thief steals a car belonging to O and sells it to A who sells to B who resells to C and so on. In such circumstances there would be great difficulty in any system of law which allowed apportionment of the loss: should apportionment be only as between O and A? Or between all the parties? And how should the loss be apportioned?

The Committee did, however, go on to make a number of other recommendations for reform of the law. They rejected the notion of fundamental alteration in the law such as would prima facie protect any bona fide purchaser for value, but went on to propose the following detailed changes.

1. The Committee recommended[1] the abolition of the distinction between contracts void for mistake and contracts voidable for fraud. Hence, in cases like *Cundy* v. *Lindsay*[2] and *Ingram* v. *Little*[3] it would become immaterial whether the contract is void or voidable. In either event the third party should be protected.[4]

2. The Committee recommend[5] reversal of the decision in *Caldwell's*[6] case: rescission of a voidable contract should require communication.

3. The third recommendation[7] is that the dicta in the *Newtons of Wembley*[8] case should be reversed and Sect. 9 of the Factors Act amended to make it clear that it enables the buyer in possession to pass a good title.

4. The Committee rejected the suggestion that any bailee should be able to pass a good title.[9]

5. The Committee strongly criticised the market overt rule as "capricious," and recommended that the rule should be replaced by a wider protective provision applicable to a sale at any retail premises.

Within the context of the existing law, the first three of these recommendations appear to be sensible and are unlikely to rouse much opposition. The fourth recommendation is more controversial but the fifth appears to be the real stumbling block to the implementation of the Report. This recommendation has raised fears that it would facilitate the disposal of stolen goods by underworld channels. Generally, the Report is a disappointing document largely because of its complete failure to search for any empirical evidence as to the way in which the present law operates.[10] The lack of this evidence makes it very difficult to justify positive proposals for change of a fundamental character. The most important question to which insufficient attention has usually been paid is the likelihood of the original owner of lost or stolen goods

---

[1] Para. 15.   [2] (1878), 3 App. Cas. 459.   [3] [1961] 1 Q.B. 31.
[4] This result is achieved by Sect. 2–403 of the U.C.C.
[5] Para. 16.   [6] [1965] 1 Q.B. 525.   [7] Para. 23.
[8] [1965] 1 Q.B. 560.   [9] Para. 29.
[10] See my criticisms of the Report in (1966), 29 *M.L.R.* 541.

being protected by insurance. Where this is the normal situation there seems good reason for giving greater protection under the law to bona fide purchasers than is done at present. A less drastic approach would, as a minimum, amalgamate some of the existing statutory provisions by reducing them to a common principle. Thus sections 2, 8 and 9 of the Factors Act could well be replaced by a principle (along the lines of Sect. 2–403 of the U.C.C.) enabling any dealer to pass a title to goods which have been entrusted to his possession. Equally, conflicts between third party purchasers and parties who, in an economic sense, hold a security interest, could be dealt with on some comprehensive and rational basis.[1]

[1] See the Crowther Committee Report, para. 4.2.9. *et seq.*

PART V

EXPORT SALES

CHAPTER 20

EXPORT SALES

THE sale of goods which are to be shipped to their destination gives rise to a host of difficult questions, adequate discussion of which would require a whole volume.[1] This is not a task which it is proposed to undertake here, but something must be said of the principal types of export contract, of the problems raised by export and import licences, and of the method of payment by bankers' commercial credits. In the first place, four types of contract will be considered whose essential terms have become standardised by commercial practice, although there is considerable variation in matters of detail.

EX-WORKS OR EX-STORE CONTRACTS

Ex-works or ex-store contracts present few difficulties in this connection. In fact these can hardly be considered as export sales at all, since it is the buyer's duty to take delivery at the works or store in question, and what he does with them after that is entirely his own affair. The property and risk will, in the absence of any contrary indication, pass when the goods are delivered in most contracts of this kind, since they are almost invariably sales of unascertained goods, and it is unlikely that there will be any appropriation (except perhaps where provision is made for inspection at an early date) prior to delivery.

It should be noted that business men frequently use the terms "ex works" or "ex store" merely to indicate the price at which the goods will be sold (as indeed they sometimes do with the term "f.o.b.") and that it should not necessarily be concluded from the use of these terms that the contract is in fact an ex-works or ex-store contract. When all the terms of the contract are examined it may be found that duties inconsistent with such a contract are imposed on the seller.

F.O.B. CONTRACTS

In an f.o.b. contract the seller's duty is to place the goods free on board a ship to be named by the buyer. The seller's obligations extend to all charges incurred before this time including loading charges, but not freight or insurance. In the absence of a contrary intention, the

---

[1] See Schmitthoff, *The Export Trade*, 5th ed; *British Shipping Laws*, Vol. 5.

buyer has the right and the responsibility of selecting both the port and the date of, and generally making the arrangements for, the shipment of the goods.[1] He must nominate a ship on which the goods may be loaded by the seller and give adequate notice to the seller of that nomination. The ship must be an "effective" ship, i.e. capable, both physically and otherwise, of receiving the cargo. If the buyer nominates a ship which cannot receive the cargo, or which cannot load in time, he may, if he still has sufficient time, substitute another vessel in place of the one first nominated.[2] Where the contract provides for a range of ports from which the goods are to be shipped it is the buyer's right and duty to select one out of the permitted number of ports, and to give the seller sufficient notice of his selection.[3]

Normally the contract for the carriage of the goods is made between the buyer (or his agents) and the shipowners.[4] When the seller delivers the goods for loading on board he normally obtains a mate's receipt which he transmits to the buyer, and the buyer exchanges this for the proper bill of lading.

In this sort of f.o.b. contract the almost universal rule is that property and risk both pass on shipment—as soon as the goods are over the ship's rail, and if it should be material, the property and risk in each part of the cargo will pass as it crosses the ship's rail.[5] The loading of the goods is usually an "unconditional appropriation" which passes the property under Sect. 18, Rule 5. If the goods are loaded together with other goods of the same description so that no unconditional appropriation of the specific goods sold then takes place, property cannot pass on shipment, but the risk will do so.[6] This is not because of any peculiarity of f.o.b. contracts but because in this type of contract the seller's duty is to *deliver* the goods f.o.b. Once they are on board the seller has delivered them to the buyer and it is natural that they should thereafter be at the buyer's risk.

It has already been seen that under Sect. 32 (1) delivery to the carrier is prima facie deemed to be delivery to the buyer himself, but despite this it has been held that Sect. 32 (3) applies to f.o.b. contracts. This subsection states that—

Unless otherwise agreed, where goods are sent by the seller to the buyer by a route involving sea transit, under circumstances in which it is usual to insure, the seller must give such notice to the buyer as may enable

[1] *Ian Stach, Ltd.* v. *Baker Bosley, Ltd.*, [1958] 2 Q.B. 130.

[2] *Agricultores Federados Argentinos* v. *Ampro S.A.*, [1965] 2 Lloyd's Rep. 157.

[3] *David T. Boyd & Co., Ltd.* v. *Louis Louca*, [1973] 1 Lloyd's Rep. 209.

[4] Hence there may be no privity of contract between sellers and shipowners; this may cause difficulty if the goods are damaged in course of loading by the shipowners before property and risk have passed to the buyers, see *Pyrene, Ltd.* v. *Scindia Navigation*, [1954] 2 Q.B. 402.

[5] *Colonial Insurance Co. of New Zealand* v. *Adelaide Marine Insurance Co.* (1886), 12 App. Cas. 128.

[6] *Inglis* v. *Stock* (1885), 10 App. Cas. 263.

him to insure them during their sea transit, and, if the seller fails to do so, the goods shall be deemed to be at his risk during such sea transit.

The construction of this subsection was the subject of some widely differing views in the Court of Appeal in *Wimble Sons & Co., Ltd.* v. *Rosenberg & Sons*[1] where the plaintiffs sold goods to the defendants f.o.b. Antwerp. The buyers sent instructions for shipping the goods leaving it to the sellers to select the ship. The sellers shipped the goods, but did not insure and the cargo was lost at sea. Vaughan Williams and Buckley, L.JJ., agreed that Sect. 32 (3) applied to f.o.b. contracts, differing from Hamilton, L.J., who thought it had no application at all to such contracts because the seller does not send the goods to the buyer but only puts them on the ship for dispatch to the buyer. The majority thought, however, that dispatch was something different from delivery, and that the seller does dispatch or send the goods to the buyer although he only delivers them to the ship, and such delivery is deemed to be delivery to the buyer by Sect. 32 (1). This was not the end of the disagreements for Buckley, L.J., thought that the sellers were not liable in this case because the buyers already had sufficient information to enable them to insure if they wished. They knew what the freight was, they knew the port of loading and they knew the port of discharge. The only information lacking was the name of the ship which would not have prevented insurance. On the other hand Vaughan Williams, L.J., thought that such a construction would destroy the efficacy of the section since it is always possible for the buyer to insure the goods by a general cover policy. However Buckley, L.J., answered this fairly by pointing out that in this case the buyer had enough information to enable him to make a particular insurance, but he agreed that the mere fact that the buyer can take out a general cover policy would not prevent the operation of Sect. 32 (3).

The net result of this case is that, though the subsection in theory applies to f.o.b. contracts, in practice it will rarely be of much importance because in most cases the buyer will already have enough information to insure the goods specifically.

The above account is a sketch of the "classic" f.o.b. contract. But in modern times there are many variants on the f.o.b. contract. In particular it is nowadays very common for the seller to be required to make some or all of the arrangements for shipping and insuring the goods, particularly where the seller is an exporter,[2] or where small parcels

---

[1] [1913] 3 K.B. 743, followed in *Northern Steel Co., Ltd.* v. *Batt* (1917), 33 T.L.R. 516.

[2] An f.o.b. sale, though contemplating the export of the goods, may be made between parties carrying on business in the same country. For example, a company which has contracted to sell goods to a foreign buyer may itself buy goods, in order to fulfil that contract, f.o.b. English port from English sellers. In that case the first sellers will not be exporters.

rather than whole cargoes are being shipped.[1] In this event it is the seller who makes the contract for the carriage of the goods with the shipowner, and he must then comply with Sect. 32 (2) of the Act. This provides—

> Unless otherwise authorised by the buyer, the seller must make such contract with the carrier on behalf of the buyer as may be reasonable having regard to the nature of the goods and the other circumstances of the case. If the seller omit so to do, and the goods are lost or damaged in course of transit, the buyer may decline to treat the delivery to the carrier as a delivery to himself, or may hold the seller responsible in damages.

In other words if this subsection applies the buyer can either reject the goods, or accept them and claim damages. It may be observed that this section differs from the proviso to Sect. 20 which is in certain respects parallel to this provision. Under the present subsection it appears that the buyer's remedies for the damage to or loss of the goods operate whether or not the loss or damage was the consequence of the seller's failure to make a reasonable contract with the carrier, whereas under Sect. 20 if either party is at fault in taking delivery of the goods the goods are at the risk of the party in fault, but only in respect of damage which might not have occurred but for such fault.

What is a "reasonable" contract for the seller to make must be judged in the light of the circumstances existing when the contract of carriage is made, and not at the date of the contract of sale.[2] Thus a contract to carry the goods by an unusual route may be reasonable if the more usual route is unavailable when the contract of carriage is made.[3]

For an illustration of the workings of Sect. 32 (2) reference may be made to *Thomas Young & Sons, Ltd.* v. *Hobson & Partners*[4] where goods were damaged in transit owing to their being insecurely fixed. Had the sellers made a reasonable contract with the carriers, i.e. had they sent the goods at company's risk, as was the usual practice for goods of that kind, instead of at owner's risk, the damage would not have occurred. The Court of Appeal held that the buyers were entitled to reject the goods.

Where the seller is responsible for shipping the goods it may be an important question whether he does so on his own account as a principal, or whether he does so merely as agent of the buyer. In particular, if the seller ships as principal, property does not usually pass on shipment, whereas if he ships as agent it does normally do so.[5] But apart from this crucial distinction, many other ancillary questions may turn on

[1] *D. H. Bain* v. *Field & Co. Ltd.* (1920), 3 Ll.L.R. 26, at p. 29.
[2] *Tsakirogolou & Co. Ltd.* v. *Noblee Thorl G.m.b.H.*, [1962] A.C. 93.
[3] Ibid. See also *Plaimar Ltd.* v. *Waters Trading Co. Ltd.* (1945), 72 C.L.R. 304.
[4] (1949), 65 T.L.R. 365. The contract here was f.o.r. (free on rail) but the legal results are the same as with a f.o.b. contract.
[5] For a recent illustration of this point, see *President of India* v. *Metcalfe Shipping Co.*, [1970] 1 Q.B. 289.

whether the seller acts as principal or agent in shipping the goods. For example, if the seller is unable to secure shipping space he would normally be liable for non-delivery if it was his duty as seller to arrange shipping;[1] whereas he would not be so liable if he were required to arrange shipping as the buyer's agent. And other issues may also turn on whether the seller ships as principal or as agent, e.g. who is to bear any increase in shipping or insurance charges after the contract of sale is made, or whether the seller is entitled to charge commission on the contract of carriage.

Whether the seller acts as principal or agent in shipping the goods usually depends on whether the parties intend that the seller should retain the bill of lading as security for payment. If this is the intention of the parties the presumption is that the seller is acting as principal in shipping the goods. This in turn may be determined by the bill of lading itself. If the bill of lading is made out in the seller's name, Sect. 19 (1) and (2) come into operation. Sect. 19 (1) has already been set out above.[2] Sect. 19 (2) provides—

> Where goods are shipped, and by the bill of lading the goods are deliverable to the order of the seller or his agent, the seller is prima facie deemed to reserve the right of disposal.

The result of these provisions is that the property will normally pass on shipment of the goods if the bill of lading is in the buyer's name, while if it is in the seller's name it will normally pass only when the bill of lading is transferred to the buyer and the price is paid or tendered.[3]

But the terms of the bill of lading are only evidence of the intention of the parties. The fact that the bill of lading is taken in the seller's name is not conclusive proof that the seller is shipping the goods as principal, or is reserving the right of disposal. He may in fact transfer the bill of lading to the buyer as soon as he receives it, which would probably indicate that he was acting as agent all along.[4] And although the taking of the bill of lading in his own name by the seller prima facie indicates that the property does not pass on shipment, it does not follow that if the bill of lading is taken in the buyer's name it must be held that the property does pass on shipment. The retention of the bill of lading by the seller may be inconsistent with an intention to pass the property until it is handed over.[5]

It must be stressed that even where property does not pass on shipment the seller normally retains the property only as security for payment, or, in modern times, as a means of obtaining bridging finance

---

[1] See, e.g., *Lewis Emmanuel & Son, Ltd.* v. *Sammut*, [1959] 2 Lloyd's Rep. 629, a c.i.f. contract, but in this respect there is no difference between such a contract and an f.o.b. contract in which the seller undertakes as principal to ship the goods.

[2] Above, p. 154.

[3] *Mirabita* v. *Imperial Ottoman Bank* (1878), 3 Ex. D. 164.

[4] *The Albazero*, [1974] 2 All E.R. 906.

[5] *Kronprinsessan Margareta*, [1921] 1 A.C. 486; cf. *The Parchim*, [1918] A.C. 157.

to cover the period of shipment.[1] Hence, once the goods are shipped the buyer has an interest in the goods so that the seller must transfer those goods to the buyer under the contract; if he transfers them to anyone else he breaks his contract with the buyer, and on tender of the price the buyer becomes entitled to sue such a third party for conversion.[2] It also follows that, even where the property does not pass to the buyer on shipment, the risk will normally do so.[3] The seller's duty is to deliver the goods f.o.b. and once delivered they are at buyer's risk; it is his business to insure the goods, and his risk if they are lost or damaged uninsured or delayed en route.[4] It is immaterial that the property has not passed.

Of course, in the last resort everything depends on the terms of the particular contract and it must not be assumed that every f.o.b. contract is identical in the obligations imposed on the parties. It would, however, be very unusual for the property to pass before shipment in an f.o.b. contract,[5] or for the risk not to pass on shipment.

C.I.F. CONTRACTS

The main features of a c.i.f. contract were lucidly described by Lord Wright in *Smyth & Co., Ltd.* v. *Bailey Son & Co., Ltd.*—[6]

The contract in question here is of a type familiar in commerce, and is described as a c.i.f. contract. The initials indicate that the price is to include cost, insurance and freight. It is a type of contract which is more widely and more frequently in use than any other contract used for purposes of sea-borne commerce. An enormous number of transactions, in value amounting to untold sums, are carried out every year under c.i.f. contracts. The essential characteristics of this contract have often been described. The seller has to ship or acquire after that shipment the contract goods, as to which, if unascertained, he is generally required to give a notice of appropriation. On or after shipment, he has to obtain proper bills of lading and proper policies of insurance. He fulfils his contract by transferring the bills of lading and the policies to the buyer. As a general rule, he does so only against payment of the price, less the freight which the buyer has to pay. In the invoice which accompanies the tender of the documents on the "prompt"—that is, the date fixed for payment—the freight is deducted, for this reason. In this course of business, the general property remains in the seller until he transfers the bill of lading . . .

By mercantile law, the bills of lading are the symbols of the goods. The general property in the goods must be in the seller if he is to be able to pledge them. The whole system of commercial credits depends upon

[1] *Ross T. Smyth & Co., Ltd.* v. *Bailey, Son & Co.*, [1940] 3 All E.R. 60, at p. 68.
[2] *Mirabita* v. *Imperial Ottoman Bank* (1878), 3 Ex. D. 164.
[3] *Inglis* v. *Stock* (1885), 10 App. Cas. 263.
[4] *Frebold* v. *Circle Products, Ltd.*, [1970] 1 Lloyd's Rep. 499.
[5] *Carlos Federspiel & Co., S.A.* v. *Chas Twigg & Co., Ltd.*, [1957] 1 Lloyd's Rep. 240, where the authorities are comprehensively reviewed by Pearson, J.
[6] [1940] 3 All E.R. 60, at pp. 67-68.

the seller's ability to give a charge on the goods and the policies of insurance.[1]

The seller's duties in a c.i.f. contract, as summarised in the above passage, relate to the following matters. First, he must ship the goods or buy goods already shipped. It would not be very common nowadays for a c.i.f. seller to buy goods afloat and in the great majority of cases the seller either already has the goods or himself buys them for shipment. Stipulations as to the time and place of shipment as specified in the contract must be strictly complied with, and are almost always treated as conditions.[2] Delay of even one day in shipping the goods will justify rejection by the buyer. Indeed, the buyer is equally justified in rejecting the goods if they are shipped too soon.[3] The seller must also insure the goods at his own expense.

Secondly, the seller must tender to the buyer proper shipping documents. These comprise (1) the seller's invoice for the price, (2) the bill of lading and (3) an insurance policy covering the goods against marine risks. The bill of lading and the insurance policy are, in a commercial sense, the buyer's guarantee that he will receive the goods in due course or, if they should be lost or damaged, that he will have recourse either against the shipowners or the insurers. In practice, as we shall see,[4] payment will often be made through a bank by means of a letter of credit, and the documents are in this case sent to a bank and not to the buyer direct.

Although Sect. 32 (1) states, as we have seen, that delivery to a carrier is prima facie deemed to be delivery to the buyer, this has no application to c.i.f. contracts in which delivery of the goods to the buyer occurs when, but not before, the documents are handed over. The peculiar feature of c.i.f. contracts is the importance attached to the shipping documents, delivery of which transfers the property and the possession in the goods to the transferee. The seller's duty to deliver the goods in these cases means only that he must deliver the documents, for even if the goods are lost at sea the seller can still insist on payment of the price in return for the documents.[5] But "that does not mean that a c.i.f. contract is a sale of documents and not of goods.[6] It contemplates the transfer of actual goods in the normal course, but if the goods are lost, the insurance policy and bill of lad-

---

[1] It may be noted that in one respect Lord Wright's speech differs from the judgment of Kennedy, L.J., in *Biddell* v. *Horst*, [1911] 1 K.B. 934, at p. 956, for Kennedy, L.J., thought that the property passed on shipment, conditionally or unconditionally, but according to Lord Wright it never passes until the bill of lading is transferred.

[2] For a recent illustration, see *Aruna Mills Ltd.* v. *Dhanrajmal Gobindran*, [1968] 1 Q.B. 655.

[3] *Bowes* v. *Shand* (1877), 2 App. Cas. 455.

[4] Chapter 22, *post*.

[5] *Manbré Saccharine Co., Ltd.* v. *Corn Products Co., Ltd.*, [1919] 1 K.B. 198.

[6] No mere academic point, for if it is not a sale of goods the Act does not apply.

ing contract—that is, the rights under them—are taken to be, in a business sense, the equivalent of the goods."[1]

Not only does a transfer of a bill of lading transfer the property and the possession in the goods, but a pledge of the documents also operates as a pledge of the goods although this is not generally true of documents of title. This transferability is of crucial importance both in law and in practice. Indeed, negotiability (in this sense) is of the very essence of a bill of lading. A non-negotiable document is not strictly speaking a bill of lading at all.[2] But "it is true generally that a bill of lading is not a negotiable instrument in the sense that a bill of exchange is, and that the transferee of a bill of lading does not get a better title than his transferor."[3]

Sect. 32 (2), which has been set out above,[4] also applies to c.i.f. contracts. This section requires the seller to make a "reasonable" contract with the shipowner. It has already been seen that what is reasonable must be judged at the time the contract of carriage is made and not when the contract of sale is made.[5] So far as c.i.f. contracts are concerned one of the most important requirements of a "reasonable" shipping contract is that it should give the buyer a right of action against the shipping company for loss or damage to the goods throughout the whole period of the voyage.[6] This means that if the goods have to be transhipped the first shipowner (who contracts with the seller, and will be liable to the buyer when the documents are transferred to him) must accept liability for the defaults of subsequent shipowners who will not be in privity with the sellers nor, therefore, with the buyers. But this may no longer be true in practice because most bills of lading today exonerate the shipowner from liability after transhipment, and if these are the only available bills of lading the seller is entitled to ship on those terms.[7]

It follows from the nature of a c.i.f. contract that Sect. 32 (3) does not apply because there is always an express agreement as to the insurance of the goods. This is still the case even if special circumstances occur as a result of which the ordinary insurance cover is not effective, and it would be advisable to take out a special cover.[8]

In c.i.f. contracts the risk once again passes on shipment, and if the goods are lost at sea the buyer is still bound to pay the price, although he will as a rule have the benefit of the insurance policy.

[1] Lord Wright in *Smyth & Co., Ltd.* v. *Bailey Son & Co., Ltd.*, [1940] 3 All E.R. 60, at p. 70.
[2] *Kum* v. *Wah Tat Bank*, [1971] 1 Lloyd's Rep. 439.
[3] *Nippon Yusen Kaisha* v. *Ramjiban Serowgee*, [1938] A.C. 429, at p. 449, *per* Lord Wright.
[4] Above, p. 223.
[5] Above, p. 223.
[6] *Hansson* v. *Hamel & Horley, Ltd.*, [1922] 2 A.C. 36.
[7] *Plaimar, Ltd.* v. *Waters Trading Co., Ltd.* (1945), 72 C.L.R. 304.
[8] *Law & Bonar* v. *American Tobacco Co., Ltd.*, [1916] 2 K.B. 605.

✓ The law is the same even if the seller knows that the goods have been lost when he tenders the shipping documents.[1]

Where c.i.f. contracts differ fundamentally from f.o.b. contracts is that the general rule, which is not easily displaced,[2] is that the property only passes when the documents are transferred and paid for.[3] Where the bill of lading is taken in the seller's name this accords with Sect. 18 and Sect. 19 (1) and (2) which have already been discussed. But where, contrary to the usual practice, the bill is taken in the buyer's name the prima facie rule is that delivery to the carrier is deemed to be an unconditional appropriation,[4] but this presumption is rebutted by the very nature of the c.i.f. contract. Under Sect. 19 (3), which has been set out above,[5] it is expressly provided that if the seller sends a bill of exchange to the buyer with the shipping documents the property does not pass unless the buyer accepts the bill of exchange. Even if the seller draws a bill of exchange on the buyer and discounts it with a bank before it has been accepted by the buyer, the property will still not pass. Although the seller may obtain payment in this way he remains under a secondary liability as drawer of the bill of exchange and so property remains in him as security for this contingency.[6] Indeed, even when the seller has received the full price in advance there may be special circumstances which give him some interest in retaining the property and it may be held that the transfer of the documents remains necessary to pass property.[7]

It should be added that in the sale of unascertained goods c.i.f. the seller is often under a duty to give notice of appropriation to the buyer, but this "is not intended to pass and does not pass the property,"[8] but merely fixes the goods to be delivered, so that it would be a breach of contract for the seller to deliver any other goods. The reason for this is that the notice is not an "unconditional" appropriation within the meaning of Sect. 18, Rule 5. It is conditional on the buyer taking up the documents and paying for the goods.

EX-SHIP CONTRACTS

In these cases "the seller has to cause delivery to be made to the buyer from a ship which has arrived at the port of delivery and has

---

[1] *Manbre Saccharine Co., Ltd.* v. *Corn Products Co., Ltd.,* [1919] 1 K.B. 198.

[2] See, e.g., *Cheetham & Co., Ltd.* v. *Thornham Spinning Co., Ltd.,* [1964] 2 Lloyd's Rep. 17, where the property was held to have been retained by the seller even after the goods had been deposited in the buyer's warehouse, the seller not having been paid and having retained the shipping documents. A similar case is *Ginzberg* v. *Barrow Haematite Steel Co., Ltd.,* [1966] 1 Lloyd's Rep. 343.

[3] *Mirabita* v. *Imperial Ottoman Bank* (1878), 3 Ex. D. 164.

[4] Sect. 18, Rule 5 (2), p. 156, *ante.*   [5] Above, p. 155.

[6] *The Prinz Adalbert,* [1917] A.C. 586; *H.M. Procurator-General* v. *M. C. Spencer,* 1945] A.C. 124.

[7] *The Gabbiano,* [1940] P. 166.

[8] *Smyth & Co., Ltd.* v. *Bailey Sons & Co., Ltd.,* [1940] 3 All E.R. 60, at p. 65, *per* Lord Wright.

reached a place therein, which is usual for the delivery of goods of the kind in question."[1] In other words the seller really is under an obligation to deliver the goods to the buyer at the port of discharge in ex-ship contracts, and the buyer has no concern with the shipment. Sect. 32 therefore has no application at all to this type of case. It also follows that if the seller fails to deliver the goods the buyer is not liable for the price, or if he has paid it, he can recover it as on a total failure of consideration. Thus in *Comptoir D'Achat et de Vente du Boerenbond Belge S.A.* v. *Luis de Ridder Limitada*,[2] the plaintiffs bought a quantity of rye "c.i.f. Antwerp," but the sellers retained the bill of lading and the insurance policy under the contract, and they also guaranteed the condition of the goods on arrival. It was held by the House of Lords that these terms were inconsistent with a true c.i.f. contract and that in fact the contract was for the sale and delivery of the goods ex ship. Consequently the seller's failure to deliver the goods through the outbreak of war enabled the buyers to recover the price as on a total failure of consideration.

Generally speaking, in contracts of this kind the property and risk will only pass on delivery.

[1] *Yangtsze Insurance Association* v. *Lukmanjee*, [1918] A.C. 585, at p. 589, *per* Lord Sumner.
[2] [1949] A.C. 293.

CHAPTER 21

EXPORT AND IMPORT LICENCES

EXPORT AND IMPORT LICENCES

IN the modern world, where trade prohibitions and restrictions abound, the obtaining of an export or import licence, or both, is often a necessary prerequisite to the performance of a contract of sale. It is, therefore, a matter of considerable importance to decide which of the parties is to obtain the licence, and what happens if he fails to do so.

The courts have refused to lay down any general principles on this question, and have insisted that each case must be decided according to its own special circumstances.[1] Nevertheless, some indications may be gleaned from the cases to show the sort of considerations which the courts will treat as relevant. It goes without saying, of course, that, if the parties have expressed a clear intention as to who is to apply for a licence, or what is to happen if it is not obtained, then the courts will give effect to that intention. The difficulties arise when the parties have not expressed any such clear intention.

In ex-works or ex-store contracts it is hardly possible to doubt that in the absence of a contrary intention it is the buyer's duty to obtain all necessary permits and licences. Indeed, one can go further and say that in such contracts the seller is not concerned with what the buyer does with the goods after he has taken delivery. Hence in such cases the question of export and import licences is irrelevant to the contract of sale.

At the other end of the scale, ex-ship contracts also do not give rise to much difficulty. In the absence of any contrary intention, it is plainly the seller's duty to obtain any necessary export licence, but probably the buyer's duty to obtain an import licence if required.

It is f.o.b. and c.i.f. contracts and their many variants which tend to give rise to the difficulties in this connection. So far as f.o.b. contracts are concerned, it was for long thought that, as a result of the decision of the Court of Appeal in *H. O. Brandt & Co.* v. *H. N. Morris & Co., Ltd.*[2] the obligation to obtain an export licence was generally on the buyer. It is obvious that this would in many circumstances be a highly inconvenient conclusion. Fortunately, it now appears from the decision of the House of Lords in *A. V. Pound & Co., Ltd.* v. *M. W. Hardy & Co., Inc.*[3] that *Brandt*'s case is not to be taken as laying down any general rule, and although the House refused to lay down any general rule itself it is

[1] *A. V. Pound & Co., Ltd.* v. *M. W. Hardy & Co., Inc.*, [1956] A.C. 588.
[2] [1917] 2 K.B. 784.
[3] [1956] A.C. 588.

possible, without undue rashness, to say that prima facie in a f.o.b. contract the duty of obtaining the export licence is on the seller. *A fortiori* is this the case in a c.i.f. contract.

The points to which attention must be given in considering whether this is so in any particular case are, *inter alia*, the following. Is the seller exporting the goods from one country to the buyer in another, or are both parties resident in the same country? The latter may, of course, be the position where the buyer is buying for export to a customer abroad, and hence himself buys the goods on f.o.b. or even c.i.f. terms. In this event, as in *Brandt*'s case, it is much easier to reach the conclusion that the duty to obtain an export licence is on the buyer, because the seller is not himself selling the goods for export. It is the buyer who wants to export the goods, and naturally therefore it is for him to obtain the licence. The case is quite different in the normal position where the seller is exporting the goods to the buyer, for if the buyer is resident in some country hundreds or thousands of miles away it would be unreasonable and impracticable to expect him to obtain the export licence.

Another point to consider is whether there are any particular circumstances rendering it easier for one party or the other to obtain the licence. If, for example, the buyer and seller are resident in different countries, and only a member of a certain trade association may be granted an export licence,[1] or if the licences are granted according to a quota system based on the seller's previous shipments,[2] it becomes virtually impossible to hold that the buyer must obtain the licence.

A third relevant factor is whether the need for a licence existed when the contract was made (and if so, whether the parties knew about it) or whether the need for a licence was only imposed after the contract was made by new legislation or controls.

The duty of obtaining an *import* licence must plainly be on the importer, i.e. the buyer, in most circumstances, if only because the relevant statutory provisions will generally impose the duty on him, and in the absence of a contrary intention, "the contract must be treated as made upon the assumption that the statutory law applicable . . . should be observed by the parties to the contract."[3] This is *a fortiori* the case in a f.o.b. sale for the seller may not even know the destination of the goods.

When it has been decided whether the duty to obtain the necessary licence is on the buyer or the seller, the next question which may arise is whether the duty is absolute, i.e. is the party in question to be taken to have warranted that he will obtain the licence, or only that he will use his best endeavours to do so? If the latter is the true position, a failure

---

[1] E.g. *Peter Cassidy Seed Co., Ltd.* v. *Osuustukkuk-Auppa I.L.*, [1957] 1 All E.R. 484.

[2] *Partabmull Rameshwar* v. *K. C. Sethia, Ltd.*, [1950] 1 All E.R. 51, aff'd. (no speeches reported) [1951] 2 All E.R. 352n.

[3] *Mitchell Cotts & Co. (Middle East) Ltd.* v. *Hairco, Ltd.* [1943] 2 All E.R. 552 *per* Scott, L.J. at 554-5.

to obtain the licence will generally mean that the contract is frustrated.[1]

In *Re Anglo-Russian Merchant Traders, Ltd.*,[2] the Court of Appeal held that generally speaking there is no absolute duty to obtain a licence, and that where a seller applies for and is refused an export licence, he is not generally liable in damages for non-delivery. In *Peter Cassidy Seed Co., Ltd.* v. *Osuustukkuk-Auppa I.L.*,[3] Devlin, J., agreed with this as a general principle.

> The person whose duty it is to apply for a licence may either warrant that he will get it, that is an absolute warranty, or he may warrant that he will use all due diligence in getting it. When nothing is said in the contract it is usually—probably almost invariably—the latter class of warranty which is implied, but each case must be decided according to its own circumstances, and the question of implication must be settled in the ordinary way in which implied terms are settled.[4]

But ultimately the learned judge held that in the particular circumstances of the case the sellers had warranted that they would obtain a licence. In this case the contract stated: "Delivery: prompt as soon as export licence granted," and the sellers had assured the buyers that this was a pure formality. On the other hand, in *Mitchell Cotts & Co. (Middle East), Ltd.* v. *Hairco, Ltd.*,[5] Scott, L.J., inclined to the view that the buyers' duty to obtain a licence (in that case, an import licence) is generally absolute, and in *Partabmull Rameshwar* v. *K. C. Sethia, Ltd.*,[6] the House of Lords held, on somewhat unusual facts, that the sellers had bound themselves to obtain an export licence.

Even an obligation by a party to use his best endeavours to obtain a licence is somewhat severely applied by the courts. In *Brauer & Co. (Great Britain), Ltd.* v. *James Clark (Brush Materials), Ltd.*[7] for instance, sellers had agreed to sell goods for shipment f.o.b. a Brazilian port, "subject to any Brazilian export licence." The sellers had applied for a licence which was refused on the ground that the price was too low. On its appearing that the sellers might have obtained a licence if they had been prepared to pay the extra (some 20 per cent above the contract price) to their own suppliers, it was held that they had not used their best endeavours to obtain a licence. On the other hand, where the seller is under a duty to apply for a licence, the buyer may nevertheless be bound to supply the seller with any information (e.g. as to the ultimate destination of the goods) which may be required by the licensing

---

[1] But only if a licence has been necessary throughout the whole period available for shipment: *Ross T. Smyth & Co. (Liverpool), Ltd.* v. *W. N. Lindsay (Leith), Ltd.* [1953] 1 W.L.R. 1280.
[2] [1917] 2 K.B. 679.
[3] [1957] 1 All E.R. 484.
[4] At p. 486.
[5] [1943] 2 All E.R. 552.
[6] [1950] 1 All E.R. 51, [1951] 2 All E.R. 352 n.
[7] [1952] 2 All E.R. 497.

authority.[1] Where a seller who is under a duty to use his best endeavours fails even to apply for a licence he has the heavy burden of proving that any application was foredoomed to failure.[2]

There is, perhaps, something slightly misleading in talking of an implied warranty by a party to obtain, or to use his best endeavours to obtain, a licence. If there is no mention of the matter in the contract then the true position is simply this. The seller is bound to deliver the goods to the buyer and the buyer is bound to take delivery from the seller. If either party will not or cannot perform his obligations he is prima facie in default, unless he can show that the contract has been frustrated. Often he can show that the contract has been frustrated by proving that a necessary licence has been refused despite his best endeavours to obtain one.[3] But where the obligation to deliver (or to take delivery) is construed as an absolute obligation, then the failure to obtain the licence does not excuse non-performance. Strictly speaking, therefore, there is no question of a person warranting that "he will get a licence," or that "he will use his best endeavours to get a licence."

---

[1] *Phoebus D. Kyprianou* v. *Cyprus Textiles, Ltd.*, [1958] 2 Lloyd's Rep. 60.
[2] *Société d'Avances Commerciales (London)* v. *A. Besse & Co. (London)*, [1952] 1 T.L.R. 644.
[3] It appears that, contrary to the general rule laid down in *Joseph Constantine Steamship Line, Ltd.* v. *Imperial Smelting Corpn., Ltd.*, [1942] A.C. 154, a party who has failed to obtain a licence must himself prove due diligence in order to invoke frustration: *Brauer & Co. (Great Britain), Ltd.* v. *James Clark (Brush Materials), Ltd.*, [1952] 2 All E.R. 497; *Vidler & Co. (London), Ltd.*, v. *R. Silcock & Sons, Ltd.*, [1960] 1 Lloyd's Rep. 509.

CHAPTER 22

BANKERS' COMMERCIAL CREDITS

PAYMENT OF PRICE BY BANKERS' COMMERCIAL CREDIT[1]

WHERE a person carrying on business in one country buys goods from a seller in another country it is common practice nowadays for the price to be paid by means of a banker's commercial credit. The normal procedure is more or less as follows, although there may frequently be variations of detail.

The buyer instructs his own bank (the issuing bank) to open a credit in favour of the seller with a bank in the seller's country (the "intermediary" or "correspondent" banker). Almost invariably the buyer instructs the issuing bank that the seller is only to be allowed to draw on the credit on presentation to the paying bank of documents showing that the goods have been shipped and are on their way to the buyer. The shipping documents will comprise the seller's invoice for the goods, the bill of lading, and frequently (always in c.i.f. contracts) an insurance policy or certificate. The intermediary banker will then notify the seller that instructions have been received to open a credit in his favour, and will inform him of the precise terms on which he will be allowed to avail himself of the credit. As soon as the goods are shipped the seller will present these documents to the intermediary banker. The bank will check the documents with the terms of the credit to ensure that the goods shipped are (so far as can be seen from the documents) the contract goods, and that everything appears to be in order, and if satisfied that this is the case, will permit the seller to draw against the credit. This may be done by accepting a bill of exchange, or discounting a bill drawn on the buyer, or by making funds available in cash.

The intermediary bank will then transmit the documents to the issuing bank which will inform the buyer that they have been received. The buyer will also satisfy himself that the documents are in order, and will in due course pay the issuing bank an amount corresponding to the price paid to the seller, together with the bank's own charges. The issuing bank will, of course, pay the intermediary bank, and will release the documents to the buyer sometimes even before it has been paid. Armed with these, the buyer will then be in a position to resell the goods and transfer the documents to a sub-buyer, or alternatively, to take delivery as soon as the goods arrive.

Virtually all bankers' credits are today granted on the terms that they

---

[1] See Gutteridge and Megrah, *The Law of Bankers' Commercial Credits*, 4th ed., 1968; Davis, *The Law Relating to Commercial Letters of Credit*, 3rd ed., 1963; Ellinger, *Documentary Letters of Credit*, 1970.

are to be governed by the Uniform Customs and Practice for Documentary Credits (3rd edition, 1962) prepared by the International Chamber of Commerce. The banks of nearly all the countries in the world use this document (hereafter referred to as the Uniform Customs) which is, therefore, to all intents and purposes a part of the law of bankers' commercial credits.

There are many variations in the forms of commercial credits, the principal distinctions being between revocable and irrevocable credits, and confirmed and unconfirmed credits. Under the Uniform Customs, an irrevocable credit constitutes a definite undertaking by the issuing bank that the credit will be made available if the seller complies with the stipulated conditions. A revocable credit does not constitute a definite undertaking by the issuing bank and may be cancelled or modified without notice. The distinction between a confirmed and unconfirmed credit turns upon whether or not the intermediary bank accepts a direct obligation to the seller to honour the credit. In the former event, the intermediary bank "confirms" the credit, i.e. undertakes (sometimes for an extra commission payable directly by the seller) to pay whether or not it is put in funds by the issuing bank; in the latter event the credit is unconfirmed, the intermediary bank merely informs the seller that the credit has been opened in his favour, and the seller will have no right of recourse against the bank in the event of its refusing to pay.

In the past, doubts have even existed as to whether the seller could sue the bank if it refused to honour a confirmed credit, on the ground that there is no contract between seller and bank, owing to the absence of consideration. But in practice banks never take this technical point, and judicial pronouncements now seem to have put their liability beyond doubt.[1]

The vital element in this commercial machinery is that the seller must not be allowed to draw against the credit unless it is quite clear, so far as can be seen from an examination of the documents, that he has fulfilled his obligations under the contract. Hence it is of the first importance that the buyer should inform the issuing bank precisely what documents are required.[2] It is equally important that the documents presented by the seller to the intermediary bank should correspond exactly with the terms of the credit (which should, of course, represent the agreed terms of sale) for otherwise the bank will refuse payment, or if it pays it does so at its peril, for the buyer (or the issuing bank) may refuse to take up the documents.

The bill of lading must, therefore, cover shipment from and to the agreed ports. It must be a "shipped" bill of lading, i.e. it must acknowledge that the goods have actually been shipped, and not merely

---

[1] See especially *per* Jenkins, L.J., in *Hamzeh Malas & Sons* v. *British Imex Industries, Ltd.*, [1958] 2 Q.B. 127, at 129; also *Urquhart, Lindsay & Co.* v. *Eastern Bank, Ltd.*, [1922] 1 K.B. 318.

[2] See Article 13 of the Uniform Customs.

received for shipment,[1] and the invoice must describe the goods exactly as stated in the credit.[2] It was formerly held that even the *de minimis* rule was excluded in this situation,[3] but Article 32 of the Uniform Customs permits a tolerance of 3 per cent more or less than the contract quantity unless the credit stipulates to the contrary.[4] In other matters than quantity the position still is that the *de minimis* rule does not apply.[5] Generally, also, the credit requires "clean" bills of lading, which means that the bill must "not contain any reservation as to the apparent good order or condition of the goods or the packing."[6] Where the documents are to include insurance policies, a certificate will not suffice unless, as is customary, the credit expressly says so. On the other hand, provided that the documents presented by the seller are in order, he is entitled to avail himself of the credit notwithstanding that the buyer may have some complaint about the quality of the goods.[7] The value of this method of payment would be considerably reduced if a claim by the buyer had the effect of preventing the seller from drawing on the credit. It appears, however, that if there has been anything in the nature of fraud on the part of the seller the court has jurisdiction to restrain the seller by injunction from drawing on the credit.[8]

From the legal point of view, a commercial credit as described above involves a pledge of the documents by the seller to the paying bank which is, in due course, transferred to the issuing bank. In the normal course of events the pledge is discharged when the buyer takes up the documents and pays off the bank. If, however, something should go wrong in the performance of the contract, e.g. if the buyer should become insolvent, the bank is in a position to enforce and realise its security, if necessary, through its possession of the documents. One result of this commercial machinery has been to render virtually obsolete the seller's right of stoppage *in transitu*, for if the buyer becomes insolvent there is no fear that he will obtain the goods since he has not

---

[1] *Diamond Alkali Export Corpn., Ltd.* v. *Bourgeois*, [1921] 3 K.B. 443; Article 18 of the Uniform Customs.

[2] It was formerly held that even the bill of lading had to do this, see *Rayner & Co., Ltd.* v. *Hambro's Bank, Ltd.*, [1943] K.B. 37. But under Art. 30 of the Uniform Customs, it is sufficient if the bill of lading describes the goods in general terms.

[3] *Moralice (London), Ltd.* v. *E. D. & F. Man*, [1954] 1 Lloyd's Rep. 526.

[4] This does not apply where the credit specifies quantity in terms of packing units or containers or individual items. Nor does this entitle the seller to draw more than the amount of the credit. It simply means that the bank will pay even if the seller ships up to 3 per cent more or less than the contract quantity.

[5] *Soproma S.p.A.* v. *Marine & Animal By-Products Corpn.*, [1966] 1 Lloyd's Rep. 367, at p. 390.

[6] *Per* Salmon, J., in *British Imex Industries, Ltd.*, v. *Midland Bank, Ltd.*, [1958] 1 Q.B. 542, at 551. See now Article 16 of the Uniform Customs. In practice, bills of lading very rarely say anything about the *actual* condition of the goods. They merely acknowledge that the goods are in apparent good order and condition. That is enough for a clean bill.

[7] *Hamzeh Malas & Sons* v. *British Imex Industries, Ltd.*, [1958] 2 Q.B. 127.

[8] Ibid.

got the necessary documents, and will not be able to get them except on paying the bank.

Although, in an ordinary contract of sale of goods, delivery and payment are concurrent conditions, in contracts in which the price is to be paid by means of a commercial credit "the seller is entitled, before he ships the goods, to be assured that, on shipment, he will get paid."[1] Hence, in the absence of any agreement to the contrary, the credit must be opened by the buyer a reasonable time before the beginning of the shipment period,[2] even if the seller has some weeks or even months in which to ship, and does not in fact ship until the end of the period. This is still the case, even where the contract is on f.o.b. terms in which the buyer is entitled to fix the date of shipment.[3] The seller cannot, of course, draw against the credit until the goods are shipped because the presentation of the shipping documents is a condition precedent to his right to use the credit, so that strictly speaking there is no violation of the rule that payment and delivery are concurrent conditions. The point is that payment by means of a banker's credit is intended to operate, and does operate, not merely as a method of payment, but as a means of guaranteeing payment. Hence the seller is entitled to know before he ships the goods that the credit has been opened, and that, as soon as he presents the documents, he will be paid.

It will be seen that payment of the price by bankers' credit is very favourable to the seller in at least three respects. First, once the credit is issued, he is reasonably assured of payment; secondly, the buyer cannot delay payment by disputing the goods' conformity to the contract; and thirdly, the cost of financing the shipment period falls on the buyer. The result is that payment by this method becomes less common in a buyer's market.

Where the contract provides for payment by means of a banker's credit, and for payment against delivery of documents to a bank, the buyer fulfils his obligations by providing the credit on the agreed terms. The seller is not entitled to disregard the credit and send the documents direct to the buyer and claim payment from him.[4] Accordingly the buyer may reject documents tendered directly to him instead of to the bank. But this does not mean that the seller can never sue the buyer for the price even if the price was agreed to be payable by bankers' credit. For example if, by some commercial mishap, the goods are actually delivered to and accepted by the buyer without payment by the

---

[1] *Per* Denning, L.J., in *Pavia & Co. S.P.A.* v. *Thurmann-Nielson*, [1952] 2 Q.B. 84, at 88.

[2] *Sinason-Teicher Inter-American Grain Corpn.* v. *Oilcakes & Oilseeds Trading Co. Ltd.*, [1954] 1 W.L.R. 1394.

[3] *Ian Stach, Ltd.* v. *Baker Bosley, Ltd.*, [1958] 2 Q.B. 130.

[4] *Soproma S.p.A.* v. *Marine & Animal By-Products Corpn.*, [1966] 1 Lloyd's Rep. 367, at pp. 385–6.

bank, the seller retains his ordinary right to sue for the price[1] unless perhaps in exceptional circumstances it may be held that he had accepted the letter of credit as absolute payment.[2] So also if the goods are sold f.o.b. and the seller does not reserve the right of disposal, property normally passes (as we have seen) on shipment. Therefore if the bank wrongfully refuses payment in such a case, the seller may still sue the buyer for the price.[3] The same is probably true if the bank fails to pay because of insolvency.[4]

[1] *W. J. Alan & Co., Ltd.* v. *El Nasr Export & Import Co.*, 1972] 2 Q.B. 179; *Saffron* v. *Société Minière Afrika* (1958–9), 100 C.L.R. 231.
[2] See Ellinger in (1961), 24 *M.L.R.* 530.
[3] *Newman Industries Ltd.* v. *Indo-British Industries Ltd.*, [1956] 2 Lloyd's Rep. 219, at p. 236; reversed on the facts, [1957] 1 Lloyd's Rep. 211.
[4] See note 3.

CHAPTER 23

THE UNIFORM LAWS ON INTERNATIONAL SALES[1]

In 1964 two international Conventions were signed at The Hague with a view to the unification of the law relating to international sales. The first Convention—the major one—contains the Uniform Law on the International Sale of Goods, and the second Convention contains the Uniform Law on the Formation of Contracts for the International Sale of Goods. The Conventions have been ratified by the United Kingdom and statutory effect is given to them by the Uniform Laws on International Sales Act, 1967,[2] which came into force on 18th August 1972. The Uniform Laws have given rise to a good deal of dissatisfaction and there are already proposals to modify them; there has certainly been no rush to ratify the Conventions as they stand. Nevertheless, since the Act of 1967 is now on the Statute book it is necessary to give some indication of its principal provisions here.

APPLICATION OF U.L.I.S.

The Uniform Law on International Sales (which is abbreviated here, for convenience, as U.L.I.S.) provides that it applies to a contract for the sale of goods entered into by parties whose places of business are in different contracting states in the following three cases—

(a) where the goods are in the course of carriage or will be carried from one State to another;
(b) where the acts constituting the offer and the acceptance have been effected in different States;
(c) where the goods are to be delivered in a State other than the place where the offer and acceptance were effected.

But the Convention permits a Contracting State to limit more drastically the cases in which U.L.I.S. will apply by providing that it is only to apply where it has been chosen by the parties to the contract of sale as the law of the contract. Sect. 1 (3) of the 1967 Act enables an Order-in-Council to be made taking advantage of this limitation and this has been done. It has, however, been made clear that this is only an interim measure and that in due course this restriction will be dropped. Until that happens, the Conventions will be of little importance in English Law. It is not entirely clear what is to happen if the contract is made between parties one of which carries on business in a State con-

[1] See Graveson, Cohn and Graveson, *Uniform Laws on International Sales Act*, 1967.
[2] See Feltham (1967), 30 *M.L.R.* 670.

239

taining this restriction, and the other in a Contracting State which does not. The problem cannot be solved by falling back on ordinary rules to determine what is the proper law of the contract because Art. 2 of the Convention excludes the rules of private international law. Probably the answer is that Sect. 1 (3) of the 1967 Act will be treated as the overriding enactment and U.L.I.S. will not apply in this situation[1]—at all events as a part of the law of the United Kingdom.

It will be seen that the scope of the Act will be very limited. Apart from the requirement that the parties must choose the law expressly, the provisions of Art. 1 of U.L.I.S. limit its application to cases in which the parties carry on business in different Contracting States. So, for instance, a sale of goods f.o.b. English port, or c.i.f. overseas port, entered into between buyers and sellers carrying on business in England would not even prima facie fall within U.L.I.S. This may be unfortunate because it may mean that in string sales of goods intended for export the different contracts may be governed by different laws. If, for instance, A, an English company, sells goods to B, also an English company, f.o.b. Liverpool for export to European firm C, to which B has sold the goods, the contract between A and B will be governed by English law while the contract between B and C may be governed by U.L.I.S.

The second restriction on the application of the Act is that it only applies as between parties whose places of business are in different Contracting States. Since very few States have so far ratified the Convention there will, at present, be few such Contracting States.

The third restriction on the application of U.L.I.S. is that Contracting States may declare (and effect can be given to such declarations under Sect. 1 (5) of the 1967 Act) that "two or more States shall not be regarded as different States". Thus, if two Contracting States have very similar systems of law so that conflict of laws problems are unlikely to arise between them, they may prefer to exclude the operation of U.L.I.S. as between themselves. It is not yet known whether the United Kingdom will take advantage of this clause in relation to other parts of the Commonwealth which may also become Contracting States if and when the restriction requiring express selection of U.L.I.S. is dropped.

Finally, it is to be observed that (even if the law applies in the absence of express provision by the parties) its effect may be excluded in whole or in part by the intention of the parties, express or implied.

SCOPE OF THE ACT

Contracts Governed by U.L.I.S.

Unlike the Sale of Goods Act, U.L.I.S. contains no definition of a contract of sale of goods. It does, however, provide that it is not

---

[1] But it will then presumably be necessary to apply ordinary rules to ascertain the proper law, and if those rules indicate that the proper law is that of the State which has not restricted the operation of U.L.I.S., it may come in by the back door as it were.

to apply to sales of securities, negotiable instruments or money; nor to the sale of any ship, vessel or aircraft which is or will be subject to registration; nor to the sale of electricity; nor to a sale by authority of law or on execution or distress.[1] It is also provided that a contract for the sale of goods to be manufactured or produced shall be considered to be a contract of sale unless the party ordering the goods supplies an "essential and substantial" part of the materials necessary for the manufacture of the completed article. This introduces a test similar to that used in English law to distinguish contracts of sale from contracts for skill and labour.

What Parts of the Contract Are Governed by U.L.I.S.

U.L.I.S. does not purport to deal exhaustively with the legal relationship of a buyer and seller. It does not deal, in particular, with the formation of the contract, nor with the transfer of the property in the goods, nor with the validity of the contract, nor with the effects of frustration or failure to obtain import and export licences. So far as formation of the contract of sale is concerned, this is the subject of the second Convention, and is also given statutory force by the 1967 Act. But the other matters remain to be governed by English law, or such other law as is the proper law of the contract. There is little doubt that this is likely to lead to complications in the future.

SUMMARY OF THE MAIN PROVISIONS OF U.L.I.S.

U.L.I.S. consists of 101 Articles many of which have been very carefully drafted. In view of the restricted nature of the law's probable operation in England a full and detailed commentary here would be out of place. It is proposed merely to summarise the main provisions of the law.

Delivery of the Goods

The seller is required to deliver the goods and hand over any documents relating thereto as required by the contract and U.L.I.S. (Art. 18). If the contract involves carriage of the goods, and no other place for delivery has been agreed upon, delivery is effected by handing over the goods to the carrier (Art. 19-2 corresponding closely with Sect. 32 (1) of the Sale of Goods Act).

The goods must be delivered at the agreed date (Art. 20). If a period for delivery is allowed the seller may deliver at any time within that period (Art. 21). If no date is fixed the goods must be delivered in a reasonable time (Art. 22, corresponding to Sect. 29 (2) of the Sale of Goods Act).

The place of delivery is prima facie the seller's place of business, but if the sale relates to specific goods which are known to be elsewhere, then that is the place of delivery. This is provided for by Art. 23, corresponding closely to Sect. 29 (1) of the Sale of Goods Act. But Art. 23 then goes on to provide that the same rule applies to goods to be manufactured or produced at a place known to the parties when the contract is made. This means that prima facie a contract for manufactured goods will be an ex-works contract under U.L.I.S. though doubtless a contrary intention will often be inferred.

Arts. 24 to 34 deal with the buyer's remedies for a failure to deliver in due time or at the right place. Such failure is a breach of the contract entitling the buyer to damages, as of course it does under the Sale of Goods Act. The effect of failure to deliver in due time does not, however, give the buyer the right to treat the contract as repudiated forthwith, as he may do under English law. Whether it has this effect depends on whether the failure is a "fundamental breach." This concept, now somewhat discredited in English law,[1] thus reappears rather surprisingly in U.L.I.S. A breach is said to be fundamental whenever the party in breach knew or ought to have known, when the contract was made, that a reasonable person in the situation of the other party would not have entered into the contract if he had foreseen the breach and its effects (Art. 10). This definition has been severely criticised on the ground that whether a reasonable person would have entered into the contract, even if he had foreseen the breach and its effects, would largely depend on whether there was a seller's market or a buyer's market.[2] But the provision is probably workable enough in practice and it is supplemented in the case of delayed delivery by Art. 28. This Article provides that, in the case of commodities for which a price is quoted on a market available to the buyer, any delay amounts to a fundamental breach.

If the seller is guilty of fundamental breach, the buyer may, as in English law, affirm the contract or treat it as at an end; but he must inform the seller of his election within a reasonable time, or the contract is at an end. If the delay does not amount to a fundamental breach the buyer may grant the seller an additional reasonable period of time for delivery and failure to deliver during this time will be a fundamental breach.[3] The effect of delivery at the wrong place also depends on whether this amounts to a fundamental breach. But in this event failure by the buyer to avoid the contract promptly means that he will be relegated to a claim for damages.

Conformity of the Goods

Arts. 33 to 49 deal with the seller's duties in respect of the quantity and quality of the goods. Under Article 33 (a) the seller must not

[1] See above, p. 126.
[2] Graveson, Cohn and Graveson, op. cit. pp. 55-7.
[3] Art. 17. Cf. the similar principle in English law that a delivery date is waived by the buyer he may thereafter give notice of a new date: Rickards v. Oppenheim, [1950] 1 K.B. 616, supra, p. 65.

deliver more or less than the contract quantity; under (*b*) he must not deliver "goods which are not those to which the contract relates or goods of a different kind"; (*c*) requires conformity with a sample; (*d*) requires the goods to "possess the qualities necessary for their ordinary or commercial use"; (*e*) stipulates that the goods must be suitable for a particular purpose contemplated by the contract; and a residuary paragraph (*f*) requires the goods generally to possess the qualities and characteristics contemplated by the contract.

Para. (*a*) of this Article corresponds to Sect. 30 of the Sale of Goods Act; para. (*b*) corresponds broadly with Sect. 13, and para. (*c*) with Sect. 15 (2) (*a*) of the Sale of Goods Act. Para. (*d*) appears to correspond broadly with Sect. 14 (2) but it will be noted that it avoids the term "merchantable quality." It is also drafted so as to accord with some earlier definitions given to the term "merchantable quality"[1] though these were later discarded in favour of the concept of "commercial saleability". One reason for discarding the earlier test of merchantability was that it did not adequately cater for the case of goods which are ordinarily used for a variety of purposes. If the goods are suitable for some ordinary purpose but not for others, difficulties may therefore arise under this paragraph.[2] Para. (*e*) corresponds with the new Sect. 14 (3) of the Sale of Goods Act. Probably the paragraph will only apply where the purpose "contemplated by the contract" is indeed a purpose for which the seller expressly or impliedly undertakes that the goods will be suitable. It is hardly to be supposed that the purpose would be regarded as "contemplated by the contract" if the seller, though knowing the buyer's purpose, makes it clear that he accepts no responsibility for deciding if the goods are suitable for that purpose. Even so it may well be that this paragraph would impose a heavier liability on a seller than Sect. 14 (3) of the Act. For instance, if a question arises as to the suitability of the goods for resale in the country into which they are to be imported, the position under the Sale of Goods Act now is that the importing buyer will not normally be treated as relying on the skill or judgment of the exporting seller.[3] It would seem that under the Uniform Law the seller might be liable in this case.

There is, however, one very important respect in which the Uniform Law imposes a less stringent duty on the seller than the Sale of Goods Act. Article 33–2 provides that breach by the seller as to the quantity of the goods, or lack of conformity, is to be ignored "where it is not material." This is a substantial departure from the position in English law exemplified by *Arcos Ltd.* v. *Ronaasen & Son.*[4] Materiality is a much

---

[1] *Supra*, p. 85.

[2] See, e.g., *B. S. Brown Ltd.* v. *Craiks Ltd.*, [1970] 1 All E.R. 823, discussed *supra*, p. 87.

[3] See *Teheran-Europe Corporation* v. *S. T. Belton Ltd.*, [1968] 2 Q.B. 545, discussed, *supra*, p. 92.

[4] [1933] A.C. 470, *supra*, p. 73.

broader concept than is allowed for by the *de minimis* rule and Art.
33–2 seems a considerable improvement on English law.

The buyer's remedies for lack of conformity depend on whether the
breach is fundamental; if it is, he may avoid the contract by giving
prompt notice to the seller (Art. 43). Otherwise he can only claim
damages (Art. 41–2). But in all cases the buyer must give prompt notice
of lack of conformity after he has examined the goods, or if defects
are revealed later, as soon as they are discovered. An overall time limit
of two years is imposed for complaints based on lack of conformity
(Art. 39). If the complaint relates to part of the goods only, the buyer
can reject that part if the breach is fundamental but he cannot
repudiate the whole contract unless the breach is fundamental in
relation to the whole contract.[1]

Documents

The Uniform Law does not deal comprehensively with the duties of
the parties under f.o.b. or c.i.f. or other export contracts. Accordingly
Art. 50 merely requires the seller to deliver any documents required by
the contract or by usage and Art. 51 gives the buyer appropriate
remedies.

Transfer of Property

Arts. 52 and 53, though headed "Transfer of Property" in fact deal
with the seller's title to the goods. These provisions avoid the difficulties
which have arisen under Sect. 12 of the Sale of Goods Act[2] by requiring
the buyer to notify the seller of any adverse third party claim to the
goods and giving the seller the opportunity to free the goods from
such a claim. If the seller does so (e.g. by paying off the claimant) the
buyer can only claim for actual loss.

Other Obligations of the Seller

If the seller is bound to dispatch the goods to the buyer Art. 54
requires him to make "in the usual way and on the usual terms" any
necessary contract for the carriage of the goods (corresponding to
Sect. 32 (2) of the 1893 Act). He is also bound to provide the buyer, on
request, with information necessary to enable the buyer to insure if the
seller is not himself bound to insure. This corresponds with Sect. 32 (3)
of the Sale of Goods Act but avoids the difficulties encountered under
that provision[3] by confining the seller's obligation to cases where the
buyer requests the information.

Obligations of the Buyer

The buyer must pay for the goods and take delivery of them as
required by the contract and the Uniform Law (Art. 56). If no price is

---

[1] This seems to be the effect of Art. 45 though the wording is not explicit.
[2] *Supra*, p. 49.　　　　　[3] *Supra*, p. 222.

fixed the buyer is bound to pay the price "generally charged by the seller at the time of the conclusion of the contract." This differs from Sects. 8 and 9 of the Sale of Goods Act which require the buyer to pay a reasonable price. This may be considered unfair to the buyer but it plainly accords with normal commercial understanding. Where no price is fixed the usual understanding is that the buyer agrees to pay the seller's usual price.

The seller is not entitled to sue for the price merely because property has passed; if it is "in conformity with usage and reasonably possible" for the seller to resell he cannot claim payment of the price but only damages (Art. 61).

The buyer is obliged to take delivery of the goods and do anything necessary to enable the seller to hand over the goods (Art. 65). Payment of the price and delivery of the goods are, as under Sect. 28 of the Sale of Goods Act, concurrent conditions (Art. 71) but the buyer is not bound to pay the price until he has had an opportunity of examining the goods.

Suspension of the Contract

Art. 73 contains a provision which appears somewhat different from anything in the Sale of Goods Act but is, in effect, a generalisation of of the seller's right of stoppage *in transitu* though it applies on the face of it to both parties. The Article is closer to Sect. 2–609 of the U.C.C. than to anything in the Sale of Goods Act. It states that where "the economic situation of the other party appears to have become so difficult that there is good reason to fear that he will not perform a material part of his obligations" the first party may suspend performance. Thus if the seller fears insolvency of the buyer he may withhold delivery, and this remains the case even if documents of title have been transferred to the buyer (Art. 73–2) but there is provision for protecting the rights of a bona fide transferee of the documents (Art. 73–3).

Discharge through Other Events

Art. 74 contains provisions which appear to be substantially in accord with English law as to discharge of the parties by reason of non-performance through impossibility. Art. 75 deals with breach in instalment sales and Art. 76 recognises the concept of anticipatory fundamental breach.

Remedies

The rules as to damages are similar to those in English law (Art. 82 and Arts. 84–87) but Art. 83 provides that if the buyer fails to pay the price at the date the seller is entitled (apart from damages) to interest at 1 per cent above bank rate of the seller's country. The principle of mitigation of the loss is also adopted (Art. 88).

Preservation of the Goods

An interesting innovation is Art. 92–2 providing that even if the buyer rejects the goods he must, if they have been dispatched to him, take possession of them on behalf of the seller provided this can be done "without unreasonable inconvenience or unreasonable expense." The buyer then has a lien on the goods for his reasonable expenses. He is also empowered to sell them on notice to the seller, if the seller unreasonably fails to take possession of the goods (Art. 94). Here again U.L.I.S. is closer to the U.C.C. (Sect. 2–603) than to the Sale of Goods Act.

Passing of Risk

Arts. 96 to 101 deal with the passing of risk. Contrary to the general rule under the Sale of Goods Act, risk does not pass with property (which is indeed not dealt with by the Uniform Law) but on delivery (Art. 97). However, the risk only passes on delivery if the goods conform to the contract, or when the buyer fails to reject the goods so delivered.[1]

If delivery is delayed through the buyer's default risk passes at the latest time when it would have passed had there been no default (Art. 98–1) but in sales of unascertained goods risk will not pass even then unless the seller has set the goods aside and notified the buyer accordingly (Art. 98–2).[2]

Some of these provisions appear to conflict with basic principles of English law as applied to f.o.b. and c.i.f. contracts but in practice there will be little difference. For instance if documents are transferred and paid for in a c.i.f. sale it is not clear in English law whether risk passes if the goods do not conform with the contract. But acceptance of the documents does not prevent subsequent rejection of the goods for breach of condition as to the quality of the goods, and therefore it is largely immaterial that the risk may have passed to the buyer. Under the Uniform Law the risk will not have passed on delivery of documents in any event. As between buyer and seller therefore, the result will be the same. The only problem will be whether practical difficulties may arise in claiming against the insurer: the buyer will have the policy but the risk will be on the seller. However, the buyer will obviously have to return the policy if he rejects the goods. In an f.o.b. contract, however, there is more likely to arise the disturbing possibility that the seller may not be able to claim against the insurer for lack of privity in this situation.

---

[1] This seems to be the effect of Art. 97–2 but the drafting leaves much to be desired.

[2] Art. 98–3 meets the case where the seller cannot set aside part only of the goods: presumably this would cover (e.g.) sale of petrol from a bulk storage tank. Cf. *Sterns* v. *Vickers*, [1923] 1 K.B. 78.

SUMMARY OF U.L.O.F.

The Second Convention—the Uniform Law on the Formation of Contracts for the International Sale of Goods (abbreviated here to U.L.O.F.)—is much shorter than the first. It applies to all contracts which "if they were concluded" would be governed by U.L.I.S.

By Art. 2, the provisions of U.L.O.F. are subject to the course of dealing between the parties, or to usage, but no offer may stipulate that silence amounts to an acceptance. By Art. 3 an offer or acceptance need not be in writing or any other form.

An offer may be revoked so long as the revocation is communicated before the acceptance is dispatched (Art. 5–4 which accords with English law). An important difference from English law is that an offer cannot be revoked if the revocation is not in good faith or in conformity with fair dealing, or if the offer indicates that it is open for a fixed time, or that it is firm or irrevocable (Art. 5–2). Such indication may be express or implied (Art. 5–3).

The acceptance may consist of a communication, or of the actual dispatch of the goods by the seller or of the price by the buyer (Art. 6).

A purported acceptance introducing additions, limitations or other modifications is, as in English law, only effective as a counter-offer (Art. 7–1). But an important difference from English law is provided for by Art. 7–2 which allows an acceptance to contain additional or different terms "which do not materially alter the terms of the offer." Unless the offeror promptly objects to these additions he will be deemed to have accepted them.

U.L.O.F. avoids directly settling the issue whether the posting of a letter of acceptance concludes a contract. But Art. 9–2 provides that the acceptance is to be treated as though it arrived in due time if it would have done so in the normal course of transmission. The practical effect of this will be similar to the English rule that posting constitutes acceptance. But it is qualified by the fact that the offeror may inform the acceptor "orally or by dispatch of a notice" that he considers his offer as having lapsed. Therefore under U.L.O.F. the *dispatch* of such a notice by the offeror after posting (but before receipt) of an acceptance by the offeree will prevent a contract coming into existence; the position in English law is to the contrary.

A useful provision is that the expression "to be communicated" means to be delivered at the address of the person to whom the communication is directed.

PART VI

THE REMEDIES OF THE SELLER

CHAPTER 24

REAL REMEDIES

SELLER'S RIGHTS AND POWERS AGAINST THE GOODS

WHERE the buyer defaults in his principal obligation, that is, payment of the price, the seller has of course, his personal action on the contract itself, but if the seller were always compelled to fall back on this remedy, his position would be in many respects unsatisfactory. The law has, therefore, developed certain real rights whereby the seller can still look to the goods as a kind of security for payment of the price. In considering these real rights four different fact situations must be distinguished.

Firstly, there may be a sale of specific goods in which the property has passed to the buyer, and the goods have been delivered to him. Here the seller has relinquished all right to look to the goods for his price, and he is relegated to his personal right of action against the buyer. If the seller attempts to enforce his right to the price by seizing the goods from the buyer's possession, the seller's conduct will be a breach of Sect. 12 of the Act,[1] and will doubtless constitute the tort of conversion as well.

Secondly, there may be a sale of specific goods in which the property has passed to the buyer, but the goods have not yet been delivered. In this case, whether the goods are still in the possession of the seller or have been dispatched to the buyer (but not yet reached him) the law confers on the seller, subject to certain conditions (*a*) the power to resell the goods and pass a good title to a third party, and powers incidental thereto, and (*b*) the right to do so vis-à-vis the first buyer. It must be emphasised that these are two very different things, for the seller may well have the power to pass a good title to a bona fide transferee without the right so to do, in other words the resale may constitute a breach of contract as against the first buyer although it validly transfers the property. Indeed, as we have seen, the seller always has the power to transfer a good title to an innocent third party so long as he is in possession of the goods, but the right to do so is more severely restricted, as will become apparent in due course.

[1] *Healing (Sales) Pty., Ltd.* v. *Inglis Electrix Pty., Ltd.* (1968), 42 A.L.J.R. 280.

Thirdly, there may be an agreement to sell specific or unascertained goods in which no property has yet passed, but in which the seller is under a personal obligation to deliver certain particular goods and no others. This is always the case where there is an agreement to sell specific goods, and it may also occur in a sale of unascertained goods when there has been sufficient appropriation to place the seller under an obligation to deliver those particular goods, although there has not been sufficient appropriation to pass the property. This may happen, for example, in a c.i.f. contract when the seller gives notice of appropriation, or in a contract for the manufacture of an article where the personal obligation to deliver the goods may come into being before the property passes.[1] In these cases the law does not need to confer a power of resale on the seller because he still has the property in the goods, and can, simply by virtue of this property, transfer a good title to another buyer. But it does not follow that the seller does not need statutory protection from the consequences of exercising this power. For example, if the buyer defaults in payment of the price on the date agreed, the seller, being still the owner of the goods, has power to resell them (and the incidental powers of retaining them, or recovering them from a carrier) but the exercise of these powers might be a breach of contract. The law, therefore, protects the seller from the consequences of availing himself of these powers, subject to certain conditions.

Fourthly, there may be an agreement to sell unascertained goods in which no property has yet passed, and in which there is no obligation to deliver any particular goods. Here no special provisions are needed at all, because the seller clearly has full power to exercise any control over the goods, and such exercise cannot be a breach of contract. For example, if a seller agrees to sell 1,000 tons of a certain type of wheat and procures wheat of that description intending to deliver it in performance of the contract, no property passes before appropriation, nor is the seller bound to deliver that particular 1,000 tons. If, therefore, the seller resells this 1,000 tons to a third party he can pass a good title thereto and his action will not be a breach of contract.

It must be said that the Act fails to draw clearly all the above distinctions, with the natural consequence that confusion results. One does not have to agree with all the conclusions of Hohfeld to acknowledge that there is a world of difference between a power and a right of resale, yet this clear distinction is obscured by the ambiguity of such phrases as "the seller has the right to do such and such," or "the seller may do such and such."[2] An examination of Sect. 39 which confers the three real rights of the unpaid seller fully reveals this confusion—

[1] *Per* Parke, B., in *Laidler* v. *Burlinson* (1837), 2 M. & W. 602, at 610-11; *Wait* v. *Baker* (1848), 2 Ex. 1, 8-9.
[2] Cf. Sects. 39, 41, 44 and 48.

(1) Subject to the provisions of this Act, and of any statute in that behalf, notwithstanding that the property in the goods may have passed to the buyer, the unpaid seller of goods, as such, has by implication of law—

(*a*) A lien on the goods or right to retain them for the price while he is in possession of them;

(*b*) In case of the insolvency of the buyer, a right of stopping the goods *in transitu* after he has parted with the possession of them;

(*c*) A right of resale as limited by this Act.

(2) Where the property in goods has not passed to the buyer, the unpaid seller has, in addition to his other remedies, a right of withholding delivery similar to and co-extensive with his rights of lien and stoppage *in transitu* where the property has passed to the buyer.

The first subsection is not likely to give much difficulty although it is not so clearly drafted as it might have been. It is clear that its object is to confer on the seller not merely the power to deal with the goods, but also the right so to do as against the buyer. This section is for the benefit of the seller and not of the third party, so that a power without a corresponding right would have been useless in this respect. But the second subsection is not so innocuous, and may well give rise to trouble in the future. It is easy to see what the draftsman had in mind when he inserted it. He clearly thought it necessary to put in the right of withholding delivery, but not the power of resale because the seller who is still owner does not need this power. But, as we have seen, this is a confusion of the right and the power. If Sect. 39 (2) only means to lay down certain powers then it is totally unnecessary because the owner of the goods has the power of withholding delivery no less than the power of passing a good title to a third person. On the other hand, if Sect. 39 (2) is meant to confer, not a power which already exists, but a right to exercise this power, as one would have thought, it follows that the right to resell the goods should have been included as well. The omission of this right might have the remarkable result that an unpaid seller could, as against the buyer, resell the goods in accordance with the Act where the property had passed to the buyer, but could not do so where the property had not passed. But whatever the literal construction of these provisions may be, the courts have shown no inclination to be too literal-minded. On the contrary it has recently been affirmed that the seller's rights of resale cannot be greater where the property has passed to the buyer than where it has not.[1]

The second defect of Sect. 39 (2) is that it states that the owner-seller's right of withholding delivery is similar to and co-extensive with, the rights of lien and stoppage *in transitu* where the property has passed. This fails to differentiate those cases where the seller is under

---

[1] *R. V. Ward, Ltd.* v. *Bignall*, [1967] 1 Q.B. 534, at p. 545.

a personal duty to deliver a particular lot of goods, and those cases where there is no such duty. In the latter event the seller's right of withholding delivery is by no means co-extensive with his right of lien. It is a far wider right, for it arises without default on the part of the buyer. Obviously where the seller's duty has not yet become attached to any particular goods there can be no question of a breach of contract by him simply because he chooses to withhold delivery of the goods which he had intended to use in performance of the contract. It is inconceivable that this section should, by a side wind as it were, alter these fundamentals in the law of sale. In proceeding to examine the three real rights of the unpaid seller, then, it must be borne in mind that we are only concerned with the second and third fact situations put above. In other words we are concerned with those cases where, but for these special rights, the seller would have a power but no right to deal with the goods by withholding delivery or reselling, and those cases where the seller would have neither the power nor the right to do so.

Who is an Unpaid Seller?

These three real rights may only be exercised by an unpaid seller, and the first question is, who exactly is an unpaid seller within the meaning of the Act. The meaning of "unpaid" is explained by Sect. 38 (1) as follows—

(1) The seller of goods is deemed to be an "unpaid seller" within the meaning of this Act—
   (a) When the whole of the price has not been paid or tendered;
   (b) When a bill of exchange or other negotiable instrument has been received as conditional payment, and the condition on which it was received has not been fulfilled by reason of the dishonour of the instrument or otherwise.

The seller is "unpaid" within the meaning of the Act even though he has sold on credit.

The meaning of a "seller", for present purposes, is explained by Sect. 38 (2) as follows—

(2) In this Part of this Act the term "seller" includes any person who is in the position of a seller, as, for instance, an agent of the seller to whom the bill of lading has been indorsed, or a consignor or agent who has himself paid, or is directly responsible for, the price.

If, for example, the seller sells the goods through an agent and the agent has paid the price, or made himself liable to pay it, he, the agent, is entitled to exercise any of the rights of the unpaid seller.[1] A buyer who has rejected goods is not, however, in the position of a seller

[1] *Ireland* v. *Livingston* (1872), L.R. 5 H.L. 395, 408; *Cassaboglou* v. *Gibb* (1883), 11 Q.B.D. 797, 804.

within the meaning of this section, and cannot claim any of the unpaid seller's rights in order to secure repayment of the price.[1] It follows that a buyer who is minded to reject goods on the ground that
they do not conform to the contract, should, if he has paid the price,
be careful to do so only if he is satisfied of the solvency of the seller.
The rejection of the goods revests the property in the seller, so if he
should prove insolvent the buyer will have worsened his position by
the rejection.

We can now pass to examine in detail the three real rights conferred
by the Act on the unpaid seller.

UNPAID SELLER'S LIEN

The seller's lien in contracts of sale of goods now depends entirely
on the Sale of Goods Act, which is quite inconsistent with any suggestion that there may be any equitable lien differing from that provided
for in the Act.[2]

The seller's lien is a right to retain the goods until the whole of the
price has been paid or tendered. It does not "strictly speaking give
to the seller any property in the goods subject to it."[3] At common law
a lien does not confer a power of sale, but the unpaid seller has a
statutory power and right of sale subject to certain conditions which
will be examined in due course. In practice, of course, the lien is often
exercised merely as a preliminary to a resale of the goods.

The seller's right of lien is a qualification upon the duty to deliver
the goods laid down by Sect. 27, and it only arises if three conditions
are satisfied.

In the first place the seller must be an unpaid seller as defined by
Sect. 38. This section has already been set out, and it is only necessary to emphasise here that the whole of the price must be paid or
tendered before the buyer can claim to have discharged the lien. This
raises important questions in connection with instalment contracts, and
it has been held that, generally speaking, the seller is entitled to exercise his lien over any part of the goods if any part of the price is outstanding. In other words he is not confined to claiming a lien over
those goods to which the unpaid part of the price may be attributed.[4]
Reference should be made here to Sect. 42 which is as follows—

> Where an unpaid seller has made part delivery of the goods he may
> exercise his right of lien . . . on the remainder, unless such part delivery
> has been made under such circumstances as to show an agreement to
> waive the lien . . .

[1] *J. L. Lyons & Co., Ltd.* v. *May & Baker, Ltd.*, [1923] 1 K.B. 685.
[2] *Transport & General Credit Corpn., Ltd.* v. *Morgan*, [1939] 2 All E.R. 17, at
p. 25, *per* Simonds, J.
[3] *Per* Fletcher Moulton, L.J., in *Lord's Trustee* v. *G.E. Railway*, [1908] 2 K.B.
at pp. 63-4.
[4] *Ex parte Chalmers* (1873), 8 Ch. App. 289; *Longbottom & Co., Ltd.* v. *Bass
Walker & Co., Ltd.*, [1922] W.N. 245.

Where, however, there is not one contract, but a number of separate contracts for goods to be separately paid for and delivered, it naturally follows that the seller cannot claim a lien over any part of the goods which have been paid for, merely because some other goods have not been paid for.[1] This would be a general lien, which may be conferred by contract, but the lien which the Act confers is only a special or particular lien. It does not follow, of course, from the mere fact that the goods are to be delivered and paid for in instalments that there is not still one contract only. On the contrary the general rule is that a contract for the sale of goods by instalments is still one contract, and the lien may therefore be exercised over any part of the goods.[2]

In the second place, the seller is not entitled to a lien if the goods have been sold on credit. If a seller agrees to allow the buyer credit this does not necessarily mean that he is prepared to deliver the goods before the price has been paid. It may only mean that the seller is not insisting on immediate payment to which he is prima facie entitled if he is ready and willing to deliver. Oddly enough, the Act appears to assume that an agreement as to credit necessarily means an agreement that the buyer shall be entitled to the goods before payment, for Sect. 41 (1) (a) says—

(1) Subject to the provisions of this Act, the unpaid seller of goods who is in possession of them is entitled to retain possession of them until payment or tender of the price in the following cases, namely:

(a) Where the goods have been sold without any stipulation as to credit;

Read literally this would mean that if a person buys goods, and asks the seller for time to pay, which the seller grants, the buyer is forthwith, without more, entitled to demand delivery. Yet in granting credit the seller may have meant no more than that he would not insist on immediate payment, and in this event the court would no doubt give effect to the intention.

Although the seller, therefore, has generally no right of lien if he sells the goods on credit, there are two exceptions to this rule, for Sect. 41 (1) proceeds to add two further cases where the lien may be claimed—

(b) Where the goods have been sold on credit, but the term of credit has expired;

(c) Where the buyer becomes insolvent.

The first of these exceptions clearly enables the seller to claim a lien on the goods where the buyer has not taken advantage of the sale on credit to take possession of the goods. But it also seems to confer a right of lien even where the seller acts wrongfully in refusing to allow

[1] *Merchant Banking Co., Ltd.* v. *Phoenix Bessemer Steel Co., Ltd.* (1877), 5 Ch. D. 205, 220.
[2] *Ex parte Chalmers* (1873), 8 Ch. App. 289.

the buyer delivery despite the agreement as to credit, although it may be that the buyer could recover damages for non-delivery in this event.

The second exception requires rather closer examination. This clause enables the seller to refuse delivery even where he has agreed to sell the goods on credit (and *a fortiori*, if he has not) if the buyer becomes insolvent. On the meaning of insolvency reference should be made to Sect. 62 (3)—

> A person is deemed to be insolvent within the meaning of this Act who either has ceased to pay his debts in the ordinary course of business, or cannot pay his debts as they become due, whether he has committed an act of bankruptcy or not . . .

It is important to note that the mere fact that the buyer has become insolvent, or even that he has announced his insolvency, does not amount to a repudiation of the contract.[1] It is, therefore, open to the trustee in bankruptcy or to a sub-buyer to tender the amount due to the seller and claim delivery of the goods. On the other hand, "If a person who has entered into a contract of this kind gives to the vendor before he has parted with the goods that which amounts in effect to this notice, 'I have parted with all my property, and am unable to pay the price agreed upon', it is equivalent to a repudiation of the contract."[2] In such a case the seller can treat the contract as at an end, and do as he pleases with the goods, and if he resells at a loss, he can prove in the bankruptcy for the remainder. For present purposes the important point is that, even if the seller has sold the goods on credit, he can refuse to deliver them if the buyer becomes insolvent, except on payment of the whole price. He cannot be compelled to deliver up the goods and relegated to his right to prove in the bankruptcy for the price.

The third essential requirement of the unpaid seller's right to a lien is that he must be in possession of the goods. The lien is the right of an "unpaid seller of goods who is in possession of them . . . to retain possession of them." It is not a right which enables the seller to regain a possession which has been given up. Possession is always a difficult subject, perhaps largely because it has not always been appreciated that possession means different things in different branches of the law.[3] Indeed, it does not always have the same meaning in the same branch of the law. In *G.E. Railway* v. *Lord's Trustee*,[4] Lord Macnaghten expressly recognised that the seller's lien differs from other liens in certain respects. It seems highly probable, for example, that the degree of control necessary to retain a seller's lien differs from that necessary

---

[1] *In re Phoenix Bessemer Steel Co., Ltd.* (1876), 4 Ch. D. 108; *Ex parte Chalmers* (1873), 8 Ch. App. 289.

[2] *Per* Jessel, M.R., in *Ex parte Stapleton* (1879), 10 Ch. D. 586, at p. 590.

[3] This now seems to have been recognised by the House of Lords, see *R.* v. *Warner*, [1969] 2 A.C. 256.

[4] [1909] A.C. 109, 115.

to retain an innkeeper's or repairer's lien. An innkeeper does not lose his lien although he permits the owner the most complete control over the goods, provided only that they are not taken out of the inn. A repairer may even retain his lien although he permits the owner to take the goods away for a limited purpose every day, provided they are returned at night.[1] It was indeed formerly thought that a seller likewise did not lose his lien if he merely delivered the goods to the buyer as his agent or bailee, but this is probably not so today, even if it ever was.[2] There is, however, no reason to doubt that some element of control over the goods by the buyer is not inconsistent with the seller's retention of his lien.

At common law a seller was only entitled to his lien if he was in possession as seller, and he lost his right of lien if he only retained possession as agent or bailee of the buyer. But the law was altered by the Act, Sect. 41 (2) of which enacts that—

> The seller may exercise his right of lien notwithstanding that he is in possession of the goods as agent or bailee . . . for the buyer.

But if the seller agrees to hold the goods as agent or bailee it may be held that he has waived his lien, the possibility of which is not excluded by this subsection.[3]

The seller's lien is twice said by the Act to be a lien for the price[4] so presumably the seller is not entitled as seller to claim a lien for storage charges or the like. The decision of the House of Lords in *Somes* v. *British Empire Shipping Co.*[5] is usually cited as laying down that the seller has no lien for storage charges in any circumstances, but in fact the case only decided that the seller cannot claim a lien in respect of storage charges which arise as a result of the seller's exercise of his lien for the price. If the seller for his own benefit declines to deliver the goods before payment, it is not unreasonable to say that the cost of storing the goods during the time before the buyer pays should not give the seller the right to a lien for those charges. But if the storage charges are not the result of the seller's refusal to deliver, but the direct consequence of the buyer's default in taking delivery, it is hard to see why the seller should not have a lien for such charges. However, the general principle is that a bailee cannot claim a lien (except by express contract) unless he has in some way undertaken to improve the goods, so that mere storage charges would not, in any event, give rise to a lien.[6]

---

[1] *Albemarle Supply Co.* v. *Hind & Co.*, [1928] 1 K.B. 307.
[2] See *Benjamin on Sale* (8th ed.) citing *Tempest* v. *Fitzgerald* (1820), 3 B. & Ald. 680. But this was a case of a buyer exercising some rights of dominion by permission of and under the supervision of the seller (exercising horse on seller's land).
[3] P. 258, *post.*   [4] Sect. 39 (1) (*a*) and Sect. 41 (1).   [5] (1860), 8 H.L.C. 338.
[6] *Re Southern Livestock Producers Ltd.*, [1963] 3 All E.R. 801.

Loss of Lien

The seller loses his lien in one of four ways—

Firstly, if the price is paid or tendered the seller ceases to be an unpaid seller and therefore loses his lien. But (apart from any question of waiver to be considered shortly) he is entitled to retain possession until payment or tender. If this is so it might seem that payment or tender is a condition precedent to the buyer's right to claim delivery, but as we have seen Sect. 28 expressly says that payment and delivery are concurrent conditions. It is usually inferred from this that actual tender of the price is not necessary provided the buyer is ready and willing to pay the price and there is judicial authority to the effect that this at any rate is the limit of the seller's duty to deliver.[1] But if the buyer sues for non-delivery without making tender it is difficult to see how the court could avoid giving effect to the unequivocal provision of Sect. 41 (1) that the seller is entitled to retain possession until payment or tender of the whole price. It could, however, be argued that the seller waives the need for such a tender if he makes it quite plain that he is not going to deliver the goods in any event.[2]

The remaining three ways in which the seller loses his lien are set out in Sect. 43 which runs—

> (1) The unpaid seller of goods loses his lien . . . thereon—
>
> (a) When he delivers the goods to a carrier or other bailee . . . for the purpose of transmission to the buyer without reserving the right of disposal of the goods;
>
> (b) When the buyer or his agent lawfully obtains possession of the goods;
>
> (c) By waiver thereof.

We have already seen that for some purposes delivery to a carrier is deemed to be delivery to the buyer,[3] but this section clearly differentiates between these two different possibilities, and as will be seen shortly, the seller's right of stoppage *in transitu* depends on this very distinction. Although the seller loses his lien on delivery to the carrier he may still have the right of stoppage *in transitu*, but it is still important to decide when the goods pass into the possession of the carrier, because the extent of the right of lien differs from that of stoppage *in transitu*. In particular, the seller can only stop the goods if the buyer is insolvent, whereas his right of lien only depends on the absence of a stipulation as to credit. It follows that the seller may well have a right of lien in circumstances in which he will have no right of stoppage once the goods have been delivered to the carrier.

The meaning of a right of disposal has already been considered in considering Sect. 19,[4] and if it means the same thing here as it does in that section it follows that a seller who takes a bill of lading in his

[1] *Levey & Co., Ltd.* v. *Goldberg*, [1922] 1 K.B. 688.

[2] See *Peter Turnbull & Co., Ltd.* v. *Mundas Trading Co., Ltd.* (1954), 90 C.L.R. 235.

[3] P. 63, *ante.*   [4] Pp. 154 and 224, *ante.*

own name will have a right of lien until he transfers the bill. It has, however, been argued that right of disposal means something different here, viz. a right of disposal of the *possession*.[1] The point is a difficult one. On the one hand it would be strange to find a different meaning attributed to the same phrase in a similar context in two parts of the same Act. On the other hand, by Sect. 39 (1) (*a*) the seller only has a lien while he is in possession of the goods and delivery to a carrier normally means that the seller no longer has possession. Moreover, by Sect. 39 (2) the seller's right to a lien is the same whether or not property has passed; but if the seller "reserves the right of disposal" within the meaning of Sect. 43 by taking a bill of lading in his own name he will in fact lose his lien when property passes. The answer to these difficulties probably lies in the principle that possession of a bill of lading (at least where it is in the name of the party in possession) confers possession of the goods. As a practical matter it seems clear that shipping the goods will not normally deprive the seller of his lien if the goods are deliverable to him (or his order) under the bill of lading. In the absence of any contrary agreement the seller may decline to transfer the bill of lading except against payment of the price.

Since possession is essential to the maintenance of a lien, it naturally follows that when the buyer or his agent lawfully obtains possession of the goods the lien is lost. It is submitted that "lawfully" here means "with the consent of the seller," so that even if the goods are obtained in circumstances amounting to a criminal offence, provided that it is with the consent of the seller, the lien will be lost. It is only by such an interpretation that the section can be brought into harmony with Sect. 25 (2) of the Sale of Goods Act and Sect. 9 of the Factors Act, which, as we have seen, enable a buyer in possession with the consent of the seller, to pass a good title to a third party. Although it may be a little odd to say that a possession obtained in circumstances amounting to an offence may be "lawfully" obtained, it is submitted that this is more consonant with the rest of the Act, and this construction would probably be adopted.[2] But if the buyer obtains possession of the goods without the consent of the seller, the lien is not lost, and even if the property has passed to the buyer it appears that he cannot pass a good title free from the lien to a third party.

---

[1] Schmitthoff, *Sale of Goods*, 2nd ed., pp. 158–9.
[2] See, e.g., *Du Jardin* v. *Beadman*, [1952] 2 Q.B. 712 (*ante* p. 195), which is inconsistent with any suggestion that the lien would bind a bona fide purchaser to whom the buyer disposes of the goods after having obtained possession by larceny by a trick. This is also confirmed by the New Zealand decision in *Jeffcott* v. *Andrews Motors, Ltd.*, [1960] N.Z.L.R. 721, holding that the bona fide purchaser is protected without deciding whether the lien survives or not. Although it may be argued that this does not preclude the possibility of the lien surviving as between seller and buyer in such circumstances it is difficult to see how the seller could enforce the lien or what significance the survival of the lien could have. It is, perhaps, arguable that if the lien did survive, a disposition by the buyer to a third party who took with notice of the circumstances would be void as against the seller.

It has already been suggested that the seller's lien cannot avail him as against third parties taking in good faith even if he delivers the goods to the buyer merely as his agent or bailee.[1] But it may be that in such a case the seller will retain his lien as against the buyer, a point which is only likely to assume practical importance in somewhat unusual circumstances.[2]

The fourth way in which the seller may lose his lien is by waiver. In a certain sense delivery of the goods to the buyer on credit is but an instance of waiver of the lien, but the seller may waive his lien without giving up possession at all. If, for example, the seller should ask the buyer's permission to retain possession by way of temporary loan, he may be held to have waived his lien. Although Sect. 41 (2) says that the seller may exercise his lien notwithstanding that he is in possession as the buyer's bailee or agent, the subsection does not say that the seller may exercise his lien notwithstanding that he has impliedly waived his lien. And, if the seller, having originally refused to sell on credit, were later to agree to the buyer taking possession before payment, this would presumably amount to a waiver of the lien, and the seller would not be able to change his mind again and insist on the lien after all.[3] Moreover, if the seller wrongly deals with the goods in a manner inconsistent with the buyer's rights he is held to have waived his lien, and cannot therefore plead lack of payment or tender if sued by the buyer in conversion.[4]

Sect. 43 (1) (c) dealing with waiver is probably to be read subject to Sect. 41 (1) (b) and (c) which confer a lien where the goods are sold on credit, but the term of credit has expired, or where the buyer has become insolvent, since both these clauses contemplate a situation in which there is a waiver followed by later events causing the lien to revive. If, therefore, the seller were originally to refuse credit, but were later to waive his lien it is probable that the subsequent insolvency of the buyer would cause the lien to revive if the seller were still in possession of the goods. This, at any rate, was the position at common law.[5]

The seller's right of lien is not affected by any sub-sale or other disposition of the goods by the buyer unless he has assented thereto. The meaning of this has already been considered.[6] It must also be remembered that if the seller allows the buyer to have possession of the documents of title, or of the goods themselves, a transfer of these to an innocent third party will defeat the right of lien.

A seller who has once lost his lien does not regain it merely because

---

[1] Pp. 209–10, ante.　　　[2] See n. 2 on p. 257, supra.

[3] Cf. Bank of Africa v. Salisbury Gold Mining Co., Ltd., [1892] A.C. 281, at p. 284, per Lord Watson.

[4] Jones v. Tarleton (1842), 9 M. & W. 675; Mulliner v. Florence (1878), 3 Q.B.D. 484.

[5] Townley v. Crump (1835), 4. A. & E. 58.

[6] Pp. 182–3, ante.

he obtains possession of the goods once more.[1] But a seller who exercises his right of stoppage *in transitu* is in effect restored to his former position, and regains his lien.

The exercise of the seller's right of lien does not of itself rescind the contract of sale. This naturally follows from the fact that failure by the buyer to pay the price at the agreed time is not a breach of condition which justifies the seller in repudiating the contract. This question will be more fully examined later.[2]

UNPAID SELLER'S RIGHT OF STOPPAGE *IN TRANSITU*

The seller's right of stoppage *in transitu* is set out in Sect. 44—

Subject to the provisions of this Act, when the buyer of goods becomes insolvent, the unpaid seller who has parted with the possession of the goods has the right of stopping them *in transitu*, that is to say, he may resume possession of the goods as long as they are in course of transit, and may retain them until payment or tender of the price.

It makes no difference whether or not the property has passed to the buyer.[3] Where the property has not passed, the seller has, in virtue of his ownership, the power to stop the goods, and the Act makes the exercise of this power rightful as against the buyer; where the property has passed the Act confers both the power and the right to stop.

It has been said that "the courts look with great favour on the right of stoppage *in transitu* on account of its intrinsic justice,"[4] and this is certainly borne out by judicial pronouncements. In *Booth Steamship Co., Ltd.* v. *Cargo Fleet Iron Co., Ltd.*,[5] for example, Lord Reading said—

It is a right founded upon the plain reason that one man's goods shall not be applied to the payment of another man's debt.

But this is mere rhetoric, and inaccurate rhetoric at that. The right of stoppage is not primarily a right to prevent one man's goods being applied to another man's debt, but a right to retake goods which have been sold to one man and to prevent those goods being applied to the payment of *his* debts. It is by no means obvious that the justice of the case is on the side of the seller when the matter is viewed from this angle.[6] However, it seems to accord with commercial morality that the seller should be treated as, in a sense, a secured creditor, looking to the goods as his security, until they have finally passed into the possession

---

[1] *Valpy* v. *Gibson*, (1847) 4 C.B. 837; *Pennington* v. *Motor Reliance Works, Ltd.*, [1923] 1 K.B. 127.

[2] P. 268, *post*.   [3] Sect. 39 (2).

[4] Chalmers, *Sale of Goods Act*, p. 124, 13th edn. (This passage has been excised from later editions.)

[5] [1916] 2 K.B. 570, at p. 580.

[6] "It is not founded on any ethical principle" *per* Brett, L.J., in *Kendall* v. *Marshall, Stevens & Co., Ltd.* (1883), 11 Q.B.D. 356, 364.

of the buyer. In modern times the development of the system of payment against documents, and in particular of payment by bankers' commercial credits has virtually rendered the right of stoppage obsolete.[1] Where the price is to be paid in this way, the seller has little to fear from the threat of the buyer's insolvency for the seller will retain the control of the goods through the documents of title until he is paid. The law relating to stoppage *in transitu* is therefore only important where the sale is on credit.

Before the seller can exercise his right of stoppage *in transitu* three conditions must be satisfied. Firstly, the seller must be an unpaid seller within the meaning of the Act. Secondly, the buyer must be insolvent, and thirdly, the goods must be in course of transit. The first two of these have already been considered, and it remains now to examine the meaning of the expression "course of transit." The decisions at common law on this subject were very numerous and in 1877 Jessel, M.R., said that "As to several of them there is great difficulty in reconciling them with principle; as to others, there is great difficulty in reconciling them with one another; and as to the whole, the law on this subject is in a very unsatisfactory state."[2] Sect. 45 of the Act has made a determined, and on the whole, successful attempt to reduce this chaos to a number of definite rules.

The goods are in transit when they have passed out of the possession of the seller into the possession of a carrier, but have not yet reached the possession of the buyer. The difficulties inherent in the concept of possession are no less here than elsewhere in the law. Generally speaking, the question "When does the transit commence?" has not given rise to nearly as much difficulty as the question, "When does the transit end?", but one ambiguity must be cleared up. If the carrier is the seller's own agent no question of the right of stoppage arises at all, for the goods, while in the possession of such agent, are still sufficiently in the possession of the seller to enable him to exercise his lien, and he need not invoke the less extensive right of stoppage. The right of stoppage only arises when the carrier is an independent contractor, who holds possession of the goods on his own behalf, as carrier.[3]

It is now necessary to examine the question, "When does the transit end?" In the first place it must be clearly understood that, although Sect. 32 (1) says that delivery to a carrier is prima facie deemed to be delivery to the buyer, this is only a constructive and not an actual delivery, and it is only an actual delivery which ends the right of stop-

---

[1] See *ante*, p. 236.

[2] *Merchant Banking Co., Ltd.* v. *Phoenix Bessemer Steel Co., Ltd.* (1877), 5 Ch. D. 205, at p. 220.

[3] It has been held in New Zealand that the Post Office is not a carrier for this purpose and that there is no right of stoppage over goods consigned by post: *Postmaster-General* v. *W. H. Jones & Co. (London), Ltd.*, [1957] N.Z.L.R. 829.

page.[1] If this were not so, of course, Sect. 32 (1) would be inconsistent with the whole concept of stoppage *in transitu*, because this right postulates delivery to a carrier, but not delivery to the buyer. This much is clear from Sect. 45 (1)—

> Goods are deemed to be in course of transit from the time when they are delivered to a carrier by land or water, or other bailee . . . for the purpose of transmission to the buyer, until the buyer, or his agent in that behalf, takes delivery of them from such carrier or other bailee. . . .

Although, therefore, delivery to a carrier is not, *ipso jure*, delivery to the buyer for this purpose, there is no reason why the buyer should not be able to show that, in the particular circumstances of the case, the carrier was his agent, and that therefore the transit was at an end, just as the seller can show that the carrier was his agent, and that the transit had never started. This possibility is expressly recognised by Sect. 45 (1) which refers to the buyer or "his agent," and by Sect. 45 (5) which says—

> When goods are delivered to a ship chartered by the buyer it is a question depending on the circumstances of the particular case, whether they are in the possession of the master as a carrier, or as agent to the buyer.

If the ship is owned by the buyer, clearly delivery of the goods to the master is a delivery to the buyer's agent which terminates the transit. Likewise, if the ship is demised to the buyer so as to vest complete control over the vessel in the buyer, the master is treated as being employed by the buyer; and then delivery to the ship is delivery to the buyer. But if the ship is merely chartered for a voyage or a fixed period as is the usual case, the master remains the servant of the shipowner, and does not become the agent of the buyer, so that delivery to the ship does not end the right of stoppage. If the seller is owner of the ship no question of the right of stoppage arises at all, of course, because the goods are still in the possession of the seller while on the ship.

It should also be noted that the mere fact that the contract is for the sale of goods f.o.b. does not exclude the right of stoppage. Although the seller's duty in a contract f.o.b. is complete when he has placed the goods on board this does not mean that he is not still interested in them and that he cannot subsequently stop them if the buyer becomes insolvent.[2] The right of stoppage is not lost merely because the seller is entitled to say, "I have done my duty, I wash my hands of the goods from now on." Similarly, the transit is not at an end merely because it is the buyer who gives the instructions for the dispatch of the goods for part or all of the voyage. "Wherever it is part of the bargain between the vendor and the vendee that the transit shall last

[1] *Ex parte Rosevear China Clay Co., Ltd.* (1879), 11 Ch. D. 560, 569.
[2] Ibid., 560.

up to a certain time, the transit continues until that time has arrived."[1] But if the buyer requests delivery to a certain place or person, the transit does not continue merely because the buyer intends ultimately to give, and does in fact give, fresh directions for the dispatch of the goods elsewhere. The law on this point was summed up by Brett, L.J., (as he then was) in *Bethell & Co., Ltd* v. *Clark & Co., Ltd.*—[2]

> Where the transit is a transit which has been caused either by the terms of the contract or by the directions of the purchaser to the vendor, the right of stoppage *in transitu* exists. But, if the goods are not in the hands of the carrier by reason either of the terms of the contract or of the directions of the purchaser to the vendor, but are *in transitu* afterwards in consequence of fresh directions given by the purchaser for a new transit, then such transit is no part of the original transit and the right to stop is gone. So also, if the purchaser gives orders that the goods shall be sent to a particular place, there to be kept till he gives fresh orders as to their destination to a new carrier, the original transit is at an end when they have reached that place.

It follows that in the ordinary way if the goods pass through successive stages of transit from one carrier to another in pursuance of the contract or of later directions given by the buyer to the seller, the transit continues and the seller retains his right to stop the goods until they reach their ultimate destination.[3] But if the buyer intercepts the goods at some stage in the course of the transit the right to stop is lost. Thus Sect. 45 (2) says—

> If the buyer or his agent in that behalf obtains delivery of the goods before their arrival at the appointed destination, the transit is at an end.

Where, therefore, the seller of goods contracted to deliver them free of charge at the buyer's premises in London, but the carriers delivered the goods at dock warehouses in accordance with instructions from the buyer, it was held that there was no right to stop.[4]

The transit is normally brought to an end by actual delivery of the goods to the buyer, but the transit is also determined if the carrier in effect attorns to the buyer, or if he wrongfully refuses to deliver to the buyer. Thus Sect. 45 (3) and (6) say—

> (3) If, after the arrival of the goods at the appointed destination, the carrier or other bailee . . . acknowledges to the buyer, or his agent, that he holds the goods on his behalf and continues in possession of them as bailee . . . for the buyer, or his agent, the transit is at an end, and it is immaterial that a further destination for the goods may have been indicated by the buyer.

[1] *Kendall* v. *Marshall, Stevens & Co., Ltd.* (1883), 11 Q.B.D. 356, at p. 369, *per* Bowen, L.J.
[2] (1888), 20 Q.B.D. 615, at p. 617. Cf. *Lyons* v. *Hoffnung* (1890), 15 App. Cas. 396.
[3] *Reddall* v. *Union Castle Mail Steamship Co.* (1915), 84 L.J.K.B. 360.
[4] *Plischke & Sohne G.m.b.H.* v. *Allison Bros., Ltd.*, [1936] 2 All E.R. 1009. Cf. *Valpy* v. *Gibson* (1847), 4 C.B. 837, *Reddall* v. *Union Castle Mail Steamship Co., supra.*

(6) Where the carrier or other bailee . . . wrongfully refuses to deliver the goods to the buyer, or his agent in that behalf, the transit is deemed to be at an end.

If, however, the buyer rejects the goods the transit is not at an end, for Sect. 45 (4) says—

If the goods are rejected by the buyer, and the carrier or other bailee . . . continues in possession of them, the transit is not deemed to be at an end, even if the seller has refused to receive them back.

It is not clear on the face of the Act whether subsect. (4) is to be read subject to subsect. (3) or vice versa. If the carrier informs the buyer that the goods have arrived, and that he holds them on his behalf, and subsequently the buyer inspects the goods and rejects them, does the transit continue or not? As the Act is doubtful resort may be had to the decisions at common law, and these seem to show that in such a case the transit is not ended because the carrier's attornment to the buyer only transfers the possession to him on the assumption that he assents thereto. Where he rejects the goods the attornment has no effect and the right to stop continues.[1]

As with the seller's lien the right of stoppage may generally be exercised over part only of the goods where some other part has been delivered. Under Sect. 45 (7)—

Where part delivery of the goods has been made to the buyer, or his agent in that behalf, the remainder of the goods may be stopped *in transitu*, unless such part delivery has been made under such circumstances as to show an agreement to give up possession of the whole of the goods.

Somewhat surprisingly, the Act does not make it clear whether the transfer of the bill of lading to the buyer is by itself sufficient to terminate the seller's right of stoppage. The U.C.C. (Sect. 2–705 (2) (*d*)) explicitly provides that negotiation of any negotiable document of title to the buyer (which of course covers transfer of a bill of lading) terminates the right of stoppage. But it seems implicit in Sect. 47 of the English Act that mere transfer of the bill of lading to the buyer does not prevent the seller from stopping the goods in transit.

The right of stoppage may also be lost by sub-dealings with the goods by the buyer. Considerable difficulties have arisen here, and it is essential to keep two points clearly distinct. The first question which arises is whether the sub-buyer or pledgee is entitled to possession of the goods free from the seller's right of stoppage, and the second question is whether, assuming the sub-buyer or pledgee to be so entitled, the seller can exercise his right of stoppage over the money paid by the sub-buyer in the event of a sale, or over the goods subject to the pledgee's rights in the event of a pledge. To take the latter possibility

[1] *Bolton* v. *Lancs. & Yorks. Railway* (1866), L.R. 1 C.P. 431; cf. *Taylor* v. *G.E. Railway* (1901), 17 T.L.R. 394.

first, there can be no doubt that the seller can still exercise his right of stoppage, notwithstanding that the goods have been pledged, but, of course, he can only do so subject to the rights of the pledgee. In other words the seller can claim the return of the goods from the carrier if he is prepared to pay off the pledgee. What is more, even if the pledgee obtains the goods in virtue of his pledge and sells them, the seller is entitled to claim that the balance of the price shall be paid directly to him, and shall not be paid to the insolvent buyer. This was decided by the House of Lords in *Kemp* v. *Falk*[1] and the decision has been incorporated in the proviso to Sect. 47 of the Act, which says that, where the documents of title to goods which the seller would otherwise be entitled to stop have been pledged, "the unpaid seller's right of lien or stoppage *in transitu* can only be exercised subject to the rights of the transferee." It is true that this section is mainly concerned to give priority to the rights of the pledgee over those of the seller (hence the word "only") but it seems necessarily to recognise that the right of stoppage may be exercised in these circumstances.

The problem is more difficult in the case of a sub-sale by the buyer. In *Ex parte Golding Davies & Co., Ltd.*[2] A sold goods to B and B resold them to C before they were dispatched by A. The bill of lading was taken in C's name, but before it was transferred to C, B became insolvent. C not yet having paid the price, A claimed that he was entitled to intercept the money before it reached B, i.e. in effect, A claimed the right of stoppage over the money. It was held by the Court of Appeal that A was entitled to do this. It is sometimes said that the basis of the judgments was that the bill of lading not having been transferred to C, the vendor still retained the right of stoppage, but it is submitted that this view is untenable because no stress was laid on the non-transfer of the bill of lading in the judgments. On the contrary the *ratio decidendi* was stated clearly by Cotton, L.J.—

> Can the vendor make effectual his right of stoppage *in transitu* without defeating in any way the interest of the sub-purchaser? In my opinion he can. He can say, "I can claim a right to retain my vendor's lien. I will not defeat the right of the sub-purchaser, but what I claim is to defeat the right of the purchaser from me, that is, to intercept the purchase money which he will get so far as it is necessary to pay me." That, in my opinion, he is entitled to do.[3]

In *Kemp* v. *Falk*[4] Lord Selborne clearly thought that *Ex parte Golding Davies & Co., Ltd.*,[5] was wrongly decided, but the other members of the House in that case expressed no opinion on the point. *Ex parte Golding Davies & Co., Ltd.*, is also not easy to reconcile with *Berndtson* v. *Strang*.[6] In this case the Chancery Court of Appeal held that where

---

[1] (1882), 7 App. Cas. 573.   [2] (1880), 13 Ch. D. 628.
[3] At 638.   [4] (1882), 7 App. Cas. at pp. 577-8.
[5] (1880), 13 Ch. D. 628.   [6] (1868), 3 Ch. App. 588.

goods are damaged in transit the unpaid seller has no right to the proceeds of an insurance policy covering the goods. His right of stoppage "is a right to stop the goods in whatever state they are. If they arrive injured and damaged in bulk or quality the right to stop *in transitu* is so far impaired."[1] Presumably it follows that if the goods are entirely lost in transit the right to stop is similarly lost, yet there seems no difference in principle between such a case, and a resale of the goods.[2] But even if *Ex parte Golding Davies & Co., Ltd.*,[3] was rightly decided at common law, the question must still be answered whether it survives the Sale of Goods Act, and the answer to this, it is conceived, must be No. The proviso to Sect. 47 says quite clearly that if the bill of lading is transferred by way of resale to a third party taking in good faith and for value, the unpaid seller's right of stoppage "is defeated." No mention is made of the possibility of transferring the right from the goods to the money. It should also be borne in mind that even if the above submissions are wrong, and *Ex parte Golding Davies & Co., Ltd.*,[3] does represent the modern law, yet there can be no shadow of a claim of stoppage when the purchase price from the sub-purchaser has actually been paid over to the insolvent buyer. This would be a blatant attempt to obtain full payment of a debt from a trustee in bankruptcy, and could not be permitted.

Position as between Vendor and Carrier

If a carrier to whom a notice of stoppage has been sent wrongly delivers the goods to the buyer, he is liable for conversion to the vendor, so it is of the utmost importance that the relationship between the carrier and the seller should be clearly defined. Oddly enough the Act does no more than lay down the methods which the seller may adopt of exercising his right of stoppage, and impose the burden of redelivery on the seller. Sect. 46 says—

(1) The unpaid seller may exercise his right of stoppage *in transitu* either by taking actual possession of the goods, or by giving notice of his claim to the carrier or other bailee . . . in whose possession the goods are. Such notice may be given either to the person in actual possession of the goods or to his principal. In the latter case the notice, to be effectual, must be given at such time and under such circumstances that the principal, by the exercise of reasonable diligence, may communicate it to his servant or agent in time to prevent a delivery to the buyer.

(2) When notice of stoppage *in transitu* is given by the seller to the carrier, or other bailee . . . in possession of the goods, he must redeliver

---

[1] *Per* Lord Cairns, at p. 591. But in most c.i.f., and in many f.o.b. contracts, the policy would be taken out by the seller and he would therefore be able to claim the proceeds himself.

[2] Presumably the result would be different if the damage or loss occurred after the seller had given notice of exercise of the right of stoppage.

[3] (1880), 13 Ch.D.628.

the goods to, or according to the directions of, the seller. The expenses of such redelivery must be borne by the seller.

The carrier has a lien on the goods for the freight due, and this lien takes priority over the seller's right of stoppage. Hence the carrier can refuse to redeliver the goods to the seller unless the latter is first prepared to discharge the amount of the freight. But any general lien which the carrier may have by contract is postponed to the seller's right of stoppage unless the seller was a party to the contract which conferred this general lien.

> A carrier of goods, whether by land or sea, has a lien on the goods for their freight, but this right, which arises from the common law is confined to the carrier's charges payable on the carriage of the particular goods. Such a lien prevails against the rights of the vendors as well as those of the consignees. On the other hand, a general lien, that is, a right to retain the goods for other freights due upon other transactions can only arise by express contract or from general usage, and such a lien, apart from contract, cannot affect the rights of the consignor.[1]

In some respects the carrier's lien is of a peculiar nature, as against the unpaid seller, for it confers on him the positive right of action to recover the amount of the freight. Moreover, an unpaid seller who stops the goods in transit is under a duty to give the carrier instructions as to the disposal or return of the goods, and if he fails to do so the carrier is not responsible for the consequences. In *Booth Steamship Co., Ltd.* v. *Cargo Fleet Iron Co., Ltd.*,[2] the defendants sold goods to X and dispatched them by the plaintiffs to Brazil. Before the vessel reached its destination, the sellers exercised their right of stoppage and requested the plaintiffs not to deliver to the buyers. The plaintiffs then asked what they were to do with the goods, but the defendants gave no instructions and refused to pay the freight. After further fruitless correspondence during which the defendants repudiated all liability for freight or landing charges, the plaintiffs finally landed the goods at their original destination, and sued for the freight. It was held by the Court of Appeal that the responsibility for what had happened lay entirely with the sellers and that the carriers were entitled to damages representing the amount of the freight and the landing charges.[3]

As is the case with the seller's lien, the exercise of the right of stoppage *in transitu* does not of itself rescind the contract of sale. The exercise of the right to stop enables the seller to resume possession of

---

[1] *Per* Lord Buckmaster in *U.S. Steel Products Co., Ltd.* v. *G.W. Railway Co.*, [1916] 1 A.C. 189, at p. 195.

[2] [1916] 2 K.B. 570.

[3] It is not easy to see what is the juristic nature of this right. If the seller was no party to the contract of carriage, it cannot be a contractual right. Nor does it appear to be tortious for the seller does nothing wrong in stopping the goods. On the other hand the claim resembles an action for damages rather than a quasi-contractual claim for restitution. In *Booth S.S. Co., Ltd.* v. *Cargo Fleet Iron Co., Ltd.*, the judges thought the claim was not contractual.

the goods, and to retain them until payment or tender of the price.[1]
It follows that if the buyer's trustee in bankruptcy chooses to tender
the whole price the seller is bound to accept it and redispatch the
goods to him, unless indeed there are grounds for inferring a repudiation of the contract by the buyer.

UNPAID SELLER'S RIGHT OF RESALE

It has already been pointed out that the seller's power of resale
must be carefully distinguished from his right of resale. The seller has
the power to resell the goods (1), if he still has the property in the
goods, or (2) if, even though the property has passed, he is in possession of the goods within Sect. 25 (1) of the Sale of Goods Act, or
Sect. 8 of the Factors Act, or (3) if, even though the property has
passed, the seller has exercised his right of lien or stoppage *in transitu*.
We need not enlarge on the first case, and the second has already
been fully discussed, but the third needs to be briefly considered. Sect.
48 (2) says—

> Where an unpaid seller who has exercised his right of lien . . . or
> stoppage *in transitu* re-sells the goods, the buyer acquires a good title
> thereto as against the original buyer.

This presumably means that, even though the property has passed to
the first buyer, if the seller exercises his right of lien or stoppage, he
has power to resell the goods passing a good title to a third party even
though he could not have done so under Sect. 25 (1) of the Sale of
Goods Act and Sect. 8 of the Factors Act. In other words this subsection envisages the possibility of a resale by a seller not in possession of the goods, and is to that extent wider than these two sections.

It is now necessary to examine the seller's right of resale. The seller
is entitled as against the buyer to resell the goods in any of the following circumstances—

1. If the seller's obligation to deliver has not yet crystallised into an
obligation to deliver any specific goods. Here it is clear that the seller
incurs no liability if he resells the goods for the simple reason that it
cannot be said which are "the goods" which he must deliver.

2. If the buyer repudiates the contract, it is again clear on principle
that the seller can accept the repudiation and may resell the goods if
he chooses. It is of course immaterial whether or not the property has
passed to the first buyer. Refusal to accept the goods by the buyer is
prima facie a repudiation of the contract, and if the seller accepts that
repudiation, the contract is thereby rescinded, and the seller may resell
the goods and sue for damages for non-acceptance. If the property
passed to the buyer on the making of the contract the rescission of the
contract by the seller's acceptance of the buyer's repudiation will

---

[1] Sect. 44.

revest the property in the seller. If, however, the seller refuses to accept the repudiation then he cannot prima facie resell the goods. He cannot do so because either the property will have passed to the buyer, or the seller will still be bound to transfer it to the buyer. In this situation the seller can only resell if authorised to do so by Sect. 48 (3) or (4) which are discussed below.[1] As we have seen, however, the mere fact that the buyer is late in paying the price is not a repudiation of the contract, but is at most a breach of warranty for which the seller may recover damages.

3. In the third place the seller has a right of resale if he has expressly reserved this right in the original contract, on default by the buyer. In this event Sect. 48 (4) comes into play—

> Where the seller expressly reserves the right of re-sale in case the buyer should make default, and on the buyer making default re-sells the goods, the original contract of sale is thereby rescinded, but without prejudice to any claim the seller may have for damages.

As we have seen Sect. 48 (1) states that—

> Subject to the provisions of this section, a contract of sale is not rescinded by the mere exercise by an unpaid seller of his right of lien . . . or stoppage *in transitu*.

4. Lastly, the unpaid seller is given a right of resale if the goods are perishable, or, in other cases, if he gives notice to the buyer that he intends to resell and the buyer still does not pay the price due. Sect. 48 (3) states that—

> Where the goods are of a perishable nature, or where the unpaid seller gives notice to the buyer of his intention to re-sell, and the buyer does not within a reasonable time pay or tender the price, the unpaid seller may re-sell the goods and recover from the original buyer damages for any loss occasioned by his breach of contract.

The first of these four possibilities has already been discussed and the second does not need enlarging upon here. The question what exactly amounts to a repudiation of the contract is never an easy one, but it is a question which belongs more properly to the general law of contract. The third and fourth cases, however, require further consideration.

It will be noted that Sect. 48 (4) explicitly provides that, where the seller resells in the exercise of an express power of resale in the contract, then "the original contract of sale is thereby rescinded." Sect. 48 (3) contains no such provision to cover the case where the goods are perishable or where the seller resells after notice. In *Gallagher* v. *Shilcock*[2] it was held by Finnemore, J., that this meant that a sale under Sect. 48 (3) did not rescind the original contract of sale. Accordingly, if the property in the goods had already passed to the buyer, then the seller was reselling

---

[1] R. V. Ward, Ltd. v. Bignall, [1967] 1 Q.B. 534.   [2] [1949] 2 K.B. 765.

the buyer's goods and was acting as a quasi-pledgee rather than as an owner. Hence, the buyer remained liable for the price (subject to credit for the resale price) and would indeed have been entitled to claim any profit made if the resale were at a higher price.

This decision was unsatisfactory in many ways and it was overruled by the Court of Appeal in *R. V. Ward, Ltd.* v. *Bignall.*[1] In this case the plaintiffs sold two cars, a Vanguard and a Zodiac, to the defendant, who almost at once repudiated the purchase and refused to pay or take delivery of the goods. The sellers at first wrote to the buyer insisting that the property in both cars had passed to him and that he was therefore liable for the price. But the sellers also gave notice that if the buyer did not pay the price within five days they would resell the cars. The buyer did not pay and the seller only succeeded in reselling the Vanguard. He therefore sued for the price of the Zodiac plus his loss on the resale of the Vanguard. The Court held that the seller could not sue for the price of the Zodiac as the resale of the Vanguard had rescinded the original contract. Hence the buyer was only liable for damages for non-acceptance, assessed in the usual way as the difference between the contract price and the market price of the Zodiac. The Court explained away the difference in the wording of Sect. 48 (3) and (4) on somewhat ingenious grounds. Failure by the buyer to pay the price is not *per se* a breach which justifies repudiation, but once the seller has given notice to the buyer to pay, time is made of the essence of payment. Hence failure to pay now amounts to repudiation and the seller accepts this by reselling the goods. The resale therefore amounts to a rescission of the contract, property revests in the seller and the buyer is no longer liable for the price. If, however, the contract contains an express provision for resale, then such a resale (apart from Sect. 48 (4)) would not necessarily amount to rescission. For in this event the resale would be an exercise of a contractual right, and not an acceptance of repudiation by the buyer. Therefore Sect. 48 (4) expressly provides that resale is a rescission of the contract. Thus the reason for the contrast is not that Sect. 48 (3) is intended to have a different result, but that the express provision is not necessary in Sect. 48 (3).

Where the contract of sale is rescinded as a result of the buyer's breach, the buyer can recover any part of the price paid in advance, though the seller can, of course, sue for damages for the breach.[2] But the buyer cannot recover a deposit paid by way of earnest to secure performance.[3] The distinction between a deposit and a part payment depends on whether the sum paid in advance is intended to be available to the seller whatever the outcome of the transaction, as a security for performance by the buyer, or whether it merely represents an advance

---

[1] [1967] 1 Q.B. 534.
[2] *Dies* v. *British & International Mining, etc., Corporation,* 1939] 1 K.B. 724.
[3] Ibid.

payment of the price. There have been suggestions that equitable relief may perhaps be available to enable a buyer to recover even a deposit (for example where a deposit substantially exceeds the amount of the seller's loss)[1] but these suggestions have not yet been acted on.[2] There is less reason to doubt that equity will at least enable the buyer to prevent the forfeiture of his deposit by extending the time for payment of the balance of the price. But the buyer must make it clear, in his claim for the assistance of equity, that he is ready and willing to complete his obligations if the time for doing so is extended by the court.[3]

---

[1] *Stockloser* v. *Johnson*, [1954] 1 Q.B. 476.

[2] See *Campbell Discount Co., Ltd.* v. *Bridge*, [1961] 1 Q.B. 445 (reversed on a different point, [1962] A.C. 600); *Galbraith* v. *Mitchenall Estates, Ltd.*, [1965] 2 Q.B. 473.

[3] *Barton, Thompson & Co. Ltd.* v. *Stapling Machines Co.*, [1966] Ch. 499.

CHAPTER 25

PERSONAL REMEDIES

ACTION FOR THE PRICE

In addition to the real rights, the seller has of course, his personal action upon the sale for breach of contract by the buyer. This action may take one of two forms. It may be an action for the price of the goods sold, or it may be an action for damages for non-acceptance. The general rule laid down in Sect. 49 (1) and Sect. 50 (1) is that an action for damages is the appropriate remedy where the property has not passed. This simple principle is unfortunately complicated by the fact that the property in the goods may pass to the buyer before they have been delivered to, and accepted by him.

Hence Sect. 49 (1) says—

Where, under a contract of sale, the property in the goods has passed to the buyer, and the buyer wrongfully neglects or refuses to pay for the goods according to the terms of the contract, the seller may maintain an action against him for the price of the goods.

Sect. 50 (1) says—

Where the buyer wrongfully neglects or refuses to accept and pay for the goods, the seller may maintain an action against him for damages for non-acceptance.

It is of course obvious that the property in the goods may have passed to the buyer, *and* he may have neglected or refused to accept and pay for them, for, as has been seen, property in the goods often passes before delivery. In such an event it seems to follow that the seller has the option of suing for the price under Sect. 49 (1) or for damages under Sect. 50 (1). In other words the seller has—

1. An action for the price where the property has passed and the buyer has accepted the goods.

2. An action for damages where the property has not passed and the buyer refuses to accept the goods.

3. An action for the price, or for damages where the property has passed and the buyer refuses to accept the goods.

The fact that the property has not passed, owing to some wrongful act of the defendant, does not enable the seller to claim the price unless the buyer is estopped by his conduct from disputing the fact that the property has passed. Hence if the buyer fails to name an effective ship in a sale f.o.b. the seller's remedy is an action for damages, not for the price.[1]

[1] *Colley* v. *Overseas Exporters, Ltd.*, [1921] 3 K.B. 302.

And if the buyer in a c.i.f. contract refuses to take up the shipping documents when tendered, the seller's remedy is once again an action for damages, not for the price.[1] There is one exceptional case in which the seller may sue for the price although the property has not passed, for under Sect. 49 (2)—

> Where, under a contract of sale, the price is payable on a day certain irrespective of delivery, and the buyer wrongfully neglects or refuses to pay such price, the seller may maintain an action for the price, although the property in the goods has not passed, and the goods have not been appropriated to the contract.

The important point to note about this subsection is that it concerns a case where the price is payable irrespective of delivery. If the price is payable *before* delivery, the seller can thus sue for the price as soon as it becomes due, so long at least as he does not treat the whole contract as repudiated. If, on the other hand, the price is payable at some date *after* delivery, the possibility of repudiation does not arise (assuming that the buyer does not purport to reject the goods), and again the seller is clearly entitled to sue for the price. But this second case is likely to fall within the ordinary rule (that the seller may sue for the price when the property passes) and does not seem to be the case contemplated by the section. Sect. 49 (2) seems to be principally concerned with a case where the price is payable before delivery; in such a case the seller's only remedy is an action for the price. He cannot claim damages for non-acceptance because the buyer may not yet have refused to accept the goods. The main difficulty in interpreting the subsection is the meaning of "a day certain". Does it mean a named, fixed date, or is it possible to invoke the maxim *certum est quod certum reddi potest*? In *Workman Clark & Co., Ltd.* v. *Lloyd Brazileno*[2] it was held that the seller, who was constructing a ship for the buyer, was entitled to sue for the instalments as they became due, although the date on which they became due was ascertained by reference to the stage which had been reached in the construction of the vessel. The Court of Appeal decided both that Sect. 49 (2) applies to instalments payable on a day certain, and that these instalments were payable on a day certain. It does not follow that the price can be sued for whenever the date for payment can be ascertained because in many cases an action for damages would be the more appropriate remedy. But in this case there would have been no ground for an action for damages and the seller would have been left without any remedy if he could not sue for the price.

The distinction between an action for the price and an action for damages is of considerable importance. In purely monetary terms there

---

[1] *Stein, Forbes & Co., Ltd.* v. *County Tailoring Co., Ltd.* (1916), 86 L.J.K.B. 448.
[2] [1908] 1 K.B. 968.

will usually be a substantial difference between the price of the goods and damages for non-acceptance. Moreover, if the property has passed to the buyer and the seller is entitled to sue for the price, he is under no obligation to mitigate his damage[1] by attempting to resell the goods or otherwise.[2] The goods now belong to the buyer and not the seller, and it is the buyer's responsibility to take delivery of the goods or otherwise dispose of them.

Obviously an action for the price is more favourable to the seller than a mere action for damages for non-acceptance. But where the goods have not been delivered, the law may in practice place the seller in a somewhat difficult situation. He may choose to take his stand on the argument that the property has passed to the buyer, disclaim all responsibility for the goods, and sue for the price. But on the other hand, if he takes this course he runs the risk that the court may eventually decide that property had not passed to the buyer, and that the seller's only remedy is for damages for non-acceptance. If the court takes this view it follows that the seller will have been responsible for mitigating the damage by (for example) attempting to resell the goods. His failure to do so may then reduce the damages to which he would have been entitled. On the other hand, if the seller attempts to mitigate the loss by reselling the goods, or part of them, or by dealing with them in some way, a court may treat this as evidence of an acceptance by the seller of repudiation of the contract by the buyer. The result of this will be that even if the property had originally passed to the buyer it will now revest in the seller and an action for the price will no longer lie. If, therefore, the seller's efforts to resell the goods have failed, he will have made his own position worse by attempting to dispose of them.[3]

These difficulties largely stem from the fact that the seller is entitled to sue for the price of the goods where the property has passed but the buyer has refused to take delivery. It is doubtful whether in modern times this is the most sensible approach to the issues which arise. The most important practical problem in this situation is this: whose responsibility is it to resell or otherwise dispose of the goods and to hold them pending resale? If this responsibility should be the buyer's then an action for the price is appropriate, but if it should rest on the seller, an action for damages for non-acceptance would be more appropriate. Which of the parties should bear this responsibility cannot, it is suggested, be answered simply by asking if the property has passed but should depend on a balance of convenience. For instance, if the seller is a dealer and the buyer is a private consumer (as has happened in several cases concerning the sale of motor vehicles) it seems more

---

[1] As to the normal duty to mitigate, see *post*, p. 275.

[2] In this sense an action for the price of goods in which property has passed is an illustration of the principle laid down by the H.L. in *White & Carter (Councils), Ltd.* v. *McGregor*, [1962] A.C. 413, see *per* Lord Keith at p. 437.

[3] See, e.g., *R. V. Ward, Ltd.* v. *Bignall*, [1967] 1 Q.B. 534.

sensible that the seller should have the responsibility of reselling the goods, and should be confined to an action for damages. Conversely, there are situations—especially in export sales—where the responsibility for taking possession of the goods and trying to resell them should be on the buyer despite the fact that property has not passed. For instance, if the buyer refuses to accept shipping documents properly tendered in an f.o.b. or c.i.f. sale, it would be extremely inconvenient for the seller to make arrangements to land, store and dispose of the goods at the place of destination. In this case it would seem more reasonable if the seller could sue for the price, and leave the buyer with the responsibility of dealing with the goods. In practice, of course, if the price is payable by a banker's credit, the seller will probably be able to sue the bank if the documents are wrongly rejected, but there are some situations in which the seller should also have an action against the buyer for the price.

In this connection it is interesting to note the provisions of Section 2–709 of the Uniform Commercial Code which seem a considerable improvement on those of the Sale of Goods Act.[1] Under Section 2–709 (1) the seller can sue for the price if the buyer has accepted the goods, or if the goods have been identified to the contract and "the seller is unable after reasonable effort to resell them at a reasonable price, or the circumstances reasonably indicate that such effort will be unavailing." Thus if the buyer refuses to take delivery of the goods the seller is in the first instance obliged to try to resell the goods unless it is clear that this will be unavailing. The mere fact that property has passed, therefore, does not entitle the seller to sue for the price. Conversely, once the seller has made reasonable efforts to resell and these have proved unavailing he may sue for the price even though property has not passed. Moreover, once the seller is entitled to sue for the price under Section 2–709 (1), Section 2–709 (2) enables the seller to resell at any time prior to judgment if such resale becomes possible, without thereby forfeiting his right to sue for the price. He must, of course, give credit for the proceeds of the resale, but his claim will then be for the contract price less the resale price, and does not become converted into an action for damages as it does under English law.

In addition to the seller's right to sue for the price, or for damages for non-acceptance, he may also have the right to claim special damages under Sect. 54, and the right to claim for any loss occasioned by the buyer's neglect to take delivery. In both cases it seems immaterial whether or not the property has passed. A claim by a seller for special damages is likely to arise but rarely in practice,[2] and the principles governing such a claim may be more suitably dealt with when we come to examine the remedies of the buyer. A word needs to be said, how-

[1] The Uniform Law on International Sales seems to produce a similar result. See Art. 61–2.

[2] For a recent example, see *Penarth Dock Engineering Co., Ltd.* v. *Pounds*, [1963] 1 Lloyd's Rep. 359.

ever, on the possibility of a claim for loss occasioned by the buyer's failure to take delivery. Sect. 37 lays down—

> When the seller is ready and willing to deliver the goods, and requests the buyer to take delivery, and the buyer does not within a reasonable time after such request take delivery of the goods, he is liable to the seller for any loss occasioned by his neglect or refusal to take delivery, and also for a reasonable charge for the care and custody of the goods: Provided that nothing in this section shall affect the rights of the seller where the neglect or refusal of the buyer to take delivery amount to a repudiation of the contract.

Where, therefore, the property in the goods has passed to the buyer and he neglects to take delivery the seller may either sue for damages, or for the price, and in the latter case he can add a claim under Sect. 37 for damages to cover the cost of care and custody, and any further loss he may have suffered, e.g. if the goods have gone bad and tainted other goods not sold to the buyer. If he sues for damages only, his claim will cover these items as a matter of course.

Where the price is due in a foreign currency, but the action is brought in England, the amount recoverable must be calculated at the rate of exchange prevailing at the time when the price was due, and not at the date of judgment.[1] If therefore the value of the foreign currency has increased in relation to English currency between these dates the seller will receive less in the foreign currency than he would have done had the price been paid when due. On the other hand if the foreign currency has depreciated between these dates in relation to English currency the seller will receive more in the foreign currency than the actual price due. This rule led to very unsatisfactory results and in 1975 the Court of Appeal decided that it was time to jettison the whole basis of the rule. They held that it was now possible to give judgment for the price *in the foreign currency itself*.[2]

ACTION FOR DAMAGES

We have already seen that the seller's only remedy where the property has not passed is an action for damages for non-acceptance, and that such an action is an alternative remedy where the property has passed but the buyer neglects to take delivery. It now becomes necessary to examine the method by which such damages are calculable, leaving aside for the moment the question of special damages.

It may be convenient, first of all, to recall the general principle of contract law that the innocent party is bound to take reasonable steps to mitigate the damage. This principle applies to contracts of sale of

---

[1] *Peyrae* v. *Wilkinson*, [1924] 2 K.B. 166; *Madeleine Vionnet et Cie.* v. *Wills*, [1940 K.B. 72.
[2] *Schorsch Meier G.m.b.H.* v. *Hennin*, [1975] 1 All E.R. 152.

goods as it applies to other contracts, and it applies equally whether the innocent party is buyer or seller. There is no need in a book of this nature to examine this principle at length, but it is mentioned here because the idea behind it underlies many of the detailed rules relating to damages in the law of sale of goods.

The general rule laid down by Sect. 50 (2) is—

> The measure of damages is the estimated loss directly and naturally resulting, in the ordinary course of events from the buyer's breach of contract.

And the general method of computing the loss directly and naturally arising from the buyer's breach is laid down by Sect. 50 (3)—

> Where there is an available market for the goods in question the measure of damages is prima facie to be ascertained by the difference between the contract price and the market or current price at the time or times when the goods ought to have been accepted or, if no time was fixed for acceptance, then at the time of the refusal to accept.

Meaning of "available market"[1]

The first question to which this subsection gives rise is, what is meant by "an available market"? It is astonishing how scanty is the authority on this point. In *Dunkirk Colliery Co., Ltd.* v. *Lever*[2] there is a dictum by James, L.J., which suggests that a market necessarily signifies some place where the goods can be sold. In *Marshall* v. *Nicoll*,[3] an appeal to the House of Lords from Scotland, it was held, in a somewhat confusing and inconclusive discussion, that there might be a market within the meaning of Sect. 51 (3)—the corresponding section dealing with non-delivery—although the goods were being specially made to order, and the market for such goods was extremely limited. Next, in *W. L. Thompson, Ltd.* v. *Robinson (Gunmakers), Ltd.*,[4] the question was fully argued before Upjohn, J., who thought himself bound to follow the dictum of James, L.J., in *Dunkirk Colliery Co., Ltd.* v. *Lever*[5] although that case was decided before the Sale of Goods Act, and although the dictum was manifestly *obiter*, and was not expressly concurred in by the other members of the Court.[6] However, the learned judge gave his valuable opinion on the matter—[7]

> Had the matter been *res integra* I think that I should have found that an "available market" merely means that the situation in the particular

---

[1] See two interesting articles on this question in 36 *Can. Bar Rev.* 360 and 43 *A.L.J.* 52, 106.

[2] (1878), 9 Ch. D. 20, 25.   [3] [1919] S.C. (H.L.) 129.

[4] [1955] Ch. 177.   [5] (1878), 9 Ch. D. 20.

[6] Moreover two valuable dicta were not cited to the learned judge. In *The Arpad*, [1934] P. 189, at p. 191, Bateson, J., said: "Market means buyers and sellers." And in *Heskell* v. *Continental Express, Ltd.*, [1950] 1 All E.R. 1033, at p. 1050, Devlin, J., said: "A market for this purpose means more than a particular place. It means also a particular level of trade."

[7] [1955] Ch. at p. 187.

trade in the particular area was such that the particular goods could freely be sold, and that there was a demand sufficient to absorb readily all the goods that were thrust on it so that if a purchaser defaulted the goods in question could readily be disposed of.[1]

It is submitted that this opinion is greatly to be preferred to that of James, L.J., as becomes clear when the facts of *W. L. Thompson, Ltd.* v. *Robinson (Gunmakers), Ltd.*,[2] are examined. The buyer contracted to buy a car from the plaintiffs, but failed to take delivery when the car was available. The sellers returned the car to the makers and claimed from the buyer damages for their loss of profit on the sale. It was found as a fact that the supply of cars exceeded the demand in that area at the time. At that time resale price maintenance was still rigidly enforced in relation to cars and other consumer goods, and consequently there was rarely any difference between the contract price and the "market" price in the sense of the fixed retail price. The buyer contended that there was a market and that there being no difference between the market price and the contract price, the sellers were only entitled to nominal damages. Had this contention succeeded it is submitted that the plaintiffs would have been deprived of damages to which they were obviously entitled. For even if the sellers had not returned the car to the makers, but resold it to another buyer, they would still have lost one sale. For, with an excess of supply over demand, the sellers would still have been able to supply the buyer with a car even had there been no breach, and thereby earned profit on both sales.[3] Fortunately Upjohn, J., was able to avoid such a result by holding that, even if there were a market, yet Sect. 50 (3) only laid down a prima facie rule, and that this rule could not be applied in this particular case.

This conclusion received the approval of the Court of Appeal in *Charter* v. *Sullivan*.[4] This case was the counterpart of *W. L. Thompson, Ltd.* v. *Robinson (Gunmakers), Ltd.*, in that, on otherwise identical facts, the plaintiff was able to dispose of all the cars he could obtain, and he was accordingly held entitled only to nominal damages. The Court of Appeal agreed with Upjohn, J., that on such facts it was immaterial whether there was an available market or not, but Jenkins, L.J., disagreed (*obiter*) as to the meaning of the term "available market." After citing the above passage from the judgment of Upjohn, J., Jenkins, L.J., proceeded as follows—

I do not find Upjohn, J.'s definition entirely satisfactory. I will not, however, attempt to improve upon it, but will content myself with the negative proposition that I doubt if there can be an available market for

[1] This definition was in fact adopted by Sellers, J., in *A.B.D.* (*Metals & Waste*), *Ltd.* v. *Anglo-Chemical & Ore Co., Ltd.*, [1955] 2 Lloyd's Rep. 456.
[2] [1955] Ch. 177.
[3] Cf. *In re Vic Mill, Ltd.*, [1913] 1 Ch. 465, and see p. 283, *post.*
[4] [1957] 2 Q.B. 117.

particular goods in any sense relevant to section 50 (3) of the Sale of Goods Act, 1893, unless those goods are available for sale in the market at the market or current price in the sense of the price, whatever it may be, fixed by reference to supply and demand as the price at which a purchaser for the goods in question can be found, be it greater or less than or equal to the contract price. The language of section 50 (3) seems to me to postulate that in the cases to which it applies there will or may be a difference between the contract price and the market or current price, which cannot be so where the goods can only be sold at a fixed retail price.[1]

Since the virtual disappearance of resale price maintenance in England this point has ceased to be of such importance. Both in retail and in commercial sales the "market price" is now likely to be the average or mid-point of a number of different prices prevailing in the market in question.

In general the question whether there is an available market is treated by the courts as a question of fact and, in some cases, even as a question of degree. There may, for instance, be evidence that sales occasionally take place of the commodity in question, but only rarely, or in small quantities.[2] Or there may be evidence that similar, though not identical, goods are readily available or disposable.[3] Or again there may be evidence that it is possible to buy or sell the goods at a different place or in smaller quantities. In all these cases the courts take a fairly broad and common-sense view of the question. The question which is usually treated as decisive is whether or not it would be reasonable for the seller to dispose of the goods through such market as is in fact available. It has, in fact, been suggested that the market price rule is best seen as an illustration of the rule that the innocent party must mitigate his loss; accordingly, attempts to define "market" in any narrow or technical sense are to be deplored. The important question is whether the seller can reasonably find a substitute purchaser and not where or how this substitute sale is to be made.[4]

Effect of Resale by Seller on "available market"

The market price rule is in principle based on the loss which the plaintiff (seller) would have suffered if, on non-acceptance by the buyer, the plaintiff had sold the goods in the market. It is thus concerned with a notional or hypothetical sale which might reasonably have been made by the seller. The rule then gives rise to problems where the seller actually has gone into the market and resold the goods. If this resale is actually at the market price there will, of course, be no difficulty; but if the resale is made at *less* than the market price, the seller may

---

[1] At p. 128.
[2] *Kwei Tek Chao* v. *British Traders & Shippers, Ltd.*, [1954] 2 Q.B. 459, 498 (held a market). Cf. *Garnac Grain Co.* v. *H. M. Faure & Fairclough*, [1968] A.C. 1130, 1138 (held, evidence on which judge could find there was a market although it was not possible to buy the contract quantity in one amount for immediate delivery).
[3] *Hinde* v. *Liddell* (1875), 10 Q.B. 265.   [4] See Ogus, *Law of Damages*, pp. 326–7.

wish to claim as damages the difference between the original contract price and the resale price, rather than the market price. Equally, if the resale takes place at a price *higher* than the market price, the buyer may claim that the damages should only represent the difference between the contract and the resale price.

In attempting to answer these questions it is necessary to distinguish between the case where the seller finds a substitute buyer immediately on non-acceptance by the buyer, and the case where the seller chooses to retain the goods for some period before reselling them. If he resells more or less forthwith on non-acceptance by the buyer at *less* than the market price the seller will clearly have difficulty in claiming damages based on this resale price. For the obvious question will be why the seller should have resold at less than the market price. Prima facie, the requirement that he should mitigate his loss would have required him to sell at not less than the market price, and unless the seller can find some very convincing reason for what he has done it is difficult to see why he should recover more than the difference between the contract and the market price. If, on the other hand, the seller succeeds in convincing the court that in the particular circumstances it was reasonable of him (despite the mitigation principle) to resell at the price which he in fact obtained, it seems improbable that the court would find that the resale price actually was lower than the market price. Such findings would be contradictory in the ordinary way, and a decision that the actual resale price was reasonable would normally connote a finding that there was no available market at which the seller could have disposed of the goods at a higher price.

If the seller resells promptly on breach by the buyer at *more* than the market price it is not wholly clear whether the buyer can take advantage of this to reduce the damages he would otherwise have to pay. The seller will, of course, face the same evidentiary problem as in the converse situation discussed in the last paragraph. That is to say the seller may have difficulty in convincing the court that there was an available market in which prices were lower than the price actually obtained, for this implies that the second buyer made a bad bargain. And although parties do, of course, make bad bargains from time to time, the situation envisaged here is one in which the seller has unexpectedly had the goods left on his hands by non-acceptance by the buyer, and in which, therefore, one would have expected the seller to be in a poor bargaining situation. However, let it be assumed that the seller is able to establish that he has resold at more than the market price. As the seller cannot claim for the loss if he sells below the market price, it may seem only fair that he should be able to retain any profit he makes by selling at above the market price. But there does seem to be a modern trend to deny recovery for a "loss" which is in fact counter-balanced by a profit and it seems probable that a court would today hold that the seller is only entitled to the difference between contract and resale price, as this is the true measure of his loss. There seems no clear authority on this point, but the present submission appears to be the correct inference from the decision of the Court of Appeal in *Campbell Mostyn (Provisions), Ltd.* v. *Barnett Trading Co.*,[1] where the seller retained the goods after the breach and subsequently resold them for more than the market price prevailing at the date of breach. It was held in these circumstances that the seller was entitled to recover the difference between contract and market price and did not have to account for the greater price at which he had in fact sold the goods. Somervell, L.J., quoted with approval this passage from Lord Wrenbury's speech in *A.K.A.S. Jamal* v. *Moolla Dawood*,[2] a Privy Council case dealing with shares—

> If the seller retains the shares after the breach the speculation as to the way the market will subsequently go is the speculation of the seller, not of the buyer; the seller cannot recover from the buyer the loss below the market price at the date of the breach if the market falls, nor is he liable to the purchaser for the profit if the market rises.

It seems a reasonable inference that the position is different where the seller resells immediately upon breach. This conclusion may be supported by the recent decision of the Court of Appeal in *R. Pagnan & Fratelli* v. *Corbisa Industrial Agropacuaria Limitada*[3] although the circumstances were rather unusual. This case concerned a breach of contract by the seller, rather than the buyer, but in general the same principles are applicable. In this case the buyers rightly rejected the goods delivered but then, as part of a settlement of the dispute, agreed to buy the same goods at a substantially lower price. This price was lower even than the market price and the buyers consequently made a handsome overall profit which exceeded their loss on the original sale. It was held that the second contract was part of a continuous course of dealing between the parties and not a wholly new and independent event. Consequently, the profit made by the buyers on the second sale had to be set-off against their loss on the first, and they were only entitled to nominal damages. While it is not wholly clear whether the result would have been the same if the second purchase had not been from the sellers the case does illustrate a modern reluctance to award damages for a "loss" which in one sense is purely notional.

Which Market?

Where there is an available market in more than one place, the relevant place is prima facie the place at which the goods were to be delivered

---

[1] [1954] 1 Lloyd's Rep. 65.

[2] [1916] 1 A.C. 175, at p. 179. McGregor *On Damages*, 13th edn., §250, appears to overlook that these two cases involved a deliberate retention of the shares (or goods) after the non-acceptance and a resale only after this delay.

[3] [1970] 1 W.L.R. 1306.

under the contract. So in *Hasell* v. *Bagot, Shakes & Lewis Ltd.*,[1] where Japanese superphosphate was sold for delivery at Adelaide, it was held that the question was whether there was a market at Adelaide and not in Japan. Had there been a market in both places, the market price at Adelaide would have been the relevant price. However, where goods are sold f.o.b. or c.i.f. for shipment to a particular market then the relevant market would prima facie be that at the place of destination.[2] The point to remember in all cases is that if the buyer refuses to accept the goods the seller will ordinarily have to find a substitute purchaser, and the question is where should the seller reasonably be expected to look for such a purchaser? Where the seller's business is limited to a particular local area, the availability of a market in that area and the market price in that area are the only relevant considerations.[3] In other cases the seller may reasonably be expected to look far afield for a substitute purchaser, e.g., where the seller is engaged in international trade.

Market Price at What Date?

Where the buyer's refusal to take the goods occurs at the time when they should have been accepted the provisions of Sect. 50 (3) are exactly in point, and the seller recovers the difference between the contract price and the market price at that time. If no time has been fixed, however, the problem is more difficult as it is still not settled whether a contract for delivery within a reasonable time is a contract for delivery at a fixed time within Sect. 50 (3). In *Millett* v. *Van Heeck*,[4] a Divisional Court held that it was not. In the Court of Appeal,[5] however, it was found unnecessary to decide the point and the appeal was dismissed on other grounds, all members of the Court reserving their opinion on the question. The actual point decided by the Court of Appeal in this case was that the market price at the date at which the buyer refuses to take delivery is quite irrelevant where his refusal takes the form of an anticipatory breach. In such a case the seller has the choice of accepting the repudiation, or of continuing to treat the contract as binding, but in either event the damages are prima facie assessable by reference to the market price at the date when delivery ought to have been accepted. If the action comes on for trial before this date arrives the court must make the best estimate it can of the probable market price at this date. In either event if the market rises between the date of repudiation and the date when delivery should have been accepted, the relevant market price is that prevailing at the latter date. In other words the seller is not entitled to

[1] (1911), 13 C.L.R. 374.
[2] *Aryeh* v. *Lawrence Kostoris & Son, Ltd.*, [1967] 1 Lloyd's Rep. 63, at p. 71, *per* Diplock, L.J.
[3] *W. L. Thompson, Ltd.* v. *Robinson (Gunmakers), Ltd.*, [1955] Ch. 177, *supra*, p. 276.
[4] [1920] 3 K.B. 535.   [5] [1921] 2 K.B. 369.

receive a higher measure of damages merely because the buyer repudiates the contract at a time when the market is lower than it is on the delivery date.[1] Otherwise he would receive more as a result of the breach than he would have received if the contract had been performed.

On the other hand where the market falls between the date of repudiation and the date when the goods ought to have been accepted, the result differs according to whether the repudiation has been accepted or not. In the former event, the seller is under a duty to mitigate his damage and should resell at once in a falling market. If he fails to do this he cannot hold the buyer liable for a greater amount than the difference between the contract price and the market price at the date of the repudiation.[2] Should the seller decline to accept the repudiation, however, as he is perfectly entitled to do[3] he is under no obligation to mitigate his damage by reselling at once. He can stand by the contract and wait until the delivery date before reselling, and in this case he is entitled to receive damages assessed in the normal way by reference to the market price at the date when the goods ought to have been accepted.[4]

The rule laid down by Sect. 50 (3) is only a prima facie method of calculating the damages, and if it would lead to an obviously incorrect assessment of the loss directly and naturally resulting from the breach, it must be discarded, and some other method of assessment, based for example, on the profit lost, must be used.[5] A fortiori, if there is no market at all the subsection is of no assistance. In these cases the amount recoverable must depend upon whether the seller has already procured or manufactured the goods for delivery, or not. If he has done so, the prima facie measure of damages is the difference between the contract price and the value of the goods at the date of breach.[6] Since there is, on this supposition, no market, there will often be practical problems in assessing the value of the goods at the time of breach but the court must do the best it can on the material available to it. Where the goods have been manufactured to some special order it may even be that they have no value at all and the seller will then be able to sue for the full price. His right to the whole of these damages will, of course, depend upon proof that the goods are useless and unsaleable, not only in their existing form, but even after reasonable alterations. For the seller must

[1] *Melachrino* v. *Nickoll & Knight*, [1920] 1 K.B. 693.

[2] *Roth* v. *Tayson* (1896), 73 L.T. 628.

[3] *Frost* v. *Knight* (1872), L.R. 7 Ex. 111. See also *Sudan Import & Export Co.* (*Khartoum*), *Ltd.* v. *Société Générale de Compensation*, [1958] 1 Lloyd's Rep. 310, where the sellers at first refused to accept the repudiation, but later agreed to do so.

[4] *Tredegar Iron & Coal Co., Ltd.* v. *Hawthorne* (1902), 18 T.L.R. 716. These principles have now received the approval of the House of Lords: *Garnac Grain Co.* v. *H. M. Faure & Fairclough*, [1968] A.C. 1130.

[5] *W. L. Thompson, Ltd.* v. *Robinson* (*Gunmakers*), *Ltd.*, [1955] Ch. 177; *Charter* v. *Sullivan*, [1957] 2 Q.B. 117; pp. 276–8, *ante*.

[6] *Harlow & Jones, Ltd.* v. *Panex* (*International*), *Ltd.*, [1967] 2 Lloyd's Rep. 509 at p. 530.

always mitigate his damage, and if he can make the goods saleable by small alterations he should do so.[1] If, on the other hand, the seller has not yet procured or manufactured the goods, he will prima facie be entitled to recover the difference between the contract price, and the cost to himself of so procuring or manufacturing the goods, that is to say, his profit. The mere fact that the non-performance of the contract which has been broken has enabled the seller to make profits on other contracts does not of itself entitle the defaulting buyer to claim that the profits so made should be set off against those which have been lost as a result of his breach, because the seller might have been able to earn both lots of profit.[2] But in *Hill & Sons* v. *Edwin Showell & Sons*[3] the House of Lords held that a buyer is entitled to give evidence to show that in fact the seller would not have been able to earn both lots of profit, for example, because his factory has been working to capacity the whole time. Although the burden of proof on the buyer in this respect is a heavy one, if he can succeed in establishing the point the seller will only be entitled to recover the difference between the profit he should have made, and the profit he actually made.

As is the case in an action for the price, the rule in an action for damages for non-acceptance abroad is that the damages must be calculated at the rate of exchange prevailing at the date of the wrong, and not at the date of the judgment.[4] It is not yet clear whether the courts' willingness to give judgment *for the price* in a foreign currency (*ante*, p. 275) will also extend to claims *for damages*.

[1] It cannot be said as a general rule that the innocent party cannot be expected to lay out money to mitigate his damages, although this may be so where the suggested expenditure would be highly speculative: *Jewelowski* v. *Propp*, [1944] K.B. 510.

[2] *In re Vic Mill, Ltd.*, [1913] 1 Ch. 465; *W. L. Thompson, Ltd.* v. *Robinson (Gunmakers), Ltd.*, [1955] Ch. 177.

[3] (1918), 87 L.J.K.B. 1106.

[4] *Société des Hôtels du Touquet-Paris-Plage* v. *Cumming*, [1921] 3 K.B. 459; *Di Ferdinando* v. *Simon Smits & Co., Ltd.*, [1920] 3 K.B. 409.

PART VII

THE REMEDIES OF THE BUYER

CHAPTER 26

REJECTION OF THE GOODS

BUYER'S RIGHT TO REJECT THE GOODS

THE buyer's first and primary remedy for a breach of contract by the seller is to repudiate the contract of sale, and to reject the goods. As we have seen this remedy is only available to the buyer when the seller's breach of contract goes to the root of the agreement, that is to say where it is a breach of condition, and not where it is a mere breach of warranty. We have already examined in some detail the implied conditions as to the quality and quantity of the goods to be delivered under the contract, breach of which entitles the buyer to repudiate the contract and to reject the goods. It is only necessary now to stress that at common law and under the Sale of Goods Act the buyer's right to reject can be exercised no matter how trivial the breach, and no matter that the loss to the seller would be much greater than any benefit to the buyer. There is much to be said for cutting down this right of rejection in certain circumstances. It is indeed arguable that the Misrepresentation Act already has the effect of enabling the court, in its discretion, to refuse rescission and award damages in lieu, whenever a buyer claims to reject goods for breach of a condition constituting a misstatement of fact.[1] But it is unlikely that the Act was intended to have this effect and unsafe to assume that it does.

Instalment Sales

It now remains to consider the position which arises in a contract for the sale of goods by instalments, where the seller is guilty of a breach of condition as to one or more instalments. Is the buyer entitled in such circumstances to reject the whole consignment of goods, or is he entitled only to reject that part in respect of which there is a breach of contract, or again is he relegated to a claim for damages? The question is posed rather than answered by Sect. 31 (2) as follows—

> Where there is a contract for the sale of goods to be delivered by stated instalments, which are to be separately paid for, and the seller makes defective deliveries in respect of one or more instalments, or the buyer

[1] See (1967), 30 *M.L.R.* at pp. 377–8.

neglects or refuses to take delivery of or pay for one or more instalments, it is a question in each case depending on the terms of the contract and the circumstances of the case, whether the breach of contract is a repudiation of the whole contract or whether it is a severable breach giving rise to a claim for compensation but not to a right to treat the whole contract as repudiated.

Non-severable Contracts

Sect. 31 (2) by its express terms, only applies where the goods are to be delivered by instalments and the instalments are to be separately paid for. But this is not an exhaustive statement of the circumstances in which a contract may be severable.[1] As will be seen later[2] there are cases in which a contract is severable in law even though the goods are not to be delivered by separate instalments or the instalments are not to be separately paid for. If the contract is not severable then it is to be treated as an entire contract. Hence, in these cases a partial breach is to be treated in the same way as a total breach and the buyer is prima facie entitled to reject all the goods. In this situation the fact that the goods are delivered in instalments is immaterial once it is found that this does not make the contract severable. The position is exactly the same as it would be if the whole consignment were delivered at once, and part of the goods were defective. In such a case it is well established that the buyer can reject the whole.[3]

Severable Contracts

Where the contract is severable because the goods are to be delivered in instalments and are to be separately paid for, the right of the buyer to reject the whole consignment depends, as stated by Sect. 31 (2), on the terms of the contract and the circumstances of the case. (If the contract is severable although the goods are not to be delivered in instalments, or the instalments are not to be separately paid for, the same rules probably apply as a matter of common law.) If the contract is silent as to the events which have occurred—

The main tests to be considered in applying the sub-section . . . are, first, the ratio quantitatively which the breach bears to the contract as a whole and secondly, the degree of probability or improbability that such a breach will be repeated.[4]

[1] This is expressly stated by Atkin, L.J., in *Longbottom & Co., Ltd.* v. *Bass Walker & Co., Ltd.*, [1922] W.N. 245, but it is also implicit in many other cases.
[2] See, *post*, p. 297.
[3] *Jackson* v. *Rotax Motor & Cycle Co., Ltd.*, [1910] 2 K.B. 937; *Re Moore & Co., Ltd., & Landauer & Co.*, [1921] 2 K.B. 519. Cf. the position where (in a case not falling within Sect. 31 (2)) the *buyer* wrongfully refuses to accept part of the goods; this does not justify repudiation by the seller unless the part rejected is substantial: *Francis* v. *Lyon* (1907), 4 C.L.R. 1023.
[4] *Maple Flock Co., Ltd.* v. *Universal Furniture Products (Wembley), Ltd.*, [1934] 1 K.B. 148, at p. 157, *per* Lord Hewart, C.J.

Two cases may be contrasted. In *Maple Flock Co., Ltd.* v. *Universal Furniture Products* (*Wembley*), *Ltd.*,[1] the plaintiffs contracted to sell 100 tons of rag flock to the defendants, delivery to be at the rate of three weekly instalments of one and a half tons each, as required, and the flock to conform to Government standards. The first fifteen loads were satisfactory, but a sample from the sixteenth load showed that that load did not conform to Government standards. In the meantime the defendants had taken delivery of four more loads all of which were satisfactory. Applying the above test the Court of Appeal held that the defendants were not entitled to repudiate the contract, as the breach only affected one and a half tons out of the flock already delivered, and it was most improbable that it would recur. On the other hand, in *R. A. Munro & Co., Ltd.* v. *Meyer*,[2] A agreed to buy 1,500 tons of meat and bone meal, delivery at the rate of 125 tons a month, from B. After more than half of the total quantity had been delivered, and discovered to be seriously defective the buyer claimed to repudiate the contract. Wright, J., held that he was entitled to do so. "Where the breach is substantial and so serious as the breach in this case and has continued so persistently, the buyer is entitled to say that he has the right to treat the whole contract as repudiated."[3]

A single contract, though severable, is not the same thing as a number of distinct and separate contracts. If parties enter into distinct contracts, breach of one would very rarely justify repudiation of the others. But a provision in a contract that each instalment or each delivery is to be treated as a separate contract does not mean that there are distinct contracts; it merely indicates that the contract is severable. Hence such a clause does not deprive a buyer of a right to throw up the whole contract if he would otherwise have such a right.[4]

It will be noticed that Sect. 31 (2) appears to assume that the buyer has one of two possible remedies: repudiation of the whole contract, or merely a claim for damages. The subsection does not appear to contemplate the third possibility of allowing the buyer to reject the defective instalments while retaining the rest of the goods. But there is no reason to suppose that the buyer cannot do this, subject to the somewhat complex rules governing the question of partial acceptance in non-instalment contracts.[5]

Consequences of Rejection

Where the buyer repudiates the contract, having the right to do so, he can of course decline to pay the price, or if he has paid it, he can recover it as on a total failure of consideration. In addition he may maintain an action for damages, for if the buyer acts within his rights

---

[1] [1934] 1 K.B. 148.   [2] [1930] 2 K.B. 312.
[3] *R. A. Munro & Co., Ltd.* v. *Meyer*, [1930] 2 K.B. 312, 331.
[4] Ibid., p. 332.   [5] See *post*, p. 298.

in rejecting the goods tendered, he can normally hold the seller guilty of non-delivery.[1] There may be some circumstances in which, after rejection by the buyer, the seller can tender delivery of a new lot of goods if he still has time to do this within the period allowed by the contract,[2] but in general it seems that the buyer is entitled to treat a wrongful delivery as itself a breach of contract which justifies repudiation by him.[3]

Where the goods are so rejected it is not the responsibility of the buyer to return the goods to the seller, for Sect. 36 states—

> Unless otherwise agreed, where goods are delivered to the buyer, and he refuses to accept them having the right so to do, he is not bound to return them to the seller, but it is sufficient if he intimates to the seller that he refuses to accept them.

As will be seen below,[4] this rule presents some problems where the buyer has redelivered the goods to a sub-buyer before they are discovered to be defective. In this situation the normal solution is simply to deny the buyer's right to reject altogether.

The acceptance by the seller of the buyer's rejection revests the property in the former if it had passed to the buyer, and also restores to him the immediate right to possession. Consequently, as we have seen, the buyer has no lien on the goods for the repayment of the purchase price.[5] "The seller, upon receipt of notice of rejection is entitled to have the goods placed at his disposal so as to allow of his resuming possession forthwith."[6]

As we have already seen,[7] it is not wholly clear whether the risk is to be treated as revesting in the seller on rejection, but the practical position seems to be that the risk does not pass at all where defective goods are delivered and then rejected by the buyer.

LOSS OF THE RIGHT TO REJECT

Even though the seller may be guilty of a breach of condition and the buyer may prima facie be entitled to repudiate the contract and reject the goods, he may in certain circumstances lose this right, and be compelled to treat the breach of condition as though it were a mere breach of warranty. He may, in other words, have to accept the goods, and be content with a claim for damages. It is now necessary to

---

[1] *Millar's Machinery Co., Ltd.* v. *David Way & Son* (1934), 40 Com. Cas. 204.

[2] *Borrowman, Phillips & Co.* v. *Free & Hollis* (1878), 4 Q.B.D. 500; *E. E. Brian Smith* (1928) *Ltd.* v. *Wheatsheaf Mills, Ltd.*, [1939] 2 K.B. 302.

[3] Sect. 11 (1) (*b*) and (*c*) both appear to assume that rejection of the goods involves repudiation of the contract, but cf. the views of Lord Devlin in, [1966] *Camb. L.J.* 192, at p. 194.

[4] *Post*, p. 291.

[5] *J. L. Lyons & Co., Ltd.* v. *May & Baker, Ltd.*, [1923] 1 K.B. 685.

[6] *Per* Bankes, L.J., in *Hardy & Co., Ltd.* v. *Hillerns & Fowler*, [1923] 2 K.B. 490, at p. 496; cf. Devlin, J., in *Kwei Tek Chao* v. *British Traders & Shippers, Ltd.*, [1954] 2 Q.B. 459, at p. 488.

[7] *Supra*, p. 167.

examine the circumstances in which this may occur, and first of all, Sect. 11 (1) (c) must be set out in full. In its original form this was as follows—

> Where a contract of sale is not severable, and the buyer has accepted the goods, or part thereof, or where the contract is for specific goods, the property in which has passed to the buyer, the breach of any condition to be fulfilled by the seller can only be treated as a breach of warranty, and not as a ground for rejecting the goods and treating the contract as repudiated, unless there be a term of the contract, express or implied, to that effect.

Loss of Right to Reject through Passing of Property

According to the plain words of Sect. 11 (1) (c), if the contract was for the sale of specific goods the buyer lost his right of rejection when the property passed to him.[1] Many writers had pointed out the difficulties which arose from this paragraph when read in conjunction with Sect. 18, Rule 1. This Rule is generally taken to mean that, in the absence of a contrary intention, in a sale of specific goods the property passes as soon as the contract is made, with the result that the right of rejection arose and was lost at the very same minute.

This was such an obviously unsatisfactory conclusion that methods of escape were sought. Firstly, in a number of cases the courts attempted to avoid the whole difficulty by holding that in most (if not all) sales of specific goods the sale was not unconditional within the meaning of Sect. 18, Rule 1. In the second place, buyers sometimes rested their case on allegations of mistake and of innocent misrepresentation. Neither of these methods of evasion of Sect. 11 (1) (c) proved very successful although the possibilities of the latter remained, to some extent, unsettled. It was plain, however, that no satisfactory solution existed to these difficulties except the repeal of the words "or where the contract is for specific goods the property in which has passed to the buyer" and this was eventually effected by Sect. 4 (1) of the Misrepresentation Act, 1967. Accordingly, the right to reject the goods is, in all cases of sales of specific and unascertained goods alike, now lost by acceptance and acceptance alone.

Loss of Right to Reject through Acceptance

The meaning of acceptance depends on the construction of Sects. 34 and 35 which in their original form were as follows—

> 34. (1) Where goods are delivered to the buyer, which he has not previously examined, he is not deemed to have accepted them unless and

---

[1] The passing of property had no effect on the right of rejection in sales of unascertained goods: *McDougall* v. *Aeromarine of Emsworth, Ltd.*, [1958] 1 W.L.R. 1126. In this respect the Sale of Goods Act may well have altered the law; see, e.g., *Perkins* v. *Bell*, [1893] 1 Q.B. 193, where buyers of unascertained goods lost their right of rejection on the passing of property.

until he has had a reasonable opportunity of examining them for the purpose of ascertaining whether they are in conformity with the contract.

(2) Unless otherwise agreed, when the seller tenders delivery of the goods to the buyer, he is bound, on request, to afford the buyer a reasonable opportunity of examining the goods for the purpose of ascertaining whether they are in conformity with the contract.

35. The buyer is deemed to have accepted the goods when he intimates to the seller that he has accepted them, or when the goods have been delivered to him, and he does any act in relation to them which is inconsistent with the ownership of the seller, or when after the lapse of a reasonable time, he retains the goods without intimating to the seller that he has rejected them.

Relationship between Sect. 34 and Sect. 35

Unfortunately the Act did not expressly state which of these was the governing section, and it therefore left open the position where the buyer had not had a reasonable opportunity of examining the goods within Sect. 34 (1), but did something which brought him within Sect. 35. It is quite possible for the buyer to do some act inconsistent with the ownership of the seller before he has had a reasonable opportunity for examining the goods, and in this event there was formerly a serious conflict between Sect. 34 and Sect. 35. The former said that in such circumstances the buyer was not deemed to have accepted the goods, and Sect. 35 said that in these circumstances the buyer was deemed to have accepted the goods.[1]

In *Hardy & Co., Ltd.* v. *Hillerns & Fowler*,[2] the Court of Appeal held that Sect. 35 was the governing section. The facts of the case illustrate the hardship to the buyer which results from this interpretation of the Act. A contracted to sell to B wheat to be shipped from South America. The ship carrying the wheat arrived at Hull on 18th March. On 21st March B resold a part of the cargo and dispatched it to the sub-buyers. On 23rd March B had his first opportunity to examine the goods, and on doing so, found them not to conform to the contract. It was held that the buyers had done an act inconsistent with the ownership of the sellers within Sect. 35, and that they had therefore accepted the goods, and lost their right of rejection.[3]

This decision was distinguished by a New Zealand Court in *Hammer & Barrow* v. *Coca-Cola*,[4] although the facts of the cases are very similar. In this case the plaintiffs contracted to sell some goods to the defendants, it being a term of the contract that the goods would be delivered to the

---

[1] One is reminded of the famous dictum of Lord Mildew, "There is too much of this damned deeming"; see *Travers* v. *Travers, Codd's Last Case*, p. 80, by Sir Alan Herbert.

[2] [1923] 2 K.B. 490.

[3] Cf. *Benaim & Co.* v. *L. S. Debono*, [1924] A.C. 514, where all the goods were actually delivered to the sub-buyer.

[4] [1962] N.Z.L.R. 723, noted in 26 *M.L.R.* 194. But see *Pelhams (Materials), Ltd.*, v. *Mercantile Commodities Syndicate*, [1953] 2 Lloyd's Rep. 281.

premises of a third party to whom the defendant had previously contracted to supply the same goods. Richmond, J., emphasised that under Sect. 35 two requirements must be satisfied before a buyer can be deemed to have accepted the goods in the second of the three ways mentioned in that section. First, the goods must have been delivered to him, and secondly, he must have done some act inconsistent with the seller's ownership. The learned judge held that, in dispatching the goods to the third party, the seller was acting as a seller delivering the goods to the buyer in accordance with the contract of sale. Nothing had been done thereafter which could be treated as inconsistent with the seller's ownership. In *E. & S. Ruben, Ltd.* v. *Faire Bros. & Co., Ltd.*,[1] on the other hand, Hilbery, J., held that, in delivering the goods to the carrier for transmission to the third party, the sellers were acting as agents for the buyer, and that the goods must be treated as notionally delivered to the buyers before they were delivered to the carriers. The delivery to the carriers was, therefore, evidence of an act subsequent to delivery to the buyer which could be treated as inconsistent with the seller's ownership.

These cases left the law in an unsatisfactory state. It is common practice for goods to be bought and resold without examination until they are delivered to the sub-buyer. In these circumstances the sub-buyer retained the right to reject the goods while the middle buyer was deemed to have "accepted" them and so was deprived of his right to reject. The law was accordingly altered by Sect. 4 (2) of the Misrepresentation Act, 1967, which inserts in Sect. 35 of the Sale of Goods Act the words "(except where section 34 of this Act otherwise provides)" thereby making it clear that Sect. 34 is the governing section. The position therefore now appears to be that the buyer is deemed to have accepted the goods—

(*a*) when he intimates to the seller that he has accepted them, or

(*b*) (except where section 34 of the Act otherwise provides) when the goods have been delivered to him, and

(i) he does any act which is inconsistent with the ownership of the seller; or

(ii) when, after lapse of a reasonable time he retains the goods without intimating to the seller that he has rejected them.[2]

There is no doubt that this is a considerable improvement in the law, but the question does arise whether it in fact goes far enough. Since the buyer cannot reject in any event unless he is in a position to restore the

---

[1] [1949] 1 K.B. 254. As pointed out by Richmond, J., it was not part of the original contract that the goods should be delivered to the third parties in that case.

[2] This subdivision into paragraphs is not in the Act itself; and it is not entirely clear whether the words in brackets which were inserted by the 1967 Act do control the third limb of the section as they clearly would if the Act were set out as indicated in the text; see 30 *M.L.R.* at p. 386.

goods to the seller,[1] why should he lose the right to reject merely because he has done an act inconsistent with the ownership of the seller and has had an opportunity to examine the goods? Suppose the buyer fails to take the opportunity, or fails to discover the defect in question, and then resells and delivers to a sub-buyer. If the sub-buyer immediately discovers the defect and returns the goods to the buyer, the buyer will still be unable to reject the goods notwithstanding the amendment to Sect. 35 made by Sect. 4 (2) of the 1967 Act. Yet the fact that the buyer does an act which *may* affect his ability to restore the goods to the seller is surely no reason for depriving him of his right to reject when in *fact* it does not affect his ability so to restore the goods. The only real problem is what is to happen where the sub-buyer rejects the goods *without returning them to the buyer.* Is the buyer then also to be entitled to reject the goods while they remain physically situated at the premises of the sub-buyer? It will be remembered that under Sect. 36 of the Act the buyer is not bound to return the goods to the seller when he rejects them; it is sufficient that he intimates to the seller that the goods are at his disposal. Similarly if the buyer arranges for the retransport of the goods from the sub-buyer, can he charge the seller with the cost of this in addition to rejecting the goods?

Prior to the passing of the Misrepresentation Act the position on this point was somewhat obscure.[2] But the position now seems to depend on whether the buyer had a reasonable opportunity to examine the goods and so lost his right to reject.

Where Buyer Has Had Reasonable Opportunity to Examine the Goods

The buyer still loses his right of rejection if he has had a reasonable opportunity to examine the goods and has resold and delivered the goods to a sub-buyer. In *Perkins* v. *Bell*[3] it was held that prima facie the place of delivery to the buyer is the place where he ought to examine the goods, and if he chooses to redispatch the goods to the sub-buyer without examining them he will (it seems) lose his right to reject. In this case the seller sold barley to the defendant for delivery at T railway station. The defendant could have examined the barley there but he sent the barley on to sub-buyers who later rejected it. The buyer was held to have lost his right to reject and the principal reason for this seems to have been the Court's view that it would be unjust to compel the seller to collect the barley from the sub-buyer's premises. What the Court did not consider was whether this injustice could not be avoided by a less drastic step than depriving the buyer of his right to reject.

[1] See *supra*, p. 287.
[2] See *Perkins* v. *Bell*, [1893] 1 Q.B. 193, decided just before the Act was passed; *Molling & Co.* v. *Dean & Son, Ltd.* (1901), 18 T.L.R. 217, which was adversely commented on in *Hardy & Co.* v. *Hillerns & Fowler*, *supra*, but is now good law again.
[3] *Supra.*

Justice would have been done and the seller's interest secured if the Court had held that the buyer could reject provided that he put the goods at the seller's disposal at the place where they were delivered to him. Unfortunately the effect of Sect. 34 and Sect. 35 is still to deprive the buyer of the right to reject in this situation.[1]

Where Buyer Has Not Had Reasonable Opportunity to Examine the Goods

But there are some cases in which the courts are prepared to hold that the place of delivery to the buyer is not a reasonable place to examine the goods,[2] and in this situation the buyer will not lose his right to reject when the goods have been resold and delivered. Moreover, in this case the responsibility for retransporting the goods to the original place of delivery will be the seller's. For instance in *Molling & Co.* v. *Dean & Son*[3] the plaintiffs made 40,000 books to the defendants' order, knowing that they were intended for shipment and resale to an American sub-buyer. Indeed the plaintiffs printed the books with the sub-buyer's imprint and packed them for shipment to him. They were delivered to the defendants who consigned them to the sub-buyers without examination. The sub-buyers rejected and the defendants brought the goods back to England at their own cost. It was held that they were entitled to reject the goods and also to recover the cost of transport on the ground that the proper place for inspection was on delivery to the sub-buyers. Hence the buyers had not had a reasonable opportunity to examine the goods. Consequently, since the Misrepresentation Act, 1967 (whatever the status of this case before then), this decision is now clearly right: the buyer would be deemed not to have accepted the goods under Sect. 34 because he had not had a reasonable opportunity to examine them under Sect. 35.

It will be seen that in this case the sellers knew perfectly well that the goods would probably be delivered to the sub-buyers without examination. In this situation it is reasonable to impose on the seller the cost of retransporting the goods back to the place of delivery. This is, in a sense, merely an application of the rule that the damages recoverable for breach of contract are prima facie controlled by what is foreseeable as the probable result of breach.

But where the seller has no reason to know or foresee that the goods may be delivered and dispatched to sub-buyers without examination it would not be right to impose the cost of retransport on the seller if the goods are rejected. However, it seems that this question cannot arise because in this situation the place of examination will be the place of delivery to the buyer; he will therefore be held to have had a reasonable

---

[1] For the possibility of avoiding this result by claiming rescission for misrepresentation, see *post*, p. 303.

[2] This is especially true of f.o.b. contracts, see *Bragg* v. *Villanova* (1923), 40 T L.R. 154; *Boks & Co.* v. *J. H. Rayner & Co.* (1921), 37 T.L.R. 800.

[3] *Supra*, p. 291, n. 2.

opportunity to examine the goods, and will consequently have lost his right to reject.[1] Hence the very circumstances which make it just to impose the retransport costs on the seller (foreseeability of sub-delivery without examination) are also the circumstances which will determine whether the buyer has had a reasonable opportunity to examine the goods and so lost his right to reject.

"Act inconsistent with the ownership of the seller"

Another unhappy feature of these two sections is the reference in Sect. 35 to an act "inconsistent with the ownership of the seller." This suggests that the ownership of the goods cannot pass until the buyer has accepted them, but of course this is not so. If the property has already passed to the buyer how can he be said to do an act inconsistent with "the ownership of the seller"? One possible answer is to be found in the judgment of Devlin, J., in *Kwei Tek Chao* v. *British Traders & Shippers, Ltd.*[2] If the property has passed in circumstances in which the buyer retains the right to reject, the passing is merely conditional—

> He [the buyer] gets only conditional property in the goods, the condition being a condition subsequent. All his dealings with the documents[3] are dealings only with that conditional property in the goods. It follows, therefore, that there can be no dealing which is inconsistent with the seller's ownership unless he deals with something more than the conditional property. If the property passes altogether, not being subject to any condition, there is no ownership left in the seller with which any inconsistent act under Sect. 35 could be committed. If the property passes conditionally the only ownership left in the seller is the reversionary interest in the property in the event of the condition subsequent operating to restore it to him. It is that reversionary interest with which the buyer must not, save with the penalty of accepting the goods, commit an inconsistent act.[4]

Although this sounds convincing at first sight, it must be said that this way of putting the law involves some circularity in reasoning, and does not help to decide when a buyer has lost his right to reject. The problem is that there is no statement or definition of the rights which the seller's reversionary interest carries. The only way of defining these rights seems to be to say that the seller is entitled to the goods in the place and condition in which they are to be found when rejected. Clearly this means that the buyer cannot reject the goods if he has resold them to a sub-buyer who does not himself reject them. Such a resale is obviously inconsistent with the seller's reversionary rights. But

---

[1] *Saunt* v. *Belcher* (1920), 26 Com. Cas. 115, at pp. 118–19.
[2] [1954] 2 Q.B. 459.
[3] The case was concerned with a sale on c.i.f. terms, but the reasoning applies to all sales of unascertained goods.
[4] At p. 487.

it is not clear why a resale should be treated as inconsistent with the seller's rights if the sub-buyer *does* reject the goods so that they are available for return to the seller. Nor does this way of putting the matter help to decide whether any other sort of act should be held inconsistent with the ownership of the seller. The truth is that the phrase "an act inconsistent with the ownership of the seller" is one with no fixed meaning.

The court is, in effect, empowered to decide whether it thinks that the buyer ought to be entitled to reject the goods according to the justice of the case. In order to ascertain what meaning the phrase has, therefore, it is necessary to examine the case law to see what acts the courts have in fact held to be inconsistent with the ownership of the seller.

It will be apparent from the above discussion that much the most common type of act "inconsistent with the ownership of the seller" is a resale and delivery of the goods.[1] The authorities do not go much beyond this. At all events, there seems to be no case in which the mere fact of a sub-sale, without more, and in particular without delivery, has been held to deprive the buyer of his right to reject.[2] It may well be that since the decision in *Kwei Tek Chao* v. *British Traders & Shippers, Ltd.*,[3] the courts will hold that nothing short of actual delivery will have this effect. Certainly it has been said that a buyer is not deemed to have accepted the goods merely because he has made inquiries with a view to their resale, even after discovering them to be defective.[4] In Australia it has also been held that a claim by the buyer against the insurer in respect of damage to the goods is not inconsistent with the seller's ownership.[5]

In consumer sales a somewhat different approach to this question may be necessary though there is little authority directly in point.[6] Probably any substantial or repeated or prolonged use would be held inconsistent with the seller's ownership if it prevented the buyer returning the goods in substantially the same condition as when purchased.[7]

---

[1] *Hardy & Co.* v. *Hillerns & Fowler*, [1923] 2 K.B. 490, which is still good law on this point.
[2] Cf. *J. & J. Cunningham* v. *R. A. Munro & Co., Ltd.* (1922), 28 Com. Cas. 42, 48.
[3] [1954] 2 Q.B. 459.
[4] *Per* Scrutton, L.J., in *Fisher Reeves & Co., Ltd.* v. *Armour & Co., Ltd.*, [1920] 3 K.B. 614, 624.
[5] *J. S. Robertson (Aust.) Pty., Ltd.* v. *Martin* (1955–56), 94 C.L.R. 30. The buyer will of course have to pay over the insurance moneys to the seller (or credit him, if he has previously paid the price) on rejection, ibid., p. 60.
[6] See *Armaghdown Motors* v. *Gray*, [1963] N.Z.L.R. 5 (registration of car in buyer's name held inconsistent with seller's ownership).
[7] The position may perhaps be different where the buyer has made repeated complaints to the owner demanding the repair of the goods, see *Farnworth Finance Facilities, Ltd.* v. *Attryde*, [1970] 2 All E.R. 774. (But this is perhaps questionable: to demand repairs implies acceptance rather than rejection of the goods.)

In the *British Traders & Shippers* case, Devlin, J., after giving his explanation of the phrase "an act inconsistent with the ownership of the seller", went on to hold that in documentary sales the buyer is not deprived of his right to reject merely by dealing with the documents.

> So long as he [the buyer] is merely dealing with the documents he is not purporting to do anything more than pledge the conditional property which he has. Similarly, if he sells the documents of title he sells the conditional property. But if, as was done in *Hardy & Co.* v. *Hillerns & Fowler*,[1] when the goods have been landed, he physically deals with the goods and delivers them to his sub-buyer, he is doing an act which is inconsistent with the seller's reversionary interest.[2]

The result of this case appeared to be that in a documentary sale the buyer had two distinct rights of rejection; a right to reject documents not conforming to the contract, and a right to reject the goods themselves if they failed to conform to the contract. A dealing with the documents might deprive the buyer of his right to reject the documents, but could not deprive him of his right to reject the goods. However, it now seems that this is not really a very satisfactory statement of the law. At least two qualifications need to be made to Devlin, J.'s exposition. The first is that the buyer's acceptance of the documents may very well deprive him of his right to reject the goods where the breach of contract relating to the documents and the breach relating to the goods are in effect one breach only, and not two distinct breaches. Thus, if the goods are shipped late, and this fact appears from the documents the seller is, in principle, in breach of his obligations both as regards the documents and as regards the goods. Nevertheless, it is unreal to treat this as involving two separate breaches, and if the buyer accepts the documents he may well be treated as having waived the seller's breach and thus be bound to accept the goods.[3] Thus, even though acceptance of (or dealing with) the documents may not amount to an act inconsistent with the seller's ownership the buyer may be unable to reject the goods on other grounds in such circumstances.

The second qualification that needs to be made to Devlin, J.'s statement of the law in the *British Traders & Shippers* case is that whatever the law may say about dealing with the documents not amounting to a dealing with the goods, in practice such a dealing may affect the buyer's power to reject the goods. If he has resold the documents, for instance, he will hardly be able to reject the goods unless the sub-buyer himself rejects—but equally he is unlikely to want to reject except in this case. In the case of a pledge, however, the position may be more difficult because the buyer may be unable to reject the goods without

---

[1] [1923] 2 K.B. 490.
[2] [1954] 2 Q.B. 459 at pp. 487–8.
[3] *Panchaud Frères S.A.* v. *Etablissements General Grain Co.*, [1970] 1 Lloyds Rep. 53.

the consent of the pledgee who may insist on being paid off first. Certainly this appears to be the effect of the Uniform Customs.[1] Therefore where the price has been paid to the seller by a banker's credit against documents, the buyer will in practice have to pay off the bank to obtain a release of the documents before he can return the documents to the seller and so reject the goods.

There can be no acceptance of goods which the seller had no right to sell, and in such a case the mere fact that the buyer has retained and used the goods does not prevent his rejecting them and recovering the full price as on a total failure of consideration.[2] It has been said, however, that "Clearly the answer would not have been the same if the buyer, with knowledge of the true facts, had continued to use the [goods] for another twelve months or so, and had then found that the market had fallen and that he would like to hand [them] back again."[3]

A buyer who is entitled to reject goods for breach of condition must, of course, mitigate his damage according to the ordinary rule. However, he cannot, it would seem, be required by this principle to accept goods when he wants to reject them (at all events when the goods are defective in quality),[4] nor to reject them when he wants to accept them.[5]

It should be observed that the buyer's right to reject defective goods may be, and very often is, qualified by express contractual provisions.[6] In some cases restrictions on the right to reject may be imposed by making the right conditional on, e.g., testing or sampling the goods. In others there may be stringent time limits within which notice of rejection may be given, and so forth. In all such cases the provisions of the contract prevail.

The question whether a buyer can be treated as having accepted the goods and lost his right to reject where the seller has been guilty of a fundamental breach has already been discussed.[7]

Acceptance of Part of the Goods

The question whether the buyer is entitled to accept part and reject part of the goods delivered is one of some difficulty. The opening words of Sect. 11 (1) (c), it will be recalled, are as follows—

[1] See Art. 8.

[2] *Rowland* v. *Divall*, [1923] 2 K.B. 500, p. 50, *ante*.

[3] *Per* Devlin, J., in *Kwei Tek Chao* v. *British Traders & Shippers, Ltd.*, [1954] 2 W.L.R. at p. 372, a passage omitted in the report at [1954] 2 Q.B. 459; see p. 54, n. 2, *ante*.

[4] *Heaven & Kesterton, Ltd.* v. *Etablissements François Albiac & Cie.*, [1956] 2 Lloyd's Rep. 316. The position might well be different if there was no physical defect in the goods but the breach was, e.g., late delivery: ibid., at p. 321, *per* Devlin, J. The reason for this is that if the buyer proposes to buy in the market it would be reasonable to reject defective goods but not necessarily reasonable to reject goods proffered by the seller which conform to the contract in quality.

[5] *Kwei Tek Chao* v. *British Traders & Shippers, Ltd.*, [1954] 2 Q.B. at p. 483.

[6] For a recent example, see *W. E. Marshall & Co.* v. *Lewis & Peat (Rubber), Ltd.* [1963] 1 Lloyd's Rep. 562.

[7] See pp. 126–8.

Where a contract of sale is not severable, and the buyer has accepted the goods or part thereof, etc.

Read literally the whole paragraph only applies to a contract of sale which is not severable; but the paragraph should probably be read as meaning—

Where the buyer has accepted the goods, or where the contract of sale is not severable and the buyer has accepted part of the goods, etc.

The point is that severability is only relevant where the buyer purports to accept part of the goods.

Assuming that this is the correct construction it seems clear that if the contract is severable the buyer is entitled to reject goods not conforming to the contract and to accept the balance of the goods if he chooses to do so. (He may also throw up the entire contract in the circumstances referred to in Sect. 31 (2), as previously discussed.)[1] Even this proposition may seem open to theoretical objections because the right to reject the goods has been said to be merely a species of the right to rescind[2] and it may seem inconsistent for the buyer to rescind the contract while retaining part of the goods. However, this objection is purely academic; as a matter of practical convenience it is plainly right that the buyer should be entitled to accept part and reject part of the goods, and there is no doubt that this is the law in the case of severable contracts.

Two further questions remain to be considered, and these are somewhat more difficult: first, what contracts are "severable" in this context and secondly when can the buyer accept part and reject part of the goods in a non-severable contract?

What Contracts Are Severable?

This is not a question which has been the subject of much judicial discussion. It will be recalled that under Sect. 31 (2) a contract is severable if the goods are to be delivered in instalments, and the instalments are to be separately paid for. But it is clear that a contract may be severable in many other situations also. For instance, a contract for the sale of a quantity of cloth was held to be severable where the cloth was to be delivered in instalments although the price was to be paid by monthly account and not separately for each instalment.[3] And a contract for the sale of some motor accessories was held to be severable purely on the ground that the contract specified "deliveries as required."[4] This was interpreted to mean that the goods would necessarily be delivered in instalments and it was assumed that this was enough to render the

[1] *Supra*, p. 285.
[2] See *Kwei Tak Chao* v. *British Traders & Shippers*, [1954] 2 Q.B. at p. 480. Sect. 11 (1) (b) and (c) both appear to assume that rejection of the goods necessarily involves repudiation of the contract.
[3] *Longbottom & Co., Ltd.* v. *Bass Walker & Co., Ltd.*, [1922] W.N. 245.
[4] *Jackson* v. *Rotax Motor & Cycle Co., Ltd.*, [1910] 2 K.B. 937.

contract severable. In other cases a buyer has been held entitled to
accept part and reject part of the goods though it has not always been
clear whether this was on the ground that the contract was severable.[1]

Export contracts often provide that the seller is entitled to ship the
goods in separate loads and that in this event each shipment is to be
considered a distinct contract. Such a clause gives the seller the option to
treat the contract as an entire contract by shipping the goods in one
load, or to treat it as severable and ship different loads.[2] If he ships the
goods in different lots it may be important for the buyer's right to
reject that the contract be treated as severable because different loads
involve different shipping documents; hence one load may be resold to
X who may reject the goods and another load to Y who does not reject.
In this situation the middle buyer will wish to have the right to reject
part and accept part of the total quantity sold to him.

Buyer's Right to Accept Part and Reject Part of Goods in Non-severable Contracts

Prima facie Sect. 11 (1) (c) would seem to prevent a buyer from accepting part and rejecting part of the goods if the contract is not severable.
But the position is much complicated by Sect. 30 (3) of the Act which
has been set out above,[3] and which provides that if the seller delivers
"the goods he contracted to sell mixed with goods of a different description" the buyer may accept the conforming goods and reject the rest.
Sect. 11 (1) (c) has been treated by the courts as subject to this provision[4]
so that, even if the contract is non-severable, the buyer may, in the
circumstances specified in Sect. 30 (3) accept part and reject part of the
goods. For example, in *Ebrahim Dawood, Ltd.* v. *Heath, Ltd.*,[5] sellers
contracted to sell 50 tons of steel sheets in varying lengths. In fact they
delivered the whole quantity in 6 foot lengths. This was plainly a non-
severable contract, yet the buyer was held entitled, under Sect. 30 (3),
to accept part of the goods and reject the rest.

But the buyer can only do this where the case falls within the precise
wording of Sect. 30 (3); therefore the buyer must show that the seller
has delivered "the goods that he contracted to sell mixed with goods
of a different description." We have already seen that[6] the courts have
construed the words "the goods he contracted to sell" as including the
case where the seller does not deliver the correct total quantity of

---

[1] See, e.g., *Molling & Co.* v. *Dean & Son, Ltd.* (1901), 18 T.L.R. 217 (sale of 40,000
books printed by plaintiffs to defendant's order).

[2] For an unusual case in which the goods were shipped on one ship but as two
lots with separate shipping documents, see *Esmail* v. *J. Rosenthal & Sons, Ltd.*,
[1965] 2 All E.R. 860.

[3] *Supra*, p. 68.

[4] *London Plywood & Timber Co., Ltd.* v. *Nasic Oak Extract Factory Co., Ltd.*,
[1939] 2 K.B. 343.

[5] [1961] 2 Lloyd's Rep. 512.

[6] *Supra*, p. 68.

contract goods. Thus if the seller contracts to sell 100 tons of wheat and he delivers 50 tons of wheat and 50 tons of barley he has delivered "the goods he contracted to sell mixed with goods of a different description."

However, Sect. 30 (3) does not apply where the goods delivered by the seller are *all* of the contract description, but some part of them are of unmerchantable quality.[1] In this situation the buyer cannot reject part and accept part of the goods under Sect. 30 (3) and will therefore only be able to do this under Sect. 11 (1) (c) if the contract is severable. Nor does Sect. 30 (3) apply where *all* the goods are unmerchantable or fail to conform to the contract. Such a case also must be governed solely by Sect. 11 (1) (c). Some hypothetical examples may make the point clearer. Suppose, for example, that a person buys 700 bags of nuts from a seller. Prima facie this is a non-severable contract, i.e. it is a contract for the sale of a quantity of nuts, the fact that they are in 700 bags being immaterial. If the seller delivers 700 bags and 600 are satisfactory, but the remaining 100 bags contain nuts which are unmerchantable, the buyer cannot accept the 600 and reject the remainder, since "the contract of sale is not severable and the buyer has accepted the goods or part thereof." On the other hand if the remaining 100 bags contained nuts of a different description the buyer could reject those bags while retaining the other 600 under Sect. 30 (3).

If the contract is a severable contract (for example because the nuts are to be delivered in instalments which are to be separately paid for) the position would be different. For instance, if the 700 bags are delivered in seven instalments of 100 bags, and the first six instalments appear satisfactory and are accepted, but the seventh contains nuts which are unmerchantable or are nuts of a different description then the buyer can reject the last bags, while retaining the other 600.

But if *all* the bags contain unmerchantable nuts or nuts of a different description the buyer cannot accept part and reject part of the bags unless the contract is severable. The somewhat illogical result is that, where the contract is not severable, if the seller is in partial breach in delivering goods, some of which are unsatisfactory, he is worse off than if he delivers goods all of which are unsatisfactory. In the former case acceptance of the part does not preclude rejection of the rest while in the latter case it does. This strange result seems to stem from the fact that if all the goods are non-contract goods it is not possible to rely on Sect. 30 which is more favourable to the buyer than Sect. 11.[2]

The explanation for this somewhat paradoxical state of the law may well be that suggested by Salter, J., in *W. Barker & Co., Ltd.* v. *E. T. Agius*,[3] namely that Sect. 30 was never intended to apply to such

[1] See *Aitken Campbell & Co., Ltd.* v. *Boullen and Gatenby*, [1908] S.C. 490.

[2] This was accepted as settled law by Roskill, J., in *Esmail* v. *J. Rosenthal & Sons, Ltd.*, [1964] 2 Lloyd's Rep. at p. 454. The point was not argued before the C.A. and the H.L. avoided pronouncing on it: [1965] 2 All E.R. 860.

[3] (1927), 33 Com. Cas. 120.

a case, but was only intended to apply where the seller delivers not only the whole of the contract goods but delivers other goods of the same or a different description together with the contract goods. If this construction were put on Sect. 30 it would follow that a buyer could never accept part and reject part of the goods covered by the contract except in the case implicitly covered by Sect. 11 (1) (c), namely where the contract is severable. But as a matter of policy it would seem a retrograde step to move in this direction. The truth is that the concept of "severability" appears far too narrow for present purposes. There seems no sound reason of commercial policy for refusing to allow the buyer to accept part and reject part of the goods delivered, whether or not the contract is severable in the technical sense, provided only that the goods constitute different "commercial units".[1] In the hypothetical examples discussed above, for instance, it is absurd that a buyer of 700 bags of nuts cannot accept 600 bags and reject the remainder merely because they are all of the same description, if they are in fact unmerchantable. It is possible that the meaning to be attached to the word "severable" in Sect. 11 (1) (c) of the Act is not so conclusively determined as to be beyond the reach of the House of Lords. If the word could be given a very wide meaning so as to bring it into line with the approach of the U.C.C., it would be unnecessary to rely on the present haphazard use of Sect. 30 to mitigate the results of applying Sect. 11 (1) (c).

---

[1] This is the test employed by Sect. 2–601 of the U.C.C. Obviously the buyer cannot be allowed to accept part and reject part (e.g.) of one piece of machinery.

CHAPTER 27

RESCISSION FOR INNOCENT MISREPRESENTATION

RESCISSION OF THE CONTRACT

IT is an astonishing fact that the relationship between the right to reject goods for breach of condition and the right to rescind for innocent misrepresentation has not yet been fully explored by the courts, although it has been said that "a right to reject is merely a particular form of the right to rescind."[1] The first question which must be answered is whether the remedy of rescission of a contract of sale of goods for innocent misrepresentation has survived the Sale of Goods Act. The point seems never to have been argued in England, and the answer depends upon whether the rules of common law saved by Sect. 61 include the rules of equity. In *Riddiford* v. *Warren*[2] the New Zealand Court of Appeal held, on the construction of an identical statute, that they did not, and that the right to rescind for innocent misrepresentation could no longer be applied to contracts for the sale of goods. The judgment of Atkin, L.J., in *Re Wait*,[3] an extract from which is quoted above, is also very much in point. Atkin, L.J., there pointed out that a Code which only set out the common law rules, and left equitable rights inconsistent with them, would have been futile.

On the other hand, there are a number of cases in which it has been assumed that a contract of sale of goods may be rescinded for innocent misrepresentation in an appropriate case. In *Abram Steamship Co., Ltd.* v. *Westville Shipping Co., Ltd.*,[4] the House of Lords, in a Scots appeal, upheld the rescission of a contract for the assignment of the benefit of a shipbuilding contract. The contract rescinded in this case was treated as a mere assignment of the shipbuilding contract, but since the ship was already under construction it seems that it also involved the sale of the ship itself. More recently the Court of Appeal has several times assumed that rescission is available for contracts of sale of goods. In particular in *Leaf* v. *International Galleries*[5] the Court of Appeal seems to have been of the opinion that the remedy was available in a suitable case, although they denied it there because of unreasonable

---

[1] *Per* Devlin, J., in *Kwei Tek Chao* v. *British Traders & Shippers, Ltd.*, [1954] 2.Q.B. at p. 480. Yet if this were strictly true it is hard to see how a buyer could ever accept part and reject part of the goods delivered, see *ante*, pp. 296–300.

[2] (1901), 20 N.Z.L.R. 572; followed in *Watt* v. *Westhoven*, [1933] V.L.R. 458. See Howard, 26 *M.L.R.* 272, at pp. 282–5.

[3] [1927] 1 Ch. 606, pp. 159–60, *ante.*

[4] [1923] A.C. 773.

[5] [1950] 2 K.B. 86.

delay. And again in *Long* v. *Lloyd*[1] the Court of Appeal was in no doubt that the remedy was available. Finally, in *Goldsmith* v. *Rodger*,[2] the Court of Appeal actually rescinded a contract of sale of goods. In this case the misrepresentor was the buyer, but the Court held that the remedy of rescission is equally open to either party.

It seems certain, therefore, that an English Court would not now follow the New Zealand Court of Appeal.

Assuming, then, that this remedy is still available, it becomes a matter of some importance to decide when exactly it can be invoked, what is the relationship between the right of rejection and the right of rescission and what is the effect of the Misrepresentation Act. The first two of these problems were considered at some length in *Leaf* v. *International Galleries*[3] and *Long* v. *Lloyd*,[4] although neither case can be regarded as wholly satisfactory owing to the many difficult points which were glossed over. But as a result of the provisions of the Misrepresentation Act these cases can now be dealt with quite shortly.

In *Leaf* v. *International Galleries*, the plaintiff bought a picture from the defendants which was stated by them to be a Constable. Some five years later the plaintiff sought rescission of the contract on the ground that this was an innocent misrepresentation (fraud was not alleged) for which the normal equitable remedy should be available. The Court of Appeal decided that, assuming the plaintiff to have this right, he was in any case too late to rescind, since five years was far more than a reasonable time. Similarly, in *Long* v. *Lloyd* the plaintiff bought a second-hand lorry from the defendant on the faith of certain statements made by the latter as to the condition of the vehicle. Despite repeated complaints by the plaintiff to the defendant—which the defendant made some attempt to meet—the plaintiff continued to use the lorry until it broke down more or less completely, though only a few days after he had bought it. Again the plaintiff claimed rescission, for misrepresentation, and again the Court decided that he was too late, apparently on the ground that the buyer had accepted the lorry.

Two questions which gave rise to difficulties in these cases have been set at rest by the Misrepresentation Act. First, it is not now material to inquire whether a statement in this kind of case becomes incorporated into the contract as a contractual term. For by Sect. 1 (*a*) of the Misrepresentation Act the fact that a representation has become a term of the contract does not in itself deprive the innocent party of the right to rescind. Secondly, the rule in *Seddon* v. *N.E. Salt Co.*[5] (sometimes also called the rule in *Angel* v. *Jay*)[6] barring rescission of an executed contract for innocent misrepresentation is now abolished by Sect. 1 (*b*)

[1] [1958] 1 W.L.R. 753.   [2] [1962] 2 Lloyd's Rep. 249.
[3] [1950] 2 K.B. 86.
[4] [1958] 1 W.L.R. 753. See further on this case a note by Grunfeld at 21 *M.L.R.* 550 and another by the writer at 22 *M.L.R.* 76.
[5] [1905] 1 Ch. 326.   [6] [1911] 1 K.B. 666.

of the Act. Therefore the vexed question whether this rule applied to contracts of sale of goods cannot now arise, at least in England. This means that rescission of such a contract will only be barred on one of the other grounds on which rescission may be barred, i.e. affirmation, lapse of time, inability to make *restitutio in integrum*, or the acquisition of rights by an innocent third party. It seems probable that, so far as concerns the right of a buyer to rescind, the effect of the Act will be to put rejection for breach of condition, and rescission for innocent misrepresentation largely on the same footing. An act which constitutes an acceptance within the meaning of Sect. 35 will presumably amount to an affirmation of the contract within normal equitable principles.

But there appear to be at least two situations in which the rules governing acceptance in Sect. 35 differ from the equitable principles governing rescission for misrepresentation. First, we have seen that under Sect. 35, if the goods are delivered to the buyer and he does not within a reasonable time intimate that he rejects the goods, he is deemed to have accepted them.[1] But in equity it seems that lapse of time by itself does not prevent rescission: it will only do so if it is evidence of affirmation or if the representor is thereby prejudiced.[2] Since it is possible that a reasonable time for rejection may elapse without the seller being prejudiced by the delay it seems that equity might allow rescission in a case where rejection would be barred under Sect. 35.

Another possible divergence concerns the buyer who has had a reasonable opportunity to examine the goods and has resold and delivered the goods to a sub-buyer. As we have seen,[3] this remains a case in which the buyer loses his right of rejection under Sects. 34 and 35 of the Act even though the buyer is willing and able to place the goods at the seller's disposal at the original place of delivery. It seems that a right to rescind for misrepresentation would not be lost in this situation. The buyer would (it seems) only lose his right to rescind if he could not make *restitutio in integrum*. For example if he cannot get the goods back from the sub-buyer he plainly cannot rescind his own purchase of the goods. But where he is in fact in a position to restore the goods to the seller it does not seem that previous dealings by the buyer will deprive him of the right to rescind.[4]

The further question which now arises is the effect of this divergence between the statutory and the equitable principles. In *Leaf* v. *International Galleries*[5] Denning, L.J., expressed the view that a right to rescind for misrepresentation cannot survive beyond the point when a right to reject for breach of condition is lost because a misrepresentation is "much less potent" than a breach of condition. But it seems that

---

[1] *Supra*, p. 289.
[2] *Allen* v. *Robles*, [1969] 1 W.L.R. 1193; *Fenton* v. *Kenny*, [1969] N.Z.L.R. 552.
[3] *Supra*, p. 291.
[4] *Abram Steamship Co. Ltd.* v. *Westville Shipping Co.*, [1923] A.C. 773.
[5] [1950] 2 K.B. 86, at pp. 90-1.

this reasoning cannot survive Sect. 1 (a) of the Misrepresentation Act which clearly permits rescission for a misrepresentation even where the misrepresentation has become a term of the contract. This being so, it would be very anomalous if the right to rescind is lost at an earlier date when the misrepresentation does *not* become a term of the contract.

The conclusion is that, whenever a buyer wishes to reject goods and the seller may wish to contend that the buyer has lost the right to reject, the buyer will be well advised to seek, in the alternative, rescission for misrepresentation. This will not, of course, be possible where the breach complained of was non-performance of a promise, and not a misstatement of fact; nor will it always be advantageous to the buyer, particularly as the court may in its discretion refuse rescission under Sect. 2 (2) of the Misrepresentation Act and award damages in lieu. As we have seen,[1] the court has no discretion to deprive a buyer of the right to reject under the Sale of Goods Act and it is unlikely that the Misrepresentation Act affects the position in this respect.

[1] *Supra*, p. 284.

CHAPTER 28

ACTION FOR DAMAGES

DAMAGES FOR NON-DELIVERY

THE buyer's action for damages for breach of contract may take one of two forms. It may be an action for damages for non-delivery, or it may be an action for damages for breach of warranty or condition in respect of goods which have been delivered. And firstly, damages for non-delivery.

Unlike the seller's remedy, the nature of which depends upon whether the property has passed or not, the buyer's action for damages for non-delivery is the same, and the damages are assessed in the same way, whether or not the property has passed. In both cases his essential complaint is the same, viz. that the seller has failed to deliver goods which he ought to have delivered, and the buyer claims damages accordingly. The only difference is that where the property has passed the buyer may have a claim in detinue or conversion, but as will be seen, in practice the result is the same in either case.

The main rules for the assessment of damages are laid down by Sect. 51—

(1) Where the seller wrongfully neglects or refuses to deliver the goods to the buyer, the buyer may maintain an action against the seller for damages for non-delivery.

(2) The measure of damages is the estimated loss directly and naturally resulting, in the ordinary course of events, from the seller's breach of contract.

(3) Where there is an available market for the goods in question the measure of damages is prima facie to be ascertained by the difference between the contract price and the market or current price of the goods at the time or times when they ought to have been delivered or, if no time was fixed, then at the time of the refusal to deliver.

The Market Price Rule

If, then, there is a market the prima facie rule is the same as in an action by the seller, that is to say, the damages are to be assessed by reference to the market price of the goods at the time when they ought to have been delivered, and by giving him the difference between the market price and the contract price the court puts the buyer in the position he would have been in had the goods been delivered. If the market price is lower than the contract price it follows of course that the buyer is only entitled to nominal damages.

The general rule is not displaced merely because the buyer has already contracted to resell the goods to a third party at a price higher or lower than the market price at the date when delivery should be made. This principle was laid down by the Court of Appeal in *Rodocanachi* v. *Milburn*[1] and was affirmed by the House of Lords in *Williams* v. *Agius*.[2] The resale price is treated as irrelevant because the buyer must, in order to fulfil his sub-sales, buy in the market if the seller fails to deliver. Damages for the non-delivery are intended to compensate for the additional cost of buying in the market.

We have already seen in dealing with the action for non-acceptance that the concluding words of Sect. 51 (3) have no relevance where there is an anticipatory breach of contract.[3] Should the seller repudiate the contract before the date for delivery arrives, the market price to be taken in the assessment of the damages is not that prevailing at the date of the repudiation, but that at the time when delivery might have been expected to be made.[4] The only qualification on this rule is that the innocent party must as always mitigate his loss as a reasonable man, and if he accepts the seller's repudiation he should buy against the contract at once if the market is rising.[5]

We have also seen that it is still doubtful whether a contract for delivery within a reasonable time is a contract for delivery at a fixed time within Sect. 51 (3). That is to say, it is doubtful whether in such a case the relevant market price is that prevailing at the date of the refusal to deliver, or at the probable date of delivery under the contract.[6]

Although the market price rule is now firmly established in English law it may be observed that there are cases in which it does not do full justice to the buyer. In particular it is unrealistic to suppose that a buyer will in practice be able to buy goods on the market on the very day on which the seller fails to deliver. The buyer will often wish to consider his position, or to negotiate with the seller on breach and some delay before he buys substitute goods is likely to be the rule rather than the exception. In this situation the Uniform Commercial Code enables the buyer to take the price of the substitute goods as the basis for the measure of damages.[7] English law, on the other hand, remains committed to the general principle that the actual price paid by the buyer for substitute goods is immaterial. Certainly the buyer will have difficulty in making out a case for higher damages where he has, after the seller's failure to deliver, bought in the market at higher than

---

[1] (1886), 18 Q.B.D. 67.   [2] [1914] A.C. 510.
[3] *Millett* v. *Van Heeck*, [1921] 2 K.B. 693.
[4] *Melachrino* v. *Nickoll & Knight*, [1920] 1 K.B. 693.
[5] *Roth* v. *Tayson* (1896), 73 L.T. 628. On the whole question see pp. 281–2, *ante*.
[6] In a c.i.f. contract the date on which the goods ought to have been delivered within Sect. 51 (3) is the date on which the documents ought to have been tendered: *C. Sharpe & Co., Ltd.* v. *Nosawa & Co., Ltd.*, [1917] 2 K.B. 814; *Garnac Grain Co.* v. *H. M. Faure & Fairclough*, [1966] 1 Q.B. 650, affirmed,[1968] A.C. 1130.
[7] Sect. 2–712.

market prices. There is, perhaps, more likelihood that the damages will be reduced if the buyer has bought at lower than market prices.[1]

Cases Where the Market Price Rule is Inapplicable

It is now necessary to examine those cases in which the damages are assessed by some other yardstick than that of market price. In the first place even where there is a market for the goods in question[2] the buyer may in some exceptional cases be able to claim damages representing the loss he has suffered on sub-sales which he has been unable to fulfil. For example, a buyer may contract to buy goods at £10 per ton and may contract to resell the same goods at £12 per ton. If the market price at the date of non-delivery to the first buyer is £11 per ton the question is whether the first buyer should recover as damages £1 per ton (the difference between market price and contract price) or £2 per ton (the difference between market price and resale price). As we have seen the normal rule is that sub-sales must be ignored in assessing the damages, but this rule only applies to damages arising directly and naturally from the breach under Sect. 51. The buyer may, in addition, be able to claim special damages, the right to which is reserved by Sect. 54, and which are based on loss not directly or naturally following from the breach, but on loss arising from special circumstances of which the parties were aware. These two different types of damages correspond to the first and second rules in *Hadley* v. *Baxendale*[3] which have recently been authoritatively restated by the House of Lords in *Koufos* v. *Czarnikow, Ltd.* (*The Heron II*).[4] According to this decision the question in every case is whether the loss which the buyer has suffered was, at the time the contract was made, reasonably foreseeable by the seller as liable or not unlikely to result.

A simple example of special damage which may be alleged by the buyer is for freight which he has had to pay despite non-delivery of the goods.[5]

But it is one thing to recognise in principle that damages may be given in respect of a resale price. It is another thing to define the precise circumstances in which a buyer is entitled to claim damages in respect of sub-sales. The leading case is the decision of the House of Lords in *Re R. & H. Hall, Ltd. and W. H. Pim (Junior) & Co.'s Arbitration*,[6] which "astonished the Temple and surprised St. Mary Axe."[7] In this case the sellers sold a specific cargo of corn in a specific ship

---

[1] See *R. Pagnan & Fratelli* v. *Corbisa Industrial Agropacuaria Limitada*, [1970] 1 W.L.R. 1306, though the facts here were rather special, see *ante*, p. 280.
[2] On the meaning of market, see pp. 276–8, *ante*.
[3] (1854), 9 Ex. 341.   [4] [1969] 1 A.C. 350.
[5] *E. Braude (London), Ltd.* v. *Porter*, [1959] 2 Lloyd's Rep. 161.
[6] [1928] All E.R. Rep. 763.
[7] See *James Finlay & Co.* v. *N.V. Kwik Hoo Tong Handel Maatschappij*, [1929] 1 K.B. 400, 417.

to the buyers at 51 shillings and ninepence per quarter. The buyers resold at 56 shillings and ninepence per quarter but when the vessel arrived the market price had fallen to 53 shillings and ninepence per quarter. The sellers failed to deliver, and the question was whether the measure of damages was the difference between the contract price and the resale price on the one hand, or the contract price and the market price, at the date when the goods should have been delivered, on the other. It was held that the former was the appropriate measure of damages but the precise *ratio decidendi* is not easy to state. It seems that there were two critical factors in the case which displaced the general principle: first, the sale was for a specific cargo on a specific ship, and it was this same specific cargo which had been resold, and secondly, the contract of sale by its terms actually provided for resale by the buyer in the sense that various provisions of the contract dealt with this eventuality.

It has been suggested that the reason why the buyer can claim a higher measure of damages where these two conditions are satisfied is that the buyer cannot fulfil his sub-sales by buying in the market. If the buyer has contracted to sell the specific goods which he has agreed to buy under the first contract he will necessarily be unable to fulfil the second contract if the goods are not delivered. Substituted goods bought in the market will not do, and accordingly the market price is irrelevant.[1] The only alternative is to assess the damages by reference to the resale price provided (and this is the second requirement) that it was known or foreseen that the goods were to be resold.

It seems clear that both requirements must be satisfied because the mere fact that sub-sales may be contemplated as a reasonable probability is not enough to displace the general principle. For as Maugham, L.J., said in *The Arpad*—[2]

> I suppose most vendors of goods and most carriers might be taken to know that if the purchaser or consignee is a trader the goods will probably be sold, or be bought for sub-sale; but the authorities seem to show conclusively that something more than that is necessary to enable the damages to be assessed by reference to a contract of sub-sale entered into before the date of delivery.[3]

But it has been said that the position may differ where "the seller knows that the buyer is buying the goods in order to fulfil an already existing special contract, and knows that if he fails to deliver the

---

[1] Ogus on *Damages*, pp. 333–5. The difficulty with this solution is that, although the buyer will not be able to fulfil his sub-sales by buying in the market where he has resold the specific goods bought, the damages payable to his sub-buyer will surely be nil if equally good substitutes are in fact available in the market.

[2] [1934] P. 189, 230.

[3] Cf. *James Finlay & Co.* v. *N.V. Kwik Hoo Tong Handel Maatschappij*, [1929] 1 K.B. 400 *per* Scrutton, L.J., at pp. 411-12 and Sankey, L.J., at pp. 417-18. Cf. also *Horne* v. *Midland Railway Co.* (1873), L.R. 8 C.P. 131.

goods the buyer will come under a specific liability to his sub-buyer."[1]

Where the two conditions are satisfied but the buyer has contracted to resell the goods at *less* than the market price the question whether the seller is able to claim the benefit of this is one which cannot be answered with any confidence until the courts have considered it. All the cases which have arisen so far in which sub-sales have been taken into account have been cases in which the buyer increased his damages by proving that his loss was more than the difference between the contract and the market price.

If the buyer can bring himself within the principle of *Hall's case* he may be entitled to recover not only his loss of profit on sub-sales (for that is what it comes to) but also any damages which he may have had to pay his sub-buyer in respect of *his* loss of profit, and indeed that of other sub-buyers in the string. Moreover, if the buyer has been sued by his sub-buyer and has had to pay damages and costs, he is entitled to claim from the seller the total sum he has had to pay in respect of damages and costs as well as a sum in respect of his own costs.[2] The only qualification on this rule is that the buyer must have acted reasonably in defending the action. In string contracts it may well be easier for the buyer to claim loss of profit than in other sales, because in such a case if the seller knows that the buyer "is not buying merely for resale generally but upon a string contract where he will resell those specific goods and where he can only honour his contract by delivering those goods and no others, the measure of profit on resale is the right measure."[3]

Where there is no market for the goods in question, the buyer's damages clearly cannot be assessed in the usual way in terms of the market price. In such a case the method to be adopted for assessing the damages depends partly on whether the buyer is a trader, buying for resale, or whether he is buying for use, and partly on what measures the buyer actually adopts to meet the seller's failure to deliver. Where he is a trader, the buyer is entitled to recover the difference between the value of the goods at the time they should have been delivered, and the contract price. The value of the goods is prima facie to be assessed at the price at which the buyer may have contracted to resell them. Putting it briefly, the buyer is able to recover his loss of profit.[4] And

---

[1] *Aryeh* v. *Lawrence Kostoris & Son, Ltd.*, [1967] 1 Lloyd's Rep. 63, at p. 68, *per* Willmer, L.J.

[2] *Hammond & Co., Ltd.* v. *Bussey* (1887). 20 Q.B.D. 79

[3] *Per* Devlin, J., in *Kwei Tek Chao* v. *British Traders & Shippers, Ltd.*, [1954] 2 Q.B. at pp. 489–90. In *Aryeh* v. *Lawrence Kostoris & Son, Ltd. (supra)*, at p. 72, Diplock, L.J., suggested that these remarks must be confined to string sales in standard form entered into by dealers on a commodity market where it is contemplated that the buyer may resell on the same terms.

[4] *J. Leavey & Co.* v. *Hirst & Co.*, [1944] K.B. 24; *Patrick* v. *Russo-British Export Co., Ltd.*, [1927] 2 K.B. 535; *Household Machines, Ltd.* v. *Cosmos Exports, Ltd.* 1947] 1 K.B. 217.

again if the buyer can prove special knowledge on the part of the seller he may also be able to recover in respect of damages which he has to pay to his sub-buyer.[1] Alternatively, the buyer may choose to buy substitutes with which to fulfil his contracts, and should these cost more than the contract goods, he can prima facie recover this excess cost, and is not bound to account for the better quality of the goods so bought.[2] In the case of goods bought for use the buyer may be able to recover damages to meet the additional cost of buying reasonable alternative goods, or of adapting or modifying alternative goods for his purposes.

It should be observed that a sub-sale price cannot be taken as conclusive evidence of the value of the goods. In particular, where it is proved that the contract of sub-sale was entered into long before the date at which delivery should have been made, and that the price of similar goods has fallen heavily in the meantime, some other mode of assessing the value of the goods must be chosen.[3]

DAMAGES FOR BREACH OF CONDITION OR WARRANTY

The seller may deliver the goods to the buyer, but may still be guilty of a breach of warranty, or of a breach of condition which the buyer chooses, or is compelled, to treat as a breach of warranty. In this event Sect. 53 applies—

(1) Where there is a breach of warranty by the seller, or where the buyer elects, or is compelled, to treat any breach of a condition on the part of the seller as a breach of warranty, the buyer is not by reason only of such breach of warranty entitled to reject the goods; but he may

(a) set up against the seller the breach of warranty in diminution or extinction of the price; or

(b) maintain an action against the seller for damages for the breach of warranty.

(2) The measure of damages for breach of warranty is the estimated loss directly and naturally resulting, in the ordinary course of events, from the breach of warranty.

Late Delivery

Where the seller's breach consists of late delivery the method of assessing the damages must again depend partly on whether the buyer is a trader buying for resale or whether he is buying for use. If he is buying for use, the appropriate damages may be calculated by con-

---

[1] In a suitable case the court may grant a declaration that the buyer is entitled to an indemnity in respect of damages and costs he may have to pay his sub-buyer: *Household Machines, Ltd.* v. *Cosmos Exports, Ltd.*, [1947] 1 K.B. 217. But this remedy is sparingly used, see, e.g., *Trans Trust* v. *Danubian Trading Co., Ltd.*, [1952] 2 Q.B. 297.
[2] *Hinde* v. *Liddell* (1875), L.R. 10 Q.B. 265.
[3] *The Arpad*, [1934] P. 189; *Heskell* v. *Continental Express, Ltd.*, [1950] 1 All E.R. 1033.

sidering how much it would have cost the buyer to hire substitute goods during the delay, or what additional costs may have been incurred by the buyer as a result of having to make do without the goods during the delay. Much will depend here on what the buyer has actually done to mitigate his loss arising out of the delay, and whether his conduct has been reasonable.

Where, on the other hand, the buyer is a trader buying for resale it seems that the normal rule is that the buyer is entitled to recover as damages the difference between the market price at the time the goods should have been delivered and the market price at the time they were in fact delivered. Oddly enough, there appears to be no clear authority to this effect in the law of sale, but this was the measure of damages awarded by the House of Lords for delayed delivery in a contract of carriage in *Koufos* v. *Czarnikow*[1] and it seems to be generally accepted that the same measure applies in a sale.[2]

Under this measure of damages it will be observed that the contract price is irrelevant. The rule is based on the assumption that the buyer resells the goods as soon as they are delivered to him; on this assumption the loss to the buyer which is caused by the delay is the fall in the market between the contract delivery date and the actual delivery date.

A difficult and controversial case is *Wertheim* v. *Chicoutimi Pulp Co., Ltd.*,[3] where A contracted to sell goods to B, but was late in delivering them. The market price at the date when the goods ought to have been delivered was 70 shillings a ton, but the market price at the date when the goods were in fact delivered was 42 shillings and sixpence a ton. The buyer, however, resold the goods at 65 shillings a ton. It was held by the Privy Council that the buyer was only entitled to the difference between 70s. and 65s. the ton. Although this case was accepted as good law in *Williams* v. *Agius*[4] by Lord Dunedin, and apparently by Lord Atkinson, it has given rise to a certain amount of criticism[5] on the ground that it conflicts with the general principle that sub-contracts are to be ignored unless they were especially contemplated. The buyer did not suffer the full loss which might have resulted from the seller's breach but this was, in a sense, due to his own business success in selling goods for 65 shillings a ton when the market price was only 42 shillings and sixpence. The buyer might, if the goods had been delivered on time, have resold those goods at their market price of 70 shillings per ton, and bought other goods to fulfil his contract. In this way he would have made a large profit of which he was deprived by the breach of contract.

---

[1] [1969] 1 A.C. 350.
[2] McGregor on *Damages*, 13th edn., §578.
[3] [1911] A.C. 301.
[4] [1914] A.C. 510.
[5] See *Slater* v. *Hoyle & Smith*, [1920] 2 K.B. 11, especially *per* Scrutton, L.J., at p. 24. See also McGregor on *Damages*, §580 and Ogus on *Damages*, p. 345.

Breach of Warranty of Quality

Different considerations arise again where goods defective in quality
are delivered. To such a case Sect. 53 (3) applies—

> In the case of breach of warranty[1] of quality such loss is prima facie
> the difference between the value of the goods at the time of delivery to the
> buyer and the value they would have had if they answered to the
> warranty.

The prima facie rule under Sect. 53 (3) is thus that the buyer is
entitled to the difference between the value of the goods actually delivered and the value which the goods would have had if they had
conformed to the contract. Of course this means that if the goods are
so seriously defective as to have no value at all, the buyer is entitled to
recover the full value which the goods should have had. The market
price of the goods is in principle irrelevant to an action for damages of
this kind, although in some cases (especially in consumer sales) the
market price of the goods as warranted may be some evidence of the
value of the goods as warranted. The value of the goods actually
delivered will often be difficult to assess, and it is hardly likely that the
defective goods will have a market price at all.

The normal rule here, as elsewhere, is that sub-sales by the buyer are
irrelevant to the buyer's claim for damages. In *Slater* v. *Hoyle & Smith*,[2]
the buyers contracted for the purchase of 3,000 pieces of unbleached
cloth of specified quality. Some 1,625 pieces of lower quality than
specified were delivered, but the buyer delivered 691 of them under
a sub-contract he had made for the higher grade material, and obtained
payment at the same rate. The Court of Appeal held that these facts
must be ignored in assessing the damages, and that the buyer was
entitled to the difference between the value of the contract goods and
the value of the goods actually delivered.

Although Sect. 53 (3) states that the relevant date for valuing the
goods actually delivered is the time of delivery to the buyer, this does
not always work well in practice. It may, for instance, be some time
after delivery that the breach of warranty is first discovered. Or the
goods may be consigned and delivered to sub-buyers before the defect
is discovered. In this last situation the courts have held that the goods
should be valued at the time and place of delivery to the sub-buyer

---

[1] It is perhaps a little curious that this section refers to a breach of *warranty* of
quality, when all the terms as to quality implied by Sects. 13–15 are conditions. This
suggests that the draftsman thought that a condition becomes a warranty if the
buyer claims damages in respect of it, but this is not so: *Wallis, Son & Wells* v.
Pratt & Haynes, [1911] A.C. 394.

[2] [1920] 2 K.B. 11.

provided that the seller knew or could have foreseen that the goods might be redelivered without examination.[1]

It will be seen that the prima facie rule laid down by Sect. 53 (3) treats the market price as irrelevant. It is the defects in the goods for which the buyer is to be compensated, and the damages are thus based on the deficiency in their value arising from the defects. If, however, the market price of the goods has fallen significantly since the contract was made the buyer is likely to reject defective goods, as he is nearly always entitled to do. In this event the buyer is able to take advantage of the seller's breach of warranty to throw on to him the loss flowing from the drop in the market. Where the buyer with full knowledge of the defective nature of the goods chooses to keep them, and merely to claim damages for the breach of warranty, the normal rule must be applied and the buyer will be able to recover only the difference between the value of the goods and their value as warranted. However, difficulties have arisen where the buyer loses his right to reject before he becomes fully aware of the defective nature of the goods. As we have already seen, this remains possible even though it is now less likely to occur since the amendment of Sects. 34 and 35 of Sale of Goods Act.[2] In this event the buyer may feel that it is unreasonable to confine him to the measure of damages prescribed by Sect. 53 (3) for he will have lost the opportunity of rejecting the goods and buying replacement goods in the market at the now lower market price. Although it is by no means obvious why any sympathy should be shown to a buyer who has thus lost the opportunity for escaping from a bad bargain, the courts have in fact come to the assistance of the buyer in two cases of this nature. Both cases concerned, not breaches of warranty of quality, but late shipment under c.i.f. contracts in which the bills of lading were wrongly antedated to make it appear that the goods had been shipped during the contract period. In the first case[3] it was held that the buyer who had lost his right to reject before being aware of the late shipment, could recover damages representing the difference between the contract and the market price at the date of delivery. This decision was, it seems, partly based on the argument that the buyer was claiming damages, not merely for the late shipment of the goods, but for the separate breach involved in tendering false bills of lading. It was because of this falsity that the buyers did not discover until too late that the goods had been shipped late, and in a sense it was therefore true to say that it was the falsity of the bills of lading which caused the buyers' loss; had the bills of lading been accurate the buyers would probably have rejected the

---

[1] *Van den Hurk* v. *R. Martens & Co., Ltd.*, [1920] 1 K.B. 850; *Saunt* v. *Belcher* (1920), 26 Com. Cas. 115. Much the same result is arrived at by the Uniform Commercial Code Section 2–714 which substitutes the place of acceptance for the place of delivery.

[2] *Supra*, pp. 289–91.

[3] *James Finlay* v. *N.V. Kwik Hoo Tong*, [1929] 1 K.B. 400.

documents (owing to the fall in the market price) on the ground of late shipment and thus escaped their bad bargain.

In the second case,[1] the buyers were again deceived by false bills of lading, but in this case they knew of the late shipment by the time the goods themselves arrived. Although it was too late for them to reject the documents they could (it was held) have still rejected the goods when they arrived, and the case had to be decided on the supposition that they had accepted the goods with knowledge of facts from which the right to reject arose. Even in this situation it was held by Devlin, J. that the buyers could recover the difference between the contract price and the market price at the date of delivery, and thus throw on to the sellers the loss caused by the drop in the market. This case seems to push this principle as far as it can be taken, and it was based on Devlin, J.'s view that a buyer who has accepted documents under a c.i.f. contract may have practical difficulties about rejecting the goods, and that his choice to accept them is therefore not a wholly free and unconstrained choice. More recently some doubts have been expressed in the Court of Appeal about the validity of the argument that there are two rights of rejection, one for the documents, and one for the goods, in a c.i.f. contract.[2] Certainly it would seem wrong to allow a buyer quite freely and voluntarily to accept goods which he is entitled to reject, and then try to place himself in the same financial position that he would have been in if he had rejected. A buyer who wants to do this should reject the goods first and then try to negotiate a new price with the seller based on the fall in the market. However, the two decisions referred to above may be justified because of the seriousness of the practice of antedating bills of lading to conceal a late shipment, and the desirability of ensuring that the seller should not be able to retain any advantage as a result. The decisions are unlikely to have much relevance where there is a breach of warranty of quality or fitness for purpose. Even in a c.i.f. contract such a breach is unlikely to be apparent from the shipping documents and there is little likelihood of such breaches being concealed by false shipping documents, although this may occasionally happen where a clean bill of lading is wrongly issued for goods whose apparent condition is manifestly unsatisfactory.

Goods Bought for Use

Sect. 53 (3) does not differentiate between goods bought for use and goods bought for resale, and the same measure of damages is thus prima facie applicable in the former as well as the latter case. The buyer can thus recover the difference between the actual value of the goods and their value as warranted, even where he buys for use. In practice,

---

[1] *Kwei Tek Chao* v. *British Traders & Shippers, Ltd.*, [1954] 2 Q.B. 459.
[2] *Panchaud Frères* v. *Etablissements General Grain Co.*, [1970] 1 Lloyd's Rep. 53, *ante*, p. 295.

however, the damages in this case are likely to take a different form, or at least to be calculated in a different manner. One possibility is that the buyer will simply have the goods modified or repaired so as to bring them up to the requisite standard. Clearly, in this event the cost of such work is likely to be treated as equal to the difference in value between the goods delivered and their value as warranted.

Peculiarly difficult problems attend the calculation of damages for breach of warranty of quality in respect of profit-earning chattels. This is partly because of the need to avoid duplicating the damages by including the same item as a capital loss and an income loss, and partly because there is a large number of ways in which loss of profits may be calculated. Difficulties of this nature led to a divided Court of Appeal in *Cullinane* v. *British "Rema" Manufacturing Co., Ltd.*,[1] but it is doubtful if any general principle can be extracted from this case.[2]

Consequential Loss

Claims for damages for consequential loss are more commonly associated with breaches of warranty of quality and the like than with claims for non-delivery. Obviously the main reason for this is that defective goods can cause damage or injury in use, and this type of claim for consequential loss is therefore more frequently made when the goods have been bought for use. Where personal injury or physical damage to property is caused by defective goods in this way the damages are assessed in much the same way as in the tort of negligence. In such circumstances the damages may run into thousands of pounds, although the inherent value of the goods may be only a few shillings, as where a child was blinded by use of a defective catapult,[3] or where a man contracted dermatitis from wearing underpants containing an excess of harmful chemicals.[4]

A different type of consequential loss is encountered where the goods are bought for resale, and that is where the buyer has resold and delivered the goods to a sub-buyer who later has claimed damages against him for the defects in the goods. We have already seen that, in the usual course of events, sub-sales are ignored in claims under Sect. 53 (3) and claims of this kind therefore are normally treated as claims for "special damages" under Sect. 54 which require proof of special knowledge of the probability of resale. But the buyer's burden of proof here is lighter than where he claims similar damages in an action for non-delivery because he need only show that sub-sales were contemplated as a reasonable probability, and need not go on to show (as it seems he must in the non-delivery cases) that he had contracted to resell the specific

[1] [1954] 1 Q.B. 292.
[2] See Macleod, [1970] *Journal of Business Law*, 19.
[3] *Godley* v. *Perry*, [1960] 1 W.L.R. 9.
[4] *Grant* v. *Australian Knitting Mills*, [1936] A.C. 85.

goods to sub-buyers. Once it is shown that the seller should have contemplated that the goods were bought for resale, any damages and costs paid to the sub-buyer as a result of defects of quality can be properly regarded as special damage recoverable under Sect. 54.[1] But it has been stressed that in order that the buyer should be able to claim such damages and costs it is an overriding requirement that the sub-contracts should have been made on the same terms and conditions as the first contract. For, clearly, if the buyer chooses to resell the goods on more onerous terms, or with more extensive warranties, he cannot fix liability on his seller for damages he has had to pay in respect of these more onerous terms or more extensive warranties. The law on this topic was well summed up by Branson, J., in *Kasler & Cohen* v. *Slavouski*—[2]

> If a man has sold goods to another in such circumstances as to fix him with special knowledge of the purpose for which those goods are being bought, and that other sells them on the same terms and conditions and then is subjected to an action because the goods do not come up to the contract quality, or for any other reason entitling him to claim damages upon such contract, the first purchaser is entitled, if he has acted reasonably in defending the action and has yet been cast in damages and costs, to claim from his seller not only the damages but also the costs he has had to pay.[3]

And if the buyer reasonably settles a claim made against him by the sub-buyer, the amount paid under such settlement is prima facie the measure of damages recoverable from the seller, and is in any event the upper limit. But it is open to the seller to contest the amount, and to show that the sum paid was excessive, for he is of course not bound by the settlement to which he was no party.[4]

DAMAGES IN TORT

Where the property and the immediate right to possession have passed to the buyer he may have, in addition to his remedies in contract, an action in tort for detinue or conversion. As between the parties to the contract the action in tort has no advantages, and is

---

[1] But a buyer claiming damages for breach of condition as to quality cannot of course tender as evidence of his loss the amount paid by him to his sub-buyers *as damages for non-delivery: Aryeh* v. *Lawrence Kostoris & Son, Ltd.*, [1967] 1 Lloyd's Rep. 63.

[2] [1928] 1 K.B. 78, at p. 85.

[3] Cf. *Bostock & Co., Ltd.* v. *Nicholsons & Co., Ltd.*, [1904] 1 K.B. 725; *Dexters* v. *Hill Crest Oil Co., Ltd.*, [1926] 1 K.B. 348, 359, *per* Scrutton, L.J. If the sub-sales are not on the same terms, *quaere* if the buyer can claim damages paid to the sub-buyer in respect of defects for which the seller would have been liable? According to Devlin J. at first instance in *Biggin & Co. Ltd.* v. *Permanite, Ltd*, [1951] 1 K.B. 422, the answer is "Yes", with qualifications.

[4] *Biggin & Co., Ltd.* v. *Permanite, Ltd.*, [1951] 2 K.B. 314.

rarely used. The buyer cannot get higher damages by suing in tort than in contract, even where the measure of damages in the former case would normally be the higher,[1] nor can he obtain a decree of specific restitution except in cases where he could obtain a decree of specific performance.[2]

The only advantage to the buyer of the action in tort is that it avails against third parties who have meddled with, or caused damage to, the goods at a time when the buyer had the property in the goods. The buyer cannot, however, sue a third party in respect of damage done to the goods *before* the property passed to him, a rule which is apt to cause some difficulty where the property in goods is transferred while they are at sea.[3]

DAMAGES FOR MISREPRESENTATION

In a work of this nature it is unnecessary to make more than a brief reference to the possibility of an action for damages for misrepresentation. Such an action lay at common law for fraud, but under Sect. 2 (1) of the Misrepresentation Act, damages may now be obtained also for negligent misrepresentation. It is to be expected that a claim for such damages will frequently be made in the alternative to a claim for breach of express warranty in the future, and it has been held at first instance that damages on the contract measure can be obtained.[4] This means that a buyer can recover sufficient damages to put him in the position he would have been in if the representation had been true, and not just in the position he would have been in if it had not been made. This is potentially a holding of great importance.

[1] *The Arpad*, [1934] P. 189. In Australia a buyer has been held entitled to exemplary damages for wrongful seizure of goods delivered to him (*Healing Sales Pty., Ltd.* v. *Inglis Electrix Pty., Ltd.* (1968), 42 A.L.J.R. 280) but it is doubtful if such damages could be awarded in England under *Rookes* v. *Barnard*, [1964] A.C. 1129.
[2] *Cohen* v. *Roche*, [1927] 1 K.B. 169.
[3] *Margarine Union G.m.b.H.* v. *Caubay Prince S.S. Co.*, [1969] 1 Q.B 219.
[4] *Watts* v. *Spence, The Times*, 12 February, 1975.

CHAPTER 29

SPECIFIC PERFORMANCE

THE buyer, but not the seller,[1] may invoke the discretion of the court and ask for a decree that the contract be specifically performed. This right is now regulated by Sect. 52 which says—

> In any action for breach of contract to deliver specific or ascertained goods the Court may, if it thinks fit, on the application of the plaintiff, by its judgment or decree direct that the contract shall be performed specifically, without giving the defendant the option of retaining the goods on payment of damages. The judgment or decree may be unconditional, or upon such terms and conditions as to damages, payment of the price, and otherwise, as to the Court may seem just, and the application by the plaintiff may be made at any time before judgment or decree.

Specific goods, as we have seen, are defined by Sect. 62 as being goods "identified and agreed upon at the time the contract is made," and it has been said that "ascertained goods" in this context probably means goods "identified in accordance with the agreement after the time a contract of sale is made."[2]

Sect. 52 applies whether or not the property has passed to the buyer,[3] although if the property has passed the buyer has the option of claiming a decree of specific restitution in an action of detinue. But even here he cannot ask for such a decree as of right. "The power of the Court in an action of detinue rests upon a footing which fully accords with Sect. 52 of the Sale of Goods Act."[4] In other words the remedy rests entirely within the discretion of the court and will not be granted in respect of chattels of no special importance. But where a chattel is of peculiar importance, and of practically unique value to the plaintiff the court will grant the necessary decree.[5]

Where the property has not passed to the buyer there can be no question of detinue, and the only claim which can be made is on the

---

[1] Although the seller has not in name a right to a decree of specific performance, the fact that he generally has a right to claim the price when the property has passed must in many cases be tantamount to a right to specific performance, for if the buyer has to pay the price the property and the right to possession will vest in him by satisfaction.

[2] *Per* Atkin, L.J., in *Re Wait*, [1927] 1 Ch. 606, 630.

[3] Ibid., p. 617, *per* Lord Hanworth, M.R.

[4] *Per* McCardie, J., in *Cohen* v. *Roche*, [1927] 1 K.B. 169, 180–1.

[5] *Behnke* v. *Bede Shipping Co., Ltd.*, [1927] 1 K.B. 649.

contract. Until recently it was generally thought that the court had no power to grant specific performance of a contract for the sale of goods as yet unidentified; and that a contract for the sale of an unidentified part of a specific whole was not a contract for the sale of specific or ascertained goods, of which specific performance could be ordered under Sect. 52.[1]

But very recently doubt has been thrown on these traditional ideas. In *Sky Petroleum, Ltd.* v. *VIP Petroleum, Ltd.*[2] the plaintiffs obtained an interlocutory injunction to restrain the defendants from breaking a contract to supply the plaintiffs with all their petroleum requirements for ten years. Goulding, J., treated the injunction as in effect a decree of specific performance, but went on to hold that the general rule was inapplicable where damages would clearly not be an adequate remedy. In the case before him there was a real danger that the plaintiffs would be forced out of business if the defendants broke their contract in the very peculiar circumstances then holding.

[1] *Re Wait*, [1927] 1 Ch. 606.
[2] [1974] 1 All E.R. 954.

PART VIII

HIRE-PURCHASE AND CONSUMER CREDIT

CHAPTER 30

NATURE OF HIRE-PURCHASE CONTRACTS

INTRODUCTORY

CONTRACTS of hire-purchase are treated by the man in the street as contracts of sale in which the price is to be paid by instalments. In law, however, as we have already seen, contracts of hire-purchase are very different from contracts of sale. In fact the *raison d'être* of hire-purchase contracts (at least till the passing of the Hire-Purchase Act, 1964) was that they should not be contracts of sale, for they were devised largely for the purpose of evading the provisions of Sect. 9 of the Factors Act, 1889, which as we have seen, enables a person who has bought or agreed to buy goods, and who is in possession of them, to pass a good title to an innocent purchaser for value.

The law of hire-purchase is principally governed by common law rules—rules for the most part of recent origin—and the Consumer Credit Act, 1974, which has now replaced the Hire-Purchase Acts. Although the common law rules are profoundly modified by this Act it is still true to say that it does not set out to state substantially the whole of the law peculiar to hire-purchase contracts in the way in which the Sale of Goods Act does with the law of sale. Moreover, there is still a considerable area in which the common law rules apply as a result of the two main limitations on the operations of the Consumer Credit Act. These are (1) that the Act only applies where the total credit does not exceed £5,000,[1] and (2) that the Act does not apply to any hire-purchase agreement in which the hirer is a corporation.[2] This latter provision, which was inserted in the 1964 Bill during its passage through Parliament, is an expression (albeit in a very crude way) of the fact that the main purpose of the Act was consumer protection. And the Consumer Credit Act has retained this restriction on its operation.

Quite apart from the existence of a codifying Act for sales of goods, the law of hire-purchase differs considerably from the law of sale owing to differences in commercial practice. A sale is such an everyday oc-

---

[1] Sect. 8 (2) of the 1974 Act. This figure has been raised from £2,000 by the Consumer Credit Act, and in addition the £5,000 only relates to the amount of credit supplied and does not include the credit charges themselves.
[2] Sect. 8 (1) of the 1974 Act.

currence, and the Sale of Goods Act covers so much of the ground, that many contracts of sale are made in which the parties express only the bare elements of the transaction. Even if the only evidence that appeared in a case was that X had agreed to sell, and Y had agreed to buy, certain goods, this might be sufficient to establish a valid contract.[1]

On the other hand, contracts of hire-purchase are almost invariably spelt out in great detail. They are a typical example of standard form contracts which have been perfected over the years to give the maximum possible protection to the owner and to impose the heaviest possible burden on the hirer although the balance is now largely redressed by statute. The result of all this is that there is far less general law governing hire-purchase contracts than sale of goods contracts. Thus, whereas a judge may have to fill in large gaps in a sale, he will rarely have any gaps to fill in a hire-purchase, since virtually every contingency will already be specially provided for either by the contract or by legislation. Moreover, although hire-purchase contracts tend to follow a fairly uniform scheme it cannot be said that there are standard hire-purchase terms. Hence an agreement to sell "on hire-purchase terms" without further explanation is too vague to constitute a legal contract.[2] This also means that an oral hire-purchase would be almost impossible even apart from the statutory requirements.

THE CONTRACT AND ITS OBLIGATIONS

As we have already seen, a hire-purchase contract generally takes the form of a bailment under which the goods are hired, together with an option to purchase subject to the conditions of the agreement being complied with. There are, however, many different variations in the details. For example, in some hire-purchase contracts the hirer is entitled to return the goods at any time before he exercises his option to purchase (and in cases to which the Consumer Credit Act applies, he is always entitled to do so[3]); while in others he may be bound to pay all the instalments. In the latter case the option to purchase may be purely derisory, as where the hirer, having paid several hundred pounds by way of rental charges, then has the "option" to purchase the goods for ten shillings or even one shilling.[4] In some cases, too, the initial payment is treated as the consideration for the option to purchase. Again, in some cases the option has to be specifically exercised by some payment on the conclusion of the period of hire, while in other cases the property passes automatically if the hirer pays all the instalments and otherwise abides by the terms of the agreement. In this event, however, the hirer must be given the option of returning the goods during

---

[1] *Hillas & Co., Ltd.* v. *Arcos, Ltd.,* [1932] All E.R. Rep. 494.
[2] *Scammell* v. *Ouston,* [1941] A.C. 251. [3] Sect. 99 of the Act of 1974.
[4] I have argued elsewhere (5 *Bus. Law Rev.* 24) that there is no conclusive authority against treating this sort of case as a sale.

the period of hire, otherwise the contract will be a conditional sale, although, as has been seen, this will now make little difference.

Nevertheless, the basic element in all true hire-purchase agreements is the combination of bailment and option to purchase. On the face of it, and accepting hire-purchase agreements as being what they purport to be, both elements would seem equally important. But in *Warman* v. *Southern Counties Car Finance Corporation, Ltd.*[1] it was held that if the owner is in breach of the implied condition as to title there is a total failure of consideration, notwithstanding that the hirer has used the goods throughout the period of hire. Finnemore, J., said—

> The essential part of the agreement is that the hirer has the option of purchase and it is common knowledge—and I suppose, common sense— that when people enter into a hire-purchase agreement they enter into it not so much for the purpose of hiring, but for the purpose of purchasing by a certain method, by what is, in effect, deferred payments . . . If at any stage the option to purchase goes, the whole value of the agreement to the hirer goes with it.[2]

This decision was obviously influenced by *Rowland* v. *Divall*,[3] and if a hire-purchase contract is regarded as in truth merely a form of sale, it would seem a reasonable conclusion from that case, although *Rowland* v. *Divall* is itself, as we have pointed out, open to criticism.[4] It is true that the case seems difficult to reconcile with the fact that the courts have so far always treated hire-purchase contracts as exactly what they purport to be, but this is now largely immaterial. The whole thrust of the Consumer Credit Act is to assimilate hire-purchase to sales on credit.

In *Kelly* v. *Lombard Banking Co., Ltd.*[5] a hire-purchase contract stated that the initial deposit was in consideration of the hirer's being granted the option to purchase. After the hirer had paid a total of £419 out of £534 a creditor levied execution against him. This being—as is common form—one of the events on which the owner was entitled to determine the agreement, the owners retook possession of the goods. The hirer then claimed that he was entitled to recover his deposit on the ground that as he had never exercised his option to purchase there was a total failure of consideration. The Court of Appeal rejected this claim on the ground that the option to purchase was an existing right as soon as the contract was signed, and could have been exercised forthwith. Thus the hirer had got what he had paid for and there was no total failure of consideration. This case is no doubt distinguishable from *Warman*'s *case* because in that case the option to purchase was valueless, since the owners had no title which could be purchased. However, it does show the difficulty of attempting to treat the option to buy as something quite separate from the bailment. The actual result in this

---

[1] [1949] 2 K.B. 576.   [2] At p. 714.   [3] [1923] 2 K.B. 500.
[4] *Supra*, p. 51.   [5] [1959] 1 W.L.R. 41.

case could not recur today because the owner would not under such circumstances be entitled to seize the goods without a court order and such an order would certainly not be granted today without giving the hirer time to pay off the remaining balance.

Another problem which arises out of the dual nature of hire-purchase contracts is to decide whether the hirer has any proprietary interest in the goods pending the exercise of the option. The practical importance of this lies in the extent of the liability of a third party to whom the hirer may purport to sell the goods. The third party will not, of course, get a good title, except in the case of motor vehicles where Part III of the Hire-Purchase Act, 1964, may apply, but if he is sued for conversion of the goods by the owner, the question arises whether he is liable for the full value of the goods at the time when he converted them, or whether he is only liable for the balance of the hire-purchase price, i.e. is he entitled to credit for instalments paid by the hirer? In *Belsize Motor Supply Co., Ltd.* v. *Cox*[1] it was held that the third party was only liable for the balance of the total price due, and this decision was approved and followed by the Court of Appeal in *Whiteley* v. *Hilt*.[2] In *United Dominions Trust, Ltd.* v. *Parkway Motors*,[3] McNair, J., distinguished these cases on the ground that in both of them the benefit of the hire-purchase agreement was assignable, whereas in the case before him assignment was expressly prohibited. But this case was overruled by the Court of Appeal in *Wickham Holdings, Ltd.* v. *Brooke House Motors, Ltd.*[4] where it was held that the finance company should only be entitled to recover from the third party the unpaid balance of the hire-purchase price. Although there are doctrinal difficulties in the reasoning of the Court in this case, it was followed in *Belvoir Finance Co., Ltd.* v. *Stapleton*.[5]

So far we have been considering hire-purchase contracts from the point of view of the option to purchase. It is now necessary to consider briefly the legal position arising out of the bailment. As between the creditor and the debtor little scope is usually left to the general law of bailment since the rights and duties of the parties *inter se* are usually spelt out in considerable detail. But where third parties are concerned the ordinary rules of bailment sometimes become important. In particular, if the debtor commits some breach which goes to the root of the agreement, whereby the goods come into the possession of a third party, the creditor may be able, on ordinary principles, to claim that he has a right to determine the agreement, and that the immediate right to possession is revested in him. This being so, he can, of course, maintain an action in conversion or detinue against the third party. Even here, however, the words of the agreement may prove decisive in the result. For example, in *North Central Wagon & Finance Co., Ltd.* v. *Graham*,[6]

[1] [1914] 1 K.B. 244. [2] [1918] 2 K.B. 808. [3] [1955] 1 W.L.R. 719.
[4] [1967] 1 W.L.R. 295. [5] [1971] 1 Q.B. 216. [6] [1950] 2 K.B. 7.

the hirer wrongfully delivered the goods—a car—to an auctioneer for sale. This was a breach of the agreement which gave the owners the option to terminate the agreement by retaking the goods. In an action for conversion against the auctioneer, it was argued that until the owners had exercised their option to terminate the agreement they had no right to possession, and could not therefore sue in conversion. This argument was rejected by the Court of Appeal which held that, whether or not the owners had terminated the agreement, they had an immediate right to possession sufficient to support an action of conversion.[1] This does not, of course, mean that where a right is expressed to be exercisable on the determination of the agreement it may be exercised merely because a right to terminate has arisen.[2] It is not clear whether these cases are still good law having regard to the need to serve a "default notice" before the owner can enforce his rights.

Somewhat similar problems arise in connection with liens, especially on the hire-purchase of vehicles. Most, if not all, hire-purchase agreements of vehicles require the hirer to maintain the vehicle in good repair. From this, and from his possession of the vehicle, it has been held that the hirer has an implied authority from the owner to create a lien. Thus if the hirer takes the car to a garage for repairs, and while the car is there he defaults in payment of the instalments, the garage owners have a lien on the vehicle for their charges which is good against the owners.[3] In order to meet this situation finance companies have taken to inserting a clause in the hire-purchase agreement expressly prohibiting the hirer from creating any lien over the vehicle. The efficacy of this device was tested in *Albemarle Supply Co., Ltd.* v. *Hind*,[4] where the Court of Appeal held that in the absence of any knowledge by the garage owners of the existence of this clause in the hire-purchase agreement, the owners could not dispute the ostensible authority of the hirer to create a lien. It is not entirely clear whether this is only so where the garage owner knows that the car is held under a hire-purchase agreement. This suggestion derives some support from *Tappenden* v. *Artus*[5] where the Court of Appeal was concerned solely with actual or presumed authority which is normally negatived by the express terms of a hire-purchase agreement, but the court appears to have treated cases of ostensible authority as resting on estoppel. This would certainly lead to the conclusion that there would be no lien unless the car was known to be held under a hire-purchase agreement.

On the other hand it may be argued that the hirer's authority to

[1] See also *Jelks* v. *Hayward*, [1905] 2 K.B. 460—goods seized in execution, sheriff liable in conversion.

[2] *Reliance Car Facilities, Ltd.* v. *Roding Motors, Ltd.*, [1952] 2 Q.B. 844.

[3] *Green* v. *All Motors, Ltd.*, [1917] 1 K.B. 625.

[4] [1928] 1 K.B. 307.

[5] [1964] 2 Q.B. 185. See also *Fisher* v. *Automobile Finance Co. of Australia* (1928), 41 C.L.R. 167.

create a lien is a real (implied) authority and not merely an ostensible authority; if this were the case it would be immaterial whether the garage owner knew of the hire-purchase agreement.

The implied authority to create a lien cannot in any case survive termination of the hire-purchase agreement. So in *Bowmaker* v. *Wycombe Motors, Ltd.*,[1] where the lien was created only after the finance company had written to the hirer terminating the agreement, it was held that the lien was not binding on them.

HIRE-PURCHASE AND CONSUMER CREDIT

After the passing of the Hire-Purchase Act of 1964, it came to be increasingly felt that there were serious anomalies in the protection afforded to the consumer as a result of the differences between the law of hire-purchase and the law of sale. Thus a cash purchaser of a car might, for example, enjoy the protection of the terms implied by the Sale of Goods Act while the person who wanted to buy on credit, and so entered into a hire-purchase agreement obtained the protection of the terms implied by the Hire-Purchase Acts—and there were a number of important differences in the two sets of implied terms. Even more important was the fact that until 1973 the implied terms under the Sale of Goods Act could be freely modified or excluded by the terms of the contract, while this was only possible to a very limited extent under the Hire-Purchase Acts.

The differences between the position of a cash purchaser and a hirer under a hire-purchase agreement were rendered even more anomalous because of the availability of other forms of credit. Thus a person might borrow money from a finance company under a "personal loan" repayable by instalments, and use the money to buy for cash a car or household goods. Such a purchase would be a cash transaction as between the purchaser and the seller, but from the purchaser's point of view there would be little difference between an arrangement of this nature and a hire-purchase agreement. Similarly, a person might agree to buy goods under a "conditional sale" agreement whereby he undertook to pay the price by instalments but was not entitled to terminate the agreement. Such an agreement differed from a hire-purchase agreement in some important respects (e.g., with regard to the application of Sect. 9 of the Factors Act) but for most purposes the consumer was unlikely to see any difference between the two.

The result of these anomalies has been the passage of legislation to broaden the protection given by the Hire-Purchase Acts to other consumers who acquire goods or services on credit. The first step in this direction was taken by the Hire-Purchase Act of 1964 which largely assimilated the position of a conditional sale to that of hire-purchase. The second major step was taken by the Supply of Goods (Implied

[1] [1946] K.B. 505.

Terms) Act, 1973,[1] which very largely assimilated the law of sale of goods and the law of hire-purchase in two major respects. First, the implied terms relating to title, and quality and fitness of the goods were termed almost identically in the one Act; and secondly, the right of the supplier of the goods to contract out of his obligations was controlled in almost identical terms in the one Act. (The sections dealing with hire-purchase have been re-enacted with some verbal changes by the Consumer Credit Act, 1974.) The next major step was taken by the Consumer Credit Act of 1974. Under this Act the law governing hire-purchase transactions has, in substance, remained largely unaltered except that the £2,000 limit has been greatly raised. However, the form of the law has been greatly changed by the new Act because the provisions of the Hire-Purchase Act have, in effect been generalised so that they apply to all forms of consumer purchase on credit. Thus under the new Act, it will often make little difference to the rights of the consumer whether he acquires goods under a hire-purchase agreement, under a sale on credit, or a conditional sale, or even under a cash sale where he has borrowed the money to acquire the goods. Although, therefore, the new Act has almost completely repealed the Hire-Purchase Acts, the new legislation has replaced those Acts with provisions which are very close to those formerly applying to hire-purchase agreements but which will in future apply to all consumer credit transactions. One result of these changes is that the old terms "hirer" and "owner" should now be replaced by the more general terms "debtor" and "creditor".

[1] See Chapters 12 and 14.

CHAPTER 31

THE MECHANICS OF HIRE-PURCHASE

THE actual mechanics of hire-purchase transactions are frequently of a very complex nature. This is particularly so where the credit is supplied by someone other than the retailer who is actually selling the goods. Some retailers, of course, finance their own hire-purchase agreements, but many others, particularly in the motor trade, prefer to rely on credit facilities supplied by outside bodies, usually called "finance companies." From the economic point of view, in hire-purchase agreements financed in this way the retailer sells the goods to the consumer, who pays for them with money borrowed from the finance company. In law, of course, the transaction takes a very different form: the retailer sells the goods to the finance company for the cash price (including the deposit which is paid directly to the retailer by the hirer) and the finance company lets them on hire-purchase to the hirer for the cash price, plus "hire-purchase charges," i.e. principally interest, usually at a very substantial rate.[1] The provisions of the Consumer Credit Act do not directly alter the legal nature of a hire-purchase contract except in relatively minor respects. But the Act does more clearly recognise the fact that the *economic* similarities between acquiring goods on hire-purchase and buying goods on credit (or with a loan) are more important than the existing legal differences. It is now necessary to examine in rather more detail the legal relationships which may arise in hire-purchase transactions which are financed in this way. Three principal parties, and frequently one or more others, are involved, and there are therefore at least three possible contractual relationships, viz. between the finance company and the hirer, between the retailer and the hirer, and between the finance company and the retailer. In addition there are often guarantors involved.

RELATIONSHIP BETWEEN FINANCE COMPANY AND HIRER

Generally speaking, the courts have upheld the reality of hire-purchase agreements, and refused to look behind the outward form of the transaction. Thus it was repeatedly held that finance companies were

---

[1] Although this is by far the commonest arrangement, other methods do exist, especially in dealing with property of particular value, such as aircraft. Here, the hire-purchase contract is frequently made between the manufacturer and the buyer direct. The buyer issues promissory notes, which are then discounted with a bank or other organisation. The use of promissory notes in this way is now prohibited by the Consumer Credit Act where the credit does not exceed £5,000, see Sects. 123–5.

not subject to the Moneylenders Acts, on the ground that they were not moneylenders.[1] To argue that the lending of money is the primary object of all hire-purchase agreements was said "to confuse the economic nature of the transaction, viz. providing credit to a purchaser of goods, with its legal nature."[2] But all this has been changed by the Consumer Credit Act, one of whose main purposes is to give greater recognition to the economic reality of hire-purchase agreements. The new Act replaces the old Moneylenders Acts with new licensing provisions which apply to hire-purchase finance companies.

Only in dealing with the Bills of Sale Acts have the courts permitted themselves to look behind the form to the substance of the transaction. Now the Bills of Sale Acts strike at transactions whereby a person in possession of goods sells them whether by way of outright sale (Bills of Sale Act, 1878) or by way of security (Bills of Sale Act, 1882) but retains the possession of them, merely giving a right to the buyer to seize the goods in certain events. Hire-purchase contracts do not generally fall within the scope of these Acts (although the mischief aimed at by them occurs in almost the same form in hire-purchase contracts) because in hire-purchase contracts there is a genuine transfer of possession from retailer to the hirer.[3] However, hire-purchase contracts are sometimes used as a device for using goods as a security for a loan. Thus a person who owns a car may raise a loan on the security of the car by "selling" it to a finance company, and then immediately taking it back from him under a hire-purchase agreement. In such circumstances the courts have held that they are bound to inquire into the real nature of the transaction. This question has been considered elsewhere.[4]

Under the Consumer Credit Act the debtor's rights against the finance company have been extended to situations where the contract between them does not take the form of a hire-purchase agreement at all. Thus, if a person borrows money under a personal loan from a finance company in order to purchase (say) a car, the debtor will sometimes be able to treat the finance company (the creditor) as liable for any breaches of contract for which the supplier of the car is liable. This has the great advantage from the debtor's point of view that he may be entitled to cease paying the instalments, and if sued by the finance company, can set up (say) a breach of warranty of quality as a partial or total defence. But he will only be able to do this if the loan was made for the "restricted-use" of enabling the debtor to buy the goods (see Sect. 75 of the 1974 Act.)

---

[1] See *Olds Discount Co., Ltd.* v. *John Playfair, Ltd.*, [1938] 3 All E.R. 275; *Transport & General Credit Corpn., Ltd.* v. *Morgan*, [1939] 2 All E.R. 17.

[2] *Premor, Ltd.* v. *Shaw Brothers.* [1964] 2 All E.R. 583, at 588, *per* Diplock, L.J.

[3] *McEntire* v. *Crossley Bros.*, [1895] A.C. 457.

[4] *Supra*, p. 11. It should be remembered that in such a case the hirer will now be treated as a seller in possession and thus able to pass title to a bona fide purchaser under Sect. 25(1); see the *Pacific Motor Auctions* case, *supra*, p. 203.

RELATIONSHIP BETWEEN RETAILER AND HIRER

In the ordinary way no contractual nexus exists at all between the supplier and the debtor under a hire-purchase agreement. The man in the street who simply "buys" something from a retailer on hire-purchase may be surprised, when it comes to the point, to discover that the forms which he signs in the shop consist of a proposal form addressed to the finance company to whom, if the finance company accept his proposal, the retailer will sell the goods. If, therefore, something goes wrong with the goods, the debtor will prima facie have no right of action against the retailer, as was held by the Court of Appeal in *Drury* v. *Victor Buckland, Ltd.*[1] The law on this point has not been altered by the Consumer Credit Act.

However, the debtor may not be entirely without remedy against the retailer. In the first place there is, particularly in the case of second-hand goods, and especially second-hand cars, the possibility of holding the retailer liable in negligence. Such liability can usually be established if it can be proved that the retailer has "put into circulation in the hands of his customer a motor-car which is in fact in a dangerous condition [and] the defect rendering the condition dangerous consists of a defect which could or ought to have been discovered by reasonable diligence on his part."[2]

In the second place, if the retailer says anything to the debtor which can be construed as an express warranty as to the quality of the goods (e.g. "It's a good little bus; I would stake my life on it") the debtor may be able to set up a separate contract between himself and the retailer, the consideration for which is the debtor's agreement to enter into the hire-purchase contract with the finance company.[3] Indeed, it is possible that this development may be taken a stage further, for it has been suggested that if any contractual nexus can be established between the retailer and the debtor, it may be possible to imply into this contract terms relating to the quality and fitness of the goods analogous to those implied by Sect. 14 of the Sale of Goods Act. Thus in *Andrews* v. *Hopkinson*[4] McNair, J., said, although plainly *obiter*—

> I feel there is much to be said for the view that in a transaction such as the present, which though not in law a transaction of sale between the parties, is closely akin to such a transaction, the Court ought to imply such a condition or warranty [sc. as in Sect. 14 (1)] if any contractual relationship between the parties can in fact be established.

[1] [1941] 1 All E.R. 269.
[2] *Per* McNair, J., in *Andrews* v. *Hopkinson*, [1957] 1 Q. B. 229, at 236.
[3] *Brown* v. *Sheen & Richmond Car Sales, Ltd.*, [1950] 1 All E.R. 1102; *Shanklin Pier, Ltd.* v. *Detel Products, Ltd.*, [1951] 2 All E.R. 47; *Andrews* v. *Hopkinson, supra.* As to the measure of damages in such a case, see *Yeoman Credit, Ltd.* v. *Odgers*, [1962] 1 All E.R. 789.
[4] [1957] 1 Q.B. at p. 237.

The only difficulty here, as McNair, J., himself pointed out, is whether this suggestion can be reconciled with *Drury* v. *Victor Buckland, Ltd.*[1] The question is, however, of little practical importance now, because the hirer will always be able to rely on the implied terms binding the finance company, and this is more effective than attempting to sue the retailer or dealer.

RELATIONSHIP BETWEEN FINANCE COMPANY AND RETAILER

Thirdly, there is the relationship between the finance company and the retailer. Primarily, of course, this is simply the relationship of buyer and seller. The dealer keeps the deposit paid by the hirer and sells the goods to the finance company for the full purchase price. Of course all this is done on paper. The goods are never delivered to the finance company, but are delivered straight to the hirer. In fact it is common knowledge that the retailer may deliver the goods even before he has received the finance company's approval to the transaction, but if he does so, it is at his peril since, if the hire-purchase agreement falls through, the retailer will not receive his price, and will have to attempt to recover the goods.[2]

However, the relationship between the retailer and the finance company is frequently a good deal more complicated than this. Frequently the finance company insists that the retailer should act as guarantor. The finance companies regard themselves as mere bankers, and if there is default in payment or any difficulty in connection with the contract, the finance company does not want (as it probably has not the facilities) to be forced to take possession of the goods. They expect the retailer to step in at this stage to pay them off the balance owing. The retailer is then left, by way of subrogation or by express assignment, to enforce the hire-purchase agreement as best he can.

Agreements of this sort again take various forms. Sometimes the dealer is *eo nomine* a guarantor. Sometimes the "recourse agreement," as it is called, takes the form of an agreement whereby the retailer binds himself to repurchase the goods from the finance company, on default by the hirer, for the balance of the price due. In such a case there is normally an implication that the guarantor will be called on to repurchase within a reasonable time of the default by the hirer.[3] This repurchase form of guarantee has its dangers for the finance company because, being an ordinary contract of sale of goods the finance company, as seller, is bound in the absence of a contrary agreement to deliver the goods to the buyer. If the goods cannot be delivered, e.g.

[1] [1941] 1 All E.R. 269.
[2] See, e.g., *Central Newbury Car Auctions, Ltd.* v. *Unity Finance, Ltd.*, [1957] 1 Q.B. 371. In such cases the inapplicability of Sect. 9 of the Factors Act is especially anomalous.
[3] *United Dominions Trust* v. *Eagle Aircraft Services*, [1968] 1 W.L.R. 74, criticised in (1968) 31 *M.L.R.* 332.

because they cannot be found, the retailer will not be liable.[1] The position is different where the agreement is a contract of guarantee or indemnity, for in this case the finance company's inability to deliver the goods will, at most, give the dealer a right to counter-claim for damages.[2]

Another aspect of the relationship between the finance company and the dealer which is of considerable importance is how far the dealer can be treated as the agent of the finance company. At common law it is doubtful if any general principles can be laid down,[3] but it has been held that in most cases the dealer is agent at least for some limited purposes, e.g. for receiving offers from the hirer, for delivering the goods to him, and for receiving notice of revocation of the hirer's offer from him.[4] But the dealer is prima facie not the finance company's agent for receiving payments from the hirer[5] nor for the purpose of fixing the finance company with knowledge of defects in title to the goods.[6] In other cases it is a question of fact depending on all the circumstances how far the dealer may be treated as agent.

Under Sects. 56 and 69 of the 1974 Act the retailer is also constituted agent for two other purposes, namely, in relation to the making of representations (whether terms of the contract or not) and also in relation to the receipt of notices of cancellation where the "cooling-off" provisions of the Consumer Credit Act apply. These sections only apply where the agreement in question is a regulated agreement within the protection of the Consumer Credit Act, but where they do apply they cannot be excluded by the agreement itself.[6]

Under Sect. 75 (2) of the Consumer Credit Act the finance company will normally have a statutory right to an indemnity from the dealer where the finance company is held liable for a breach of the hire-purchase agreement as a result of the dealer's acts.

FINANCE COMPANY AND GUARANTOR

As we have seen, a retailer may himself, by one means or another, guarantee payment to the finance company. But this, of course, is for the protection of the finance company, not the retailer. In practice, therefore, it is common to find that the debtor is requested to find his own guarantor, who will also be required to sign a standard guarantee agreement, either as part of the hire-purchase agreement, or as a separate agreement. Apart from the complications introduced by the Consumer Credit Act the liability of the guarantor depends on the ordinary

---

[1] *Watling Trust, Ltd.* v. *Biffault Range Co., Ltd.*, [1938] 1 All E.R. 525.
[2] *Bowmaker (Commercial), Ltd.* v. *Smith*, [1965] 2 All E.R. 304.
[3] *Branwhite* v. *Worcester Works Finance, Ltd.*, [1969] 1 A.C. 552.
[4] Ibid.; *Financings, Ltd.* v. *Stimson*, [1962] 3 All E.R. 386; [1962] 1 W.L.R. 1184.
[5] *Car & Universal Finance, Ltd.* v. *Caldwell*, [1965] 1 Q.B. 525.
[6] Sect. 173 of the 1974 Act.

law, and does not raise many special difficulties in hire-purchase transactions. Two particular problems, however, do arise, the first of which is the effect of granting indulgence to the debtor. In the absence of specific agreement to the contrary, a creditor who grants any indulgence to his debtor (provided it is legally binding) impliedly discharges the guarantor by changing the extent of the obligations which are guaranteed. In hire-purchase contracts, an extension of time even for one instalment will discharge the guarantor completely.[1] Obviously this is an extremely inconvenient doctrine to the creditor, and it is customary for hire-purchase contracts of guarantee to permit the finance company to grant extended time for payment, or show other indulgences, without losing its rights against the guarantor. Sometimes the contract requires notice to be given to the guarantor if the time for payment is extended beyond a certain limit.[2] It has been held that the assignment by a hire-purchase company of its rights under a hire-purchase agreement does not discharge a guarantor because his rights are in no way impaired by the assignment.[3]

The second problem which has come to light in recent years is the extent of the liability (if any) of a guarantor when the hirer determines the agreement either under the terms of the agreement itself or under Sect. 99 of the 1974 Act. In these circumstances the liability of a true guarantor is co-extensive with the liability of the hirer, and if the hirer discharges his legal liabilities in full no further payment can be exacted from the guarantor even though the amounts paid fall short of the total which the finance company would have received had the agreement run its full course.[4] At common law it was held that there was no reason why an indemnity should not be so phrased as to impose liability for the balance of the total hire-purchase price, although, no doubt, clear words were needed to produce this result.[5] But this is no longer permissible in the case of regulated agreements under the Consumer Credit Act. Sect. 113 of this Act makes it clear that a surety is in no circumstances to be liable to a greater extent than the debtor himself.

When a guarantor discharges a liability owed by the principal debtor he is entitled by subrogation (as reinforced by Sect. 5 of the Mercantile Law Amendment Act, 1856) to stand in the creditor's place and to use the creditor's remedies against the principal debtor. It has been said that the right of seizure of the goods cannot pass to the guarantor by virtue of this doctrine,[6] but it is difficult to see why this should be so. Presumably on paying off the balance the guarantor steps into the shoes of the

---

[1] *Midland Motor Showroom, Ltd.* v. *Newman*, [1929] 2 K.B. 256.
[2] As to when a debt is "overdue" see *Midland Counties Motor Finance Co., Ltd.* v. *Slade*, [1951] 1 K.B. 346.
[3] *Chatterton* v. *Maclean*, [1951] 1 All E.R. 761.
[4] *Western Credit, Ltd.* v. *Alberry*, [1964] 2 All E.R. 938.
[5] *Goulston Discount Co., Ltd.* v. *Clark*, [1967] 2 Q.B. 493.
[6] *Chatterton* v. *Maclean*, [1951] 1 All E.R. 761, at p. 766.

finance company, and acquires its title to the goods. But unless he can seize the goods, of what use is the title?

Finally, a number of statutory provisions bearing on the position of guarantors should be mentioned. First, a guarantor, no less than the hirer, is protected from liability in the event of a hire-purchase agreement within the Acts not complying with the statutory formalities.[1] Secondly, a guarantor is entitled to a copy of the contract of guarantee as well as the hire-purchase agreement.[2] Thirdly, a guarantor (like the hirer himself) will be exonerated from any liability if the owner wrongfully seizes the goods without a court order after a third of the price has been paid.[3] Finally, it is to be observed that the statutory provision relating to the position of a guarantor apply to a contract of indemnity as well as to a contract of guarantee.[4]

[1] See *post*, Chapter 32.   [2] Sects. 107–8 of the 1974 Act.
[3] Sects. 91 and 113 of the 1974 Act, *post* p. 342, and see *Unity Finance, Ltd.* v. *Woodcock*, [1963] 2 All E.R. 270.
[4] See the definitions of "security" and "surety" in Sect. 189 (1) of the Consumer Credit Act.

FORMATION OF HIRE-PURCHASE CONTRACTS

FORMALITIES

CERTAIN formalities for hire-purchase contracts are prescribed under the Consumer Credit Act, 1974, for "regulated" contracts, that is, contracts in which credit not exceeding £5,000 is given to an individual. The old Hire-Purchase Acts provided that before any hire-purchase agreement was entered into the owner was required to state in writing to the hirer the cash price of the goods. However, this requirement was regarded as satisfied if the hirer had seen price labels or tickets attached to the goods, or if he had selected the goods from a catalogue or other document which stated the price. Under the new Consumer Credit Act these pre-contract requirements are now left to be specified in Regulations, and at the time of writing no Regulations have yet been made. It is assumed that on matters of this sort the new Regulations will follow the old law fairly closely.

The new Act also contains a sweeping power to make Regulations with respect to the form and content of regulated consumer credit contracts. These regulations will have to contain provisions requiring the contract to inform the debtor of his rights and duties under the Act, and otherwise, specifying the amount and rate of the charge for credit, and, where the agreement is subject to the "cooling-off" provisions, of the debtor's rights in that respect also. In addition, Sect. 61 (1) of the Act itself contains provisions regarding the signature of the agreement. The agreement must be signed both "by the debtor" and "by or on behalf of the creditor". This difference in wording makes it clear that the debtor must sign personally, and cannot sign through an agent. This was certainly the law under the old Hire-Purchase Acts,[1] and the new Act appears to confirm the law on this point.[2] Moreover, the debtor must not sign blank forms to be filled in subsequently by the creditor or supplier, for as was said in a case under the old Hire-Purchase Acts, "the object of the provision must be that the hirer should know and understand what he is agreeing to".[3]

If any of the statutory requirements relating to the form of the agreement are not complied with, the creditor is not entitled to enforce the hire-purchase agreement without an order of the court. Under Sect. 127 of the Act, the court is given wide powers to make appropriate

---

[1] *Eastern Distributors, Ltd.* v. *Goldring*, [1957] 2 Q.B. 600.
[2] The point seems to be put beyond doubt by Sect. 61 (1) (*c*) of the Act.
[3] *Eastern Distributors, Ltd.* v. *Goldring*, [1957] 2 Q.B. 600, at p. 612.

orders where there has been some technical or trivial failure to comply with the Act or with Regulations. But without such an order, the creditor can neither enforce the agreement nor retake the goods from the debtor, even if the debtor stops paying the instalments. Under the old law, it seems that the creditor could recover the goods from a third party if, for instance, the debtor had wrongfully disposed of them.[3] The effect of the new Act on this point is not entirely clear.

[3] Ibid.

CHAPTER 33

THE DUTIES OF THE PARTIES

THE DUTIES OF THE OWNER

SINCE the coming into force of the Supply of Goods (Implied Terms) Act, 1973, the duties of the owner under a hire-purchase agreement are, for all practical purposes, identical with those of a seller under a contract of sale of goods. Sects. 8–11 of the 1973 Act provide for implied terms in all hire-purchase contracts (with no financial limit) corresponding to the new terms implied in contracts of sale. Sect. 12 also prohibits contracting out in a consumer hire-purchase agreement and restricts contracting out in other cases in virtually identical terms as the new Sect. 55 of the Sale of Goods Act. It is consequently unnecessary now to give the subject any extended treatment. Conceivably it is still open to the courts to imply a term at common-law in a hire-purchase agreement which differs from the statutory terms, but in practice this is a remote possibility and can safely be ignored. The only points which need to be made are that the 1973 Act, in replacing the provisions of the Hire-Purchase Act of 1965, has made two important changes of principle, as well as many minor changes in the wording of the implied conditions; first, the 1973 Act applies to all hire-purchase agreements with no financial limit, and secondly it now protects corporations as well as individuals. Sects. 8–12 of the 1973 Act are re-enacted, with verbal alterations only, in Schedule 4 of the Consumer Credit Act, 1974.

THE DUTIES OF THE DEBTOR

It is virtually impossible to lay down any general rules of law relating to the duties of the debtor in a hire-purchase contract. As we have already seen, it is not possible to make a contract "on hire-purchase terms" without specifying those terms in some detail, and in fact the duties of the debtor are invariably specified in great detail. Since these duties vary considerably from contract to contract it is not possible to do more than indicate the sort of terms which are likely to be encountered in practice. It is not yet clear what changes may be made by the sweeping new powers to make Regulations as to the contents of consumer credit agreements.

In the first place the debtor will, of course, be under some obligation as regards the rental. As has been shown, in some contracts the debtor is bound to pay all the instalments at the agreed dates, and it is only after he has done this that his option to purchase arises. In other cases the debtor is only bound to pay the instalments—or hire charges, which in this case is the more appropriate expression—so long as the agreement continues in force. If the agreement is terminated the debtor may then become liable for some further payment, which may give rise to difficult questions of law. This is dealt with later.[1] We have also seen that if the case is covered by the Consumer Credit Act the debtor is always entitled to determine the agreement at any time before the final payment falls due.[2] In this event the hirer is liable under the Act to pay (1) any instalments in arrears; (2) enough to make up his total payments to fifty per cent of the total price (if they do not already reach this figure); and (3) damages for failure to take reasonable care of the goods, where that is the case. However, under Sect. 100 of the 1974 Act, if the creditor's loss is less than half the hire-purchase price this will be the limit of the debtor's liability. If, for example, the debtor terminates the agreement at an early stage and the goods are resold by the finance company without a substantial drop in price, the debtor's total liability may be less than half the total price.

Secondly, the contract will almost invariably require the hirer to take reasonable care of the goods, and in most cases also to maintain them in a proper state of repair. In the case of motor vehicles there is almost always an obligation to take out a comprehensive insurance policy for the full value of the goods.

Thirdly, there will usually be found a number of ancillary obligations, often spelt out in great detail so as to leave no loophole to the hirer. These provisions will usually prohibit the hirer from moving the goods from the place where they are normally kept (or garaging them in a different place from usual in the case of vehicles); they will usually prohibit him from reselling the goods, or even offering or advertising them for sale; from pledging them, or hiring them; from parting with the possession of them, or creating a lien over them, and so forth. It seems probable that the more oppressive of these clauses will be banned under the new Regulations.

Finally, mention may be made of the statutory obligation imposed on a debtor by Sect. 80 of the 1974 Act to inform the owner, on request, of the whereabouts of the goods. Breach of this requirement is a summary offence.

In addition to these duties, *stricto sensu*, the contract will usually provide that the owner is entitled to exercise his remedy of retaking the goods and claiming the minimum payment in certain other events which can hardly be regarded as breaches of contract. These usually include having execution levied against the hirer's goods, the commis-

---

[1] *Post*, p. 343.   [2] Sect. 99 of the 1974 Act.

sion of an act of bankruptcy by him, death of the hirer,[1] or, in the case of a company, going into liquidation. The owner's remedies in such circumstances are discussed later.[2]

[1] But the 1974 Act contains elaborate provisions to safeguard the family of a deceased hirer: Sect. 86
[2] *Post*, p. 343.

CHAPTER 34

THE REMEDIES OF THE CREDITOR

ONCE again general rules are difficult to lay down, since most hire-purchase contracts specify in detail what are the creditor's remedies, and when they are exercisable. It is not yet clear to what extent the new regulation-making power as to the contents of hire-purchase agreements will be used to produce a standardised form of contract laying down standard rights and duties and remedies. In a work of this kind it is only possible to deal very briefly with the main questions which arise. The creditor's two chief remedies are to sue the debtor, claiming either instalments in arrears, or general damages for breach of contract, or to attempt to retake possession of the goods with a view to their resale.

ACTION FOR INSTALMENTS OR DAMAGES

Agreements not Regulated by the Consumer Credit Act

In the law of sale, it will be recalled, the seller is, generally speaking, entitled to sue for the price only when the property has passed to the buyer. Until then, the seller's remedy is an action for damages for non-acceptance. Analogous principles apply to hire-purchase contracts, but the time of delivery is generally taken as the critical date, in lieu of the time of passing of the property. The owner cannot, therefore, sue for instalments until they fall due.

It is common practice for hire-purchase agreements to provide that if the debtor fails to pay an instalment on the due date, the whole amount will become due and payable forthwith. A provision of this sort is perfectly valid in the case of a non-regulated agreement, unless it is unenforceable as a penalty or could be attacked as an extortionate bargain under the general provisions of the 1974 Act. These two possibilities are dealt with later.

Where the debtor has refused to accept delivery of the goods, the creditor's only remedy appears to be to claim damages for non-acceptance, and this is probably so whatever the contract may say.[1] Damages in such circumstances are assessed on similar principles to those applicable in sales cases, i.e. the correct measure of damages depends on the state of the market. If the creditor is able to meet all the demand without difficulty, the measure of his loss is the total amount payable under the contract throughout its entire life, subject to appro-

[1] *National Cash Register Co., Ltd.* v. *Stanley*, [1921] 3 K.B. 292; *Karsales (Harrow), Ltd.* v. *Wallis*, [1956] 1 W.L.R. 936.

priate deductions, e.g., in respect of depreciation which will not occur if the goods are never delivered.[1] In effect, the creditor recovers for loss of profit. Damages so assessed may, of course, be very substantial, and may even exceed the sum due under a minimum payments clause. Where, on the other hand, demand exceeds supply, then repudiation by the debtor prior to delivery may, as in cases of sale,[2] cause the creditor no loss at all, or at most loss of the amount of rental (subject again to appropriate deductions) during the time which elapses while he finds a new debtor.

Actions for damages for breach of hire-purchase agreements *after* delivery were rarely brought prior to 1961 because hire-purchase finance companies preferred to sue on the minimum payments clauses which such agreements always contained. But in that year the decision of the House of Lords in *Bridge* v. *Campbell Discount Co., Ltd.*[3] made it clear that minimum payments clauses might fall foul of the law relating to penalties,[4] and actions for damages accordingly suddenly sprang into prominence in this field. After some initial difficulties the courts laid down the law in the form of two principal propositions.

First, if the debtor repudiates the contract, either in express terms, or by committing breaches which go to the root of the contract (e.g., repeated and persistent failure to pay instalments) the creditor is entitled to accept the repudiation and sue for general damages. The damages will be the total amount payable under the contract, subject to appropriate deductions.[5] In order to establish his right to damages under this heading, it is essential for the creditor to show that he has accepted the debtor's repudiation.

Secondly, if the debtor's breach does not amount to repudiation, the damages recoverable are prima facie the instalments in arrears up to the date of commencement of the action (or, if the goods have been repossessed, up to the date of repossession),[6] together with any damages for failure to keep the goods in a proper state of repair if, as is usual, the agreement contains a clause to that effect.[7]

---

[1] *Inter-Office Telephones, Ltd.* v. *Robert Freeman Co., Ltd.,* [1958] 1 Q.B. 190. In *Yeoman Credit, Ltd.* v. *Waragowski,* [1961] 1 W.L.R. 1124 it seems to have been held that this is still the case even if the debtor has the option to terminate the agreement, but see criticisms of this by Lord Denning M.R. in *Financings, Ltd.* v. *Baldock,* [1963] 2 Q.B. 104, at pp. 113–14, and see also 24 *M.L.R.* 792. The point is rendered of greater importance because all regulated agreements are terminable by the debtor under Sect. 99 of the Consumer Credit Act.

[2] *Charter* v. *Sullivan,* [1957] 1 Q.B. 117.

[3] [1962] A.C. 600.   [4] See *post,* p. 343.

[5] *Yeoman Credit, Ltd.* v. *Waragowski,* [1961] 1 W.L.R. 1124; *Overstone, Ltd.* v. *Shipway,* [1962] 1 W.L.R. 117. The deductions should include (1) an amount equivalent to the value of the goods if and when repossessed, and (2) a figure which takes into account that the owner receives payment in a lump sum instead of spread out over the period of hire.

[6] *Financings, Ltd.* v. *Baldock,* [1963] 2 Q.B. 104; *Charterhouse Credit Co., Ltd* v. *Tolly,* [1963] 2 Q.B. 683.

[7] *Brady* v. *St. Margaret's Trust, Ltd.,* [1963] 2 Q.B. 494.

Regulated Agreements

The provisions of the Consumer Credit Act appear to prevent the creditor from having any absolute right to claim instalments or damages from the buyers. However the creditor frames his action, it seems clear from Sect. 129 of the Act that the court has the power to make a "time order" giving the debtor additional time to pay. Although the Act does not expressly give the court the power to discharge the debtor, or release him from his obligations, it is possible (as experience under the Hire-Purchase Acts has shown) for a purely nominal order to be made. For example, in appropriate circumstances, the court could order the debtor to pay the instalments at the rate of 10p per week.

Sect. 129 appears to apply even to an action for damages, and even to a case where the debtor has wholly repudiated the agreement (whether before or after delivery of the goods). Consequently, it seems immaterial precisely what remedy the creditor may have in the case of a regulated agreement. The result will always lie in the discretion of the court under Sect. 129.

SEIZURE OF THE GOODS

Hire-purchase contracts invariably provide that the creditor is entitled to retake possession of the goods in any one of a large number of events. These events fall into two categories, namely (1) where there is a breach of the agreement by the debtor, usually a failure to pay instalments; and (2) where there is no such breach, for example on the death of the debtor or in the event of any other person levying execution against him. The right to retake the goods is in any event profoundly modified by the 1974 Act in the case of regulated agreements, that is where the debtor is not a company, and the credit does not exceed £5,000.

In the case of an unregulated agreement, the right to retake the goods is largely a matter for the agreement itself. At common law there is nothing to prevent the creditor retaking the goods even after nine-tenths of the price has been paid if the agreement allows him to do so, as it usually does. But even in the case of an unregulated agreement, it is probable that financial relief could now be available under the 1974 Act in this sort of case, under the new provisions relating to extortionate agreements.[1]

In the case of regulated agreements, the Consumer Credit Act imposes severe restrictions on the creditor's right to recover possession. First, under Sect. 87, the creditor cannot terminate the agreement or recover possession (or indeed, exercise any other remedy except probably sue for instalments due) unless he has first served a default notice on the debtor, giving him at least seven days in which to remedy any

[1] See *post*, p. 346.

breach of the agreement. This provision (first enacted in the Hire-Purchase Act of 1964) reflects an important principle, namely that the creditor should not be able to bring to bear the powerful remedies at his disposal as a result of some minor breach by the debtor (e.g., lateness in paying a single instalment) without fair warning. The default notice must comply strictly with the statutory requirements.[1] Secondly, under Sect. 90 of the Act, where one-third of the total price has been paid by the debtor, the creditor is no longer entitled to take possession of the goods without a court order unless the agreement has been terminated by the debtor himself. If the creditor retakes the goods in contravention of this section, Sect. 91 provides that the debtor is released from all liability under the agreement, and is entitled to recover from the creditor all sums paid by him under the agreement. There is probably no right to damages for the retaking itself.[2] It was held under the old Hire-Purchase Acts that there was no breach of the corresponding provisions of those Acts if the hirer consented to the owner's recovery of possession,[3] nor if the hirer totally abandoned the goods so that they were no longer in his possession.[4] These decisions appear to be confirmed by the new Act.[5]

The third restriction on the creditor's right to recover possession is that under Sect. 92 of the new Act the creditor is not entitled, without an order of the court, to enter the debtor's premises to retake the possession of any goods let under a hire-purchase agreement. This applies whether or not one-third of the price has been paid, although here again the debtor may consent to the creditor's entry into the premises for the purpose of retaking the goods.

In an action to recover possession of the goods the court is given a wide discretion under Sects. 129 to 136 of the new Act to make a reasonable order, irrespective of the terms of the contract. Thus, the court may make an order for the immediate delivery of the goods to the creditor, or it may make an order for delivery but postpone its operation and give the debtor the opportunity to pay the balance due "by such instalments, payable at such times as the court, having regard to the means of the debtor or hirer, and of any surety, considers reasonable". Alternatively, the court may apportion the goods, ordering part to be returned to the creditor, and transferring his title in the remainder to the debtor. The normal procedure under the old Hire-Purchase Acts has been for the court to postpone the operation of a delivery order on the terms that the hirer pays off the balance by in-

---

[1] *Eshun* v. *Moorgate Mercantile, Ltd.*, [1971] 1 W.L.R. 722.

[2] So held under the corresponding provision of the Hire-Purchase Act in *Carr* v. *James Broderick & Co., Ltd.*, [1942] 2 K.B. 275, and apparently confirmed by Sect. 170 of the new Act.

[3] *Mercantile Credit Co., Ltd.* v. *Cross*, [1965] 2 Q.B. 194.

[4] *Bentinck, Ltd.* v. *Cromwell Engineering Co., Ltd.*, [1971] 1 Q.B. 324.

[5] See Sect. 173 (3) as to the first decision, and as to the second, the words "from the debtor" in Sect. 90 (1).

stalments as fixed by the court. This usually means that the hirer in practice obtains additional time to pay, the instalments being reduced in amount, having regard to his ability to pay, but being continued for an additional period.

MINIMUM PAYMENTS AND FORFEITURE CLAUSES

1. At Common Law

Hire-purchase agreements invariably provide that on the seizure of the goods or on their voluntary return by the hirer (if he has the right to return them) the hirer is not entitled to recover any payments already made, and is also liable to pay to the owner certain further sums, sufficient to bring his total payments up to a certain proportion of the full price, usually 50 per cent, $66\frac{2}{3}$ per cent or 75 per cent, if his payments do not already reach this figure. This provision is usually called a minimum payments clause, and is intended to guard against depreciation. It is quite independent of any damage to the goods, which is always separately provided for. It remains to be seen whether use will (or indeed can) be made of the new statutory powers to regulate the content of consumer credit agreements so as to prohibit or control use of minimum payment claims.

As regards the question of forfeiture, it has generally been assumed that provisions of this sort are valid, so that, even if the hirer has paid £490 out of £500, default by him entitles the owner to retake the goods and keep all the payments.[1] It would be surprising if this were so because there is in substance no distinction between a penalty provision and a provision for forfeiting sums already paid. The only difference is that the roles of the plaintiff and the defendant are reversed. But despite dicta in the Court of Appeal[2] in favour of some form of equitable relief it has recently been held that there can be none.[3]

As regards the second point—the minimum payments clause—the position is more difficult. The first question here is whether the law relating to penalties is applicable to minimum payments clauses, and the courts have had a good deal of difficulty with this question.

The first properly reported case on the point is *Associated Distributors, Ltd.* v. *Hall*,[4] where the contract provided that the hirer might return the goods at any time if he paid enough to bring his total payments under the contract to half the total price. It was held by the Court of Appeal that this was valid and that no question of penalties arose at all, since this was simply an agreement to pay a sum on a certain event, and not agreed damages for breach. This ingenious argument (which,

---

[1] See *Hewison* v. *Ricketts* (1894), 63 L.J.Q.B. 711.

[2] *Stockloser* v. *Johnson*, [1954] 1 Q.B. 476.

[3] *Galbraith* v. *Mitchenall Estates, Ltd.*, [1965] 2 Q.B. 473, and see also *Campbell Discount Co., Ltd.* v. *Bridge*, [1961] 1 Q.B. 445, reversed on another point: [1962] A.C. 600. Cf. *Barton Thompson & Co* v. *Stapling Machines Co.*, [1966] Ch. 499.

[4] [1938] K.B. 83.

if carefully used by draftsmen, could circumvent the law relating to penalties altogether) was again accepted in *Re Apex Supply Co., Ltd.*[1] In this case the hirers were a company, and the contract provided that if they went into liquidation the owners could retake the goods and also claim payment of enough to bring the total sums paid to a figure equal to about five-sixths of the total price.

The first judicial stand against the success of this argument was made in *Cooden Engineering, Ltd.* v. *Stanford*,[2] where the Court of Appeal by a majority held that if the owners retook the goods from the hirer because of his default in not paying the instalments the question of penalties did arise, and the minimum payment clause in this case being clearly penal (it required the hirer to pay the whole price) it was held void. This decision was followed in *Lamdon Trust, Ltd.* v. *Hurrell*,[3] where a similar clause with a minimum payments clause of 75 per cent was held void. In this case Denning, L.J., threw out the suggestion that *Re Apex Supply Co., Ltd.* was inconsistent with *Cooden Engineering, Ltd.* v. *Stanford* and should not be followed. This no doubt inspired the argument put forward in *Campbell Discount Co., Ltd.* v. *Bridge*[4] which, however, failed to convince the Court of Appeal. An appeal to the House of Lords[5] unfortunately failed to settle this question. The appellant in this case distinguished himself in being (it is safe to say) the first person to win an appeal by persuading the House that on the facts he had been guilty of a breach of contract. On the important legal issue in the case two[6] of their lordships were prepared to uphold the Court of Appeal, two[7] were in favour of overruling *Associated Distributors* v. *Hall*, and the fifth[8] reserved his opinion. The result was that the Court of Appeal's decision stood and the law is committed to a rule which says that if the hirer honestly returns the goods because he cannot pay, he is exposed to the full rigours of the minimum payments clause, whereas if he deliberately breaks the contract and defaults he can invoke the law relating to penalties to protect himself.[9] The consequence is just what might have been expected, namely that the courts prefer to treat the hirer as having broken his contract if the facts can be so interpreted.[10] Indeed it has been said that a voluntary return of the goods by the hirer should not be treated as a return in accordance with his contractual rights unless he was fully aware of the consequences; it should instead be treated as a breach of contract by him.[11]

---

[1] [1942] Ch. 108.   [2] [1953] 1 Q.B. 86.
[3] [1955] 1 W.L.R. 391.   [4] [1961] 1 Q.B. 445.
[5] *Sub. nom. Bridge* v. *Campbell Discount Co., Ltd.*, [1962] A.C. 600.
[6] Lords Simonds and Morton.
[7] Lords Denning and Devlin.
[8] Lord Radcliffe.
[9] I discussed this problem in 5 *Bus. Law Rev.* 24.
[10] As in *Bridge* v. *Campbell Discount Co., Ltd.*, in the House of Lords, and in *United Dominions Trust* v. *Ennis*, [1968] 1 Q.B. 54.
[11] *United Dominions Trust* v. *Ennis* (*supra*).

The position is, therefore, that a minimum payments clause *may* amount to a penalty clause, and therefore be unenforceable, insofar as it provides for payment on a breach of contract by the hirer. The question whether any particular clause amounts to a penalty clause depends on the general principles relating to penalties laid down in *Dunlop Pneumatic Tyre Co., Ltd.* v. *New Garage & Motor Co., Ltd.,*[1] but these have been amplified in the context of hire-purchase agreements by several other decisions.[2] The result of these decisions is to make it exceedingly doubtful whether any minimum payments clause can be so drafted as to amount to a genuine pre-estimate of the damages, because it seems that the two concepts are inherently incompatible. Most minimum payments clauses provide that the *later* the breach, the less is the amount payable, whereas a true pre-estimate of the damages would do just the reverse since the value of the goods is bound to depreciate the longer the hiring lasts. The purpose of a minimum payments clause is to ensure that the finance company recovers a fixed proportion of the hire-purchase price whatever the outcome of events, whereas the object of damages is to compensate it for loss arising from the hirer's breach of contract. Since the amount of the loss must depend primarily on the value of the goods when and if recovered, it might have been thought that a clause providing that the hirer should be liable for an amount sufficient to bring his payments up to the full hire-purchase price, but giving credit for the value of the goods recovered, would have satisfied the courts. But in *Anglo-Auto Finance, Ltd.* v. *James*[3] the Court of Appeal struck down a clause even in these terms. It may be that this decision turned on the fact that the clause in question purported to provide compensation for the mere termination of the hiring agreement, and made no separate provision for depreciation. It is at all events difficult to see how a minimum payments clause could ever escape being a penalty clause if it takes no account of the value of any goods repossessed.

The net result of the cases, therefore, is that a minimum payments clause is only valid at common law (1) insofar as it provides for payment on an event other than a breach of contract by the hirer, and (2) insofar as it provides for payment on breach, if it is a genuine pre-estimate of the damage.

2. Under the Consumer Credit Act

The common law and equitable provisions set out above are now of little practical importance, although unfortunately they cannot be said to be wholly obsolete in their application to credit agreements. The

---

[1] [1915] A.C. 79.
[2] *Bridge* v. *Campbell Discount Co., Ltd.*, [1962] A.C. 600; *Lombank, Ltd.* v. *Excell*, [1964] 1 Q.B. 415; *Anglo-Auto Finance, Ltd.* v. *James*, [1963] 1 W.L.R. 1042.
[3] [1963] 1 W.L.R. 1042.

Consumer Credit Act, however, contains provisions which mean that in most cases no reliance need be placed on the rules of common law and equity. The Act has two sets of provisions bearing on the enforcement of clauses of this kind; the first set are general and apply to all credit agreements; the second apply to regulated agreements.

General Provisions

Sects. 137 to 140 of the new Act contain some very important provisions relating to extortionate credit bargains, which represent a generalisation and modernisation of certain rules formerly applicable only to "moneylending" transactions. These new provisions apply to all credit agreements, and not merely to regulated agreements, that is to say they apply even where the debtor is a corporation, and they apply irrespective of the amount of the credit.

Under Sect. 138 of the Act a credit bargain is "extortionate" and liable to be set aside or reopened under Sect. 139 if it requires the debtor to make payments (whether unconditionally or on certain contingencies) which are grossly exorbitant, or if the agreement otherwise grossly contravenes ordinary principles of fair dealing. In determining whether a credit bargain is extortionate the court must have regard to a variety of factors mentioned in the Act, including in particular, interest rates and the experience and business capacity of the borrower, and the degree to which he was under financial pressure at the time of making the bargain. The degree of risk accepted by the creditor is also an important relevant factor. If the court holds that the agreement is extortionate it may reopen the transaction, and the court then has sweeping powers to adjust the rights and duties of the parties under Sect. 139 (2). In particular, the court may set aside or reduce any obligation imposed on the debtor, or it may require the creditor to repay any sums paid by the debtor.

It seems plain that these provisions are apt to cover minimum payments and forfeiture clauses, and if they are dealt with under the Act, it will be immaterial whether the agreement is regulated or not, whether the debtor is or is not in breach of his obligations under the agreement or whether the clause is or is not valid as a matter of common law. While it is obviously difficult to predict how the courts will operate the very wide discretionary powers here entrusted to them, it seems reasonable to suppose that they will accept the underlying principle of the whole Consumer Credit Act, which is that the creditor under the hire-purchase agreement is to be treated as a financier with a security. Consequently, it is to be expected that the courts will generally insist that an agreement is extortionate insofar as it contains provisions which would give the creditor significantly more than the repayment of his capital together with interest at the agreed rate—assuming that rate itself not to be extortionate. Such an approach would mean that minimum payments and forfeiture clauses would normally be un-enforceable unless they merely provide for sufficient payments to make good any loss to the creditor caused by the debtor's breach or other act.

Provisions Dealing with Regulated Agreements

Further weapons against minimum payments and forfeiture clauses are contained in the sections of the new Act governing regulated agree-ments. So far as forfeiture clauses are concerned, the debtor's protection lies in the provisions already discussed which prevent the creditor re-taking possession of the goods without a court order when one-third of the price has been paid. The court will not normally allow the creditor to retake the goods in this event without giving the debtor every opportunity of paying the balance and so avoiding any forfeiture. And as we have seen, the court has other powers, such as apportioning the goods where this is practicable, which could be used to avoid forfeiture. Where the debtor has not paid one-third of the price, the Act does not prevent the creditor from retaking the goods so long as he first serves a notice of default, and provided that he does not have to enter the debtor's premises to do so. In this event there is nothing to prevent forfeiture of the amounts paid by the hirer except the general provisions relating to extortionate agreements. These are not likely to be applicable in this situation, since the amounts paid by the debtor (being less than one-third of the price) will rarely be sufficient to cover the drop in the value of the goods, unless the goods were secondhand.

As regards minimum payments clauses, by Sect. 99 of the 1974 Act, a debtor is entitled to terminate the agreement at any time before the final payment falls due, and in this event the Act itself provides for a sort of minimum payments clause. Prima facie the debtor in this situ-ation is liable to pay enough to bring his total payments up to one-half of the total price, but if it is shown that the creditor's loss is less than this amount, then that is the maximum of his liability.

In the other cases—for example where the contract is terminated because of a breach by the debtor or for any other reason—the debtor's protection lies in the simple fact that the court has such sweeping powers under Sect. 129 to 136 to make any reasonable order irrespec-tive of the agreement. Here again, it is reasonable to assume that the courts will be guided by the principle that the creditor should never be better off as a result of a premature termination of the agreement than he would have been if the agreement had been complied with.

CHAPTER 35

THE REMEDIES OF THE DEBTOR

LITTLE remains to be said here. The nature and applicability of the debtor's remedies is apparent from what we have said concerning the duties of the creditor, and the Consumer Credit Act. Many of the problems as to remedies which arise in the law of sale rarely do so in hire-purchase agreements, though there are conversely a number of remedies of exclusive relevance to consumer credit agreements.

REJECTION OF THE GOODS

Plainly, the debtor has a right to reject the goods for breach of condition by the creditor. The relevant conditions are those enacted by the Supply of Goods (Implied Terms) Act, 1973, as restated by the Consumer Credit Act.

There are no statutory provisions corresponding to Sect. 11 (1) (c) or Sects. 34 and 35 as to the buyer's right of rejection, in the case of hire-purchase contracts.[1] The courts must therefore fall back on general principles of contract law so that the question would be whether the debtor had elected to repudiate or to affirm the contract. Authority on this point is scanty, although in one case it was held that a hirer had not affirmed a hire-purchase agreement, despite considerable use of the goods, because he had repeatedly insisted on the goods being repaired.[2]

DAMAGES

Authority on the proper measure of damages recoverable by the debtor for breach of condition is also scanty. This is probably because, in practice, the debtor under a hire-purchase agreement is not likely to claim damages at all; if the goods are defective he is more likely to simply refuse to pay the instalments, and await attack by the creditor. On principle, it would seem that the proper measure of damages should be the difference between the value of the goods as warranted and their value as actually delivered. But it has been held that the measure of damages due to the debtor is a sum equal to the cost of hiring similar goods on similar terms less a deduction for the use he has had of the goods, and that the amount due under the agreement in question can prima facie be taken as the appropriate figure.[3] In this case the court

---

[1] The uncertainty of the law on this point is reflected in Sect. 14 of the Supply of Goods Act, 1973.

[2] *Farnworth Finance Facilities, Ltd.* v. *Attryde*, [1970] 2 All E.R. 774.

[3] *Charterhouse Credit Co., Ltd.* v. *Tolly*, [1963] 2 Q.B. 683.

rejected the argument that the measure of damages was the cost of putting the goods into a proper state of repair on the ground that in a contract of hire-purchase, it is not for the hirer to repair the goods. This seems unrealistic because it fails to pay adequate attention to the real commercial nature of a hire-purchase contract, and now that the Consumer Credit Act shows more clearly what that is, a different approach may well be justified. In *Doobay* v. *Mohabeer*[1] the Privy Council suggested that the appropriate measure might vary according to the circumstances of the case. For instance, it may be that where the debtor does keep the goods and have them repaired, the cost of the repairs is the appropriate measure of damages; while if the debtor rejects the goods, a different measure would be required.

TERMINATION UNDER SECT. 99

As we have already seen, in a regulated hire-purchase agreement, the debtor is entitled to terminate the agreement at any time before the final payment falls due, by simply giving notice to the creditor. The debtor is not even obliged to physically return the goods to the creditor, though he must, of course, hand them over when the creditor calls to collect them.[2] In a conditional sale agreement in which the price is payable by instalments, the buyer is similarly entitled to determine the agreement, and may do so even after the property has passed to him provided he has not already sold the goods to a third party.

COOLING-OFF PERIOD

Sects. 68 to 73 of the 1974 Act contain provisions substantially reproducing and generalising the cooling-off provisions of the old Hire-Purchase Act. These provisions enable the debtor to cancel the agreement not later than five days after service on him of a copy of the agreement, if the agreement has not been signed at the premises of the creditor, or the supplier or some associated party. They are, of course, aimed at contracts signed by the consumer at his own home under the pressure of door-to-door salesmen. It would be beyond the scope of this work to examine the details of the Act on this point, but its principal provisions may be summarised as follows. In order to exercise his right to cancel the agreement the debtor can give a "notice of cancellation" to the creditor or his agent (which by virtue of Sect. 69 (6) includes the supplier of the goods). The notice need not take any particular form so long as the intention to withdraw is clearly indicated. It may be sent by post, and to facilitate service in this way the agreement must give the name and address of a person to whom the notice may be sent.

---

[1] [1967] 2. A.C. 278. See also *Lowe* v. *Lombank*, Ltd., [1960] 1 All E.R. 611 where the damages seem to have been based on the cost of repairs, though no question was raised as to the measure of damages.

[2] *Capital Finance, Ltd.* v. *Bray* [1964] 1 All E.R. 603.

Regulations to be made under the Act will probably provide for a "tear-off" slip to be attached to the agreement which the debtor can simply fill in and post. Service of a notice of cancellation operates to cancel the agreement as to the provision of credit and also any "linked transaction", for example, an agreement for the maintenance of some consumer appliance entered into at the same time as the hire-purchase agreement. After service of the notice the debtor is bound to take reasonable care of the goods (if they have already been delivered to him) for 21 days. He is not bound to return the goods but must, of course, allow the creditor to collect them. He may, however, insist on being repaid anything he has paid before he allows the owner to retake the goods. Special provisions exist to deal with the possibility of the debtor having traded in goods in part exchange to the supplier. These must be returned to him, or an amount equal to the part-exchange allowance repaid to him.

Under the Consumer Credit Act these cooling-off provisions have been extended to a wide variety of other consumer transactions, and are no longer restricted to hire-purchase agreements. For example, a simple loan of an amount not exceeding £5,000 will be subject to the cooling-off provisions if the agreement is signed at the debtor's own house. In this event the money must be repaid on cancellation.

REBATE FOR EARLY PAYMENT

The new Act contains for the first time, provisions entitling the debtor to pay off the whole amount due under a hire-purchase (or other credit agreement) at any time. Sect. 95 of the Act provides that Regulations may be made to give the debtor a right to a rebate on the credit charges where there is early payment. The amount of the rebate will depend on a formula to be contained in the Regulations when they are made.

INDEX